INNOVATION MANAGEMENT

Strategies, Implementation, and Profits

Second Edition

ALLAN AFUAH
University of Michigan

New York   Oxford
OXFORD UNIVERSITY PRESS
2003

Oxford   New York
Auckland   Bangkok   Buenos Aires   Cape Town   Chennai
Dar es Salaam   Delhi   Hong Kong   Istanbul   Karachi   Kolkata
Kuala Lumpur   Madrid   Melbourne   Mexico City   Mumbai
Nairobi   São Paulo   Shanghai   Taipei   Tokyo   Toronto

Published by Oxford University Press, Inc.,
198 Madison Avenue, New York, New York 10016
http://www.oup-usa.org

Oxford is a registered trademark of Oxford University Press

Library of Congress Cataloging-in-Publication Data

Afuah, Allan.
Innovation management : strategies, implementation and profits / Allan
Afuah.—2nd ed.
     p. cm.
Includes bibliographical references and index.
ISBN 0-19-514230-6 (hardcover : alk. paper)
1. Organizational change. 2. Industrial management. 3.
Corporations—Finance. 4. Product management. 5. Strategic planning.
I. Title.
HD58.8 .A394 2003
658.4'06—dc21
          2002154341

10 9 8 7 6 5 4 3 2 1
Printed in the United States of America
on acid-free paper

To my grandmother
Veronica Masang-Namang Nkweta
I miss you mom

To the Swiss Basel Mission
without whose missionary work in Cameroon
thousands of people, including me,
would be illiterate

To the American Peace Corps program
without which I wouldn't have been exposed to
physics at an early age and without physics
there would have been no Silicon Valley,
Route 128, or MIT for me

CONTENTS

Appendixes

PREFACE

The times for students of innovation have never been better, more promising, or more challenging. In CEO speech after speech, in business school functional areas from strategy to finance to marketing, and even in annual financial statements, the word *innovation* is pervasive. It has even been suggested that innovation will be to the 2000s what total quality management was to the 1970s, what time-based management was to the 1980s, and what efficiency was to the 1990s—that is, a precondition for gaining or maintaining a competitive advantage. Unfortunately, while academic research in innovation has had very important implications for the practicing manager, the journal articles or books reporting this research have generally emphasized only a single point of view or drawn on a single discipline, often with inconsistent definitions of important terms, including the term *innovation* itself. They have not provided the type of integrative framework that can allow students of innovation to get their minds around this increasingly important field—a framework that allows them to build on and make cause-and-effect predictions. The goal of this book is to provide such a framework.

Throughout the book, seven themes underpin the synthesis and presentation of the integrative framework. First, while for the MBA, engineer, or practicing manager, a critical goal is to apply innovation concepts to real-life problems, there is still "no better practice than good theory." Jay Barney put it best when he said: "there really isn't anything quite as practical as a good theory." Accordingly, I draw on the latest in academic research and emphasize the theoretical underpinnings of any implications for practice.

Second, for many firms, competitive advantage is gained and maintained through innovation. It is also lost when firms do not innovate and their competitors do. As such, I have drawn on the literature in strategy, especially the product-market position and resource-based views of the firm. I have emphasized the link between new ideas and continued profits. The focus is on a firm that wants to profit from an innovation. Third, innovation is not limited to high technology. Surely Glaxo's blockbuster ulcer drug, Zantac, was an innovation. But so was Federal Express's offering of overnight package delivery. Innovations do not have to be breakthroughs either.

Fourth, innovation usually means *change,* both in the organizational and the economic sense, and therefore any models that seek to understand the phenomenon are necessarily multidisciplinary. The concepts, models, and theories in this book all draw on various fields, including economics and organizational theory. Fifth, both strategy and its implementations are critical to successful exploitation of innovation. Many innovation strategies fail not because there is something fundamentally wrong with them, but because they are not well implemented. The book stresses the fact that it takes a good strategy, but that it also takes an appropriate organizational structure, systems, and the right people to implement the strategy. Yes, it takes people.

Sixth, innovation entails dealing with new knowledge—collecting information and turning it into new products or services. How successful a firm is in doing so is a function of the firm's capacity to collect and process that information, and of the nature of the information itself. Finally, one needs to understand theory in order to apply it, and concepts, models, and theories that are learned and not practiced evaporate quickly. As such, I have taken several measures to facilitate the grasping and retention of the material. First, in the conceptual and theoretical discussions, I have included examples whenever possible. Second, at the end of most of the chapters, I have included a short practice case designed to illustrate key concepts. These cases are then followed by a listing of key terms and questions designed to stimulate more probing and discussion.

My interest in innovation management dates back to when I worked in the Silicon Valley and, later, Route 128. I was intrigued then by why some semiconductor firms lagged their competitors in inventing or embracing change. For example, did the lag in embracing new technologies occur because these laggards deliberately delayed entry, as a strategy, or because they just didn't have what it takes to get off first? And if so, why? When I returned to graduate school to find answers to such questions, I was confronted with many journal articles and books, each of which advanced a single view or drew only on one discipline, such as economics or organizational theory. This book is the result of many years of trying to find a framework that integrates these different views, an introductory text that draws on the latest in innovation research to provide a framework that students and practicing managers alike can sink their teeth into. While the book was designed for first- or second-year MBA students, engineering management students, and the practicing manager, scientists, engineers, and anyone who is involved in the process of turning new knowledge into new products or services that customers want would also find the book very useful.

In the rush to publish the first edition of the book, I forgot to thank my professors at MIT, especially Professors Tom Allen, Rebecca Henderson, Ed Roberts, and Jim Utterback, whose pioneering work in management of technology gave me the foundation to build upon and grow. I would also like to thank Ken MacLeod and John Bauco, who did a superb job as editor and project manager, respectively, of the book. I am still grateful to the three anonymous reviewers who reviewed the first edition of this book.

CHANGES IN THE SECOND EDITION

Three factors greatly influenced the second edition of *Innovation Management*. First, since the book rests on research in the evolving fields of management of technology and strategic management, the knowledge generated by scholars in both fields has increased considerably since I wrote the first edition. Second, since the pace of technological innovation has been very fast, scholars have been able to apply the theories, concepts, and tools explored in the first edition to learn more about their applications to exploiting innovation. Third and equally important, the professors who used the first edition in their classes offered important suggestions on how I could improve it.

When I wrote the first edition, the terminology used in strategic management's resource-based view of the firm was still evolving. In fact, it is still evolving. After a lot of reading and feedback from users, I decided to change the term "endowment" to "assets" and refine the definition of capabilities. As a result, I have had to substantially revise Chapters 3 and 7 to reflect the more popular terminology in the resource-based view of the firm. The contents of both chapters in the second edition are conceptually and logically consistent with those in the first edition.

In keeping with my goal of giving the reader a framework that he or she can put his or her mind around, I have taken several steps to separate strategy issues from implementation ones, even though the line between the two is sometimes very difficult to draw. First, I have moved what used to be Chapter 12 in the first edition to Part II: Strategizing, since the chapter is about the strategies that allow a firm to sustain a competitive advantage from innovation. It is now Chapter 10. Second, I have moved some of the concepts that were organized under implementation in what used to be Chapter 11 (now Chapter 12) to the new Chapter 10. I have also moved the implementation concepts that used to be in Chapter 10 to Chapter 12. Additionally, I have added some substantive material to Chapter 10, including what strategies to pursue when.

In what used to be Chapter 10 and is now Chapter 11, Financing Entrepreneurial Activity, I have added a section on "Complementary Assets from Co-opetitors" as a source of financing for start-ups. In Chapter 13, I have added a model that can be used to explore which mechanism a firm can use to better exploit innovations in new countries.

Finally, I have added a new chapter, Chapter 16, The Internet: A Case in Technological Change. In some ways, the Internet is a godsend for scholars of innovation. I have applied many of the concepts, theories, and tools of the book to explore some questions raised by the Internet. For example, could one have explained the potential outcome of the competition between start-up dot.coms and incumbents?

I am immensely grateful to the many professors who adopted the book for use in teaching their technology and innovation courses. I would like to thank Professors Christopher Tucci, Oscar Hauptman, Elias G. Carayannis, Donna Marie De Carolis, and Terry W. Noel for their suggestions to the changes that I have made to the first edition that have resulted in this second edition.

Ann Arbor, Michigan   **A. A.**
June 2003

For course materials, teaching guidelines, and sample cases, visit the author's
website at http://www-personal.umich.edu/~afuah/innovation.html

1

INTRODUCTION AND OVERVIEW

"I have traveled the length and breadth of this country and talked with the best people, and I can assure you that data processing is a fad that won't last out the year."
—*The editor in charge of business books for Prentice Hall, 1957.*

Most successful firms have, at one time or the other, used new knowledge to offer new products or services that customers want or have been in a position to exploit other firm's innovations. Intel's prosperity in the 1990s could be attributed to its invention of the microprocessor in 1972, while Cisco's prosperity in the late 1990s could be attributed to its ability to offer routers for the Internet. Pfizer's own prosperity in the late 1990s and early 2000s can be attributed both to its invention of Viagra as well as its exploitation of the cholesterol-bursting drug Lipitor, which was invented by Parke Davis, a division of Warner Lambert. Wal-Mart's decision to locate in small towns and saturate contiguous towns with stores, its integration of information technology and operations, its logistics, and its smart utilization of its human resources allowed the small-town Arkansas firm to become the world's largest retailer. Although many individual investors lost money during the Internet bubble, some also profited from it or should have profited from it. These examples are but the tip of an iceberg of the numerous firms that profit from innovation.

But the path to the innovation profit bank is also littered with the bodies of firms that did not innovate and lost their competitive advantage. In particular, it is strewn with the bodies of firms that did not recognize the potential of an innovation on time, did not have the right strategies to exploit the innovation once they recognized it, did not know how best to implement the strategies, or did not know how to protect their profits from competitors. Individual investors and institutions that blindly invested in dot.com companies at the peak of the bubble lost fortunes. NCR saw its leadership position in electromechanical cash registers erode when it did not recognize the potential of electronic cash registers. Swiss watchmakers did not quite see the invasion of digital watches. Kmart did not see the wisdom in locating discount stores in small towns or investing heavily in information technology and logistics until it had been overtaken by the innovative Wal-Mart. After decades of trying, Kmart filed for bankruptcy in 2002. IBM invented a technology called

RISC in 1975, shelved it, and in 2001 was still trying to use it to unseat Intel, a company it had helped crown king of microprocessors. Microsoft, the leading maker of personal computer software, was taken by surprise by the sudden importance of the World Wide Web and Netscape, a new entrant in the software business. Microsoft, unlike Kmart, recovered from its earlier myopia to overtake Netscape.

All these cases raise some very interesting questions for the student of innovation and strategy. Why is it so difficult to recognize the potential of an innovation? Can anything be done about these difficulties? How does a firm know which innovation is the right one for it to exploit? Where do the innovations come from to begin with? Are some regions or nations better environments for innovation than others and why? Can a firm control its local environment through innovation? Aren't competitors equally interested in also exploiting the same innovations? Once a firm has recognized the potential of an innovation, what is the best way to adopt it? Can it do anything about the fear of cannibalization, the emotional attachment to existing products or services, or the perils of organizational political power? How does a firm finance the innovations? Should it use existing assets or issue debt or equity to finance the innovation? Should a firm be cooperating with its competitors in adopting an innovation, and when might it be best to do so? Once a firm starts making profits from an innovation, how can it protect the profits from competitors? How does a firm in one country profit from innovating in other countries? What is the best globalization strategy for innovation? Are there any differences between profiting from an innovation in an emerging economy and in an established one? What is the role of national governments in innovation?

THE PROFIT CHAIN

This book explores these questions via the profit chain shown in Figure 1.1. Starting from the end of the chain, a firm makes profits by offering products or services at a lower cost than its competitors or by offering differentiated products at premium prices that more than compensate for the extra cost of differentiation.[1] The question is, how do low-cost and differentiated products come about, and why is it that some firms can offer them better than others? Firms create and deliver low-cost or differentiated products by performing the activities of their value configuration (value chain, value network, or value shop).[1] To perform these activities, a firm needs resources or assets such as plants, equipment, patents, scientists, brand name recognition, geographic location, client relations, distribution channels, and trade secrets. A firm's ability to use these assets to perform the activities of its value configuration in creating and delivering products and services to its customers is its competence.[2] These abilities can be anything from designing high-performance automotive engines to finding attractive markets and locating the right products or services in the right positions in these markets. A firm's assets and competences, together, make up its capabilities. As an example, consider Intel's profit chain. The firm's capabilities in integrated-circuit design and semiconductor manufacturing allowed it to invent the microprocessor. In the process of invention and commercialization as well as the subsequent incremental innovations that the firm made to

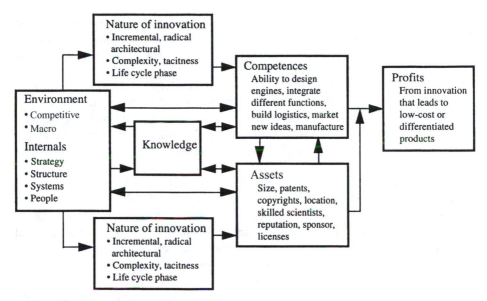

FIGURE 1.1. The profit chain.

the microprocessor, it accumulated assets such as patents, copyrights, a huge installed base of personal computers that use its microprocessors, and a reputation. With its intellectual property protected, it is difficult for other firms to imitate its microprocessor, allowing it to offer a differentiated product.

Competences and assets reinforce each other and, together, underpin the firm's profitability. They are themselves a function of technological and market knowledge. Intel's competences in integrated-circuit design and semiconductor manufacturing enabled it to accrue patents, copyrights, a reputation, and an installed base, which, in turn, also reinforce its ability to offer differentiated microprocessors. The firm has also built competences in how to protect its intellectual property and in bringing next-generation products to the market faster (than imitators) while making sure that they are compatible with earlier generations. Its ability to design and manufacture microprocessors rests on its knowledge of semiconductor device physics, logic, circuit design, and semiconductor process technology.

Technological and market knowledge, competences, and assets are, in turn, a function of the firm's strategy, organizational structure, systems, people, local environment, and chance events.[3] A firm's strategic decisions affect its competences and assets and therefore its ability to offer low-cost or differentiated products. Intel's strategic decisions over the life of its microprocessor have played a significant role in its profitability. Its decision early in the life of its microprocessor to license it to competitors played a role in IBM's choice of microprocessor for the PC. So did Intel's decision to stop licensing the design to other firms when its architecture emerged as the standard for PC microprocessors and its decision to sue NEC and AMD for violating its copyrights.

A firm whose organizational structure offers little coordination and integration of activities between R&D and marketing reduces its ability to offer new products.[4] The types of performance measures and reward systems that a firm puts in place can also affect the kinds of capabilities that it builds. The class of people a firm hires, the culture it cultivates, and the type of leadership it supports also have a bearing on its ability to carry out the activities that underpin its ability to offer low-cost or differentiated products. A firm's competitive and macro environments also impact its ability to innovate. Some environments are better at providing the suppliers, customers, financial institutions, educated work forces, and government policies that make them more conducive to innovation. Chance events can also play a role.

The nature of the innovation also matters. The new knowledge or new way of offering the new product or service can originate from the firm exploiting it but often is from its environment of competitors, suppliers, customers, government, or other institutions. How well a firm can exploit this new knowledge is a function of how different the new knowledge is from the firm's existing knowledge. It is a function of whether the new knowledge builds on the firm's existing capabilities or is very different—it is a function of whether the change is radical, incremental, or architectural to the firm. The question still remains, what exactly is the role of innovation in the profit chain?

PROFITS AND INNOVATION

So far we have not been explicit about what innovation has to do with profitability. We now look at that link.

Profits

A firm makes profits from selling a product or service when the revenues it receives from the product are greater than the cost of offering it. This can be represented by the expression

$$\text{Profits} = \text{Revenues} - \text{Cost} = P(z, q) \cdot q(z) - C(q, z). \tag{1}$$

Revenues are a function of the price the firm can charge for a product and the quantity it sells. Price, in turn, is a function of product attributes and the quantity being sold. The cost of the product also depends on the product's attributes and the quantity being produced. Thus firms would like to offer products with superior attributes for which they can charge high prices while keeping costs low and competitors out. The question is, how can they do that? This is where innovation comes in.

Innovation

Innovation is the use of new technological and market knowledge[5] to offer a new product or service that customers will want (Figure 1.2). The product is new in that

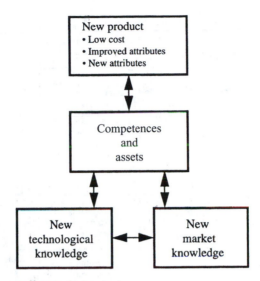

FIGURE 1.2. Innovation.

its cost is lower, its attributes are improved, it now has attributes it never had before, or it never existed in that market before. Often the new product itself is called an innovation, reflecting the fact that it is the creation of new technological or market knowledge, or it is new to customers. As shown in Equation (1), lower cost for a given price means more profits. Better or new attributes that command a price premium for a given cost also mean more profits, all else being equal. The new technological or market knowledge that is used to offer the new product or service can underpin any of the chain of activities that the firm must perform in order to offer the new product. It can be in the design of the product or in the way the product is advertised. The knowledge is new because the firm has never used it before or because it used it but only for applications unrelated to the one for which the new product is earmarked.

This book, then, is about how to recognize the link between new knowledge (technological and market) on the one hand, and low-cost, improved, or new product attributes as perceived by customers on the other. It is about how to exploit that link and generate profits. It is about how to protect those profits.

EXPLORING THE PROFIT CHAIN: AN OVERVIEW

There are four parts to the book (Figure 1.3). Part I, which consists of Chapters 2, 3, and 4, reviews some important concepts in innovation and strategy that are fundamental to understanding the questions that underpin how firms profit from innovation, the subject of Parts II, III, and IV. Part II explores questions related to the strategies that a firm must put in place in order to profit from an innovation, whereas Part III explores questions related to implementing the strategies. Part IV

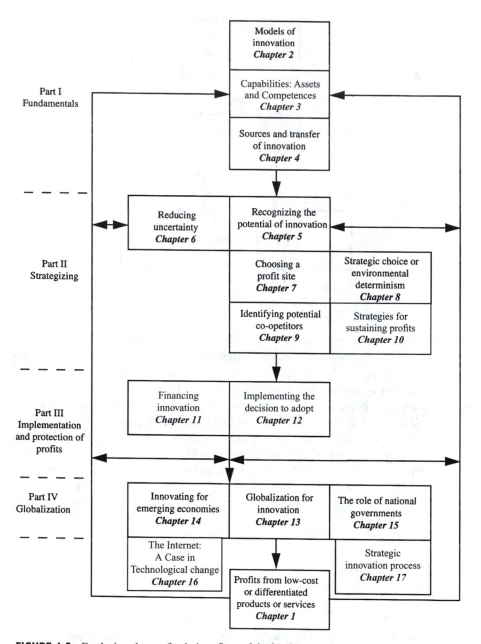

FIGURE I.3. Exploring the profit chain—flow of the book.

examines the globalization of innovation. Throughout the book, the goal of a firm is to generate profits.

Part I: Fundamentals

In Chapter 2 we explore some of the models that have been developed over the years in an effort to explain why some firms are more successful at innovation than others. From these models we synthesize an integrative framework that can be used to explore the factors that allow some firms to profit from innovation better than others. This framework is the profit chain of Figure 1.1. It argues that understanding what it takes to profit from an innovation entails exploring four questions: the *how, who, what,* and *when* of innovation. How different is the knowledge that underpins the innovation from a firm's existing knowledge? Is the innovation incremental, radical, or architectural? Is it competence enhancing or destroying? How much of the new knowledge is there, and how tacit is it? To whom is the innovation radical? What is it about some firms that allows them to use new knowledge to offer low-cost or differentiated products better than competitors, and why can't these competitors offer the same products? When in the innovation life cycle does the firm want to exploit it?

In Chapter 3 we discuss what we mean by low-cost and differentiated products, and we explore why some firms can offer them better than others. We argue that the ability of a firm to offer differentiated or low-cost products or services is a function of its ability to perform value chain activities, such as design, testing, manufacturing, marketing, merchandising, purchasing, and winning new clients, and the extent to which it possesses distinctive capabilities. How differentiated or lower cost these products or services are than competitors' and for how long they stay so, are a function of how unique or difficult it is to imitate or trade the firm's capabilities.[6] These capabilities rest on technological and market knowledge. For example, Honda's ability to offer high-performance engines rests on its knowledge of combustion engineering, lightweight durable materials, fuel injection, and of how all these components interact. How long the firm continues to exploit its competences and assets is a function of whether technological or market discontinuities render them obsolete.

Chapter 4 explores the sources of innovation and what it takes to transfer innovations effectively from their sources to exploitation sites. An innovation can originate not only from any of the functions of a firm's value chain, but also from its local environment of competitors, suppliers, customers, complementary innovators, related industries, universities, and research laboratories. Effective transfer from any of these sources is a function of the nature of the innovation, the cultural differences between receiver and transmitter, the timing of the transfer, and the absorptive and transmission capacities of the receiver and the transmitter.

Part II: Strategizing

With the foundation laid in Part I, we turn to the first key question in exploiting innovation: why do firms have such difficulties recognizing the potential of an innovation, and what, if anything, can be done about it? These difficulties are the result of two factors. The first is the way the firm collects and processes information. We argue in Chapter 5 that a firm's ability to recognize the potential of an innovation is a function of its strategy, structure, processes, people, environment, and top management's dominant logic. We also discuss some solutions to this endemic problem.

The second reason is the technological and market uncertainties that are associated with innovation. In Chapter 6 we focus on two major uncertainties that firms face: what technology is likely to invade an existing technology, and what markets are likely to open up? We argue that by observing simple patterns in markets and technological evolution, firms can learn a lot about the potential of an innovation. For example, most of the products in the American home today were first used in factories or businesses, and with advances in the technologies that underlie their production, they moved to the house. From there portable versions that customers could "take along" followed. In some cases, versions for the car also followed. Radio, audio tapes, and VCRs are examples. We argue that a critical evaluation of these trends, coupled with a firm's strategy, can reduce uncertainty considerably and increase the firm's ability to recognize the potential of an innovation. That is, a firm can reduce uncertainty by analyzing trends and taking control of its future by its strategic actions.

Now suppose a firm has recognized the potential of an innovation. The question becomes: where should it position itself along the innovation value-added chain, if at all, in order to best profit from the innovation? That is, if a firm has found out in the 1980s that an innovation called the personal computer is going to experience high growth in the 1990s, where should it place its bets? Should it make the personal computers, supply chips for them, develop software for them, distribute them, start a desktop publishing business using the computer, or stay out of the market entirely? Chapter 7 suggests a three-step process to determine a profit site. First, the firm uses Porter's[7] five forces to determine the competitive forces exerted on each industry along the innovation value-added chain of suppliers, manufacturers, complementary innovators, distributors, or customers. Second, it determines what capabilities are needed to succeed as a supplier, manufacturer, complementary innovator, distributor, or customer and the extent to which its own capabilities match them or how quickly it can acquire them. Third, the firm determines how many of these capabilities it has or how quickly it can build them. This analysis is performed for each phase of the innovation life cycle.

In Chapter 8 we explore the role of a firm's local environment in its innovativeness. We explore how a firm's suppliers, customers, related industries, competitors, and the government impact its ability to profit from an innovation. In particular, we explore how a firm can, through its strategic choices and innovation, control its competitive environment.

While a firm is finding ways to exploit an innovation, its competitors are probably doing the same. It is important for a firm to know not only who these competitors are likely to be, but also with whom it may want to cooperate. Chapter 9 is dedicated to determining a firm's potential co-opetitors—the firms with whom it may want to cooperate or have to compete with—in the face of an innovation.

Once a firm has adopted an innovation and is profiting from it, its competitors are going to want a piece of the action. Chapter 10 details generic strategies that a firm can use to protect its innovation profits. Depending on the type of industry, the product life cycle phase, the firm's capabilities, and its corporate strategy, a firm can use a combination of three strategies: (1) to *block*—the firm prevents others from imitating its innovation, (2) to *team up*—the firm allies with others, and (3) to *run*—the firm frequently introduces new products to stay ahead, sometimes cannibalizing its own products before someone else does.

Part III: Implementation and Protection of Profits

Before a firm can implement its decision to adopt an innovation, it must find the money to finance it. In Chapter 11 we argue that, depending on the type of innovation in question, a firm faces two major problems in finding the money that it needs to carry out the innovation successfully. First, because of the uncertainty inherent in the innovation, some innovations may not be able to clear company hurdle. Second, if the firm goes for outside financing, it must deal with the problems of adverse selection and moral hazard that often accompany information asymmetries. We present some fundamentals about financing an innovation and suggest some solutions for these problems.

Having determined the potential opportunities and threats of an innovation, identified potential co-opetitors, and secured financing for the innovation, a firm must now decide if and when to adopt. In Chapter 12 we discuss the obstacles that firms often face in implementing the decision to adopt. The fear of cannibalization, political coalitions, and emotional attachment to existing technologies as well as existing top managerial dominant logic and the firm's organizational structure and processes often impede progress. Successful implementation is a function of the right adoption strategies, organizational structures, processes or systems, and people; the type of innovation; and the local environment.

Part IV: Globalization

The increasing interdependence of world markets for many goods and services suggests that a firm must take a global perspective in its innovation strategies. Chapter 13 explores what global strategies are best for innovation, that is, how best to organize in a global context so as to recognize the potential of innovations, exploit them, and protect the profits. The theme that emerges is to put people where the uncertainties are.

Chapter 14 focuses on how best to innovate for emerging economies. The chapter explores strategies and implementation mechanisms that a firm with a certain value stock—the stock of end products, modified end products, core products, and capabilities—can use to profit from innovating in an emerging economy.

Governments play a critical role, largely indirectly, in innovation and global competitiveness. In Chapter 15 we discuss this role of government. We focus on its financing of R&D through universities, firms, and private laboratories and on its regulation of the firm's inventive and commercialization activities. We also explore government's other policies, including the intended and unintended effects on innovativeness.

The Internet is a godsend for students of technological change, especially when it comes to exploring the *how, what, who,* and *where* of innovation. In Chapter 16, we apply some of the theories, models, tools, and concepts of the book to answer some basic questions about the Internet.

Chapter 17 presents a strategic innovation process—the systematic process by which a firm examines its goals, innovation opportunities and threats, and capabilities. From these it chooses a profit site and determines its business, innovation, globalization, and functional strategies. Based on these strategies, it puts together the organizational structure, systems, and people that will allow it to exploit the innovation successfully.

Appendix 1 explores what it takes to win a standard or dominant design and the related benefits. Appendix 2 examines the features of project, functional, and matrix organizational structures. The glossary of terms provides brief definitions of key terms in innovation.

NOTES

1. See Porter, M. E. "Towards a dynamic theory of strategy." *Strategic Management Journal* *12:*95–117, 1991.

2. The literature on the so-called resource-based view of the firm has rather confusing definitions of competences and capabilities. We will discuss these definitions in more detail in Chapter 3.

3. See, for example, Miles, R. E., and C. C. Snow. *Organizational Strategy, Structure, and Process.* New York: McGraw-Hill, 1978. Porter, M. E. *The Competitive Advantage of Nations.* New York: Free Press, 1990.

4. Wheelwright, S. C., and K. B. Clark. *Revolutionizing Product Development.* New York: Free Press, 1992.

5. *New knowledge* here means knowledge that has not been used before to offer the product or service in question. New knowledge as used here includes breakthrough knowledge—knowledge that never existed before, such as the transistor when it was discovered. But it is not limited to breakthrough knowledge as used elsewhere. Drucker, for example, uses new knowledge to mean only breakthrough knowledge. See Drucker, P. F. "The discipline of innovation." In *Innovation,* edited by *Harvard Business Review.* Cambridge, MA: Harvard Business School Press, 1991.

6. *Resources* and *capabilities* are used interchangeably in this book.

7. Porter, M. E. *Competitive Strategy: Techniques for Analyzing Industries and Competitors.* New York: Free Press, 1980.

FUNDAMENTALS

C H A P T E R

2

MODELS OF INNOVATION

One question has interested management scholars for years: what type of firm is most likely to innovate? In this chapter we explore some of the models that have been advanced in an effort to better answer this question. This exploration provides some background definitions and concepts that are crucial to an understanding of the main theme of this book: recognizing the potential of an innovation, profiting from it, and protecting those profits. We first define innovation and then describe each model, pointing out its shortcomings and contributions. From these models we synthesize a framework for exploring who is likely to introduce and exploit innovation.

DEFINITION OF INNOVATION

Innovation is the use of new knowledge to offer a new product or service that customers want. It is invention + commercialization.[1] It is, according to Porter, "a new way of doing things (termed invention by some authors) that is *commercialized*. The process of innovation cannot be separated from a firm's strategic and competitive context."[2] The new knowledge[3] can be technological or market related. Technological knowledge is knowledge of components, linkages between components, methods, processes, and techniques that go into a product or service. Market knowledge is knowledge of distribution channels, product applications, and customer expectations, preferences, needs, and wants. The product or service is new in that its cost is lower, its attributes are improved, it now has new attributes it never had before, or it never existed in that market before. Often the new product or service itself is called an innovation, reflecting the fact that it is the creation of new technological or market knowledge. Thus the discovery and development of Merck's cholesterol-bursting drug Mevacor was an innovation, as were Wal-Mart's location of discount retail stores in small towns in the southwestern United States and Federal Express's one-day delivery service.

Innovation has also been defined as "the adoption of ideas that are new to the adopting organization."[4] This book is about profiting from innovation. Generating good ideas or adopting a new one, in and of itself, is only a start. To be an innovation, an idea must be converted into a product or service that customers want. Coming up with the idea or prototype—invention—is one thing. Championing it, shepherding it, and nurturing it into a product or service that customers want is another. Innovation entails both invention and commercialization.

A distinction has also been made between *technical* and *administrative* innovation.[5] Technical innovation is about improved products, services, or processes or completely new ones. This contrasts with administrative innovation, which pertains to organizational structure and administrative processes and may or may not affect technical innovation. Technical innovation may or may not require administrative innovation. A technical innovation can be a *product* or a *process*. According to Damanpour, product innovations "are new products or services introduced to meet an external and market need," whereas process innovations are "new elements introduced into an organization's production or service operations—input materials, task specifications, work and information flow mechanisms, and equipment used to produce a product or render a service."[6] Thus, to the extent that technical innovations use new technological or market knowledge to offer new products or services to customers, they fit the definition of innovation in this book.

WHO INNOVATES?

The debate over who is most likely to innovate dates back to, at least, Schumpeter, who first suggested that small entrepreneurial firms were the sources of most innovations.[7] Later he changed his view and suggested that, for several reasons, large firms with some degree of monopoly power were more likely to be the sources of technological innovation. He argued that large firms have the production and other complementary assets that are necessary to commercialize an invention; have the size to exploit the economies of scale that are prevalent in R&D; are more diversified and therefore more willing to take the kind of risk that is inherent in R&D projects; have better access to capital than smaller firms; and, as monopolists, do not have competitors ready to imitate their innovations and therefore are more likely to invest in them.[8] Empirical studies in search of support for either position have not been able to establish a clear relationship between a firm's size and market power and its innovative activity.[9] By shifting the focus to the *type* of innovation, however, some research suggests that whether incumbents or new entrants are able to introduce and exploit innovation is a function of whether the innovation is *incremental* or *radical*, that is, a function of how *new* the new knowledge and the new product (in our definition of innovation) are.[10]

STATIC MODELS

Incremental versus Radical Innovation

An innovation has two kinds of impact on a firm. In the first place, since knowledge underpins a firm's ability to offer products, a change in knowledge implies a change in the firm's ability to offer a new product (Figure 2.1). Thus innovation can be defined in terms of the extent to which it impacts a firm's capabilities. This is what is usually referred to as the organizational view (of classifying innovations). In this view, an innovation is said to be *radical* if the technological knowledge required to exploit it is very different from existing knowledge, rendering existing knowledge obsolete. Such innovations are said to be *competence destroying*.[11] Refrigerators were a radical innovation because making them required firms to integrate knowledge of thermodynamics, coolants, and electric motors, which was very different from knowledge of harvesting and hauling ice. At the other end of the dichotomy is *incremental* innovation. In it, the knowledge required to offer a product builds on existing knowledge. It is, according to Tushman and Anderson, *competence enhancing*. For example, a "shrink" of Intel's Pentium chip to make it run at 200 MHz is an incremental innovation in the organizational sense since the knowledge required to do so builds on the firm's knowledge in microprocessor development. Most innovations are incremental.

In the second place, since innovation results in superior products (lower cost, better or new features), it can also be classified as a function of the extent to which it renders old products noncompetitive. This is the so-called economic (competitiveness) view. In this view, an innovation is said to be radical (drastic) if it results in a product that is so superior (lower cost, better attributes, or new attributes) that existing products are rendered noncompetitive. For example, the mechanical cash register could not compete with electronic point-of-sale systems (EPOSs). Thus EPOSs were a radical innovation in the economic sense. Very often, however, the innovation still allows existing products to stay competitive. In that case it is said to be incremental or nondrastic. Both diet and caffeine-free sodas are incremental in-

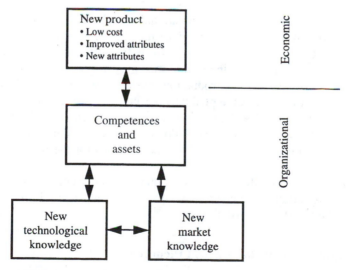

FIGURE 2.1. Innovation: Organizational and economic implications.

novations in the economic sense because their introduction allowed the standard colas to remain competitive.

These organizational and competitiveness definitions of incremental and radical innovation serve as the basis for two views of who is likely to innovate: the *strategic incentive* (to invest) and the *organizational capabilities* views.

Strategic Incentive (to Invest)

In the strategic incentive to invest view, the type of innovation—whether it is radical or incremental in the economic sense—determines what type of firm is likely to invest to be the first to innovate. Given that a radical innovation renders an incumbent's existing products noncompetitive, an incumbent with market power may be reluctant to invest in the innovation for fear of cannibalizing its existing products if, in doing so, it advances the date of introduction of the innovation.[12] New entrants, on the other hand, have less to lose. If they do not invest in the innovation, they have no products to sell in that market. On the other hand, incumbents would be more willing to invest in incremental innovations since such investments allow their existing products to stay competitive in the market.[13]

One major shortcoming of this model is that it assumes that firms have recognized the potential of the innovation, and in the case of a radical innovation, that only the fear of cannibalization prevents them from exploiting it. This is not always the case, especially with radical innovations. In any case, the model may explain why some new entrants have been the first to embrace radical innovation and incumbents have been responsible for the bulk of incremental innovations. It does not, however, explain why incumbents who invest in radical innovation may still fail. This is where the organizational capabilities view comes in.

Organizational Capabilities

If an innovation is radical in the organizational sense, incumbents have two problems in exploiting it. In the first place, since the change is competence destroying, they do not have the capabilities to exploit it.[14] In the second place, and perhaps more important, the firm's existing capabilities may not only be useless, they may actually be a handicap to the introduction and development of the innovation.[15] Firms find it difficult to break their habits, the routines and procedures they had put in place to exploit the old technology. They must unlearn the old ways of doing things. New entrants, on the other hand, do not have the burden of the old technology and can go on unencumbered to build capabilities for the innovation and exploit it.

If, on the other hand, the innovation is incremental, incumbents tend to dominate since the required knowledge builds on what they already have, but new entrants would have to build it from scratch.

Issues with the Incremental–Radical Dichotomy

One implication of these definitions is that new entrants are more likely to do well in the face of a radical innovation, whereas incumbents are more likely to fare bet-

Innovation

	Incremental	Radical
Incumbent	Mostek and Intel lost their industry market leadership positions in the transition from 64K to 256K DRAM	GE was successful in the transitions from X rays to CAT scans to MRI IBM successfully made the transitions from vacuum tubes to transistors to integrated circuits in mainframe computers
New entrant		

(Axis label: Type of firm)

FIGURE 2.2. Counterexamples to predictions by incremental and radical models.

ter when the innovation is incremental. In many industries, however, incumbents have been the first to introduce or exploit radical innovations and, in some cases, have failed to exploit incremental innovations. Figure 2.2 gives some examples. Intel and Mostek lost their leadership positions in DRAM memory chips during the transition from the 64K to the 256K chip, an incremental innovation in the organizational sense, despite being very strong incumbents and investing heavily in the 256K DRAM. On the other hand, GE, an incumbent in the diagnostic medical equipment industry, maintained its leadership position in the transition from X rays to CAT scans to MRI, relatively radical innovations. IBM was able to maintain its dominant position in the computer industry during the radical transitions from vacuum tubes to transistors to integrated circuits.

The counterexamples illustrated in Figure 2.2 suggest that we need more than the incremental–radical model to predict the outcome of technological change. We need more models that explain why some incumbents are the first to embrace or exploit radical technological change and why they sometimes fail to exploit some incremental innovations.

Abernathy–Clark Model

The Abernathy–Clark model offers one explanation why incumbents may outperform new entrants in the face of some "radical" innovations.[16] The model suggests that there are actually two kinds of knowledge that underpin an innovation: technological and market. Thus a firm's technological capabilities could become obsolete while its market capabilities remain intact. If such market capabilities are important and difficult to acquire, an incumbent whose technological capabilities have

Market capabilities \ Technical capabilities	Preserved	Destroyed
Preserved	Regular	Revolutionary
Destroyed	Niche	Architectural

FIGURE 2.3. Abernathy–Clark terminology—role of technological and market capabilities.

been destroyed can use the market ones to its advantage over a new entrant. Focusing on the perspective of the innovating firm, the model classifies innovations according to their impact on the existing technological and market knowledge of the manufacturer (Figure 2.3). An innovation is *regular* if it conserves the manufacturer's existing technological and market capabilities, *niche* if it conserves technological capabilities but obsoletes market capabilities, *revolutionary* if it obsoletes technological capabilities but enhances market capabilities, and *architectural* if both technological and market capabilities become obsolete.

While these different categories of innovation are illuminating, the point to note in this model is that market knowledge can be just as important as technological knowledge. For example, GE's market capabilities were instrumental to its performance in the transition from one generation of technologically radical innovation to another in the medical diagnostics equipment industry.[17] It was not the first to introduce each new technology, but it successfully transitioned from X rays to CAT scans to MRI, all technologically competence-destroying innovations.

Henderson–Clark Model

Henderson and Clark were puzzled why some incumbents have so much difficulty in dealing with what appear to be "incremental" innovations—seemingly minute changes in existing technologies. Xerox stumbled for many years before finally developing a good small plain-paper copier, despite being the pioneer of the core technology of xerography.[18] RCA was never able to lead in the market for portable transistor radios despite its experience in the components (transistors, audio amplifiers, and loudspeakers) that went into the portable radio. From their research, Henderson and Clark suggested that since products are normally made up of components connected together, building them must require two kinds of knowledge: knowledge of the components and knowledge of the linkages between them, which they call *architectural* knowledge. An innovation, then, can impact either compo-

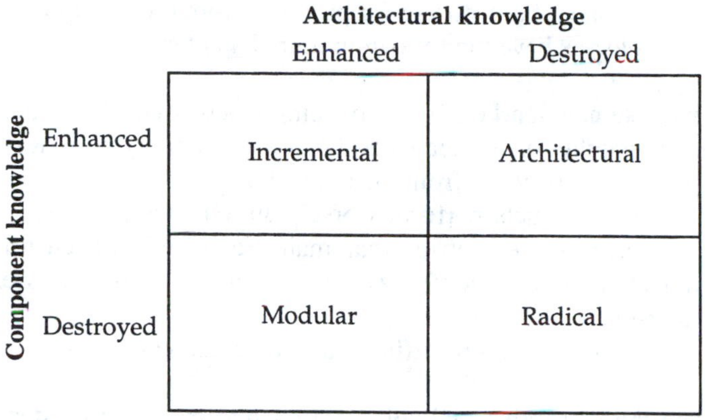

Architectural knowledge

	Enhanced	Destroyed
Enhanced	Incremental	Architectural
Destroyed	Modular	Radical

(left axis label: **Component knowledge**)

FIGURE 2.4. Architectural innovation.
Source: Reprinted from "Architectural innovation: The reconfiguration of existing product technologies and the failure of established firms" by R. Henderson and K. B. Clark, published in *Administrative Science Quarterly* 35(1). March 1990, by permission of Administrative Science Quarterly. Copyright © 1990 by Cornell University.

nent knowledge or architectural knowledge, or both, with different consequences for the firm adopting it. They went on to define four kinds of innovations, as illustrated in Figure 2.4. If the innovation enhances both component and architectural knowledge, it is *incremental;* if it destroys both component and architectural knowledge, it is *radical.* However, if only the architectural knowledge is destroyed and the component knowledge enhanced, the innovation is *architectural.* The last case, where component knowledge is destroyed but architectural knowledge enhanced, is called *modular* innovation.

With these definitions it became clear why firms had problems with what appeared to be incremental innovation. They may have mistaken architectural innovation for incremental innovation. While the component knowledge required to exploit the innovations had not changed (and therefore the semblance of incremental innovation), architectural knowledge had changed. Architectural knowledge is often tacit and embedded in the routines and procedures of an organization, making changes in it difficult to discern and respond to.

Disruptive Technological Change Model

According to the disruptive technological change model, advanced by Professor Clayton Christensen, incumbents fail to exploit disruptive technologies not so much because these firms do not "get it," as suggested by the architectural innovation model, or because the technologies are competence destroying to them, as suggested by the incremental–radical model.[19] Rather, incumbents fail because they spend too much time listening to and meeting the needs of their existing mainstream customers who, initially, have no use for products from the disruptive technology. Disruptive technologies have the following four characteristics:

1. They create new markets by introducing a new kind of product or service.
2. The new product or service from the new technology costs less than existing products or services from the old technology.
3. Initially, the products perform worse than existing products when judged by the performance metrics that mainstream existing customers value. Eventually, however, the performance catches up and addresses the needs of mainstream customers.
4. The technology should be difficult to protect using patents.

To understand the disruptive technological change model, consider a firm that has been successful in exploiting an existing technology to offer products to its mainstream customers. The firm's capabilities—what it can or cannot do—are a function of its resources, processes, and values. Its resources are assets such as product designs, brands, relationships with suppliers, customers, distribution, people, plants and equipment, technologies, and cash reserves. Its processes are the systems that the firm has put in place to transform resources into better customer value. These systems are designed to make task performance more efficient and are difficult to change, especially when they have been embedded into organizational culture. Suppose A is one of the products that the firm develops using an existing technology and that, in Year 2, more than meets the key performance attributes that the firm's mainstream customers want (B) in the product (Figure 2.5). Also suppose that in Year 2, a new product C, which costs less than A, is introduced. Initially, C's performance is inferior to that of A and does not

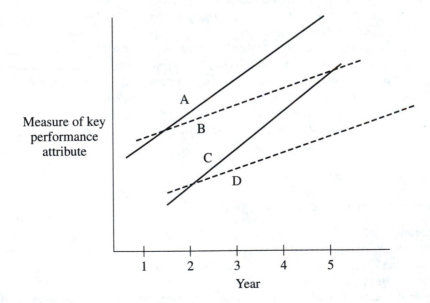

FIGURE 2.5. Disruptive technological change.

meet the performance requirements demanded by B. The firm that has produced A over the years and has been successful at doing so focuses its attention on satisfying the requirements of its key existing customers and therefore does not pay attention to developing the necessary capabilities, processes, and culture to build product C, which meets the performance attributes D that are needed by a different market. Start-ups and other entrants produce C and keep improving its performance. In Year 5, say, C's performance improves to a point where it now meets the needs of the market with demand B—the firm's mainstream customers. Because C is lower in cost than A, the firm's mainstream customers abandon it for the start-ups who offer C. At this time, it is too late for the firm and other producers of A to quickly shed their processes, values, and culture that served them so well with the old technology (in developing A) to develop C and gain a product advantage. Start-ups and other entrants take the leadership position in producing C.

Innovation Value-Added Chain

The innovation value-added chain[20] model can explain both why an incumbent can outperform new entrants at radical innovation and why it may also fail at incremental innovation. It differs from previous models in that while these other models focus on the impact of innovation on a firm's capabilities and competitiveness, it focuses on what the innovation does to the competitiveness and capabilities of a firm's suppliers, customers, and complementary innovators.[21] That is, previous models addressed the question: what does the electric car do to Ford's technological and market capabilities? But innovation also has implications for suppliers, customers, and complementary innovators, implications that can have far-reaching effects on the manufacturer.[22] Thus the electric car has implications not only for Ford's technical and market knowledge, but also for that of its suppliers (e.g., suppliers of electronic fuel injection systems), customers, and complementary innovators, such as gas station owners and oil companies. An innovation that is incremental to a manufacturer can be radical to its customers and complementary innovators and incremental to its suppliers. For example, the DSK (Dvorak simplified keyboard) keyboard arrangement that by some estimates performs 20–40 percent better than the QWERTY arrangement, which most of today's keyboards have, was competence enhancing to its innovator, Dvorak, and other typewriter manufacturers.[23] All they had to do was rearrange the position of the keys if they wanted to manufacture the DSK. But it was competence destroying to customers who had already learned how to type with the QWERTY keyboard since to use the new keyboard, they would have to relearn how to touch-type again. The various phases of this innovation at the different stages of the innovation value-added chain are shown in Figure 2.6.

Another example (also illustrated in Figure 2.6) is Cray Computer's decision in 1988 to develop and market a supercomputer that would use gallium arsenide (GaAs)[24] chips—a technology that yields very fast chips and consumes very little power, but was still relatively unproven then—instead of the proven silicon chip technology in which its suppliers had built their competences. While the super-

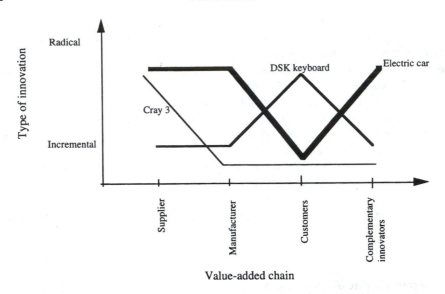

FIGURE 2.6. Innovation value-added chain. An innovation has implications not only for the firm but also for its suppliers, customers, and complementary innovators.

computer design was competence enhancing to Cray, its decision to use gallium arsenide was competence destroying to its traditional silicon chip supplier base.

In each of these examples, the innovation may have a different impact at each of the stages of the innovation value-added chain, suggesting that an innovation that is incremental to the manufacturer may not be to suppliers, customers, or complementary innovators. Thus incumbents for whom an innovation is competence destroying may still do well if the innovation is competence enhancing to their value chain, and relations with the chain are important and difficult to establish. The implications are that a firm's success in exploiting an innovation may depend as much on what the innovation does to the capabilities of the firm as on what it does to the capabilities of its innovation value-added chain of suppliers, customers, and complementary innovators (Figure 2.7).

Strategic Leadership View

The strategic leadership view argues that the strategic incentive to invest in an innovation or the failure to exploit it as a result of destroyed competence come only after a firm's top management has recognized the potential of the innovation.[25] Top management makes the decisions to invest in an innovation, or if such decisions are made by lower level managers, they still reflect the beliefs and values of top management.[26] But its incentive to invest in an innovation or its ability to embrace and exploit the innovation is a function of the extent to which the firm's top management recognizes the potential of the innovation. This ability of top management to recognize the potential of an innovation is a function of its *managerial logic,* or view of the world,[27] which, in turn, depends on management experiences, organi-

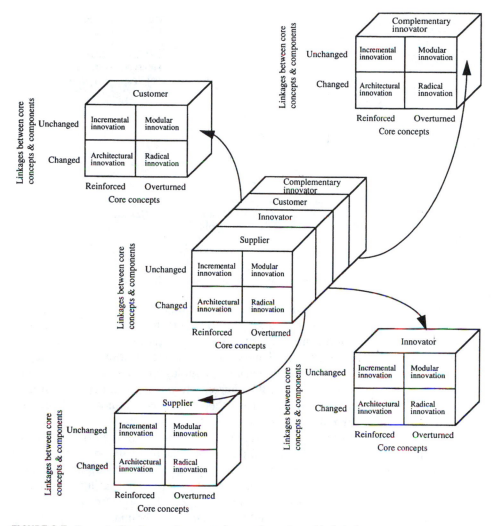

FIGURE 2.7. Impact of an innovation on an innovation value-added chain.

Source: Reprinted from *Research Policy* 24, A. N. Afuah and N. Bahram, "The hypercube of innovation," pp. 51–76, 1995, with kind permission of Elsevier Science—NL. Sara Burgerhart-straat 25, 1055 KV Amsterdam. The Netherlands.

zational logic, and industry logic. Thus whether a firm is a new entrant or an incumbent may not matter much. What matters is the strategic leadership's dominant logic.

Familiarity Matrix

Suppose top management has recognized the potential of an innovation and decided to adopt it. Is the firm going to be successful? It depends on the mechanism

Fundamentals

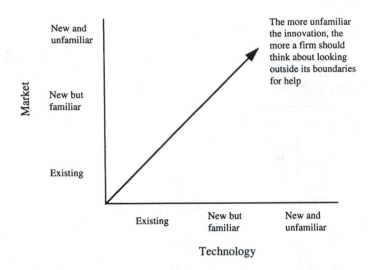

FIGURE 2.8. How to adopt an innovation, given its familiarity.

that the firm uses to adopt the innovation, Roberts and Berry argued.[28] They suggested that, in adopting an innovation, a firm can choose from seven mechanisms—internal development, acquisitions, licensing, internal ventures, joint ventures or alliances, venture capital and nurturing, and educational acquisition—depending on how familiar or unfamiliar the technology (that underpins the innovation) and the market are. That is, the appropriate mechanism depends on how radical the innovation is to the firm. The Roberts and Berry model will be discussed in much more detail in Chapter 12.

Briefly, however, if technology and market are familiar to the firm—an incremental innovation—the firm is better off developing the innovation internally since it has the capabilities to do so. If market and technology are both new and unfamiliar, the firm may be better off using venture capital, venture nurturing, and educational acquisitions to enter. As illustrated in Figure 2.8, the more radical an innovation is to a firm, the more the firm should look outside its boundaries for help.

Quantity and Quality of the New Knowledge

The incremental, radical, and architectural terminologies all describe different types of *changes* in knowledge. They describe how *new* the new knowledge is. An innovation can also be described as a function of how *much* knowledge goes into it and the *form* the knowledge takes.

Positive-Feedback Effects

Arthur groups products and services into *bulk processing* and *knowledge based.*[29] Bulk-processing products such as coal, heavy chemicals, plantains, lumber, and aniline dyes are heavy on natural resources and light on know-how. On the other hand, knowledge-based products such as aircraft, pharmaceuticals, computers, software, telecommunications equipment, missiles, factory automation, and biotechnologicals are low on natural resources and heavy on know-how. These are so-called high-technology products, which are complicated and costly to develop, manufacture, and offer to customers. Bulk-processing products exhibit diminishing returns. For example, since the supply of plantain depends on the land on which it is grown, expanding the production of plantains means that there would eventually be less land available for plantains, thus limiting supply. Thus there is an optimum scale of operations—minimum efficient scale—beyond which costs start to increase.

Knowledge-based products exhibit increasing returns, or positive feedback.[30] Typically, the up-front costs for these products are very high, but the per-unit production costs thereafter are very low. For example, in pharmaceuticals, the cost of developing and launching a new drug can be as high as $500 million. But per-unit costs after that first unit can be as low as $0.10. These costs keep falling as more and more customers can be found. As another example, developing the first copy of a software product can cost as much as $60 million. Thereafter a copy can cost as little as $0.70 to produce.

Knowledge-based products often exhibit network effects,[31] that is, the more people who use these products, the more valuable they become. The increased value comes from two factors. First, it comes from the "sharing" effect. For example, the reader's telephone would be useless if the only person he or she could talk to were the author of this book. But the more other people there are on the telephone network, the more valuable it is to the reader since he or she can talk to more people. Second, the more people who use a product, the more complementary products can be developed. For example, the more people who use a particular computer standard, the more software is developed for that particular computer. The products may also require customers to invest in a fair amount of learning in order to use them effectively. A computer user must learn how to use the operating systems. A user of a Boeing 747 must learn how to maintain and safely operate the plane. This learning makes it difficult for a user to switch to a new system. To some extent, the customer is locked-in. Table 2.1 summarizes the differences between bulk-processing products and knowledge-based products.

The network externality and the customer lock-in properties of knowledge-based products suggest that technology B may win over competing technology A, even when A is superior to B. For example, if a user has learned how to use an operating system and bought applications software that runs on it, it may be difficult to switch to a newer operating system, even when the new one is superior in performance. The positive-feedback property also suggests that strategic actions or chance events that give a technology a lead early in its life can be amplified via positive feedback to give the technology a dominant position. Strategic actions include setting low prices (sometimes, literally giving away the product), forming alliances, and making preproduct announcements.[32] Whether or not a firm is successful with positive-feedback products is a function of the strategic actions that the firm takes early in its life, chance events, and whether or not the firm is the first to

TABLE 2.1. Differences between bulk-processing and knowledge-based products.

	Bulk processing	Knowledge based
Knowledge demands	Low on know-how	High on know-how
Up-front cost	Low	High
Network externalities	Low	High
Customer lock-in	Low	High
Economics	Negative feedback	Positive feedback

introduce the product. Not all products that are high on know-how require the same amount of knowledge. The amount of knowledge required is also a function of the complexity of the innovation. For example, a personal computer and a jumbo jet plane are both heavy on know-how but require different amounts of knowledge.

Tacitness of the New Knowledge

How *much* knowledge a firm has to collect and process in exploiting an innovation is one thing. The other is the form that it takes; in particular, whether it is tacit or explicit.

Knowledge is *explicit* (articulated, codified) if it is spelled out in writing, verbalized, or coded in drawings, computer programs, or other products.[33] *Tacit* knowledge is uncoded and nonverbalized. It may not even be verbalizable or articulatable. It can be acquired largely through personal experience such as learning by doing. It is often embedded in the routines of organizations or in an individual's actions and therefore very difficult to copy. Performing most activities requires both types of knowledge. Take flying a plane, for example. A student pilot can read about the different instruments and equipment in the cockpit. This is explicit knowledge. However, there are certain things about flying a plane that can only be learned by actually flying the plane and interacting with a trained pilot. The reader would probably hesitate to be flown by a pilot who learned how to fly by reading a manual but has never been in a plane before.

Thus in addition to asking how *new* the new knowledge is (that is, how radical the innovation), it is also important to ask how *much* of the new knowledge one needs and how *tacit* it is. As an example, take the two-piece aluminum can and the Boeing 777. The change from the three-piece tin-plated steel can to a two-piece aluminum can requires new knowledge.[34] So does the change from the Boeing 767 to the 777. To some functions along the value chain of each product, it is radical. The 777 with its numerous components, interfaces, and dimensions of merit and its many suppliers, customers, and regulators is more complex than the two-piece aluminum can. It requires more knowledge than the can. The final product does not have to be complex to require lots of knowledge. Most pharmaceutical drugs are very simple but require a tremendous amount of know-how.

Imitability and Complementary Assets: The Teece Model

While not explicitly categorizing innovations as radical, incremental, or otherwise, Teece proposed a model that, like the Abernathy–Clark model, helps explain why incumbents can still profit from technologically radical innovations.[35] Puzzled by such questions as why RC Cola introduced the first diet cola only to see Coca Cola and Pepsi collect most of the profits from it, or why EMI invented and first commercialized the CAT scan only to surrender its early leadership position to GE, Teece argued that two factors are instrumental to profiting from an innovation: *imitability* and *complementary assets.* Inimitability is the extent to which the technology can be imitated. Imitability may come from the intellectual property (patents, copyrights, trademarks, and trade secrets) protection of the technology, or from the fact that imitators just do not have the competences to imitate the given technology.[36] Complementary assets are all the other capabilities—apart from those that underpin the technology—that the firm needs to exploit the technology. These include manufacturing, marketing, distribution channels, service, reputation, brand name, and complementary technologies.

Figure 2.9 suggests when an innovator is likely to profit from an innovation in this model. If imitability is high in that the technology can easily be imitated, it is difficult for the innovator to make money if complementary assets are easily available or unimportant (cell I in Figure 2.9). If, however, complementary assets are tightly held and important, the owner of such assets makes money (cell II). For example, CAT scans were easy to imitate, and EMI did not have complementary assets such as distribution channels and the relations with U.S. hospitals that are critical to selling such expensive medical equipment. GE had these assets and quickly captured the leadership position by imitating the innovation. Coca Cola and Pepsi

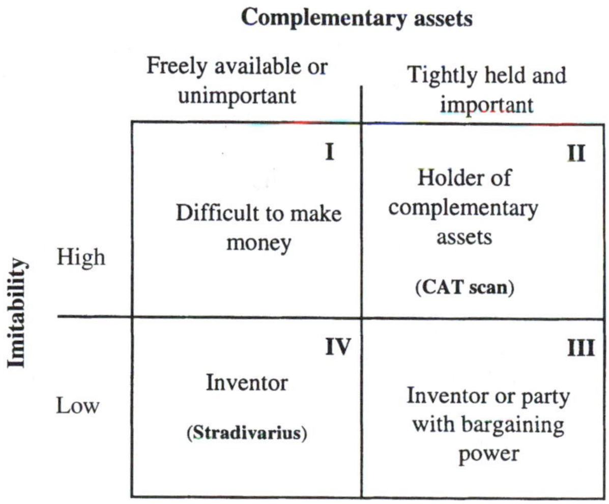

FIGURE 2.9. Who profits from innovations?

were able to profit from RC Cola's innovations because they had brand name reputation and distribution channels that RC did not, and the innovations were easy to imitate.

If imitability is low in that it is difficult to imitate the technology, the innovator stands to profit from it if complementary assets are freely available or unimportant (cell IV). For example, the owner of the Stradivarius profited enormously since no one could imitate it, and complementary assets for it were neither difficult to acquire nor important. If, as in cell III, imitability is low and complementary assets are important and difficult to acquire, whoever has both, or the more important of the two, wins. The better negotiator can also make money. Pixar is a good example. Imitability of some of its digital studio technology is low, given the copyrights it holds on its software. But offering customers movies made with that technology requires distribution channels, brand name recognition, and financing, which are tightly held by the likes of Disney and Columbia Pictures. Pixar formed an alliance with Disney to make the very successful *Toy Story,* and, so far, both firms have profited from the alliance.[37]

Local Environment

The suggestion, for example, that an innovation can be competence destroying to a firm implies that the ability of a firm to exploit the innovation may depend on something outside the firm—its environment. Indeed, several authors have argued that a firm's ability to innovate is a function of its environment. Thomas, for example, suggests that a very demanding environment can be conducive to innovation.[38] He compared the industrial policies of ten nations and found that pharmaceutical firms in the United States and the United Kingdom, where strict government regulations require proof of safety and efficacy, were more innovative than those in countries such as France, which had lenient regulation and low prices. Porter argued that the innovativenss of a firm is a function of four characteristics of its local environment, which he collectively called the "diamond."[39] These are factor conditions; demand conditions; related and supporting industries; and firm strategy, structure, and rivalry. Factor conditions, such as natural resources, skilled labor, capital, educational institutions (local universities), and private research laboratories that are repositories of scientific, technological, and market knowledge, can be sources of local advantage. It is from such repositories of knowledge that new ideas that could be nurtured into products or services often spring. It is also from them that support or nurturing for ideas from elsewhere often comes. Given that such knowledge is often tacit and therefore best transferred in person, local firms have an advantage in exploiting innovation. On the other hand, the lack of certain factors can constitute an advantage. For example, Swedish firms are leaders in prefabricated housing partly because of the short building season and the high wages of construction workers in Sweden.

The nature of local demand for products or service is also important to a local firm's ability to innovate. A firm's products tend to reflect local customer needs. One reason for this is the tacit nature of market knowledge. Customers may not be able to articulate these preferences and expectations without repeated contact with manufacturers who can help flesh out the needs. Such contact can be very costly and difficult if both manufacturer and customer are not local. Even when customer needs are well articulated, a manufacturer may not be able to understand them without repeated physical meetings, which are easier and less costly if local. Thus if local customers are very sophisticated, their needs will be reflected in local products, allowing manufacturers to be able to serve less sophisticated customers outside the locality.

In some industries, suppliers of components and equipment are critical to generating new product or service ideas, and in supporting them through subsequent development and commercialization. The technological knowledge that underlies the use of some components and equipment may be tacit, and exploiting this knowledge requires close and frequent interaction with suppliers. Sometimes it may take a lot of input from the manufacturer to develop the component or equipment. Such frequent interaction is less costly and more probable when suppliers are local, and both parties stand to gain.

For several reasons local rivalry also improves the ability of firms to innovate. First, the rivals benefit from spillover effects. That is, by picking up knowledge from each other and building on it, everyone is better off. Second, to survive in the crowded (by rivals) environment, firms have to work harder at building their capabilities and emerge as better competitors.

Government policies also play a critical role. For example, the U.S. government provides funding for research through bodies such as the National Institutes of Health (NIH). Ward and Dranove showed that such research greatly stimulates privately funded research by local firms.[40] The role of MITI in establishing Japan as a post–World War II economic power has also been widely explored. The break of the U.S. stranglehold on commercial jet aircraft by Airbus Industry was greatly aided by the policies of some European governments.

Strategic Choice

The strategic choice view argues that if an incumbent is not the first to introduce an innovation, it may not be because it has no incentive to invest, its competence has been destroyed, it has not recognized the potential of the innovation, it does not have the complementary assets, it did not use the right adoption mechanism, or it is in an environment that is not conducive to innovation. It may be because of the firm's innovation strategy—its goals, timing, actions, and resource allocation in using new knowledge to offer new products or services. By making the right choices early, a firm can build the right competences and complementary assets, or even shape the kind of environment in which it is going to operate.[41] Freeman suggests several innovation strategies: offensive, defensive, imitative, dependent, traditional, and opportunistic.[42] A firm with an *offensive* strategy is the first to introduce new products. If its strategy is to be the first to innovate, it will invest in the innovation and build the capabilities to do so. Wal-Mart, through systematic strategic choices, has become the largest retailer in the world. In a *defensive* innovation strategy, a firm waits for a competitor with an offensive strategy to introduce a product first and resolve some of the uncertainties confronting the innovation. The defensive firm then introduces its own product, correcting any mistakes that pioneers may have made. For example, IBM let Altair and Apple establish that there was a market for personal computers before deciding to launch the PC, targeting the corporate customer. Firms pursuing a defensive strategy normally have very strong complementary assets—capabilities such as manufacturing, marketing, distribution channels, and reputation, which allow a firm to commercialize an invention—and when they decide to move, they do so very quickly. They usually have strong R&D since it takes knowledge to absorb knowledge.[43] The product is not an imitation of the pioneer's version but rather a differentiated product, often with better features and lower cost. The firm, in effect, catches up with or leapfrogs the pioneer. Thus not being the first to introduce an innovation may not be a sign of a lack of incentive to invest, competence destruction, absence of appropriate complementary assets, inappropriate adoption mechanism, or being in the wrong environment. It may be because the firm in question has a defensive strategy.

While a firm with a defensive strategy would like to differentiate its products, one with an *imitative* strategy would like to produce a clone of the pioneer's product. It has very little intention of catching up with or leapfrogging the pioneer. It usually has such low-cost capabilities as lower labor costs, access to raw materials, and strong manufacturing. In the *dependent* strategy the firm accepts a subordinate role to a stronger firm. It imitates product changes only when requested by the customer or superior. Many large Japanese firms have these satellite firms. The *traditional* strategy makes very few changes to products, only striving to offer the lowest cost possible. In the *opportunistic* strategy the firm looks for some unique needs of a market segment that are not being met—it looks for a niche market. The point in all these other strategies is that a firm's failure to introduce a product first can be due to its deliberate strategy.

Summary

The impact of an innovation on the heterogeneous capability and competitiveness of a firm as portrayed by the models of innovation discussed so far is summarized in Table 2.2. From an economic point of view, the incremental–radical dichotomy focuses on the extent to which existing products are rendered noncompetitive. From an organizational point of view, the dichotomy focuses on technological knowledge. The Abernathy–Clark model draws attention to market knowledge and helps explain why some incumbents do so well in the face of a radical innovation: their technological knowledge is destroyed but their market knowledge is intact, giving incumbents with such market capabilities an advantage over new entrants in innovations where market capabilities are important and difficult to establish. Both the incremental–radical dichotomy and the Abernathy–Clark model bundle component and architectural knowledge and therefore may see no difference between some architectural and incremental innovations. The Henderson–Clark model unbundles component and architectural knowledge, and it becomes clear that what appear to be

TABLE 2.2. Relationship between static models.

Model	Key features	Value added
Schumpeter I Schumpeter II	Entrepreneurs are the most likely to innovate. Large firms with some degree of monopoly power are the most likely to innovate.	Attempt to answer the question: who is most likely to innovate? The type of firm is what matters.
Incremental–radical dichotomy	*Strategic incentive to invest:* defines innovation as incremental if it leaves existing products competitive; radical if it renders existing products noncompetitive. *Organizational capabilities:* defines innovation as incremental if capabilities required to exploit it build on existing ones; radical if capabilities required are very different from existing ones. Focus on technological component of innovation; bundles technological and market knowledge; bundles component and architectural knowledge.	The type of innovation determines the type of firm that innovates. Incumbents are more likely to exploit incremental innovation, whereas new entrants are more likely to exploit radical innovation.
Abernathy–Clark	Unbundles technological and market knowledge. Highlights the importance of market capabilities.	Explains why incumbents may do well at radical technological innovations.
Henderson–Clark	Unbundles technological knowledge into component and architectural. Defines innovation as: incremental if both architectural and component knowledge are enhanced; architectural if component knowledge is enhanced but architectural knowledge is destroyed.	Explains why incumbents fail at what appears to be incremental innovations. These are actually architectural innovations.
Disruptive technological change	*Disruptive technologies* create new markets by introducing a new kind of product or service; the new product or service costs less than existing products or services; initially, the products perform worse than existing products when judged by the performance metrics that mainstream existing customers value; eventually, performance catches up and addresses the needs of mainstream customers; the technology should be difficult to protect using patents. Disruptive technologies require resources, processes and values that are very different from those that were acquired in exploiting the older technology. When incumbents eventually decide to adopt the new technology, it's too late.	Listening to customers too much can be a problem. Incumbents need special organizational arrangements to help them develop the new resources, processes, and values for the new technology without being encumbered by the old resources, processes, and values of the old technology.

TABLE 2.2. *Continued*

Model	Key features	Value added
Innovation value-added chain	Extends emphasis to the whole innovation value-added chain of suppliers, customers, and complementary innovators. The competence of a firm's ecosystem matters too.	Explains why incumbents may fail at incremental innovations and why they may succeed at radical innovations.
Strategic leadership	Explores the role of top management and argues that whether or not a firm adopts an innovation is a function of top management's dominant logic.	Explains why some incumbents are the first to embrace radical innovations.
Familiarity matrix	Suggests that success in adopting an innovation is a function of the adoption mechanism used.	It is how a firm adopts an innovation that determines its success or failure.

"incremental" innovations may actually be architectural innovations that destroy the knowledge of linkages between components. While the incremental–radical dichotomy, the Abernathy–Clark model, and the Henderson–Clark model focus on the impact of an innovation on a firm's capabilities, the innovation value-added chain model explores the impact of the innovation on the firm's local environment of suppliers, customers, and complementary innovators. It suggests that as important as a manufacturer's capabilities are in the face of an innovation, those of its suppliers, customers, and complementary innovators can be just as important.

The strategic leadership view argues that the ability of a firm to embrace and exploit an innovation is a function of the firm's top management dominant logic; of how this logic enables top management to recognize the potential of an innovation and therefore to better allocate resources for exploiting it. Roberts and Berry suggest strategies for adopting an innovation given that a firm understands the potential of the innovation and the extent to which it obsoletes existing technological and market capabilities.

The quantity and quality of new knowledge model suggests that while it is important how *new* the new knowledge is that underpins an innovation, how *much* of it there is and the *quality* of its composition are also important. Whether the innovation is bulk processing or knowledge based and how tacit that knowledge is both play a role in who is most likely to profit from it.

While not explicitly categorizing innovation, the Teece model explains why a firm can still be unable to exploit an innovation, even when it has the technological capabilities. Capabilities other than technological ones—complementary assets— matter. Advocates of the environment as a driver of innovation argue that a firm's ability to innovate is a function of its local environment. Finally, the strategic choice view suggests that a firm's innovation strategy is what determines when it introduces an innovation, and how it exploits it.

DYNAMIC MODELS

A major shortcoming of all the models we have examined so far is that they are static. Only the cross-sectional view of a firm's capabilities and the knowledge that underpins them as well as the firm's incentive to invest at a point in time are explored. For example, we say that the electric car will be a radical innovation for Ford in 2005 because in that year, the skills that Ford needs to exploit electric car technology are very different from those it uses to exploit its existing internal combustion engine technology. The models do not look at what happens with the innovation following first adoption. The only "dynamism" in them is that there is a change from the old to the new. The models that follow are dynamic in that they take a longitudinal view of innovation and explore its evolution following introduction. They view a technology as having a life of its own with radical and incremental phases, each of which may take a different type of firm to succeed.

Utterback–Abernathy Dynamic Model of Innovation

Utterback and Abernathy detailed the dynamic processes that take place within an industry and its firms during the evolution of a technology from the *fluid* phase through a *transitional* phase to the *specific* phase.[44] In the fluid phase there are a lot of technological and market uncertainties. Technology is in a state of flux, and firms have no clear idea whether, when, or where to invest in R&D. Custom designs are common, with the new product technology often crude, expensive, and unreliable, but able to meet the requirements of some market niches. These designs are in some ways but experiments in the marketplace, and they change as producers learn more about market needs and customers understand more about the potential of the evolving technology. Process innovation accounts for very little in the fluid phase. Input materials are largely off the shelf, and manufacturing equipment is mostly general purpose. The basis of competition is largely on product features.

The evolution enters the transitional phase when, as producers learn more about how to meet customer needs through producer–customer interaction and through product experimentation, some standardization of components, market needs, and product design features takes place, and a *dominant design* emerges, signaling a substantial reduction in uncertainty, experimentation, and major design changes. A dominant design is one whose major components and underlying core concepts do not vary substantially from one product model to the other, and the design commands a high percentage of the market share. Competitive emphasis shifts to meeting the needs of specific customers, which have now become more clearly understood. The rate of product innovations decreases, and emphasis shifts to process innovation. Materials and equipment become more specialized and expensive. Competition is on the basis of differentiated products.

In the specific phase, products built around the dominant design proliferate, and there is more and more emphasis on process innovation, with product innovations being largely incremental. Materials are now very specialized, and equipment is highly specialized. The basis for competition becomes low cost. Products are highly defined with differences between competitors' products often fewer than similarities.

The pattern just described repeats itself when a new technology with the potential to render the old one noncompetitive is introduced, often by a competitor from outside the established industry. This results in a discontinuity, plunging the innovation cycle back to the fluid phase, with another wave of entering firms.

The implications of this model are that as a technology evolves through the different phases, a firm needs different kinds of capabilities in order to profit from the technology. Thus in the fluid phase, firms with product innovation competences that allow them to differentiate their products are more likely to perform better than those that do not. In the specific phase, low-cost competences are particularly important. Since control of a standard can be an asset, ex ante measures to win such a standard can also be instrumental in determining who succeeds in exploiting an innovation.

Tushman–Rosenkopf Technology Life Cycle Model

An important question in exploring the dynamics of an innovation is, to what extent can a firm influence the evolution of the innovation? For example, to what extent can a firm guide its design to an industry standard? Tushman and Rosenkopf argue that this depends on the amount of technological uncertainty which, in turn, depends on the complexity of the technology and the stage of evolution.[45] Complexity is a function of (1) the innovation's dimensions of merit—its attributes as perceived by its local environment, (2) the number of interfaces between the innovation and complementary innovations, (3) the number of components that make up the innovation and the linkages between them, and (4) the number of organizations in the innovation's local environment that are impacted by it. On this complexity scale, simple nonassembled products such as paper or glass have the least complexity since their primary attributes are cost per unit, they have limited interface with other products, and their primary focus is on customers. Open systems such as computers, radio, or telephone networks are the most complex. Computers, for example, have several dimensions of merit: type of operating system, amount of memory, disk capacity, upgradability, speed, power consumption, weight, user-friendliness, and the ability to run old software. Interfacing with other computers, networks, and other software and hardware is important. And in a computer innovation, customers, independent software vendors, hardware suppliers, and communications network providers may be impacted. The more complex an innovation, the greater the role of nontechnical factors such as complementary assets and organizations in the local environment during the innovation's life cycle. That is, the best technology is more likely to win in simple products such as glass than it is in more complex ones such as computers.

Tushman and Rosenkopf's technology life cycle starts with a *technological discontinuity* that can be either competence enhancing or competence destroying. Technological discontinuities are "those rare, unpredictable innovations which advance a relevant technological frontier by an order of magnitude and which involve fundamentally different product or process design *and* that command a decisive cost, performance or quality advantage over prior product forms."[46] Following the discontinuity is the *era of ferment,* when there is a significant amount of technological and market uncertainty. There is competition for acceptance between different designs using the new technology, each of which may have a different technical approach. Within each technical approach there is also competition. There is also competition between the old and new technologies. Eventually, out of these different competing approaches emerges a *dominant design,* "a single design that establishes dominance in a product class."[47] The more complex the technology, the more likely it is that factors other than the technical superiority of the technology will determine what design emerges as the standard. The emergence of a dominant design substantially reduces technological uncertainty and ushers in the beginning of the *era of incremental change.* Critical technological problems are defined, product features are established, and attention is turned to incremental innovation. The technology gathers momentum until it is slowed down or replaced by a technological discontinuity. As illustrated in Figure 2.10, the more complex the technology and the earlier in its life cycle, the higher the uncertainty and the larger the influence of nontechnical factors.

As was the case with the Utterback–Abernathy model, the implications of the Tushman–Rosenkopf model are that to be successful at each phase of the life cycle, a firm may need different capabilities. How effective these competences are in influencing the evolution of the technology is a function of the complexity of the product, that is, the more complex an innovation, the more intrusion can be expected from sociopolitical factors during evolution of the technology.

Both the Utterback–Abernathy model and the Tushman–Rosenkopf model have some shortcomings. It is not easy to tell when each phase (or era) begins and ends. Not all products have dominant designs, and when they do, it is difficult to predict their emergence. Following the emergence of a dominant design, the number of firms in the industry does not always decline. In fact, it goes up if the winner of the standard decides to make it an open standard and licenses its technology to anyone who wants it. The PC is an example. Process innovation does not always follow product innovations. Intel was committed to MOS (metal oxide semiconductor) process technology well before its invention of such major products as the microprocessor and the DRAM. Of course, major process technological changes also took place after the invention of these products.[48]

S Curve

The Utterback–Abernathy and Tushman–Rosenkopf models both suggest that a specific state (or era of incremental change) ends with the arrival of a technological discontinuity. One problem: it is difficult to predict when this discontinuity will arrive. It has been suggested that a firm can predict when it has reached the limit of its technology life cycle using knowledge of the technology's physical limits.[49] Foster, for example, argued that the rate of advance of a technology is a function of the amount of effort put into the technology and follows the S curve shown in Fig-

State of evolution

	Era of ferment	Era of incremental change
High	Highest uncertainty Influence of nontechnical factors is highest	Medium uncertainty Influence of nontechnical factors is high
Low	Some uncertainty Influence of nontechnical factors is low	Lowest uncertainty Influence of nontechnical factors is lowest

(Complexity — vertical axis, High/Low)

FIGURE 2.10. Uncertainty and role of nontechnical factors.

ure 2.11.[50] Technological progress starts off slowly, then increases very rapidly, and finally diminishes as the physical limits of the technology are approached. Eventually the return on efforts becomes extremely small. A new technology whose underlying physical properties allow it to overcome the physical limit of the old technology must be used. Supercomputers serve as a good example.[51] For years they were designed using single-processor architectures, until their ability to compute started approaching a physical limit—the speed of light. Multiprocessor architectures such as massively parallel processors give rise to a new S curve, as shown in Figure 2.12, with a new physical limit now being the communications bottlenecks from the many processors whose actions must be coordinated. According to Foster, computer makers should have been able to foresee the end of the single-processor architectures by looking at the diminishing returns on efforts put into improving single-processor designs.

As a predictor of whether and when to adopt a radical innovation, the S curve has some shortcomings, which we will explore in more detail in Chapter 6.

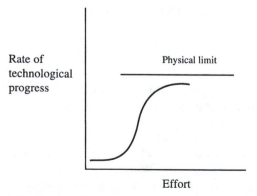

FIGURE 2.11. Foster's S curve.

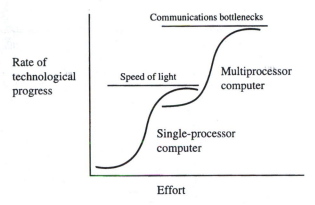

FIGURE 2.12. Supercomputer S curves.

Summary

The key features of each dynamic model and the value it adds to innovation models in predicting who is most likely to innovate are summarized in Table 2.3. The Utterback–Abernathy model introduces dynamism and the concept of a dominant design. It also suggests that industries evolve in a relatively predictable manner from one phase to the other. The Tushman–Rosenkopf model argues that technological progress depends on factors other than those internal to the technology. The more complex the technology, the more it is underdetermined by factors internal to it. Foster's S curve provides one way of predicting the end of an existing technology and the arrival of a technological discontinuity.

People

All the models discussed so far do not explicitly say anything about the role of individuals. In innovation research, five kinds of individuals have been identified to play key roles in recognizing the potential of an innovation and exploiting it: idea generators, gatekeepers and boundary spanners, champions, sponsors, and project managers. The more effective these individuals are, the better their firm will perform.

Idea Generators

These are individuals who have the ability to sift through jungles of market and technological information to find ideas that lead to new products or services.[52] They possess the talent and knowledge to find new cost- or time-effective procedures, approaches, or problem-solving strategies for problems. They possess T-skills,[53] that is, deep expertise in one discipline combined with broad enough knowledge in others to see the linkages between them. Such skills are critical in integrating different functions (R&D, design, marketing, manufacturing, customer

TABLE 2.3. Value added by each dynamic model.

Model	Key features	Value added
Utterback–Abernathy	Three phases in an innovation's life cycle—fluid, transitional, and specific.	Introduces dynamism.
	Dominant design defines a critical point in the life of an innovation.	Concept of dominant design.
	From radical product innovation to dominant design to incremental innovation. From major product innovation to major process innovation. From many small firms offering unique products to few firms offering similar products. From profitable firms to less profitable ones.	Industries evolve relatively predictably from one phase to the other.
Tushman–Rosenkopf	Similar in features to the Utterback–Abernathy model: technological discontinuity, era of ferment, emergence of a dominant design, and era of incremental change.	Technological progress depends on factors other than those internal to the technology. The more complex the technology, the more it is underdetermined by factors internal to it.
	The more complex an innovation, the more intrusion from sociopolitical factors during evolution of the technology.	
Foster's S curve	The returns on the effort put into a technology fall off as the limits to the technology are approached.	How to predict the end of an existing technology and the arrival of a technological discontinuity.
	The limits of a technology can be predicted from knowledge of its physical limits.	

service) to synthesize a product or service, in seeing the connection between a technology and its applications, or in turning customer expectations into products.

Gatekeepers and Boundary Spanners

The idea generator's ideas can originate from outside his or her organization (department, firm) or can be greatly complemented by ideas from the outside. One problem: information within an organization is often localized in that it may be a strong function of the culture, language, needs, and history of the organization. Gatekeepers link the local organization with external information sources.[54] They act as transducers between their organization and the outside. They understand the idiosyncrasies of the firm and those of the outside, and they can take internal questions, translate them into a language that the outside world can understand, obtain answers, and translate them to the organizational localized language. They also function as a repository of some kinds of knowledge for their organizations. Sometimes all they do is steer individuals to the right sources of information. While the gatekeeper is the transducer for interfirm information, the boundary scanner is the transducer for intrafirm information.

Champions

Champions, who are sometimes called entrepreneurs or evangelists, take an idea (theirs or that of an idea generator) for a new product or service and do all they can within their power to ensure the success of the innovation.[55] In the process they risk their positions, reputation, and prestige. They actively promote the idea, inspiring others with their vision of the potential of the innovation. They must be able to relate with the whole value chain and therefore require T-skills. Despite frequent opposition, especially in the face of radical innovation, champions persist in their articulation and promotion of their vision of the innovation. They usually emerge from the ranks of the organization and cannot be hired and groomed for the purpose of being champions. By evangelically communicating the vision of the potential of an innovation, a champion can go a long way in helping an organization to better understand the rationale behind the innovation and its potential.

Sponsors

Also called a coach or mentor, a sponsor is a senior-level manager who provides behind-the-scenes support, access to resources, and protection from political foes. Such support and protection serves two purposes.[56] First, it sends a signal to political foes of the innovation that they are messing with the senior manager and sponsor. Second, it reassures the champion and other key individuals that they have the support of a senior manager. Lee Iaoccoca, CEO of Chrysler, was the sponsor of the company's minivan. Edward Hagenlocker, Ford's vice president for truck operations, backed and boosted funds for a radical new approach to designing new cars, which was instrumental to the success of its trucks such as the F-150.[57]

Project Managers

While champions are leaders with a vision of the potential of an innovation and the ability to communicate that vision to the rest of the organization, project managers are the planners with an accountant's discipline who carefully and methodically plot out who should do what and when. The project manager is to meeting schedules what the innovation champion is to articulating his or her vision of the potential of the innovation. She or he is the "one-stop shop" for decision making, questions, and information on the project.

SUMMARY: AN INTEGRATIVE DYNAMIC FRAMEWORK

Each of the models we have explored makes a contribution toward our understanding of who is likely to introduce or exploit an innovation. These contributions can be summarized by four questions, which are at the core of the information collection and processing that underpin the introduction and exploitation of innovation— the *how, who, what,* and *when* of innovation.

How, Who, What, and When?

How

The first question is, how different is the new knowledge (required to offer the new product) from a firm's existing knowledge, and how different is the new product from existing products? That is, how new is the new knowledge? Is the innovation incremental, architectural, or radical? How obsolete does the innovation render existing products? How much of the new knowledge is required? How tacit is it? How central is the innovation to the products that the firm produces?

Who

Radical to whom? That is, when we say that an innovation is incremental, architectural, or radical, the question is, to whom? This question can have three different contexts: inside the firm; along the firm's innovation value-added chain of suppliers, customers, and complementary innovators; and in the global context within which the firm is operating. Inside the firm, the question becomes, is the innovation radical to R&D, manufacturing, marketing, or some other function? If an innovation is radical to R&D but not to marketing, an incumbent can take advantage of its marketing prowess to profit from it, if such marketing capabilities are important and difficult to replicate. Is the innovation radical to top management? If it is radical to most firms in an industry but not to the top management of a firm, that firm can embrace the innovation earlier than its competitors.[58] Looking outside the firm, along its innovation value-added chain, the question becomes, is the innovation radical to suppliers, customers, and complementary innovators? If it is radical to, say, suppliers but not to the manufacturer, such a manufacturer may encounter problems with exploiting the innovation. For example, in semiconductors, the feature size of devices has been decreasing steadily, but largely in incremental steps. Lately the implications of such decreases for suppliers of lithography equipment have been radical as they move from photolithography to X-ray lithography. This can present problems for manufacturers who have relied on suppliers for whom the innovation is now radical. At the global level, the question becomes, radical to which region or country? While electronic fuel injection may be standard in the United States, in some African countries it would be a radical innovation in both the economic and the organizational sense.

What

What is it about some firms that allows them to innovate better than their competitors? Why can't other firms acquire this what? It can be internal or external to the firm. Internally, is it the ability of a firm to perform certain activities? What activities? Is it the firm's ability to recognize the potential of an innovation or to build new capabilities quickly? Is it the type of people that the firm attracts—the best product champions, sponsors, project managers, and gatekeepers? Is it the intellectual property that the firm has accumulated? Is it the firm's strategies? Looking outside the firm, the question becomes, what is it about the firm's local environment that makes local firms more innovative? What drives a firm's ability to recognize the potential of an innovation?

When

The next question is, when in the life of the innovation are we answering the *how, who,* and *what* questions? The extent to which an innovation is radical, incremental, or architectural and how much of the new knowledge the firm must deal with are a function of the innovation's life cycle. The capabilities that allow a firm to perform well early in the life of an innovation may not be appropriate in the mature stage of the innovation. For example, while the ability to recognize the potential of an innovation may be critical early in the life of the innovation, the ability to manufacture at lower cost may prevail in the mature stage.

The Profit Chain

Exploring answers to these questions leads to the profit chain model of Figure 2.13. In the model the unit of performance is profits. A firm profits from an innovation by using new knowledge to offer new products or services at a lower cost than its competitors, offer differentiated products at premium prices that more than compensate for the extra cost of differentiation, or both.[59] To offer these products, a firm must carry out certain activities better than its competitors. To do so, a firm relies on its capabilities (competences and endowments). Underpinning these capabilities are technological and market knowledge. In the face of an innovation, how different the new knowledge (required to offer the new products or service) is from the old is critical to how well the firm can recognize and exploit the innovation. The same holds true for how much of the new knowledge is needed to carry out the innovation successfully and the extent to which the new knowledge is tacit.

A firm's capabilities are also a function of its strategy, structure, and systems; the people that make up the firm; and its local environment. A firm with an offensive innovation strategy, for example, works harder to be the first to introduce new products and therefore builds its capabilities accordingly. Implementing its strategies means building the right organizational structure, systems, and people. The more demanding, for example, an environment, the more local firms fine-tune their capabilities to meet the expectations. Competitors can introduce radical technological changes, thereby rendering a firm's existing competences obsolete. Government deregulation or regulation can render existing capabilities and underlying knowledge obsolete. Chance events sometimes play a role. We will revisit some of these factors from time to time in this book.

How, When, Who

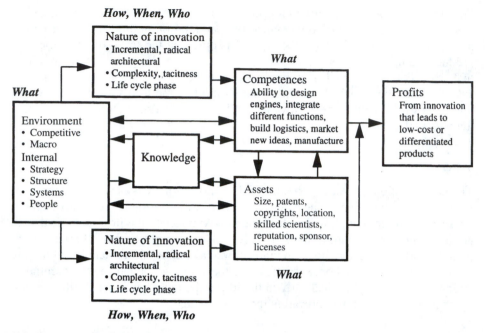

FIGURE 2.13. Integrative model for exploring how to profit from an innovation.

KEY TERMS

Administrative innovation
Appropriability regime
Architectural innovation
Boundary spanner
Champion
Competence destroying
Competence enhancing
Complementary assets
Complexity
Component knowledge
Defensive and offensive strategies
Disruptive Technology
Dominant design
Drastic innovation
Era of ferment
Era of incremental innovation
Fluid, transitional, and specific phases
Gatekeeper
Idea generation

Imitability
Incremental innovation
Innovation
Innovation value-added chain
Invention
Knowledge-based products
Positive feedback
Positive-feedback products
Process innovation
Project manager
Quality of knowledge
Quantity of knowledge
S curve
Sponsor
Strategic incentive to invest
T-skills
Tacit knowledge
Technological discontinuity

QUESTIONS AND EXERCISES

1. Can innovation be radical in the organizational sense and yet be incremental in the economic sense? How about vice versa? Give some examples.
2. What is the difference between static and dynamic models of innovation? Is this difference important?
3. What is the relationship between a firm's competitive advantage and innovation?
4. Looking at Figure 2.13, should there be an arrow from the profit box pointing back at the other boxes? Which boxes and why?
5. What is the difference between an architectural innovation and a disruptive technological change?

NOTES

1. Freeman, C. *The Economics of Industrial Innovation.* Cambridge, MA: MIT Press, 1982. Roberts, E. B. "What we've learned: Managing invention and innovation." *Research Technology Management* **31**(1):11–29, 1988.
2. Porter, M. E. *The Competitive Advantage of Nations.* New York: Free Press, 1990, p. 780.
3. *New knowledge:* See note 5 in Chapter 1 for a definition.
4. Rogers, E. M. *Diffusion of Innovations.* New York: Free Press, 1983. Downs, G. W., and L. B. Mohr. "Conceptual issues in the study of innovation." *Administrative Science Quarterly* **21**:700–14, 1976.
5. Damanpour, F. "Organizational innovation: A meta-analysis of effects of determinants and moderators." *Academy of Management Journal* **34**:355–590, 1991.
6. Damanpour, F. "Organizational innovation: A meta-analysis of effects of determinants and moderators" (1991). Utterback, J. M., and W. Abernathy. "A dynamic model of process and product innovation." *Omega* **33**:639–56, 1975.
7. Both of Schumpeter's positions are outlined in Schumpeter, J. A. *Capitalism, Socialism and Democracy,* 3d ed. New York: Harper, 1950. Schumpeter, J. A. *The Theory of Economic Development.* Boston, MA: Harvard, 1934. (A translation of the German version, *Theorie der wirtschaftlichen Entwicklung.* Leipzig: Duncker & Humboldt, 1912.)
8. Schumpeter, J. A. *Capitalism, Socialism and Democracy.* (1950). Tirole, J. *The Theory of Industrial Organization.* Cambridge, MA: MIT Press, 1988, p. 390.
9. Kamien, M. I., and Schwartz, N. L. "Market structure and innovation: A survey." *Journal of Economic Literature,* 1975. Cohen, W. ' 'Empirical studies of innovative activity." In *Handbook of Economics of Innovation and Technological Change;* P. Stoneman (Ed.). Oxford, UK: Blackwell, 1995.
10. Tushman, M. L., and P. Anderson. "Technological discontinuities and organizational environments." *Administrative Science Quarterly* **31**:439–65, 1986. Tirole, J. *The Theory of Industrial Organization.* (1988).
11. Tushman, M. L., and P. Anderson. "Technological discontinuities and organizational environments" (1986).
12. Reinganum, J. F. "The timing of innovation: Research, development, and diffusion." In

Handbook of Industrial Organization, vol. I; R. Schmalensee and Willig (Eds.). Amsterdam: Elservier Science Publishers, 1989. Henderson, R. M. "Underinvestment and incompetence as responses to radical innovation: Evidence from the photolithographic alignment equipment industry." *Rand Journal of Economics* **24**(2):248–69, 1993.

13. Arrow, K. J. "Economic welfare and the allocation of resources for invention." In *The Rate and Direction of Inventive Activity;* Richard Nelson (Ed.). Princeton, NJ.: Princeton University Press, 1962, pp. 609–26. Gilbert, R. J., and D. M. Newberry. "Preemptive patenting and the persistence of monopoly." *American Economic Review* 514–95, June 1982. Gilbert, R. J., and D. M. Newberry. "Preemptive patenting and the persistence of monopoly. Reply." *American Economic Review* 251–53, June 1984. Henderson, R. M. "Underinvestment and incompetence as responses to radical innovation: Evidence from the photolithographic alignment equipment industry" (1993).

14. Ettlie, J. E., W. P. Bridges, and R. D. O'Keefe. "Organization strategy and structural differences for radical versus incremental innovation." *Management Science* **30:**682–95, 1984. Dewar, R. D., and J. E. Dutton. "The adoption of radical and incremental innovations: An empirical analysis." *Management Science* **32:**1422–33, 1986. Tushman, M. L., and P. Anderson. "Technological discontinuities and organizational environments" (1986).

15. Leonard-Barton, D. "Core capabilities and core rigidities: A paradox in managing new product development." *Strategic Management Journal* **13:**111–26, 1992.

16. Abernathy, W., and K. B. Clark. "Mapping the winds of creative destruction." *Research Policy* **14:**3–22, 1985.

17. Mitchell, W. "Are more good things better or will technical and market capabilities conflict when a firm expands?" *Industrial and Corporate Change* **1:**327–46, 1992.

18. Henderson, R., and K. B. Clark. "Architectural innovation: The reconfiguration of existing product technologies and the failure of established firms." *Administrative Science Quarterly* **35:**9–30, 1990.

19. Christensen, C. M. *The Innovator's Dilemma.* Boston: Harvard Business School Press, 1997. See also Christensen, C. M., and M. Overdort. "Meeting the challenge of disruptive change." *Harvard Business Review* 67–76, March–April 2000.

20. *Innovation value-added chain,* as used in this text, refers to the suppliers, customers, and complementary innovators who add value to an innovation from a "manufacturer." This is different from Porter's *value chain,* which refers to the internal functions of a firm, such as operations, marketing, and sales. Porter, M. E. *Competitive Advantage: Creating and Sustaining Superior Performance.* New York: Free Press, 1985.

21. Complementary innovators are firms that provide complementary products or technologies for the manufacturer's product or technology, usually directly to customers. For example, Microsoft is a complementary innovator for makers of personal computers.

22. Afuah, A. N., and N. Bahram. "The hypercube of innovation." *Research Policy* **24:**51–76, 1995.

23. For a good account of the QWERTY story, see David, P. A. "Clio and the economics of QWERTY." *American Economic Review* **75**(2):332–36, 1985.

24. Gallium arsenide is a chip technology that can result in chips that are three and one-half times as fast, and consume half as much power as their silicon counterparts. The technology still has many problems.

25. Afuah, A. N. "Maintaining a competitive advantage in the face of a radical technological change: The role of strategic leadership and dominant logic." Working Paper, University of Michigan Business School, 1996.

26. Hambrick, D. C., and P. Mason. "Upper echelons: The organization as a reflection of its top managers." *Academy of Management Review* **9**:193–206, 1984.

27. Finkelstein, S., and D. C. Hambrick. "Top-management-team tenure and organizational outcomes: The moderating role of management discretion." *Administrative Science Quarterly* **35**:484–503, 1990. Hamel, G. M., and C. K. Prahalad. *Competing for the Future.* Boston, MA: Harvard Business School Press, 1994. Dominant logic has also been referred to by names such as *givens* (March and Simon, 1958) or *structure, mental frames,* and numerous other names.

28. Roberts, E. B., and C. A. Berry. "Entering new businesses: Selecting strategies for success." *Sloan Management Review* **26**(3):3–17, 1985.

29. Arthur, B. "Increasing returns and the new world of business." *Harvard Business Review* July–August 1996. Arthur, B. *Increasing Returns and Path Dependence in the Economy. Ann Arbor, MI: University of Michigan Press, 1994.*

30. For a good discussion of positive-feedback industries, see Bettis, R. A., and M. A. Hitt. "The new competitive landscape." *Strategic Management Journal* 7–19, 1995.

31. Katz, M. L., and C. Shapiro. "Network externalities, competition and compatibility." *American Economic Review* **75**(3):424–40, 1985.

32. Tirole, J. *The Theory of Industrial Organization* (1988).

33. Polanyi, M. *Personal Knowledge: Towards a Post Critical Philosophy.* London: Routledge, 1962.

34. Gordon, K. D., J. P. Reed, and R. Hamermesh. "Crown Cork and Seal Company, Inc. (condensed)." Harvard Business School Case #9–388-096, p. 2, 1988.

35. Teece, D. J. "Profiting from technological innovation: Implications for integration, collaboration, licensing and public policy." *Research Policy* **15**:285–306, 1986.

36. Rumelt, R. P. "Towards a strategic theory of the firm." In *Competitive Strategic Management;* R. B. Lamb (Ed.). Englewood Cliffs, NJ: Prentice Hall, 1984.

37. Schlender, B. "Steve Jobs' amazing movie adventure; Disney is betting on computerdom's ex-boy wonder to deliver this year's." *Fortune,* September 18, 1995.

38. Thomas, L. G. "Spare the rod and spoil the industry: Vigorous competition and vigorous regulation promote global competitive advantage: A ten nation study of government industrial policies and corporate pharmaceutical advantage." Working Paper, Columbia Business School, 1989. Thomas, G. L. "Implicit industrial policy: The triumph of Britain and the failure of France in global pharmaceuticals." Working Paper, School of Business, Emory University, February 1993.

39. Porter, M. E. *The Competitive Advantage of Nations* (1990).

40. Ward, M., and D. Dranove. "The vertical chain of research and development in the pharmaceutical industry." Mimeo, Northwestern University, 1991.

41. Child, J. "Organizational structure, environment and performance: The role of strategic choice." *Sociology* **6:** 1–22, 1972. Hamel, G. M., and C. K. Prahalad. *Competing for the Future* (1994).

42. Freeman, C. *The Economics of Industrial Innovation* (1982). Several other names have been used in the literature. Firms with an offensive strategy have been called *leaders* (or *innovators*), whereas those with defensive strategies have been called *fast followers,* and those with imitative, dependent, traditional, or opportunistic strategies have been lumped into the category of *followers* or *imitators.* Miles, R. E., and C. C. Snow. *Organizational Strategy, Structure, and Process.* New York: McGraw-Hill, 1978, use the terms *prospector, analyzer, reactor,* and *defender.* See also Ansoff, H. I., and J. M. Stewart. "Strategies for a technology-based business." *Harvard Business Review,* 1967.

43. Firms, whether offensive or defensive, need to have some absorptive capacity. That is, they need to do enough R&D to allow them to understand, evaluate, and learn from the pioneer's product. See, for example, Arrow, K. J. *The Limits of Organizations.* New York: Norton, 1974. Cohen, W., and D. Levinthal. "Absorptive capacity: A new perspective on learning and innovation." *Administrative Science Quarterly* **35:**128–52, 1990. Freeman, *The Economics of Industrial Innovation* (1982).

44. Abernathy, W. J., and J. M. Utterback. "Patterns of innovation in technology." *Technology Review* **80**(7):40–47, 1978.

45. Tushman, M. L., and L. Rosenkopf. "Organizational determinants of technological change: Towards a sociology of technological evolution." *Research in Organizational Behavior* **14:**311–47, 1992.

46. Tushman, M. L., and L. Rosenkopf. "Organizational determinants of technological change: Towards a sociology of technological evolution" (1992, p. 318).

47. Tushman, M. L., and L. Rosenkopf. "Organizational determinants of technological change: Towards a sociology of technological evolution" (1992).

48. For example, DRAMs started out with the MOS process, then CMOS, and, much later, BiC-MOS. Some day, there will be galium arsenide.

49. See, for example, Constant, E. W. *The Origins of the Turbojet Revolution.* Baltimore, MD: Johns Hopkins University Press, 1980. Sahal, D. "Technological guideposts and innovation avenues." *Research Policy* **14:**61–82, 1985.

50. Foster, R. *Innovation: The Attacker's Advantage.* New York: Summit Books, 1986.

51. Afuah, A. N., and J. M. Utterback. "The emergence of a new supercomputer architecture." *Technology Forecasting and Social Change* **40:**315–28, 1991.

52. A discussion of idea generators can be found in Roberts, E. B., and A. R. Fusfeld. "Staffing the innovative technology-based organization." *Sloan Management Review* 19–34, 1981.

53. The terminology of T-skills is from Iansiti, M. "Real-world R&D. Jumping the product generation gap." *Harvard Business Review* 138–47, May–June 1993.

54. The concept of gatekeepers was originated by Allen. See Allen, T. *Managing the Flow of Technology.* Cambridge, MA: MIT Press, 1984. See also Tushman, M., and D. Nadler. "Organizing for innovation." *California Management Review* **28**(3):74–92, 1986.

55. The concept of champions was first developed by Schön in his seminal article: Schön, D. A. "Champions for radical new inventions." *Harvard Business Review* **41:**77–86, 1963. See also Howell, J. M., and C. A. Higgins. "Champions of technological innovation." *Administrative Science Quarterly* **35:**317–341, 1990. Roberts, E. B., and A. R. Fusfeld. "Staffing the innovative technology-based organization" (1981).

56. Roberts, E. B., and A. R. Fusfeld. "Staffing the innovative technology-based organization" (1981). Maidique, M. A. "Entrepreneurs, champions, and technological innovation." *Sloan Management Review* 59–76, Winter 1980.

57. Naughton, K. "How Ford's F-150 lapped the competition." *Business Week,* July 29, 1996.

58. Afuah, A. N. "Maintaining a competitive advantage in the face of a radical technological change: The role of strategic leadership and dominant logic." Working Paper, University of Michigan Business School, 1996.

59. Porter, M. E. "Towards a dynamic theory of strategy." *Strategic Management Journal* **12:**95–117, 1991.

3

THE UNDERPINNINGS OF PROFITS:
COMPETENCES, ASSETS,
AND KNOWLEDGE

A firm profits from innovation by using new knowledge to offer products at a lower cost than its competitors or products that are differentiated enough to command a premium price, which more than compensates for the extra cost of differentiation.[1] This raises the *what* question that we touched on at the end of Chapter 2: what is it about such a firm that enables it to offer these products, and why can't other firms offer the same products and erode the firm's profits? In this chapter we argue that the answer lies in two words: distinctive capabilities. Performing the activities of a firm's value configuration requires assets or resources and an ability to use them. This ability to use assets to create value and profit from it is called a competence. Assets and competences together form a firm's capabilities.[2] For example, an investment bank's knowledge in mergers and acquisitions underpins its ability to win new clients. A carmaker's knowledge in combustion engineering, materials, and electronic fuel injection underpins its ability to design new engines.

The fact that assets and competences underpin profits raises two very important questions: where do they come from, and why can't we expect firms to outbid themselves in the process of acquiring these capabilities and end up with capabilities that are too expensive? We will touch on these questions only briefly (to raise consciousness) in this chapter, postponing detailed treatment to later chapters. We will suggest that a firm's environment, its strategy, structure, systems, and people, as well as chance events are the sources of its competences and assets and of the technological and market knowledge that underlies these capabilities. These relationships are summarized in Figure 3.1.

First, we describe briefly what we mean by low-cost and differentiated products. We then sketch the activities that underlie the provision of low-cost or differentiated products or services as a precursor to exploring assets and competences. Next we define assets and competences, detail their properties, and explore the relationship between them. In particular, we explore the relationship between these properties and profitability. We then argue that technological and market knowl-

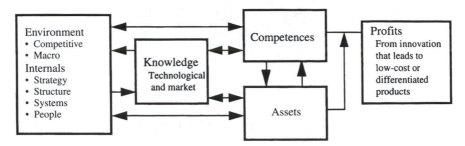

FIGURE 3.1. Position of competences and endowments in the profit chain.

edge is the bedrock of competences and assets, and we examine what that means to a firm's value chain. Finally, we explore the sources of competences and assets and some implications for competition.

LOW-COST AND DIFFERENTIATED PRODUCTS

A product is differentiated if customers perceive it as having something valuable to them that other products do not have. Porter and Barney offer seven different ways in which a firm can differentiate its products: product features, timing, location, product mix, linkage between functions, linkage with other firms, and reputation.[3]

A firm can differentiate its products by offering features that competitors' products do not have. For example, a pharmaceutical company can differentiate its drugs from those of its competitors by offering medicines that are taken once a day instead of three times daily. A maker of memory chips may differentiate itself by emphasizing the speed of its chips. For years, Silicon Graphics differentiated its computer workstations from its competitors' by emphasizing the superiority of its graphics performance—the type of performance that allowed its workstations to be used in the production of the movie *Jurassic Park*.

A firm can also differentiate its products by being the first to introduce the products. Since such products are the only ones in the market, they are, by default, differentiated since no other product has their features. Thus two personal computers with identical physical attributes—speed, amount of main memory, disk capacity, operating system, and number of applications running on it—are seen as highly differentiated if one is produced in 1994 and the other in 1995. For a while, Compaq differentiated its IBM-compatible personal computers by being the first to introduce products that used the latest versions of Intel microprocessors.

Two products with identical features can still be differentiated by virtue of their locations. One differentiating factor may be the ease of access to the products. For example, although two sandwiches may be all bologna, the one in New York City is not the same as the one in Paris if the customer is someone who lives in New York. A firm's products may also be differentiated by the service the customer would get if such service were ever needed. In many countries one of the most important things in buying a car, no matter how beautiful, fuel efficient, zippy, or superior in performance the car may be, is the availability of service. Thus a car firm in one of these countries can differentiate its cars by offering excellent service.

The mix of products that a firm sells can also be a source of product differentiation. Customers who prefer one-stop shopping would find such product mixes valuable. For example, some lawyers may prefer computer systems that already have custom-made law software loaded rather than having to buy the components separately and assemble them. Association with another firm can also be a source of differentiation. Firms that offered IBM-compatible computers in the 1970s and 1980s were actually differentiating their products by having the IBM association.

Finally, a firm's reputation can go a long way toward making customers perceive its products as being different. Mercedes Benz has a reputation for making durable cars, BMW for high-performance cars, and Maytag for durable dishwashers. Whether these reputations are deserved or are perceptions built through promotion is not always easy to determine. But they can last for a while, helping differentiate products.

VALUE CONFIGURATIONS

To create and deliver low-cost or differentiated products, a firm must perform a series of activities. The set of different functions that performs each of these activities is called a value configuration since each function adds value. There are three types of value configurations: the value chain, value network, and value chain.[4] To provide some background for the discussion on assets and competences that follows, we briefly explore these value configurations.

Value Chain

In a value chain, the activities that different departments perform are sequentially interdependent with, for example, the output of activity A forming the input of activity B and so on (Figure 3.2). Value is added at each stage to the product or service-to-be, and passed on to the next stage for more value to be added. For an automobile company, for example, A could be design, B manufacturing, C marketing, and D distribution. The design department adds value by conceptualizing and specifying how the automobile will be built. Manufacturing adds value by taking components from suppliers and assembling them according to the design. Marketing adds value by influencing customers' perception of the automobile, while distribution takes the automobile to the location where customers can take delivery. Most manufacturing industries employ the value chain. These include automobiles, airplanes, computers, microchips, appliances, jet engines, gasoline, plastics, glass, and so on. Since stage B depends on stage A for its input and on stage C to dispose of its output, and so on, the activities must be coordinated.

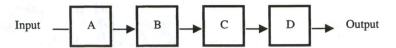

FIGURE 3.2. The value chain.

Value Network

In a value network, the departments of a firm add value by mediating between clients who want to be interdependent (Figure 3.3). Examples include commercial banks that mediate between borrowers and depositors, investment banks that mediate between issuers of equity and investors, and dating agencies that mediate between people who want dates. Value networks exhibit the property of network externalities in that the more clients there are in each mediating network, the more valuable the network is to clients. The more clients that there are at a dating agency, the better the chances of a client finding a date become. The more depositors there are at a bank, the better will be the chances of a borrower finding a loan at the bank.

Value Shop

Value creation in hospitals, consulting services, universities, R&D labs, and law firms is through the value shop. In a value shop, a client brings a problem to the organization and, depending on the nature of the problem, the organization can use one or more of input resources W, X, Y, and Z (Figure 3.4) to solve the problem. If the client is a patient, for example, the hospital can choose from lab testing, surgery, anesthesiology, and physical therapy. Which of the resources, what combinations of them are used, and in what order are functions of the type of problem and feedback from the previous problem-solving step. In the hospital example, whether

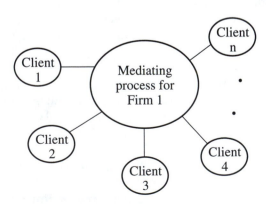

FIGURE 3.3. The value network.

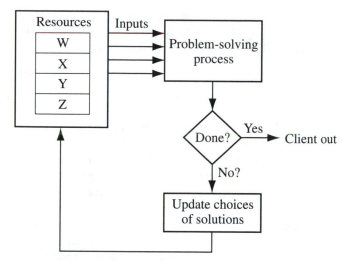

FIGURE 3.4. Value shop.

surgery is conducted on a patient may depend on the results of a lab test or consultation with a doctor.

In performing the activities of a value configuration, a firm often must interact with suppliers, customers, complementors, and firms from other industries. These other firms have value configurations of their own. What we really have, then, is a system of value configurations called a value system.

So What?

Depending on the industry and the firm's strategy, the activities that a firm undertakes in order to generate profits can be a subset or a superset of the ones just sketched in the value configurations. But even within the same industry, firms that pursue similar activities often do not earn similar profits. For example, in the 1990s, Intel, Motorola, and AMD pursued very similar activities in offering microprocessors for personal computers, but their profits from microprocessors varied considerably, with Intel making most of them. Sears, Kmart, and Wal-Mart pursued similar activities in retail, but their profits also varied considerably. This begs the question: why the differences?

In what follows we argue that these differences are a function of two factors: assets and competences, which in turn, are a function of the technological and market knowledge that underpins them.

ASSETS AND COMPETENCES

In performing the activities of a value configuration, a firm needs resources or assets such as plants, equipment, patents, skilled scientists, brand name reputation, geographic location, client relations, distribution channels, and trade secrets. A firm's ability to use these assets to perform these activities to create and deliver products and services to its customers is its competence.

Assets

Assets or resources can be grouped into tangible, intangible, and human. Tangible assets are both physical and financial, these are usually identified and accounted for in financial statements under "assets." These include plants, equipment, and cash reserves. Intangible assets are the nonphysical and nonfinancial assets that are usually not accounted for in financial statements. These include patents, copyrights, reputation, brands, trade secrets, relationships with customers, relationships between employees, and knowledge embedded in different forms such as databases containing customer vital statistics and market research findings. A patent or trade secret, for example, that gives a firm exclusive access to a product or process may allow the firm to be the only one producing a product with certain attributes, making the product highly differentiated and profitable. Examples abound: for a while, the copyright for Intel's microcode allowed it to offer differentiated microprocessors to makers of personal computers. Coca Cola's secret formula allowed it to make a soft drink with a taste that is perceived by some customers as unique. LSI Logic's reusable proprietary microchip building blocks or "cores" helped the company deliver standard functions to its customers. Human assets are the skills and knowledge that employees carry with them.

Coreness

Assets can be classified as core or noncore depending on how central they are to a firm's business. In investment banking, for example, client relationships are core since they are critical to winning new business from large clients, but patents may not be. Skilled individuals can also be core assets. In pharmaceuticals, for example, Sir James Black is credited with the discovery of blockbuster drugs at two different pharmaceutical companies: ICI and SmithKline.[5]

Imitability

Given the role that assets can play in a firm's ability to offer low-cost or differentiated products, the question is, why wouldn't competitors want to imitate such assets? In fact, they want to and often do. But imitability may not be easy for certain types of resource. Some of them, like patents or copyrights, are protected legally. Others, as we will see later, are the result of chance. Because of the uncertainty and complexity associated with the creation of some, it may be very difficult to imitate them. For example, trying to groom another Sir James Black may be very difficult, because we may not really fully understand what makes him so successful. Some, like brand name reputation, take so long to build that even if competitors knew exactly how to imitate, the time lag alone may be discouraging. The next question is, why can't competitors buy assets from someone else? They sometimes do, but it is not always easy or possible. Buying a Sir James Black may not work all the time. His success may be a unique combination of the environment he works in and his talents, and not all pharmaceutical firms can provide that type of environment. It may be that being among fellow Brits is what makes him tick, and the six figures that a Merck may be willing to pay him just wouldn't do. Others, like reputation, have to be earned. If a firm bought the Federal Express brand name and did not deliver packages on time, the reputation would gradually sink.

Profits

Figure 3.5 illustrates the role that assets can play in the ability of a firm to offer low-cost or differentiated products and therefore make profits. If the imitability of core assets is low, the owner is likely to earn some long-term profits. If it is high, the firm may be able to earn some short-term profits—long enough until the assets are imitated or bought. If the assets are noncore, then the firm stands to earn no profits when imitability is low, and negligible profits when it is high.

Competences

Assets, in and of themselves, do not customer value and profits make. Customers would not scramble to a firm's doors because the firm has great plants, geniuses, or a war chest from an initial public offering (IPO). Assets must be converted into something that customers want. To do so, a firm needs competences—the ability to

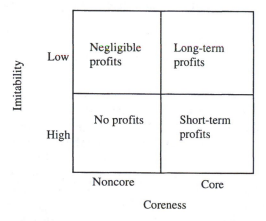

FIGURE 3.5. Core assets, imitability, and profits.

use assets to perform its value-creating activities. This usually entails the use or integration of more than one asset. LSI Logic's ability to quickly turn its "cores" into products that customers want is a competence. Intel's ability to develop microprocessors that exploit its copyrighted microcode and that are compatible with its installed base of microprocessors is a competence. So is Coca Cola's ability to turn its secret formula into a product that many customers perceive as being preferable to rivals' products.

Coreness

Competences vary in the extent to which they are at the center of a firm's ability to offer low cost or differentiated products or services. For example, Honda's ability to design high-performance engines is more at the core of its ability to offer quality cars to its customers than is its ability to find financing for customers. Hamel and Prahalad[6] have classified competences as a function of whether they are at the periphery or at the center of a firm's long-term success. If they are at the periphery, they are called *noncore* competences; if at the center, *core* competences. To be at the center, competences must meet three criteria: customer value, competitor differentiation, and extendability. The *customer value* criterion requires that a core competence must make an unusually high contribution to the value that customers perceive. For example, Apple Computer's expertise in developing graphical user interface (GUI) software makes its computers some of the most user-friendly. Such user-friendliness is valued by many customers. A competence is *competitor differentiating* if it is uniquely held or, if widely held, the firm's level of the competence is higher than that of its competitors. In the example of Apple's user-friendly computer interface, there are many companies with the ability to develop user-friendly interfaces. But Apple Computer's GUI is still arguably the most user-friendly. A competence is *extendable* if it is used in more than one product area. For example, Honda's ability to design excellent engines has allowed it to offer engines not only for cars but also for portable electric generators, lawnmowers, and marine vehicles.

Imitability

If a firm is making profits from core competences, the question is, why can't other firms imitate it and build similar competences? This takes us to one more property of competences: *imitability*—the extent to which a competence can be duplicated or substituted by competitors. A firm would rather have competences that are difficult to duplicate or substitute. The question is, how? If the knowledge that underpins the competences is tacit in that it is not coded but rather embedded in organizational routines and cumulatively learned over time,[7] potential imitators have three problems. In the first place, it is difficult to know just what it is that one wants to imitate. In the second place, even if a firm knew exactly what it is that it wants to imitate, the firm may not know how to go about it since the competences rest on tacit knowledge and are learned cumulatively over the years and embedded in individuals or routines of firms.[8] In the third place, since the competences take time to build, imitators may find themselves always lagging as they spend time imitating while the original owners of the competences move on to higher levels of the competences.

If a competitor cannot build competences, the next question is, why not buy them? One answer is that competences may not be tradable or easily moved from one firm to another. Two reasons have been advanced for why.[9] First, because of the tacit nature of the underlying knowledge, it may be difficult to tell just what it is that one wants to trade and who has the property rights for what parts of the underlying knowledge. What is it that we will buy from Honda that allows us to build zippy engines for cars, motorcycles, lawnmowers, and marine vehicles? Who has the rights for what part of the technological knowledge that underlies this competence? Second, the underlying knowledge may be sticky in that it is too costly to transfer.[10] Because of the tacit nature of the data, one may need to observe the seller over long periods in order to learn. This may be too complex and expensive.

Profits

A firm's ability to profit from its competences, then, is a function of how core the competences are *(coreness)* and the extent to which competitors can quickly acquire such competences—*imitability*). Figure 3.6 explores the impact of coreness and imitability on profits. (The profits come from the low-cost or differen-

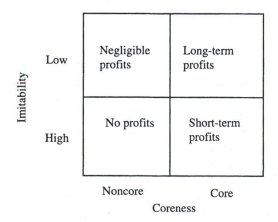

FIGURE 3.6. Core competences, imitability, and profits.

tiated products that the firm can make as a result of having the inimitable core competences.) If a competence is noncore and imitability is high, then one may not be able to make profits from it, all else being equal (Figure 3.6). If it is noncore but inimitable, the firm may be able to make some negligible profits, from it. If, however, the competence is core but easily imitated, the firm can make some profits, but these will only be temporary as competitors will have time to imitate. Finally, if the competence is core and inimitable, then the firm can make long-term profits.

Relationship between Competences and Assets

The examples explored so far suggest that there is a strong relationship between competences and assets. In the first place, a primary source of assets is competence. For example, a firm's ability to perform good research and win patents or copyrights allows it to accumulate intellectual property. It can then use such a property to limit the extent to which its products are imitated, and it can therefore increase its ability to offer low-cost or differentiated products. The ability of the human resources department of a firm to recruit and retain employees can result in the firm having a select group of gifted engineers, who can be a valuable resource in product development. Brand name reputation is achieved partly through advertising and delivering products or services that customers want. Shelf space in grocery stores or landing slots for airlines, all require certain competences and some luck to acquire.

In the second place, assets, in turn, help build competences. For example, in defending its microprocessor patents, Intel has developed strong competences in intellectual property protection. In protecting its installed base of personal computers, Intel has also improved its ability to design products that are compatible with older generations. Investment bankers who use their client relationships to win merger and acquisition businesses can help build yet stronger relationships or reputations.

Finally, and perhaps most important, there is the leveraging effect that assets have on the effectiveness of competences in delivering low-cost or differentiated products (Figure 3.7). The more core an asset is, the more effective a competence is in delivering low-cost or differentiated products. Two examples serve to illustrate this important assertion. If a firm's license or patent gives it exclusive access to a cost-reducing technology, the firm's costs would be lower than that of equally competent competitors, all else being equal. Two firms that are equally skilled in making violins can end up with two very different violins if one of them uses a secret coating, the formula of which no one else in the world knows. In each case one can say that the asset has leveraged the firm's competence, amplifying its effects. That is, if two firms A and B are equally competent at something, but A has more relevant core assets, A is likely to be more profitable. This statement is summarized in Figure 3.7. Thus although Intel's ability to design microprocessors cannot be questioned, its installed base and intellectual property protection play an important role in its ability to offer the kind of differentiated product it does.

Profits

Since competences and assets underpin low-cost and differentiated products (and hence profits), we can summarize the relationship between a firm's profitability on the one hand, and inimitability of competences and assets on the other, as shown in Figure 3.8. Effectively, firms make profits when they have core capabilities (competences and endowments) that are inimitable. The profits are not as high if either competence or endowment is noncore, and no profits can be expected if both are noncore.

KNOWLEDGE

A firm's ability to perform an activity rests on its knowledge of that activity, that is, competences rest on technological and market knowledge. As we defined in Chapter 2, technological knowledge is knowledge of components, linkages between components, methods, processes, and techniques that go into a product or service. Market knowledge is knowledge of distribution channels, product applications, and customer expectations, preferences, needs, and wants. Together, technological knowledge and market knowledge are the bedrock of capabilities. Boeing's ability to build airplanes, for example, rests on its knowledge in aircraft engines, control systems, navigation, and fuselage and how they can be linked together. It also depends on its knowledge of transportation, the airline industry, what airlines and passengers want, and how to translate all of these into an airplane. Merck is able to quickly synthesize new drugs only because of its stock of knowledge in combina-

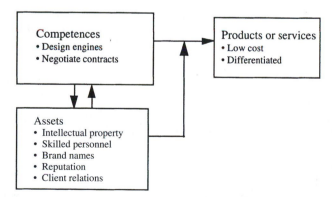

FIGURE 3.7. Relationship between assets and competences.

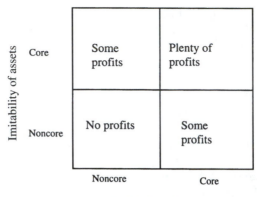

FIGURE 3.8. Profitability and capabilities.

torial chemistry, physiology, pharmacology, and its ability to integrate them. Intel's knowledge in semiconductor device physics, circuit design, logic, instruction set architecture, and layout design as well as its accumulated intellectual property underpin its ability to offer microprocessors.

Three properties of knowledge determine how well a firm performs the activities that rest on the knowledge: newness, quantity, and tacitness. We discussed the first two in considerable detail in Chapter 2 and will only summarize them here.

Newness

One critical property of the knowledge that underpins an activity is how new it is to the function or organization performing the activity. If it is very different from existing knowledge, it is said to be radical or competence destroying. If it builds on existing knowledge, it is said to be incremental or competence enhancing. The newer the knowledge, the more difficult it is for firms to perform the activities.

Quantity

The newness of the knowledge is just one factor. How much of the new knowledge is another. The move from a three-piece tin-plated steel can to a two-piece aluminum can and the move from a Boeing 747 to a 777 both entail new knowledge. But the amount of knowledge needed for the plane is a lot larger than that needed for the can. This amount is a function of the complexity of the activities that go into the product, which may or may not result in a complex product. For example, the activities that go into the discovery and development of pharmaceutical products are complex and knowledge intensive. Yet the final product is simple. The activities that go into making a plane are also complex and knowledge intensive, and the final product is also complex.

Tacitness

Knowledge can be *explicit* (articulated, codified) or *tacit*. As we saw in Chapter 2, it is explicit if it is spelled out in writing, verbalized, or coded in drawings, computer programs, or other products. It is tacit if uncoded and nonverbalized. Tacit knowledge may not even be verbalizable or articulatable.[11] Tacit knowledge can be converted to explicit and vice versa. An individual has his or her own image of his or her tacit knowledge. That image must be articulated in writing, drawing, products, or actions. A customer may have some image of what she needs in a product, but may not be able to articulate it. Nonaka et al. suggest that knowledge can be converted from tacit to explicit via metaphors, analogies, and models. Metaphors allow one to understand something by seeing it in terms of something else. "Analogy helps us understand the unknown through the known and bridges the gap between an image and a logical model."[12]

BASIS FOR DIFFERENCES IN CAPABILITIES

Although we discussed why it is sometimes difficult to imitate competitors' capabilities, we said nothing about why those differences exist to begin with. We offer one reason for competences and another for assets.

Bounded Rationality

An individual's ability to perform a task depends on his or her ability to collect and process information. The problem, though, is that individuals and organizations are cognitively limited and therefore do not always know everything that is relevant to the decisions they make. They are only boundedly rational. According to Williamson:[13]

Bounded rationality involves neurophysiological limits on the one hand and language limits on the other. The physical limits take the form of rate and storage limits on the powers of individuals to receive, store, retrieve, and process information without error. . . . Language limits refer to the inability of individuals to articulate their knowledge or feelings by use of words, numbers, or graphics in ways which permit them to be understood by others. Despite their best efforts, parties may find that language fails them (possibly because they do not posses the

requisite vocabulary or the necessary vocabulary has not been devised) and they resort to other means of communications instead. Demonstrations, learning-by-doing,
and the like may be the only means of achieving understanding when such language
difficulties develop.

Thus because individuals and organizations are cognitively limited, they may not
even understand or be able to accurately articulate how they perform certain activities or what their mental image of a situation is. The knowledge may be embedded
in their actions. It is thus difficult for the pilot of a 747 to describe exactly how she
or he feels in the cockpit of a plane and how she or he reacts to different situations,
at least not enough for an aspiring 747 pilot not to have to fly the plane himself and
learn. In the case of an organization, the knowledge may be embedded in the organizational strategies, structure, routines, and systems.

Because of these cognitive limitations, no two individuals or organizations can
have exactly the same stock of knowledge.[14] Since knowledge underpins capabilities, this suggests that no two firms would have the exact same capabilities at any
one time.

Limited Assets

The idea that some assets, by their nature, are limited, giving their owners an advantage, goes back to Ricardo, an economist.[15] He suggested that "original, unaug-
mentable, and indestructible gifts of nature" such as land are in short supply and
therefore inelastic. That is, supply is relatively fixed and does not respond to price
changes. Economic profits from such factors of production that are in short supply
have come to be known as Ricardian rents. (This is in contrast to monopoly rents,
which come from a monopolist deliberately limiting supply.) The owner of such a
limited resource stands to make a lot of money until one of two things happens.
First, if demand falls, the rents will diminish. Second, innovation may change the
basis for competition. Suppose someone invented something called fertilizer,
which can be used to increase the yield per acre of land, or skyscrapers, which can
increase the number of square feet of floor space per acre of land. Prices are likely
to fall. Land suddenly becomes elastic.

Today land is not the only asset that may be limited. Certain kinds of management talent may also be. Top chip designers are a scarce resource. So are top pharmaceutical researchers and MBAs with unique leadership skills. Taxi cap licenses
in certain cities, landing rights at major airports, and NFL franchises are also
scarce resources. Any manager who controls any of these resources has an advantage over his or her competitors, all else being equal.

SOURCES OF ASSETS AND COMPETENCES

Having established the importance of core competences and assets; we now turn to two important questions about them. Where do they come from? Why, in the process of acquiring these capabilities, do firms not outbid themselves and end up with capabilities that are too expensive to generate profits?[16] As shown in Figure 3.1, a firm's capabilities are a function of (1) its local environment; (2) its strategy, structure, systems, and people; and (3) chance events. These factors will be the subject of later chapters. In Chapters 5 and 12, for example, we will see that a firm's strategy, structure, systems and processes, and people play a critical role in how a firm builds and exploits knowledge. For example, the competences and standard that JVC and Sony built in developing the VCR are a strong function of their strategies in developing the technology. According to Rosenbloom and Cusumano:[17]

> Lacking consistent strategic direction from the top, the leading American rivals—Ampex and RCA—failed to sustain a focus for technical development and fell short. . . . Strategic consistency, then, differentiated the successful VCR pioneers from the others. . . . At Sony, top managers explicitly and consistently guided the direction of VCR development efforts. At Ampex, top management direction was sporadic and inconsistent over time; engineers on their own failed to develop a fruitful direction for technical development.

The story of Microsoft, which we will see again in later chapters, illustrates the role that chance events, firm strategy, and experience play in building the competences of a firm. In 1980, when IBM decided to enter the personal computer market, it went to Microsoft for software. It just happened that, at the time, Paul Allen (a cofounder of Microsoft) was in the process of buying an operating system called Q-DOS (quick and dirty operating system) from Seattle Computer. Microsoft bought Q-DOS, turned around, and sold it to IBM. As detailed in Chapter 7, Microsoft made sure that it retained the rights to sell DOS to any firms that cloned IBM's PCs. DOS would emerge as the standard for personal computer operating systems. Now it has a large installed base of personal computers with software that can only run on its operating system. More importantly, the copyright to the operating system is protected and competitors cannot copy it.

Overspending on Capabilities

Given that competence and assets are so important, why do firms not outbid each other in the process of acquiring a capability so that whoever ends up with it has paid so much for it that it is no longer profitable? In some cases firms have actually paid too much for capabilities. Some failed acquisitions can be placed in this category.[18] For two reasons, however, winners can still end up with profitable capabilities.[19] First, because firms may not even know explicitly if there is competition going on or what capability it is that they are competing for, there may not be enough competitors to overbid them for the capability. For example, not all firms knew that IBM was looking for an operating system to buy for its personal computers and therefore did not have a chance to compete for the standard. Second, not all firms have the right complementary assets that are sometimes critical to building a capability. For example, as detailed in Chapter 7, not all firms have a Bill Gates, whose shrewdness and experience helped make DOS a standard.

IMPLICATIONS FOR COMPETITION

The fact that performing the activities at each stage of a value configuration requires certain capabilities (competences and assets) and results in some output suggests that competition by firms is for more than just a low-cost or differentiated end product at the end of the chain. Each stage can be considered a competitive point, where firms compete for two things.[20] First, they compete for capabilities and the technological and market knowledge that underpins them. Second, they also compete for the output at that stage. Such an output is either sold or used as the input to the next stage, or both (Figure 3.9). Thus at the idea generation level, the race may be for the ability to select good ideas for development as well as for the technological knowledge that underpins this ability. The output may be for patents, licenses, trade secrets, or copyrights. The firm does not have to keep the intellectual property for its own exclusive use. It can license or trade for something else. For example, Texas Instruments collects royalties on some of the same patents that it uses to make its semiconductor products.

At the development level, firms are not only competing for skilled designers and the ability to, say, design for manufacturability, they are also competing for forging alliances that can enable them to win the dominant design or standard.[21] In the race for a dominant design or standard, assets such as firm size and reputation as well as a compatible installed base can be valuable. For example, IBM's size and reputation were instrumental to its winning the PC standard. In fact, IBM was said to have legitimized[22] the PC when it introduced a personal computer some years after many smaller companies, including Apple Computers, had been making and selling personal computers. A firm can sell its designs or manufacture them itself.

At the manufacturing level, the firm is competing for process technologies and the ability to deliver quality core products at low cost and on time. For example, one reason why Intel was the first company to ship DRAMs in volume was because it had a better process technology than AMS, the designer of the first DRAM. The output of manufacturing can be an end or a core product. A classic example of a firm that uses both core and end products to compete is Cannon, which makes laser printer engines for HP and Apple to be used in their popular printers, and also of-

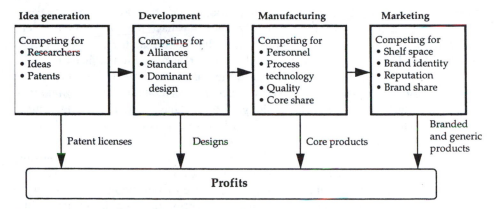

FIGURE 3.9. Competition for profits exists at all the stages of the value chain.

fers its own printers. In some industries, firms sell two kinds of end products. The first is the generic end product, which retailers buy and sell under their brand names. The second is the branded end product, which the manufacturer sells under its own brand name. For example, Allergen makes contact lens accessories and sells generic versions to Target stores, which label them with the Target brand. These Target brands (the generic brands) are sold in Target stores side by side with the same product from Allergen, with the only difference being that this second product is labeled with Allergen's own brand. At the marketing level, then, competition is not only for core products but also for brand name recognition and reputation as well as for generic and end-product market share.

An important implication of this multilevel, multistage competition is that a failed end-product launch for a firm may not really constitute "failure" since the firm may have built a stock of assets and competences as well as technological and market knowledge that can be used to offer other products or services. We will have more to say about this in Chapter 12.

INNOVATION AND COMPETENCES

As pointed out in Chapter 2, a central question in innovation management is, who is most likely to profit from an innovation? As explored in that chapter, the answer depends on the type of innovation. If, for example, the innovation is radical in both the economic and organizational sense in that it renders existing capabilities obsolete and existing products noncompetitive, new entrants are more likely to succeed at the expense of incumbents. Our exploration of the underpinnings of firm performance—of assets, competences, and knowledge—offers another answer to the question of who is more likely to perform well in the face of a technological change. Since capabilities are critical to creating value for customers, one can expect them to play a critical role during innovation. Firms that do well in the face of a technological change are likely to be the ones that have the capabilities to perform the activities of the value configuration that underpins the creation of customer value. Thus, to determine who is likely to perform well in the face of a technological change, one might start by answering the question: what does it take—in terms of assets, competences, and knowledge—to create and offer new value that customers want, using the new technology? Whoever has the underpinning nonimitable assets and competences should win. A firm's value configuration can be conceptualized as being made up of invention or technology and complementary assets. Recall from Chapter 2 that complementary assets are everything else, outside of the invention or technology, that it takes to create and offer the value that customers want. Also recall that according to the Teece model, two things determine the extent to which a firm can profit from its invention or technology: imitability and complementary assets (Figure 3.10). Imitability is the extent to which the technology can be copied, substituted for, or leapfrogged by competitors while complementary assets are all the other capabilities—apart from those that underpin the technology or invention—that the firm needs to exploit the technology. In the face of a technological change, incumbents usually have complementary assets while new entrants have none and often may have to build them from scratch. On the other hand, new entrants are usually the first to introduce the new technology. Thus, in innovations where complementary assets are tightly held and important, incumbents who own such assets can copy the technology and therefore have a chance to catch new entrants. If the technology is difficult to imitate, new entrants have a better chance of winning. Thus, in industries where complementary assets are tightly held and important, incumbents are more likely to profit from technological changes that allow existing complementary assets to be used in a exploiting the new technology.

SUMMARY

Firms make profits by selling low-cost or differentiated products. Underlying these products are competences and assets. A firm's competence is its ability to perform an activity. Assets are things such as intellectual property protection or reputation, which corroborate or complement a firm's competences in its offering of low-cost or differentiated products or services. These assets and competences, which we call capabilities, can be anywhere along a firm's value chain. Two properties of a firm's capabilities determine its profitability: coreness and imitability. The coreness of a competence or asset is the extent to which the capability is central to the firm's offering of low-cost or differentiated products. To be core, a capability must meet three criteria: customer value, competitor differentiation, and extendability. The imitability of a capability is the extent to which the capability can be imitated by other firms. The more core and inimitable a capability, the more profitable it is for its owner.

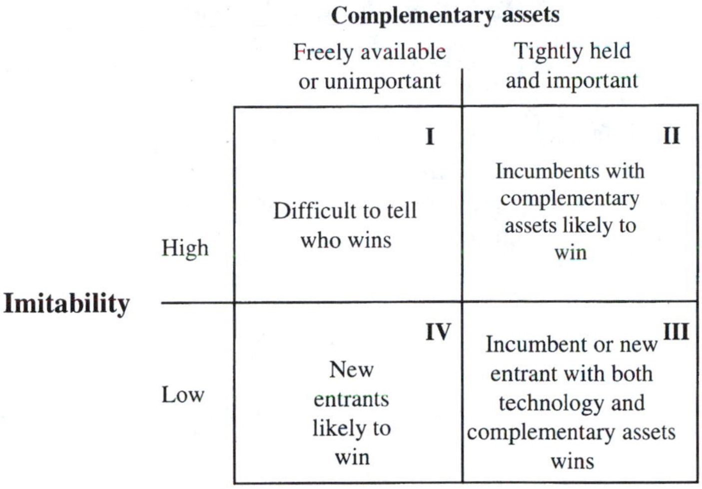

Complementary assets

	Freely available or unimportant	Tightly held and important
High	**I** Difficult to tell who wins	**II** Incumbents with complementary assets likely to win
Low	**IV** New entrants likely to win	**III** Incumbent or new entrant with both technology and complementary assets wins

Imitability

FIGURE 3.10. Who profits from innovation.

The bedrock of competences and assets is knowledge—technological and market. Knowledge has three properties that impact the ability of a firm to perform value chain activities: newness, tacitness, and quantity. Newness refers to the extent to which the knowledge required to perform an activity is new, that is, whether the innovation is radical or incremental. Tacit knowledge is uncoded, difficult to articulate or verbalize on paper or in electronic form. The quantity refers to how much of the knowledge is needed to perform the activity.

Competition is not just for end products. It is also for knowledge, capabilities, and core products.

KEY TERMS

Assets
Bounded rationality
Capabilities
Competences
Competitor differentiation
Core competences
Core products
Coreness
Customer value
Differentiated product

Extendability
Imitability
Low-cost and differentiated products
Monopoly rents
Product-market position
Profit chain
Resource-based theory of the firm
Ricardian rents
Tacit knowledge
Value chain

QUESTIONS AND EXERCISES

1. What is the relationship between competences and assets? Give examples from five industries.

2. What is the difference between monopoly and Ricardian rents?

3. Define the key terms above for a particular industry and suggest how these terms apply to the most profitable firm in that industry. Why have competitors not been able to imitate that firm?

NOTES

1. Porter, M. E. "Towards a dynamic theory of strategy." *Strategic Management Journal* **12:**95–117, 1991.

2. In the so-called resource-based view of the firm, which is the basis for this chapter, competences, resources, capabilities, and firm-specific assets have some very confusing definitions.

3. Porter, M. E. *Competitive Advantage: Creating and Sustaining Superior Performance.* New York: Free Press, 1985. Barney, J. B. *Gaining and Sustaining Competitive Advantage.* Reading, MA: Addison-Wesley, 1997.

4. Stabell, C. B., and O. D. Fjeldstad. "Configuring value for competitive advantage: On chains, shops, and networks." *Strategic Management Journal* **19:**413–37, 1998. The underpinnings of these value configurations are in Thompson, J. D. *Organizations in Action.* New York: McGraw-Hill, 1967.

5. "Harder going; in search of a cure." *The Economist,* February 7, 1987.

6. Hamel, G. M., and C. K. Prahalad. *Competing for the Future* (1994, p. 203).

7. See, for example, Dierickx, I., and K. Cool. "Asset stock accumulation and sustainability of competitive advantage." *Management Science* **35**(12):1504–13, 1989. Barney, J. B. "Firm resources and sustained competitive advantage." *Journal of Management* **17**(1):99–120, 1991. Peteraf, M. A. "The cornerstones of competitive advantage: A resource-based view." *Strategic Management Journal* **14:**179–91, 1993.

8. Properties 1 and 2 are normally attributable to causal ambiguity. Lippman, S., and R. P. Rumelt. "Uncertain imitability: An analysis of interfirm differences in efficiency under competition." *Bell Journal of Economics* **13:**418–38, 1982.

9. See, for example, Peteraf, M. A. "The cornerstones of competitive advantage: A resource-based view" (1993). Rumelt, R. P. "Towards a strategic theory of the firm." In *Competitive Strategic Management;* R. B. Lamb (Ed.). Englewood Cliffs, NJ: Prentice Hall, 1984. Rumelt, R. P. "Theory, strategy, and entrepreneurship." In *The Competitive Challenge;* D. Teece (Ed.). Cambridge, MA: Ballinger, 1987, pp. 137–58.

10. The concept of *sticky* data was conceived by von Hippel, E. " 'Sticky information' and the locus of problem solving: Implications for innovation." *Management Science* **40**(4):429–39, 1994.

11. See, for example, Polanyi, M. *Personal Knowledge: Towards a Post Critical Philosophy.* London: Routledge, 1962. Hedlund, G. "A model of knowledge management and the *n*-form corporation." *Strategic Management Journal* **15:**73–90, 1994.

12. Nonaka, I., H. Takeuchi, and K. Umemoto. "A theory of organizational knowledge creation." *Internal Journal of Technology Management,* **11:**833–45, 1996.

13. Williamson, O. *Markets and Hierarchies.* New York: Free Press, 1975, p. 21. Conner, K., and C. K. Prahalad. "A resource-based theory of the firm: Knowledge versus opportunism." *Organization Science* **7**(5):477–501, 1995.

14. This is one of Conner and Prahalad's arguments. See Conner, K., and C. K. Prahalad. "A resource-based theory of the firm: Knowledge versus opportunism" (1995).

15. Ricardo, D. *Principles of Political Economy and Taxation.* London: J. Murray, 1817.

16. This was one of the questions explored by Peteraf, M. A. "The cornerstones of competitive advantage: A resource-based view" (1993).

17. Rosenbloom, R. S., and M. Cusumano. "Technological pioneering and competitive advantage: The birth of the VCR industry." *California Management Review* **29**(4):68, 1987.

18. Hill, C. W. L., and G. R. Jones. *Strategic Management: An Integrated Approach.* Boston: Houghton Mifflin, 1995.

19. Peteraf, M. A. "The cornerstones of competitive advantage: A resource-based view" (1993).

20. Prahalad suggests that there are three phases for competition. The first is for "product concepts, technology choices, and building of competence bases." The second is for building of alliances to win the standard. The last is competition for end-product market share and profits. See Prahalad, C. K. "Weak signals versus strong paradigms." *Journal of Marketing Research,* **22**:iii–viii, 1995.

21. See Appendix 1 for more on dominant designs.

22. In response to statements that IBM had legitimized the PC, Apple Computer developed a product promotion that was never released. It went something like this: "They say that IBM has legitimized the PC. The bastards say, welcome."

SOURCES AND TRANSFER

OF INNOVATION

In Chapter 3 we explored how a firm's assets and competences can allow it to take new ideas and turn them into new products better than its competitors. The question is, where do the new ideas come from? Do they come from inside or outside the firm? How do these ideas get transferred to where they are best converted into new products? Knowing the sources of innovation can, for example, allow a firm or nation to allocate resources better in its search for innovations, allow a firm to improve its chances of recognizing the potential of an innovation, and help a firm better understand who its potential competitors are. In this chapter we explore these questions. We first discuss the sources of the technological and market ideas that are the basis for innovation. We then examine the difficulties associated with transferring technological and market knowledge and how they can be overcome. We also explore the differences between science and technology.

SOURCES OF INNOVATION

We explore two types of sources of innovation: *functional*[1] and *circumstantial*. Functional sources answer the question: where do the innovations come from? Do they come from within or from outside a firm? Where exactly within the firm? Circumstantial sources answer the question: when or under what circumstances can one expect the innovations?

Functional Sources of Innovation

There are five major functional sources of innovation for a firm: (1) its own internal value chain functions; (2) its external value-added chain of suppliers, customers, and complementary innovators; (3) university, government, and private laborato-

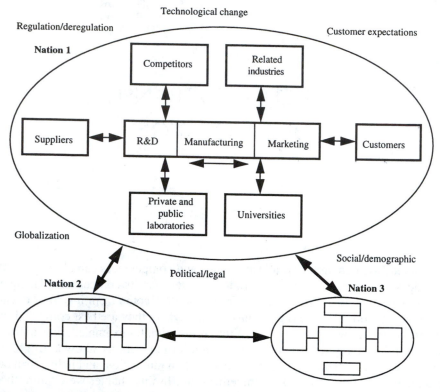

FIGURE 4.1. Functional sources of innovation.

ries; (4) competitors and related industries; and, (5) other nations or regions (Figure 4.1).

Internal Value Chain

Any of the functions within a firm's value chain can be a source of innovation. An idea can, for example, be generated and developed in R&D, the design transferred to manufacturing for production, and pricing, promotion, and positioning performed in marketing. These ideas can be in the type and number of components used in the design, the core concepts that underpin each component, and the relationships among them. Some of the more innovative firms such as 3M, Merck, and Intel spend a high percentage of their revenues every year on R&D to generate ideas for innovation. But ideas for innovation do not always come out of R&D. In performing their value-adding activities, manufacturing, marketing, and service also have an opportunity to innovate. For some industries low cost and product differentiation come largely from innovations in manufacturing. These are mainly so-called process innovations—new methods, techniques, input materials, types of equipment used, and information flow mechanisms that are used to manufacture a product or offer a service. The quality councils of the 1970s and early 1980s were designed to help generate new ideas to improve manufacturing.

In marketing, a new idea can be turned into an advertising campaign that alters the customers' perception of a product and therefore differentiates the product from those of competitors. Such a campaign can also build a firm's brand name recognition, further differentiating other products. In pricing, marketing can decide to give away some products so as to help win a standard. New ideas in how to position a product can also be critical. Financial innovations from the finance department can result in lower cost of capital, which translates into lower cost for new products. In short, any part of a firm's value chain can be the source of innovations.

Spillovers from Competitors

When a firm benefits from the findings of another firm's R&D, it is said to have benefited from spillovers. Spillovers can be anything from basic scientific knowledge to advertising ideas, both of which often cost a lot of money to develop. For example, a firm conducting research on cholesterol drugs may see some of its findings on how the body makes cholesterol spill over to its competitors. It may also see the chemical structure of its new blockbuster cholesterol-reducing drug copied by the same competitors. Some firms live off spillovers from others. They engage in strategies such as fast follower, imitator, follower, and cloner, all of which wait for other firms to invent products first. Microsoft did not invent most of the software products in which it has a commanding market share lead. Diet and caffeine-free colas were not invented by Coca Cola, although the firm is the leader in both markets. Spillovers are a function of the extent to which the scientific knowledge or invention can be protected from imitators—a function of its appropriability regime.[2] This is, as we saw in Chapter 2, a function of the protection accorded the intellectual property and of the tacitness and quantity of knowledge in question. Copyright protection is more tight than patent protection, and patent protection is tighter in pharmaceuticals than in semi-conductors. The more tacit and the more knowledge based, the more difficult it is to imitate.

Given that a firm's research findings can sometimes be easily imitated, the question is, why do so many firms still perform R&D? First, a firm's ability to absorb spillovers is a function of how much of the related knowledge it has, that is, it is a function of the firm's absorptive capacity.[3] One way to build this capacity is to perform related research. Second, there are first-mover advantages associated with being first to invent and commercialize, even when the invention is easy to imitate. By the time an innovation is copied, the innovator must have collected lots of rent or moved on to the next innovation.

Suppliers, Customers, and Complementary Innovators

Von Hippel showed that manufacturers are not always the source of innovations.[4] Suppliers, customers, complementary innovators, financiers, distributors, and any other entity that benefits from an innovation can also be a source of the innovation. These benefits can be economic or strategic. To see how, we explore the cases of suppliers, customers, and complementary innovators.

A supplier of component C to manufacturers can take two strategic innovation steps to increase the sale of C. First, it can invent a new product that uses component C as input.[5] For example, Alcoa and Reynolds Aluminum invented the two-piece aluminum can to compete with the three-piece tin-plated steel can.[6] Their intention was to turn the process over to can manufacturers so as to increase sales of their aluminum. Second, a supplier can also develop another product, B, that is complementary to component C. That way the customer can demand more of C. For example, a maker of microprocessors can give away software. Thus as more software becomes available for personal computers, more of them will sell, and the firm will sell more microprocessors.

Customers who require special features in a product they use may add these features to the product. If these are features that other customers can use, the manufacturer can incorporate them into its products. For example, a firm that uses a computer may decide to modify the operating system, adding features that other firms could use. The software maker can then incorporate these features into its next version of the operating system. Innovations originating from customers do not have to be incremental. When Singer needed electronic cash registers for its retail stores and NCR, the dominant manufacturer of electromechanical cash registers, would not listen to the idea of an electronic cash register, Singer was forced to invent one. Singer, a customer, originated a radical innovation in the electronic cash register that has evolved to today's electronic point-of-sale register. Singer may also be classified as a lead user. These are users whose needs are similar to those of other customers, except that they have these needs months or years before the bulk of the marketplace does, and stand to benefit significantly by fulfilling these needs earlier than the rest of the customers.[7] Lead users can be very good sources of ideas.

As we defined in Chapter 2, a complementary innovator is a firm whose products are critical to the success of a manufacturer, but over whom the manufacturer has very little or no direct control. For example, Microsoft's software is critical to the success of personal computer makers such as Compaq, yet Compaq has no direct control over Microsoft. To build good complementary products, a complementary innovator often has to understand some aspects of the primary product very well. This gives it an opportunity to be the source of innovations for the product. This can happen in one of three ways. First, like suppliers, a complementary innovator may make innovations in the primary product so as to sell more of its complementary products. For example, Microsoft can define a microprocessor architecture in order to sell more of its new operating system. Microsoft's efforts in offering a so-called networked personal computer are efforts to sell more of its software. Second, like a customer, the complementary innovator may need to add some features to the primary product to make its job of developing complementary products easier. For example, in developing applications software for a personal computer, a software maker may have to devise a memory management scheme to overcome the memory limitations of the personal computer's operating system. Third, a complementary innovator may find out that by adding some features to the primary product, its complementary products work and sell better. For example, a maker of electric car batteries can redesign the electronic control unit (of the electric car) to increase battery life.

University, Government, and Private Laboratories

Although basic scientific research is usually performed without any particular product or service in mind (that is, it is performed to gain scientific knowledge for knowledge's own sake), it can be a source of inventions that firms can commercialize. It is performed by universities, government research institutions such as the United States' National Institutes of Health, related industries, and competitors. (We explore the role of government in more detail in Chapter 15.) Popular examples of the results or consequences of basic research by universities and government and private laboratories include DNA, the Internet, and nuclear science. The results of basic research are normally disseminated in the form of journal papers and conference presentations and are usually available to anyone who wants them. If a firm believes that some of these results are promising (are potential inventions), it can perform more research on them, and this time with a particular application targeted, that is, applied research.

The research performed by universities and government and private laboratories is not limited to basic research. It extends to applied research. Popular examples include the computer, the jet engine, nuclear power, and the World Wide Web. Again, to take advantage of the results of R&D performed by these institutions, a firm needs to perform related research and build an absorptive capacity.

International

In Chapter 2 we saw that some nations are better at certain kinds of innovations than others. The United States leads in pharmaceuticals, biotechnology, software, movie and television entertainment, airplane manufacturing, and so on. Japan and Korea lead in facsimile machines and many other electronic components. Germany dominates in machine tools and chemicals, and Italy in shoes and specialty leather. These examples suggest that different nations can be better sources of certain innovations than other nations.

Complementarity of Sources and Timing

It is important to note the interacting and complementary nature of these sources. Consider this case. A U.S. pharmaceutical firm recognizes the potential of a market for cholesterol-lowering drugs and is determined to capitalize on it. It wants to develop a drug that curbs the ability of the body to produce cholesterol as compared to existing drugs, which try to use up the cholesterol that has already been produced and is in the blood stream. Meanwhile, years earlier, a Japanese firm has discovered a compound that inhibits cholesterol synthesis in cultured human cells. With public funding, U.S. scientists help the medical community, through publications and presentations, to better understand the scientific basis for this inhibition and, in the process, pick up a Nobel Prize in Medicine. The U.S. firm invests lots of money and effort in performing its own search for similar compounds. It successfully discovers a similar compound and turns it into a blockbuster drug of more than a billion dollars in annual sales. Thus the firm's own research, spillovers from a Japanese firm, and basic research from U.S. scientists all contribute to the technological knowledge that underlies the development of the billion-dollar-a-year drug. Often it is this ability to integrate information from different sources that is critical.

Circumstantial Sources of Innovation

So far we have explored where a firm can expect innovations to come from and said little about when or under what circumstances the firm can expect the innovations. Here we explore a few such sources. In general, it is difficult to tell when to expect an innovation.

Planned Firm Activities

Some innovations come from planned firm activities. This is what many people think about when they think of innovation. A manufacturer invests in R&D and other activities, and out of these investments come new ideas that are nurtured into new products. A customer, in the normal course of using a product, adds something to the product to make it easier to use. A complementary innovator adds some features to the main product to facilitate the use of its complementary products. Universities and government laboratories, in their normal course of research, hit a breakthrough (such as DNA or the transistor) that firms can build on to offer new products. In a way this is what we saw in exploring the functional sources of innovation.

Unexpected Occurrences

During the planned activities just discussed, unexpected occurrences, such as failure, can be good sources of innovation.[8] For example, when minoxidil was tested for efficacy in treating high blood pressure, Upjohn, the developer of the drug, did not expect one of the side effects to be hair growth. The firm took advantage of this unexpected occurrence and now markets minoxdil as Rogaine to treat baldness. IBM developed the first modern accounting machine earmarked for banks in the 1930s.[9] But banks then did not buy new equipment. IBM turned to the New York Public Library, which then had more money than banks to spend on equipment.

Change: Creative Destruction

Technological discontinuities, regulation and deregulation, globalization, changing customer expectations, and macroeconomic, social, or demographic changes are also sources of innovation. Biotechnology, the Web, fiber optics, digital movies, cable modems, massively parallel processors, and electric cars are all technological discontinuities of some sort as they offer an order of magnitude performance advantage over previous technologies. They also result in some sort of capabilities obsolescence. Schumpeter referred to such changes where an old order is destroyed by technological innovation as *creative destruction*.

In the United States, deregulation in telecommunications is allowing cable companies, regional phone companies, computer companies, long-distance phone companies, and even utility companies to vie for the delivery of voice, text, and images to customers. Deregulation and privatization are also taking place in Europe. Customers demand and expect certain levels of quality and price versus performance in the product that they buy. For various reasons, firms are no longer limiting their activities to their country of origin. Social or demographic changes, such as the changes from planned economies to capitalist ones, are also discontinuities, or baby boomers in the United States looking for luxury goods or ways of managing their own investments. These are all sources of new ideas from which to profit.

INNOVATION TRANSFER

Knowing the sources of innovation is one thing. Successfully transferring the innovation across functional, organizational, and national boundaries is another. We use the word *innovation,* instead of *technology* as in most texts, to emphasize the fact that both technological and market knowledge may be involved in the transfer.

Transfer across Functional and Organizational Boundaries

No matter what the source of an innovation, a firm that wants to exploit it is likely to be confronted with having to transfer it. If an idea is generated in R&D, for example, the prototype or blueprints may have to be transferred to the manufacturing function. If the idea is from a university, the firm must transfer it to its functions. The effectiveness of such a transfer is a function of four factors: the absorptive and transmission capacities of the receiving and transmitting organizations, the difference in the cultures of the receiving and transmitting entities, the type of innovation, and the timing of the transfer (Figure 4.2)

Absorptive and Transmission Capacities

Since it takes related knowledge to absorb knowledge, the effectiveness of the transfer of a technology from one entity to another is a function of the extent to which the receiving entity has related knowledge to allow it to absorb the knowledge being transferred. Take the transfer of a design from R&D to manufacturing. Was the manufacturing group consulting with and contributing to the R&D during the design process? Is manufacturing familiar with the idiosyncrasies of the design? In some firms, manufacturing works with design throughout the design phase so that by the time the transfer has to be made, there are no surprises. If the transfer is from one firm to the other, the questions are similar. Did the receiving firm perform research in related technologies? Does the firm have good gatekeepers to act as transducers between the two firms? Absorptive capacity is not limited to knowledge only. It can also mean having the right complementary assets. A phar-

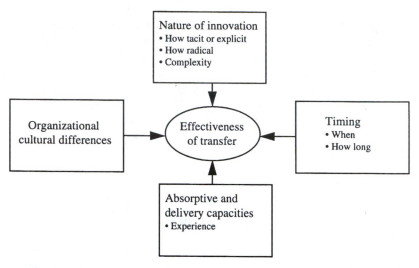

FIGURE 4.2. Determinants of innovation transfer effectiveness.

maceutical firm with the best scientists that wants to start producing bioengineered drugs is likely to run into trouble if it does not have the right manufacturing plants.

In order to play its role in the transfer successfully, the transmitter needs a certain level of delivery capacity. It must be capable of articulating what the innovation is all about. For example, the transfer of the two-piece aluminum can from aluminum producers to can makers depends as much on the aluminum producer's knowledge of can making and aluminum as it does on that of the can makers.

Difference in Cultures

An organization's culture is "a system of shared values (what is important) and beliefs (how things work) that interact with the organization's people, organizational structures, and systems to produce behavioral norms (the way we do things around here)."[10] Depending on how strong a corporate culture is, there can be subcultures within the firm. Such subcultures can have an effect on intrafirm technology transfer. If manufacturing views R&D as "a bunch of ivory tower academics" while R&D has equally little regard for manufacturing, there is less likely to be cooperation than if they viewed each other as partners in innovation.[11]

Differences in culture between transmitting and receiving firms can make the transfer of innovation very difficult. Take HP, which espouses teamwork and openness, the so-called HP way:[12]

It includes a participative management style that supports, even demands, individual freedom and initiative while emphasizing commonness of purpose and teamwork. . . . According to this style, the company provides employees direction in the form of well-defined negotiated goals, shared data, and the support of necessary resources.

Yet employees are expected to create their own ways of contributing to the company's success.

Transfers between a firm with such a culture and IBM with its more structured ways can run into roadblocks when, for example, an IBM employee may not understand why HP employees want to create their own ways of doing things instead of following the IBM way.

There is also the not-invented-here (NIH) syndrome from which the receiving organization may suffer. An organization suffers from NIH if it rejects ideas from the outside not on their merit but just because they are from the outside. U.S. automobile companies suffered from this syndrome in the 1970s when it was suggested that they could learn from Japanese automobile manufacturers. They wised up eventually.

Nature of Innovation

The transfer of an innovation also depends on the nature of the innovation, specifically, whether it is radical or incremental, whether it is complex or simple, how tacit the underlying knowledge is, and whether it is knowledge based or bulk processing.[13] Complexity is, as we saw in Chapter 2, a function of (1) the number of primary components and linkages between them that go into the innovation, (2) the innovation's dimensions of merit—its attributes as perceived by its local environment, (3) the number of interfaces between the innovation and peripheral innovations and their interrelatedness, and (4) the number of organizations in the innovation's local environment that are impacted by it. The more complex the innovation, the larger the quantity of knowledge that must be transferred, and therefore the more difficult it is to transfer it. If the innovation is radical in the organizational sense, the transmitter may not even know what it is that it wants to transmit, and the receiver may not have the absorptive capacity to receive the innovation. How easily the knowledge is transferred is also a function of how tacit it is. The more tacit, the more personal interaction between transmitter and receiver is required. The more knowledge based, the more absorptive and transmission capacity is needed.

Timing

For some innovations there is a certain time window—window of opportunity—within which an organization can undertake the activities that allow it to optimize its design or process. For example, during the early stage of an innovation, firms can experiment with different components, designs, and features. But once the dominant design emerges, it may be difficult to make substantial changes in some of the components or features. IBM had an opportunity to develop its own operating system or microprocessor for its PC, but it did not. Some time after its PC design emerged as the dominant design, it tried to introduce its own operating system and microprocessor into the PC standard. Both attempts have not been very successful so far. There are several reasons why this window closes. First, for products that exhibit network externalities and customer lock in, there is resistance by customers and

complementary innovators to any changes that destroy their networks or competences. In the IBM case, many customers did not want to learn a new operating system and therefore did not switch to IBM's new operating system. Second, once a
dominant design emerges, attention tends to focus on processes and incremental innovations that are critical to competition at that stage of the innovation's evolution.
Thus if any technological or market knowledge is intended for such a product, it
may have to be transferred during the window, or it might never be used again.

The effectiveness of the transfer is also a function of when during the life cycle
of the innovation the transfer takes place. Early in the life cycle of an innovation,
when there is still a lot of uncertainty surrounding it, transfer is likely to be less effective than later in the life cycle, when uncertainty is reduced and both transmitter
and receiver have had a chance to build absorptive and transmission capacities.

Transfer across National Boundaries

In this age of globalization, innovation transfer often involves crossing national
boundaries. The effectiveness of the transfer is still a function of the four factors
that affect cross-functional and cross-organizational transfers, namely, the differences in the cultures of the two entities, the absorptive and delivery capacities of
the receiving and transmitting entities, the timing of the transfer process, and the
nature of the technology. However, there are certain differences between nations
that can make transfer particularly difficult. We focus on these. A fifth factor is also
important in cross-country transfers (Figure 4.3): co-opetitors—the suppliers, customers, competitors, and complementary innovators with whom a firm must collaborate or compete in order to succeed.[14]

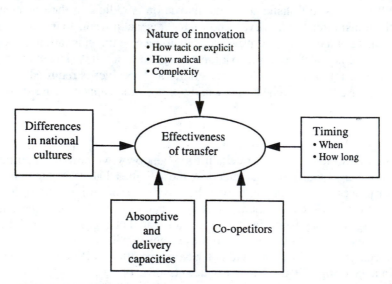

FIGURE 4.3. Determinants of the effectiveness of cross-national innovation
transfers.

Difference in Cultures

Earlier we defined an organization's culture as a system of shared values (what is important) and beliefs (how things work) that interact with the organization's people, organizational structures, and systems to produce behavioral norms (the way we do things around here). This culture is, in many ways, closely related to the culture of the nation in which the firm operates. In this definition, "the way we do things around here" can mean "here, in this country." Browning's account of the experiences of engineers from Siemens (a German company), IBM (an American company), and Toshiba (a Japanese company) while working on the development of the 256M DRAM memory chip in Fishkill, New York, illustrates how international cultural differences can dampen the rate of transfer of technological knowledge.[15] Toshiba engineers were used to working together in big rooms that look more like classrooms than American offices. This allows for informal communications that can be important in generating new ideas—ideas that may not come easily if one had to go to someone else's office and hope that he or she were free to talk à la IBM. By working together, the Toshiba engineers can also overhear conversations and know what others are doing, even family matters. Supervisors look over subordinates' shoulders.

The one person per office was fine with Siemens's engineers. What appalled them was the fact that the offices had no windows. What the offices had were narrow panes of glass on doors for visitors to see whether occupants were busy before trying to enter. German and Japanese engineers sometimes hung their coats over the glass, annoying IBMers. IBM's strict no-smoking policy meant that Japanese and German engineers had to go outside to smoke—not too pleasant an experience during the cold winters. IBM engineers, suffering from an NIH syndrome, resisted well-thought-out ideas from a Siemens engineer to improve an IBM pilot manufacturing system.

While examples such as the type of office or a no-smoking policy may be brushed off as easy problems that can be solved, they do illustrate how cultural differences can, unknown to participants, hinder innovation transfer. Other differences, however, included managerial styles. Siemens described the way American managers criticize their subordinates as America's "hamburger style of management." Managers start with sweet talk—the top of the hamburger bun. Then the criticism is slipped in—the meat. Finally, some encouraging words—the bottom bun. With the Germans, all one gets is the meat. With the Japanese, all one gets is the buns; one has to smell the meat.

Absorptive and Transmission Capacities

Differences in national educational institutions, concentration of competitors, and related industries suggest that there are likely to be national differences between absorptive and transmission capacities of firms. The presence of research universities means more opportunities to take advantage of the research being performed and build a firm's knowledge. A high concentration of competitors and related industries suggests two things. First, firms are more likely to benefit from spillovers.

Second, during the transfer process, a firm has more opportunities to communicate with local firms and obtain some of the absorptive capacity that it needs via, for example, informal know-how trading.

Timing

As posited by Vernon and detailed in Chapter 14, countries stand ready to accept products at different times during the life cycle of a product, when the cost of the product has dropped and these countries have built enough absorptive capacity to receive the innovation.[16]

Type of Innovation

What may be an incremental innovation in one country may be a radical innovation in another. While innovations in electronic fuel injection may be incremental innovations to firms in Germany and the United States, they may be radical innovations in Cameroon. Thus one party may have the incentive and capability to invest in the transfer whereas the other may not.

Co-opetitors

In the transfer of innovation within a nation or region, the system of suppliers, factor conditions, customers, related industries, and competitors that supports an innovation is likely to be the same for the transmitting and receiving entities. Across national boundaries, however, there can be considerable differences between co-opetitors from one nation to the other. For example, the supplier networks, excellent highway systems, and cheap and readily available gasoline of the U.S. environment may not be available in an emerging economy to which GM wants to transfer its automobile technology. Focusing only on the transmission and absorptive capacities of the sender and the receiver of the innovation in question, and leaving out the impact on co-opetitors, can be misleading. Thus in exploring transnational innovation transfer, it is important to consider not only the impedance mismatch between transmitting and receiving entities. It is important to consider the mismatch between the receiver's and the transmitter's co-opetitors. Several questions must be asked of the receiver and its new local environment (Figure 4.4). Do suppliers, competitors, customers and complementary innovators exist? It is not enough only to ask, as is traditionally done, whether customers exist for the innovation. How does the innovation impact the capabilities of these co-opetitors? Extensive research has shown, for example, that in many industries tight links to suppliers are critical to the success of manufacturers.[17] In such industries, successful transnational transfer of innovation requires the presence of capable suppliers in the receiving nation. In some cases this entails transferring supplier technology too. Japanese automobile manufacturers who established manufacturing plants in the United States had to build U.S. auto parts supplier networks. In entering Russia in 1990, McDonald's had to invest heavily in the growing of potatoes and beef to supply its hamburger restaurants.[18]

For innovations that require complementary products, a manufacturer may

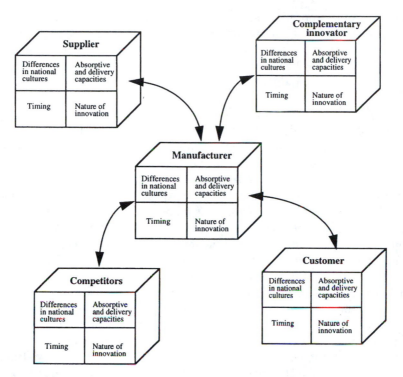

FIGURE 4.4. An innovation's co-opetitors during international innovation transfer.

need to establish the same kinds of relationships with complementary innovators as it does with suppliers. What use is there for home movie videos if there are no VCRs? In some cases collaboration with competitors may be necessary to lend some credibility to the innovation and to convince complementary innovators to invest in complementary product development.

The extent to which co-opetitors matter is a function of the complexity of the innovation. Complexity is, as we just saw, a function of (1) the number of primary components and linkages between them that go into the innovation; (2) the innovation's dimensions of merit—its attributes, as perceived by its local environment; (3) the number of interfaces between the innovation and peripheral innovations and their interrelatedness; and (4) the number of organizations in the innovation's local environment that are impacted by it. The more complex the innovation, the more likely it is that co-opetitors will play a critical role in the receiving nation.

Overcoming the Impediments to Innovation Transfer

In order to overcome the impediments associated with innovation transfer, a firm needs an organizational structure, strategies, systems, and people[19] that enable it to

(1) quickly spot ideas or innovations, (2) boost the absorptive and transmission capacities of receiving and transmitting entities, and (3) reduce the impedance mismatch between transmitter and receiver that has been created by physical, cultural, national, and knowledge gaps between the two entities.

Cross-Functional along the Value Chain

Boundary spanners act as transducers between their function and other functions of a firm's value chain. They understand the idiosyncrasies of their function and those of the other functions of the firm and can take function-specific questions, translate them into a language that other functions can understand, obtain answers, and translate them to their localized language. For example, a boundary spanner between R&D and marketing would understand both the technological and the marketing languages and be able to translate ideas from one function to the other. Champions help articulate a vision of the innovation that both receiving and transmitting functions can identify with. Sponsors use their considerable influence to "encourage" different functions to cooperate.

Allen's research suggests that locating people physically together enables them to communicate more frequently, and it is through such in-person, sometimes informal communications that new ideas can be spotted and exchanged.[20] Thus having marketing and R&D located physically next to each other gives them more opportunities to exchange both technological and marketing knowledge. Having an R&D group in a separate building far removed from everyone else not only creates a psychological barrier ("those ivory tower academics"), but also deprives the group of being near marketing to brainstorm on the latest customer needs. Spotting and transferring innovation should be a critical component in designing a building for an innovation-oriented firm.

Prior to initiating the transfer, there are several measures that a firm can take. The functions that are going to be involved in the transfer can jointly plan it, staff it, acquire the knowledge that they will need, and agree on transfer mechanisms.[21] If the transfer is, for example, of a design from R&D to manufacturing, people should be moved from manufacturing and marketing to R&D during the design of the product, well before the start of the transfer process. This serves several purposes. First, the employees from manufacturing and marketing carry with them tacit knowledge about what manufacturing needs to be able to manufacture the product well and what customers want, knowledge that can be incorporated into the design. Second, they acquire knowledge about the design as it evolves and will be in a better position to spread it when they take the design back to their functions during the transfer process. Third, they build interorganizational political networks that can come handy during the transfer.

During the transfer, employees can be moved around from the transmitter function to the receiver function. The developers of a product can move along with their design from R&D to manufacturing, and on to marketing along with the manufacturing and marketing personnel who had moved to the R&D function prior to the transfer. The originator of an idea from marketing moves on with it to the R&D group that is converting the idea into a product. In some cases, joint problem-solving meetings may be able to replace the movement of people. In others, special transfer groups have been created to effect transfers.[22]

Performance and reward systems that emphasize innovation transfer can also facilitate the transfer process. Information technology systems such as intranets also facilitate the transfer process.

Cross-Organizational

If the idea or innovation is from a competitor, research laboratory, customer, or supplier, gatekeepers play an important role in its transfer. They act as transducers between their organization and the outside. They understand the idiosyncrasies of their firm and those of the outside, and they can take internal questions, translate them into a language that the outside world can understand, obtain answers, and translate them to the organizational localized language. Although the gatekeeper is important, he or she is not the only one who should be communicating with the outside world. As is the case with cross-functional communications, cross-organizational communications should be continuous and not just at the start and the conclusion of the transfer process.[23]

A firm can also hire the person with the ideas, whether he or she is from suppliers, customers, competitors, an university, or a private research laboratory. It can also reverse-engineer inventions to learn more about them. In the 1970s and 1980s there was at least one firm whose job it was to open up and analyze microchips in order to facilitate copying by would-be imitators. Alliances with universities, competitors, or suppliers are also a good transfer mechanism. Then there is informal know-how trading. Firms trade information informally, but they will do so only when they believe that giving away the information will not hurt them.[24] Conferences in which engineers go to showcase their research talents are also good places to go for information. In any case, the firm needs to build its own absorptive capacity through such things as performing its own R&D.

Cross-National

Several steps can be taken to reduce the impediments of cross-border transfer of knowledge. Prior to the transfer, employees of the receiver can be sent to the transmitter's country to study at universities or work at research centers or related industries. This allows these employees not only to build up some absorptive capacity by acquiring the relevant knowledge that underpins the innovation, but also to learn something about the transmitter's language and culture and to build human networks. Training sessions in which members from both nations explore their cultures can help diffuse some of the tensions that we saw earlier in the IBM, Toshiba, and Siemens case. The receiver also needs someone similar to a gatekeeper. Such a person should preferably be one who understands the languages of both nations and has spent some time at the transmitter nation studying or working. An understanding of both cultures is preferred.

The transfer can take the form of joint ventures, other alliances, or acquisitions. During the transfer, continued workshops in the challenges of cultural differences can help reduce the impedance mismatch between the two firms.

Ease of Transfer Can Be Bad

So far we have treated the difficulty of transferring innovation as something bad. Often, however, a firm would like its technology to be difficult to transfer. That is because the more difficult an innovation is to transfer, the more difficult it is to be copied by imitators. Thus firms that want to keep an innovation proprietary would prefer to have one that is difficult to transfer.

RELATIONSHIP BETWEEN SCIENCE
AND TECHNOLOGY

We suggested earlier that one of the sources of innovation is the scientific research that firms, universities, and government laboratories perform. But when we defined innovation, we said it was the use of new technological or market knowledge to offer new products or services that customers want. The question then is, how does scientific knowledge get to become technological knowledge? Or does it? Better still, what is the relationship between science and technology?

There are at least three views of the relationship between science and technology. The first is the unidirectional model where basic science yields discoveries, which then lead to applied research, which, in turn, leads to invention and commercialization.[25] While in basic scientific research knowledge was generic and explicit and often encoded in written form, in applied research, the knowledge, now technological, is more specific to the firm's culture and environment, more tacit, and often encoded in products and services. For example, basic research in physics leads to the discovery of the transistor. Applied research then focuses on how to build a product, say a radio receiver, using the transistor. The knowledge that underlies the transistor radio is now technological, as it now reflects the firm's strategies, culture, and experiences.

The second model suggests that science and technology actually travel their own separate paths. According to advocates of this position, science and technology progress independently of each other.[26] Science has, as its inputs, verbally coded information such as discussions or papers and as outputs, publications. Technology also has as its inputs verbally coded information, but its outputs are physically encoded information in the form of products and services. Technology also has a by-product—verbally encoded information in the form of documentation for the product or service. Even scientists who perform scientific research, and engineers who pursue technological knowledge, are very different kinds of people.[27] Science students, for example, place a higher value on independence and learning for its own sake and value education as an end in itself. Engineering students, on

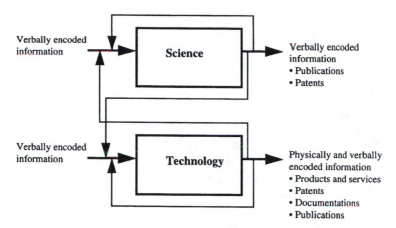

FIGURE 4.5. Relationship between science and technology.

the other hand, are concerned with success and professional preparation and view education only as a means to an end.

The third model agrees with the first in that scientific knowledge can underpin technological knowledge, but it disagrees with the implication that the relationship is unidirectional. Yes, scientific knowledge of electricity and magnetism was the basis for electrical engineering, and molecular biology is the scientific basis for biotechnology. But computer science came out of computer technology, and the development of the steam engine had a huge impact on the science of thermodynamics. The first model also disagrees with the assertion of the second model that science and technology grow independently of each other. Science and technology feed off[28] and complement each other, as shown in Figure 4.5. Science can lead to technology and technology can lead to science. Technological discoveries may need science to further understand and refine them for better commercialization. Computers and computer science are a good example. The field of computer science grew only after the invention of the computer, and then helped improve the computer. Scientific discoveries can lead to products, which in turn help us better understand the underlying science.

SUMMARY

A firm's R&D is not the only source of innovations. Its whole value chain is the source of various kinds of innovations. The value chain is not the only source of innovations either. Suppliers, customers, competitors, related industries, public and private laboratories, universities, and other nations are also sources.

Spotting and transferring these innovations to and within a firm is not easy. How effective a firm is at transferring innovation within and across its organizational boundaries is a function of the cultural differences between transmitting and receiving units, the nature of the innovation, timing, and absorptive and transmitting capacities of the two units. Across borders, these factors, in addition to the differences in co-opetitors between the two countries, also matter.

Several measures can be taken to increase the effectiveness of innovation transfer. If the transfer is internal to the firm, the relevant functions plan the transfer jointly, staff it, acquire the knowledge that they will need, and agree on transfer mechanisms. People can be moved from the receiving to the transmitting function to participate in the development of the technology. During the transfer, employees from the transmitter function move with the innovation to the receiver function. Locating participating functions physically close allows for more communications and better transfer. Boundary spanners and champions play key roles in acting as transducers and articulators of the vision of the innovation. Performance and reward systems that emphasize innovation transfer can also facilitate the transfer process.

If the transfer is across firm boundaries, the firm can hire the person with the ideas, whether he or she is from suppliers, customers, competitors, a university, or a private research laboratory. A firm can also reverse-engineer inventions to learn more about them. Alliances with universities, competitors, suppliers, or related industries are also good transfer mechanisms. Then there is informal know-how trading, in which firms trade information informally, but do so only when they believe that the information will not hurt their firms. Gatekeepers and sponsors also play key roles in the transfer. So does frequent and continuous communication with the outside. Prior to the transfer process, the firm should also have been building the relevant absorptive capacity through such functions as R&D.

Several steps can be taken to make cross-border transfers more effective. Prior to the transfer, employees of the receiver can be sent to the transmitter's country to study at universities or work at research centers or in related industries. Training sessions in which members from both nations explore their cultures can help diffuse tensions. The transfer can take the form of joint ventures, other alliances, or acquisitions. During the transfer, continued workshops in the challenges of cultural differences can help reduce the impedance mismatch between the two firms.

KEY TERMS

Absorptive capacity	*Creative destruction*
Breakthrough knowledge	*Functional sources of innovation*
Circumstantial sources of innovation	*Science and technology*
Co-opetitors	*Spillovers*
Corporate culture	*Transmission capacity*

QUESTIONS AND EXERCISES

1. Pick an industry of your choice and list the most likely sources of innovation.

2. What innovation transfer mechanisms are most effective and when? Why?

NOTES

1. The phrase *functional sources of innovation* was coined by Eric von Hippel. He was classifying individuals and firms in terms of the *functional* relationship through which they derive benefits from an innovation. In this classification, if a firm benefits from an innovation by using it, it is a customer. If it benefits by manufacturing it, it is a manufacturer. And so on. See von Hippel, E. *The Sources of Innovation.* New York: Oxford University Press, 1988.

2. Teece, D. J. "Profiting from technological innovation: Implications for integration, collaboration, licensing and public policy." *Research Policy* **15:**285–306, 1986.

3. Cohen, W., and D. Levinthal. "Absorptive capacity: A new perspective on learning and innovation." *Administrative Science Quarterly* **35:**128–52, 1990.

4. von Hippel, E. *The Sources of Innovation* (1988). Von Hippel's research concentrated on suppliers, manufacturers, and customers, which he called functional sources of innovation.

5. Harhoff, D. "Strategic spillover production, vertical integration, and incentives for research and development." Unpublished Ph.D. Dissertation, MIT, 1991.

6. Gordon, K. D., J. P. Reed, and R. Hamermesh. "Crown Cork and Seal Company, Inc. (condensed)." Harvard Business School Case #9–388-096, p. 2, 1988.

7. von Hippel, E. *The Sources of Innovation* (1988).

8. Drucker, P. F. "The discipline of innovation." In *Innovation,* edited by *Harvard Business Review.* Cambridge, MA: Harvard Business School Press, 1991.

9. This example is from Drucker, P. F. "The discipline of innovation" (1991).

10. Uttal, B., and J. Fierman. "The corporate culture vultures." *Fortune,* October 17, 1983. For a detailed discussion on culture, see, for example, Schein, E. *Organizational Culture and Leadership.* San Francisco, CA: Jossey-Bass, 1990.

11. Allen, T. J. "People and technology transfer." Working Paper #10–90, International Center for Research on Management of Technology, MIT, 1990.

12. von Werssowetz, R. O., and M. Beer. "Human resources at Hewlett-Packard." Harvard Business School Case #9–482-125, 1982.

13. See, for example, Winter, S. "Knowledge and competence as strategic assets." In *The Competitive Challenge;* D. Teece (Ed.). Cambridge, MA: Ballinger, 1987, pp. 137–58.

14. The term *co-opetitors* comes from Brandenburger, A., and B. Nalebuff. *Co-opetition.* New York: Doubleday, 1996.

15. This fascinating case is detailed by Browning, E. S. "Side by side: Computer chip project brings rivals together, but the cultures clash; foreign work habits get in way of creative leaps, hobbling joint research; softball is not the answer." *Wall Street Journal,* p. A1, May 3, 1994.

16. Vernon, R. "International investment and international trade in the product life cycle." *Quarterly Journal of Economics* 190–207, May 1966.

17. See, for example, Clark, K. B. "Project scope and project performance: The effect of parts strategy and supplier involvement on product development." *Management Science* **35**(1):1247–63, 1989. Schrader, S. "Organization of the supplier–manufacturer interface: The importance of domain specific communication." Working Paper, MIT Sloan School of Management, 1994.

18. "McDonald's in Moscow; slow food." *The Economist,* February 3, 1990.

19. The foursome of strategy, structure, systems, and people is discussed in more detail in Chapter 5.

20. Allen, T. *Managing the Flow of Technology.* Cambridge, MA: MIT Press, 1984.

21. Roberts, E. B. "Stimulating technological innovation: Organizational approaches." *Research Management* **18**(2), 1979. Tyre, M. J., and O. Hauptman. "Effectiveness of organizational responses to technological change in the production process." *Organization Science* **3**(3), 1992.

22. Roberts, E. B. "Stimulating technological innovation: Organizational approaches" (1979).

23. Allen, T. *Managing the Flow of Technology* (1984).

24. For evidence, see Schrader, S. "Information technology transfer between firms: Cooperation through information trading." *Research Policy* **20:**153–70, 1991.

25. See, for example, David, P. A. "Path-dependence and predictability in dynamic system with local network externalities: A paradigm for historic economics." In *Technology and the Wealth of Nations;* D. Foray and C. Freeman (Eds.). London: Pinter, 1993.

26. Price, D. J. "Is technology historically independent of science?" *Technology and Culture* **6**(4):553, 1965. Allen, T. *Managing the Flow of Technology* (1984).

27. Krulee, G. K., and E. B Nadler. "Studies of education for science and engineering: Student value and curriculum choice." *IEEE Transactions on Engineering Management* **7:**146–58, 1960.

28. Ziman, J. *An Introduction to Science Studies.* Cambridge, UK: Cambridge University Press, 1988.

STRATEGIZING

C   H   A   5   T   E   R

RECOGNIZING THE POTENTIAL OF
AN INNOVATION

"This 'telephone' has too many shortcomings to be seriously considered as a means of communication. The device is inherently of no value to us."
—*Western Union internal memo, 1876.*

"I think there is a world market for maybe five computers."
—*Thomas Watson, chairman of IBM. 1943.*

"The concept is interesting and well-formed, but in order to earn better than a 'C,' the idea must be feasible."
—*A Yale University management professor in response to Fred Smith's paper proposing reliable overnight delivery service. (Smith went on to found Federal Express.)*

As the above quotes suggest, it is not easy to recognize the potential of an innovation. That is, if, for example, a new technology came along, it is not always easy to understand the concepts that underpin each component of the technology and the relationships among the components. Nor is it always easy to understand how linking these components would result in a lower cost or a differentiated product or in an entirely new product that customers want. The question, then, is, why do firms have such a difficult time recognizing the potential of innovations? In this chapter and the next, we attribute these difficulties to two factors. The first is the uncertainty that often plagues innovation, especially in its very early stages. There is usually a lack of information and of clarity as to exactly what technologies will go into the product or service or what customers want. Firms must collect and process information to understand the rationale behind the innovation and its applications. This leads to the second reason for the difficulties in recognizing the potential of an innovation: the way firms collect and process information. In this chapter we argue that because of the differences in their managerial logics, strategies, structures, systems, people, and local environments, firms turn to different sources for information, consider only certain parts of that information to be relevant, and are limited and constrained in the way they process the information. Depending on the type of innovation, different firms will "see" the information differently and therefore perceive the feasibility and benefits of an innovation differently. The other reason why firms have difficulties recognizing the potential of an innovation—the uncertainty associated with the innovation—is explored in Chapter 6.

In the next section we set the stage for what follows by looking at some examples of opportunities that knocked on several boardroom doors with rather different responses. Then, in the remaining sections, we argue that a firm's ability to recognize the potential of an innovation is a function of how it collects and processes information, which, in turn, depends on the nature of the innovation and the existing organizational structure, systems, people, local environment, and managerial dominant logic.

SOME EXAMPLES

Some of the most tragic stories of firms are those recounting opportunities that passed them by. Fortunately or unfortunately, we may never know about all of them. Some are not so tragic, though. In 1995 Intel made $3.6 billion in profits, most of them from selling its microprocessor to be used in personal computers. Yet a 1970s proposal to build a home (personal) computer using Intel's microprocessor was rejected by none other than the firm's cofounder and chairman, Gordon Moore. "I personally didn't see anything useful in it [the personal computer], so we never gave it another thought," he would later say.[1]

In fact, when Intel started the design of the 80286, the fifth member of its now famous family of microprocessors, in 1978, its list of major applications for the microprocessor did not even include personal computers.

Not many firms are as lucky as Intel to recover from not promptly recognizing potential opportunities. Xerox is one of them. Its inability to recognize the potential of its inventions has to top the list for any one firm.[2] Its Palo Alto Research Center (PARC) built the first personal computer in 1973, long before Apple Computer was ever founded and eight years before IBM introduced a personal computer. It also developed the first hand-held mouse and the first graphics-oriented monitor, both of which would later form the basis for Apple's Macintosh and, later, Microsoft's Windows. Xerox also invented the first word processing program many years before Microsoft was founded and let alone before it dreamed of its best-selling Microsoft Word. The first laser printer, local area network, and object oriented programming language were also from Xerox.[3] Of course, the first computer workstation was also built at Xerox.

Xerox is certainly not alone. In 1975 IBM invented RISC (reduced instruction set computer) and sat on it while professors David Patterson of the University of California and John Hennessy of Stanford University evangelized the virtues of the invention. Then in 1981 it chose to use Intel's microprocessor in its personal computer (the PC). In 1995, 25 years after inventing RISC, IBM was trying to use it to dethrone the same Intel that it had helped crown king in the PC world (while leaving its RISC processor to rot on the shelf).[4] It was also trying to use RISC in its other product lines (servers, mainframes, and supercomputers), having done so with workstations in 1990. In 1983 it had seen RISC only as a technology for workstations—not personal computers, not minicomputers, not mainframes, and not supercomputers. IBM also helped crown Microsoft as king of the personal computer software by giving it the rights to DOS when it could have either bought it outright or introduced its own operating system.

In some ways, what Intel, Xerox, and IBM faced were more opportunities for new businesses than threats to existing businesses (arguable in IBM's case). In the Xerox case, billions of dollars were left on the table, but Xerox's main copier business was not threatened by the firm's inability to exploit the laser printer, the workstation, and other information technology inventions. In many cases, however, the impending technology threatens existing products and the firm still does not recognize the threat. NCR watched a mechanical cash register business, in which it had maintained a dominant market position, being invaded by electronic point of sale systems. Swiss mechanical watchmakers sat and watched their market shares being eroded by electronic watches, and mechanical calculator makers also watched their market shares being eroded by electronic calculators.

Why?

These examples beg a simple question: why was it so difficult for all these firms to recognize the potential of these innovations? The goal of this chapter is to explore this question. The elements of the arguments are shown in Figure 5.1. A firm's ability to recognize the potential of an innovation rests on the way it collects and

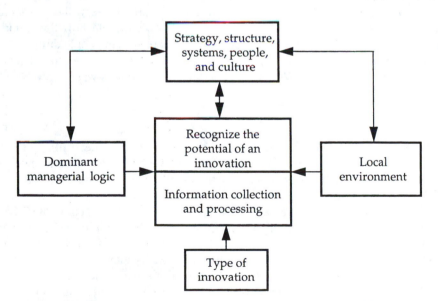

FIGURE 5.1. Factors that underpin a firm ability to recognize the potential of an innovation.

processes information and is a function of four factors: (1) its strategies, organizational structure, systems, and people; (2) its local environment, (3) its dominant managerial logic; and (4) the type of innovation in question. We explore these factors next. But first we define what we mean by recognizing the potential of an innovation and describe the information collection and processing process that underpins it.

RECOGNIZING THE POTENTIAL OF
AN INNOVATION

Recognizing the potential of an innovation consists of two parts: (1) understanding the rationale behind the invention and what it takes to commercialize it and (2) recognizing the different applications to which the new product or service can be put.

Rationale Behind an Innovation

Understanding the rationale behind an innovation consists of determining just what the components (and the core concepts underlying them) that go into the product are, and how they are linked together to deliver the new low-cost or differentiated features to customers. For a firm facing an innovation, understanding the rationale behind it may involve asking the question: can the new mousetrap be built using the new knowledge? For example, when the idea of building an electronic cash register first surfaced in the late 1960s, the question was: can a firm actually build a cash register using transistors instead of the gears, levers, ratchets, and motors that have been used all these years? How do transistors work, and how does linking them result in calculations? Would such a register actually get people through a supermarket line faster than existing ones? What will it take to build and deliver the new product to customers? What kind of service do customers want?

Applications

The other part of recognizing the potential of an innovation is determining the applications for the new product. That is, answering the question: will the new product be used in new markets as well as in existing ones? For example, will transistor radios only allow the innovator to sell to the home where vacuum tube radios have done well so far, or will they create a new market in portable and car radios? There are three categories of such applications. In the first, the innovation replaces an old solution for an old problem, because it has either a lower cost or better features than the old innovation (Table 5.1). For example, steel-belted radial tires replaced bias tires because of their superior performance (tire life and fuel efficiency).[5]

In the second category, the innovation solves an old problem as well as new one(s). For example, the personal computer replaced the typewriter as a product to

TABLE 5.1. Market competence and applications for the innovation.

Applications	Examples	Possible impact on market competence
Better solution to an old problem	Steel-belted radial tires	Enhancing
Better solution to an old problem; also a solution to new problem(s)	Personal computer replaced the typewriter and solved numerous other problems	Destroying
Solution to only new problems	8-inch disk drives were a solution to minicomputer secondary memory	Destroying

type documents and also proves valuable in other applications, such as document storage, electronic distribution, electronic merging, editing, and processing. Since the innovation solves old problems and a lot more, existing marketing competences may not be enough to exploit the full potential of the innovation.

Finally, the innovation can have a completely new application. In that case the market knowledge and the relationships that the firm had accumulated in serving the old application may not only be useless, but may actually constitute a handicap. For example, disk drive manufacturers who supplied makers of mainframe computers with 12-inch disk drives had difficulties adopting 8-inch drives early. One reason for this failure to adopt early was that 8-inch drive manufacturers worked hard to satisfy the needs of their mainframe customers who, early in the life of the disks, had little use for 8-inch drives, which were better suited for minicomputers than for mainframes.[6]

INFORMATION COLLECTION AND PROCESSING

"When I first became prime minister 15 years ago, it was a cultural shock to many Norwegians. Today, four-year-olds ask their mummies: 'But can a man be prime minister?' "
    —*Norwegian Prime Minister Gro Harlem Brundtland at the UN's Fourth Conference on Women in Beijing, China, September 15, 1995.*[7]

One way to explore why it is so difficult to recognize the potential of an innovation is to view the process of understanding the rationale behind an innovation and its applications as a problem-solving process in which a firm collects and processes information. Problem-solving involves knowing where to look for the information *(information channels),* how to screen it *(information filtering),* and how to process it *(information processing).* A firm must also deal with the cost of acquiring, transferring, and using the desired information *(information stickiness).*

Information Channels, Filters, and Stickiness

The process of innovation usually starts with an idea on how to use new technological or market knowledge to offer a new product or service. To determine the feasibility of the idea, the firm must collect and evaluate information on it. The sources to which the firm turns for the ideas (and the information to evaluate them) have been called information channels.[8] These channels depend on the stage of the value chain from which the idea is coming, and vary from industry to industry. For example, at the idea generation level, the R&D group of a pharmaceutical company may comb through biological science publications to look for potential ideas on drugs to reduce cholesterol levels. An automobile maker may go to the mechanical engineering department of a major university for new ideas on improving fuel efficiency. When an employee has a problem with software, he or she calls the computer services group of his or her company or the nerd next door. At the development level, firms may turn to competitors or the repertoire of design expertise within the firm.

Each of these channels usually contains much more information than a firm would ever need for the problem at hand. A firm must use its information filters to screen what it believes it does not need. For example, if Ford went to a local university to gather information on how to improve automobile gas mileage, it probably would pay little attention to electric car control units if it believes that the units have no relevance to the problem at hand.

Even if a firm chooses the right information channel and has the right filters to keep out what it does not need, it might still not be able to get enough of the desired information to solve its problem because it is too costly to acquire, transfer, and use. In that case the information is said to be sticky. Von Hippel suggests three factors that contribute to information stickiness: the nature of the information, the shear amount of it that must be transferred, and the attributes of providers and seekers of information.[9] The nature of the information refers to how tacit (versus explicit or generic) the information is. Since tacit information is not coded but, rather, embedded in organizational or individual routines, it may have to be transferred in person. For example, a doctor's knowledge of how to diagnose certain diseases may be difficult to spell out in a book, and therefore interns may have to follow her when she makes her hospital rounds. The amount of information that a firm needs can affect how difficult it is to acquire and transfer information. For example, the amount of data needed to diagnose a heart attack may be greater than that needed to detect a fractured shin. Finally, the stickiness of information depends on the providers and seekers. Information is less sticky when being transferred to an entity that has a stock of related knowledge. It takes knowledge to absorb new knowledge.[10] Thus it is easier for an intern to understand how the doctor is diagnosing the condition than it would be for an electrical engineer. We explore this in more detail shortly.

SOME FACTORS THAT IMPACT RECOGNITION
OF THE POTENTIAL OF INNOVATION

Having defined what we mean by recognizing the potential of an innovation and described the information collection and processing that leads to it, we now turn to the factors that determine a firm's ability to recognize the potential of an innovation (Figure 5.1). It is important to remember that the variables (boxes) and the relationships (arrows) shown in Figure 5.1 are not exhaustive.

DOMINANT MANAGERIAL LOGIC

The first factor that impacts a firm's ability to recognize the potential of an innovation is the firm's dominant managerial logic. Each manager brings to each management problem a set of biases, beliefs, and assumptions about the market that his or her firm serves, whom to hire, what technology to use to compete in the market, who the firm's competitors are, and how to conduct business.[11] This set of biases, assumptions, and beliefs is a manager's managerial logic. It defines the frame within which a manager is likely to scan for information and approach problem solving. It is the mental model that a manager brings to any innovation circumstance. Depending on a firm's strategies, systems, technology, organizational structure, culture, and how successful it has been, there usually emerges a *dominant* logic, a common way of viewing how best to do business as a manager in the firm. Dominant logic is very good for a firm as long as there are no radical changes.

The kind of organizational structure, strategies, systems, and people that exist in a firm tend to reflect management's dominant logic because management put them in place or they selected the management. These factors, in turn, reinforce the logic as the firm successfully carries out its activities. The longer the management has been at the company and industry, and the more successful the firm has been, the more dominant the logic and the more likely management will try to maintain the status quo.[12]

Figure 5.2 illustrates the role of dominant logic in the collection and processing of information. Of the universe of data that is available to a firm, its dominant logic only allows it to search for data in certain parts of the universe—certain information channels. Of the data in any of the channels that the firm searches, only the data that are consistent with its dominant logic will be allowed to go through.

The more successful a firm is in solving a problem using certain channels, filters, and problem-solving strategies, the more it will turn to them each time it has a problem. Higher performance reinforces the logic. Changes to a firm's logic are triggered by a problem or crisis.[13] Such a crisis may force the firm to seek information in different channels with filters that have been modified to reflect the crisis. Problem solving also changes, reflecting the extent to which the firm has unlearned the old problem-solving strategies and learned the new ones.

According to Hamel and Prahalad, firms need some kind of genetic variety in

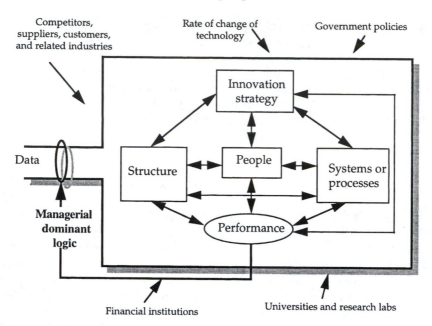

FIGURE 5.2. Dominant logic.

their management if they are to be more likely to break out of the old logic and exploit new opportunities.[14] An example from RISC technology will help illustrate the value of genetic variety to recognizing the potential or threat of an innovation early.[15] The contrasting styles of HP and Sun, who recognized the potential of RISC early, on the one hand, and those of DEC and IBM, who did so late, on the other hand, can be partly attributed to the mix of upper level management that each of these firms had. In 1980 HP hired Joel Birmbaum from IBM, where he had supervised John Cocke, the inventor of RISC. As vice president of R&D and a believer in RISC, Mr. Birnbaum represented some new blood in an HP upper level management that was largely ingrained in CISC technology. When he arrived at HP, several CISC projects had been started in an effort to replace the company's ailing 16-bit minicomputer architecture. As the vice president for R&D whose inputs to corporate decisions were valued, and as a believer in RISC, he sought and got approval from HP's board to adopt RISC for all of HP's computer products, back in 1983. Thus HP was the first company to adopt RISC for all its computer products, six years before DEC and ten years before IBM.

At DEC and IBM the picture was different. At DEC its vice president for R&D had been a designer of its very, in the parlance of the industry, CISCy VAX computers. Other higher level managers were very much into the frame of the VAX. That may explain why DEC just didn't understand "why RISC?" At IBM the picture was not very different. IBM invented[16] RISC in 1975 but, as discussed at the introduction of this chapter, neither the minicomputer, the mainframe, the supercomputer, nor the personal computer groups recognized the potential of the technology until the 1990s.

STRATEGY, STRUCTURE, SYSTEMS, AND PEOPLE (S³P)

A firm's ability to collect and process information is also a function of its innovation strategies, structure, systems, people, and local environment (S³PE).[17] In this section we briefly describe each and show how they affect the collection and processing of information that goes into recognizing the potential of an innovation (Figure 5.3).

Innovation Strategy

As we suggested in Chapter 2, there are six innovation strategies that a firm can pursue: offensive, defensive, imitative, dependent, traditional, and opportunistic. A firm that pursues an offensive strategy is the first to introduce new products.[18] Thus the capabilities it builds and the actions that it takes are earmarked toward generating new ideas and turning them into products before competitors do. Such firms usually invest a lot in R&D. Innovators such as 3M, Intel, and Merck spend large amounts of money on R&D. The R in R&D is actually the searching part—searching for new ideas that will lead to new products or services. If a firm does not invest in (re)search, it is difficult for it to find anything. Even stories of serendipity—discovery by accident—like penicillin, 3M's ScotchGard fabric protector, G. D. Searle's aspartame, or Raytheon's microwave oven are all stories of people who were performing research to begin with and, in the process, stumbled on the discoveries. Moreover, even if the ideas come from outside a firm, it still needs the absorptive capacity to understand and assimilate them.[19] Put simply, it takes knowledge to gain knowledge.

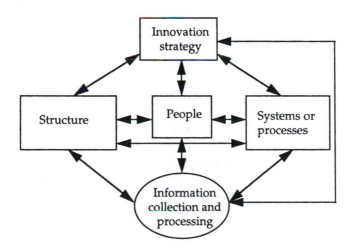

FIGURE 5.3. The role of S³P in recognizing the potential of an innovation.

A firm with a defensive strategy waits for a pioneer to introduce a product first, and then it can introduce its own products, correcting any mistakes that the pioneer may have made. As a follower, the defensive firm learns a lot about the potential of the product from the pioneer. But since its product is not a clone of the pioneer's product but rather a differentiated imitation, the defensive firm still has to invest heavily in R&D too. Moreover, since it takes knowledge to absorb knowledge, the defensive firm needs to perform R&D. Firms pursuing the remaining four strategies face somewhat the same problems as the defensive firm.

Thus firms pursuing an offensive innovation strategy are more likely to look outside their information channels for new ideas, be more receptive to them, and be more objective in processing the information than firms with defensive strategies. They want the new products more than their defensive strategy counterparts.

A firm's problem-solving strategies can also have an effect on how quickly it can recognize the potential of an innovation. As an example, take the two approaches to problem solving: *inductive* and *deductive*.[20] In the deductive approach one starts with the problem and looks for a solution to match. In the inductive, one starts with solutions and finds problems to match. As logical as the deductive approach sounds, it may actually be better, when exploring the potential of an innovation, to take the inductive approach. An example may help illustrate when and why. The typewriter was used for decades to type business and personal documents. So when word processors and, later, personal computers came along, it was very tempting for office managers to view them only as solutions to an old problem—typing documents. But these new products solved other problems. They allowed the user to store and retrieve documents at any time, print the information in different fonts, reproduce copies instantaneously, send the documents electronically, merge different documents, and edit them more easily. In fact, a famous test to see whether word processors were any match for typewriters had secretaries type one-page letters. Independent judges were asked to examine the letters and envelopes for neatness and attractiveness. The judges concluded that there was no significant difference between the quality of work from the two machines. Thus rather than take innovations and force-fit them to replace old solutions that solve old problems, these innovations should be looked at as solutions looking for problems to solve.

Organizational Structure

An innovation strategy tells us what actions a firm will take, when, and how it allocates its innovation resources. The structure of a firm tells us who is supposed to report to whom, and who is responsible for what, so as to carry out the innovation strategies. In searching for the right structure, two questions must be explored. First, there is the question of *coordination.* How do R&D and marketing, for example, keep exchanging information as the firm searches for new ideas and implements them? Second, there is the *differentiation and integration* problem. A firm's R&D and manufacturing groups are maintained as separate functions because each one necessarily has to specialize in what it does in order to keep building the stock of knowledge that underpins innovation—each one has its own unique tasks and roles to play. This is differentiation. At the same time, most innovations require cross-functional interaction. That is, the differentiated activities of the different functions must be integrated for optimal innovation.[21] Development of a car, for example, is more successful if designers, marketers, manufacturing, sales, component makers, and suppliers all work together,[22] that is, if their activities are integrated.

Organizational structures are some variation of two major types: *functional* and *project*. In the functional organization, people are grouped and perform their tasks according to traditional functions such as R&D, manufacturing, marketing, and so on (see Appendix 2). By grouping people with similar competences and knowledge, they can learn from each other and increase the stock of knowledge of the firm in the particular area. Communication is largely vertical, up and down the hierarchy of each function. In the project structure, employees are organized not by functional area, but by the project on which they are working. For example, if the project is to develop a minivan, employees from marketing, design, manufacturing, engine, and other relevant functions are assigned to the project and work for the project manager, not their functional managers. Communication is largely lateral, an advantage for innovation.

The functional organization has the advantage that since members of each function communicate with each other often, they are likely to increase their expertise in their functional areas; that is, they increase the tail of their T-skills.[23] (It will be recalled from Chapter 2 that T-skills are a deep expertise in one discipline combined with a broad enough knowledge in others to see the linkages between them.) The top of their T-skills, however, diminishes as they have little opportunity to learn from other functions. The project organization has the opposite effect. Their members run the risk of falling behind in their area of specialty, that is, losing the tail of their T-skills. This poses a dilemma for the designer of a structure that allows employees to maintain both the tail and the hat of their T-skills.

There are two solutions to this dilemma. The first was suggested by Allen, and the second is the *matrix* organizational structure.[24] Allen noted that how quickly the tail of the T-skills of a project group is rendered obsolete is a function of three factors: (1) the rate of change of the technology that underpins the industry in question, (2) the duration of the project, and (3) the amount of interrelatedness of the different components or subsystems of the product in question. Thus a choice of either the functional or the project structure that is contingent on these three factors can avoid the obsolescence of skills. The elements of this model are summarized in Figure 5.4. If the project is very long and the rate of change of the technological knowledge that underpins different functions is also changing very fast, the firm may want to stay with the functional structure. This allows employees to stay in their functional groups where, through interaction with functional colleagues, they can keep their functional skills updated (the tail of their T-skills), which are critical to the firm's success. If the product or service development is of short duration and the rate of change of knowledge that underlies functional areas is not very high, the firm is better off with a project structure. The choice of structure is also a function of how much coordination of intraproject activities is needed and how frequently. These coordination demands are a function of how interrelated the different components of the product or service are. For example, assembling an airplane requires more coordination than assembling a stereo system, given the interrelatedness of the components of the plane compared to that of the components of a stereo. The

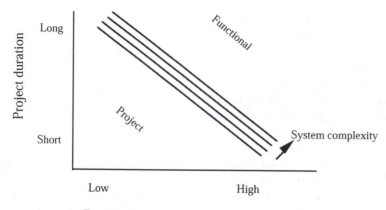

FIGURE 5.4. Choosing between functional and project structures.

Source: Adapted from Allen. T. J. "Organizational structure, information technology, and R&D productivity." *IEEE Transactions on Engineering Management* **EM-33**(4):212–217, 1986. © 1986 by IEEE.

more coordination a firm needs, the more it may want to use the project structure. There may be some situations where it is not quite clear which structure to use. For example, if the project duration is long but the rate of change of the underlying knowledge is low, it may not be quite clear which of the two to use. This is where the matrix organization comes in.

In the matrix organization (see Appendix 2) individuals from different functional areas are assigned to a project, but rather than reporting only to the project manager, they report to both their functional managers and the project manager. In some cases an employee may actually be working on more than one project. She or he may still be physically located in her or his functional area, losing out on one of the key benefits of the project organization—the frequent and sometimes unplanned interaction between the project members from different functional areas. The matrix organization has two advantages. First, since the rate of change of knowledge is likely to vary from one function to another, employees can spend time on project management commensurate with the rate of change of the knowledge in their functional areas. For example, if the rate of change of the underlying design technology is high whereas that for manufacturing is not, employees from design can spend less time on the project and be physically located in the design engineering area whereas employees from manufacturing can move to the project's location and spend more of their time on the project. Second, employees can keep their T-skills sharpened since they have a chance to interact with both their project teams and the functional groups. The disadvantage lies in the difficulty in managing two bosses and allocating allegiance.

Organizational structures can be characterized as *organic* or *mechanistic*.[25] In the organic structure, communication is lateral and not vertical, as is the case with mechanistic structures, that is, product designers talk directly to marketing rather

TABLE 5.2. Organizational structure and the collection and processing of information.

Organic	*Mechanistic*
Communication is lateral, allowing, for example, marketing and engineering to talk to each other directly and more often.	Communication is vertical along hierarchical lines, largely from boss to subordinate, telling them what to do.
Those with expertise or knowledge have the influence.	Influence rests more with those higher up in the hierarchy.
Job responsibilities are not well defined, allowing for objectivity in receiving and evaluating new ideas.	Well-defined job responsibility.
Emphasis is in exchange of ideas and not unidirectional top-down flow of information.	Emphasis is on unidirectional top-down flow of information.
Most conducive to recognizing the potential of an innovation.	Least conducive to recognizing the potential of an innovation.

than through their boss. This allows for better exchange of ideas. Second, in the organic structure, employees with the most influence are those with the technological or market knowledge and not those high up in the organizational hierarchy. This allows them to make the best informed decisions. Third, job responsibilities are more loosely defined, giving the employee more opportunities to be more receptive to new ideas and more objective about how best to use these ideas. Finally, the organic form emphasizes the exchange of information rather than unidirectional information flow from some central authority. These differences are summarized in Table 5.2.

As a firm exploits an innovation and grows, no matter which organizational structure it uses, the tendency is for it to become more mechanistic as more layers of management are added. Some firms deal with this by keeping divisions small. When the sales of a new product or service grow up to some amount, the group is spun off as a separate division. This has the added advantage that the prospect of having one's own division becomes an incentive for employees to innovate. At 3M, for example, divisions are kept small at about $200 million. At HP, when a unit reaches a certain size in sales, it is also spun off to a different division with a great deal of autonomy.

The more organic an organization, the more receptive it is to new ideas and the more flexible in processing information, and therefore the more likely it is to recognize the potential of a radical innovation.

Systems

An organizational structure tells us who does what, but says very little about how to keep people motivated as they carry out their assigned tasks and responsibilities.[26] Management must be able to monitor performance and to reward and punish individuals, functions, divisions, and organizations in some agreed upon and understood way. It must establish systems whereby information will flow in the shortest possible time to the right targets for decision making. Organizational control systems or processes and information delivery systems do that. Control systems range anywhere from market control to organizational culture. Market controls are measures such as stock prices, return on investment (ROI), and transfer pricing that reflect how a firm or division is performing in the market.

According to innovators like HP and 3M, performance criteria have to go beyond financial controls if a firm is going to innovate. Employees are told that they are expected to innovate and will be evaluated by "what is new." This can be expressed in a number of ways. At 3M it is that 25 percent of a division's sales in any year must be from products introduced within the last five years.[27] At Rubbermaid the number is 30 percent. Employees are also told to stretch, that is, set more ambitious innovation goals, and to keep trying to reach them. Resources are then allocated to back the expectations. At 3M employees are expected to spend 15 percent of their workweek on anything they want, as long as it is product-related (at HP the time is 12 percent). If an employee has a feasible idea, the employee can get a grant of up to $50,000 to pursue it. Sony uses its policy of "self-promotion" to allow employees to move around.[28] Engineers can seek out projects elsewhere in the company without notifying their supervisors.

Employees who innovate are rewarded commensurably. The rewards can range anywhere from small cash bonuses or pay raises to promotions. An employee can become the president of a division if his or her innovation grows large enough to become a division. 3M has an award ceremony once a year on its Oscar night to celebrate innovators. Failure, however, is tolerated. Management must assure employees that failure is OK, especially if the firm learns from the failure. General Mills and 3M do that. General Mills's very successful practice of putting athletes or sports events on boxes of Wheaties cereal came out of an idea that failed at first.

In addition to performance and reward systems, information flow systems are also critical. These can be grouped into two: information and communication technologies and physical building layout. The availability of information and communications systems makes it possible for, say, the CEO of Microsoft to see new product ideas from an engineer deep down the organization's hierarchy via electronic mail seconds after the engineer presses a button. If such information had to go up through the hierarchy, it would take much longer and there is a good chance that it would be distorted. An area manager for an American multinational who is resident in France does not have to go through hoops to obtain information on a new product being developed in the United States. All she has to do is go to the company's web site in the company's intranet to get undistorted up-to-date information on the product. A German driver should be able to test-drive a car in a virtual reality site in Stuttgart, Germany, and have the results fed instantly to designers in Detroit, Los Angeles, and Tokyo.

Often, however, information is very tacit and not very easily communicated via an intranet. Physical interaction may be necessary. Some ideas also pop up during unplanned accidental meetings. Allen's research suggests that the physical layout of buildings plays a critical role in the amount of communications that takes place between people.[29] The closer people are located to each other physically, the more they are likely to exchange ideas. If marketing, R&D, and manufacturing are located in the same area, eat in the same cafeteria, share the same bathrooms, and bump into each other often, they are more likely to exchange new ideas than if they were located in different buildings or regions. Firms such as Steel Case have designed their buildings with idea flow in mind.

People

Establishing control and reward systems that motivate employees and building information systems that provide them with the best information for decision making is one thing. Whether these people are motivated or not, or make the right decisions with the available information, is another—it is also a function of the type of people in the organization. It is a function of many questions: to what extent do employees share common goals? Is the manager of the brake division of a car company interested in building a personal empire or doing the best he can to make sure that his company builds the best car possible in the shortest possible time with the best brake system that can be manufactured most efficiently? Does the manufacturing group see R&D as a "bunch of ivory tower, money-spending snobs" or as colleagues with whom they can work to build the best cars in the shortest possible time at the lowest cost? To what extent do the employees have the knowledge that underpins the various activities of the firm's value chain? How much is such knowledge valued? What really is the core competence of the firm, and where does it reside—in people or in organizational routines and endowments of the firm? What does it take to motivate employees? Pay checks, job security, stock options, seeing their ideas implemented, being respected, or being "seen" as a person? Does management see unions as the adversary or as members of a team with shared goals who are there as part of the checks and balances that are necessary to keep steering toward the firm's goals? Are managers leaders or systematic planners?

As we saw in Chapter 2, five kinds of individuals have been identified to play key roles in recognizing the potential of an innovation: idea generators, gatekeepers and boundary spanners, champions, sponsors, and project managers. The more effective each of these individuals is, the better the chance of a firm recognizing the potential of the innovation. For example, champions are individuals who take an idea (theirs or that of an idea generator) for a new product or service and do all they can within their power to ensure the success of the innovation. By actively promoting the idea, communicating and inspiring others with their vision of the potential of the innovation, champions can help their organizations realize the potential of an innovation. Thus champions with charisma and an ability to articulate their vision of a product or service to others are more effective than those that do not.[30] So are idea generators who possess T-skills with very deep tails and very broad arms.

Having gatekeepers and boundary scanners is critical to collecting information. Without ties to any particular functional organization, project, or product in the firm, gatekeepers are more likely to be objective when collecting new ideas from the outside. The danger is that a gatekeeper may also develop the same information filters that successful functions do. Some human resources practices ensure that there are two promotion ladders at their firms: a technical ladder and the more traditional administrative one. The idea here is to free inventors or gatekeepers from administrative tasks to spend their time doing what they do best, and still get rewarded as much as the administrative stars who get promoted to management positions.

How well people perform their roles in the firm is a function of the firm's culture. As we saw in Chapter 4, an organization's culture is a system of shared values (what is important) and beliefs (how things work) that interact with the organization's people, organizational structures, and systems to produce behavioral norms (the way we do things around here).[31] Whether a culture is good at recognizing the potential of an innovation or not is a function of the type of culture. An entrepreneurial culture that keeps employees on the lookout for new ideas and holds the employees in high esteem when they turn those ideas to new products can be an asset in recognizing the potential of an innovation. However, some cultures can lead into the four evils of the not-invented-here (NIH) syndrome, I already know it (IAKI), prove it to me (PITM), and how on earth could my firm possibly do that.

Different firms use different strategies to avoid such evils. For example, Sony looks for people who are *neyaka,* that is, people who are open minded, optimistic, and wide ranging in their interests.[32] It also goes for generalists as compared to specialists. Says Sony's founder, Ibuka, "specialists are inclined to argue why you can't do something, while our emphasis has always been to make something out of nothing."[33]

LOCAL ENVIRONMENT

Some environments are more conducive to recognizing the potential of innovations than others. Here we consider five attributes of such environments: a system that provides financial support and rewards for innovation, a culture that tolerates failure, the presence of related industries, universities and other research institutions, and government policies.

Financial Support and Rewards: IPOs and Venture Capital

The rewards for innovation in the United States can be astronomical, and this may be a factor in how much effort people put into finding new ideas to turn into innovations. These come in several forms. First, there is the initial public offering (IPO), in which firms sell their stock to the public for the first time. In one day an individual can become a billionaire while many others see their personal wealth go up by millions of dollars. A firm can also push up its net worth by spinning out an entrepreneurial unit and offering its stock for purchase. The expectation of such rewards can be a very good incentive for the kind of effort that increases the chances of recognizing the potential of an innovation. As James H. Clark, chairman of Netscape, put it, "Without IPOs, you would not have any startups. IPOs supply the fuel that makes these dreams go. Without it, you die."[34] The availability of venture capital, partly as a result of expectations for financial rewards, also plays a critical role. By making money available for projects that would normally be considered too risky by banks and other sources of financing, venture capitalists allow firms to be more daring in their pursuits of new ideas. Some entrepreneurs use personal or family savings or loans from friends to finance their innovations, again in anticipation of the rewards. The anticipation of such rewards, coupled with readily available venture capital, allow more people to search for more ideas in more places with more combined determination. Many of those who make it usually reinvest in other innovation-searching activities.

Culture That Tolerates Failure

Many startups never make it to the payoff at the IPO. They simply fail. For several reasons such failures stop neither the entrepreneurs nor the venture capitalists who finance the innovations. First, those who fail learn in the process, and this can improve their chances of doing well the next time around. They acquire competences that can be used to tackle another innovation. Even if all they learn is what not to do next time, that can be useful too. Second, venture capital firms have seen many failures before and have found ways to reduce their risks by, for example, offering management expertise to ventures (see Chapter 11). Moreover, some of the venture capital comes from entrepreneurs who had made it only after having failed before. During the author's stint in the Silicon Valley, he does not remember seeing anyone pointing a finger at another and saying, "that's the entrepreneur who failed." Whereas bankruptcy laws are harsh in Europe and entrepreneurs who fail are stigmatized, in the Silicon Valley "bankruptcy is seen almost as a sign of prowess—a dueling scar if you wish."[35]

Sources of Innovation

As we saw in Chapter 4, the environment constitutes a very important source of innovations. Since tacit technological and market knowledge is best transferred by personal interaction, local environments that are good sources of innovation can make it easier for local firms to recognize the potential of an innovation. Take the presence of related industries. Being close to suppliers or complementary innovators increases the chances of a firm's being able to pick up useful ideas from them. For example, Intel, Microsoft, and Compaq all benefited from being in IBM's local environment (the United States) when IBM helped establish the PC as the standard.

Being close to universities or other research institutions helps in two ways. First, these institutions train personnel who can go on to work for firms or found their own companies. The knowledge that they acquire gives them the absorptive capacity to be able to assimilate new ideas from competitors and related industries. Second, scientific publications from the basic research often act as catalysts for investment by firms in applied research.[36]

Finally, as will be detailed in Chapter 15, governments play a critical role in the ability of firms to recognize the potential of innovations. Their role can be direct or indirect. The direct role may be in the sponsoring of research, such as the one conducted by the National Institutes of Health or under the sponsorship of the Defense Department. The Internet, which has laid the foundation for many innovations worldwide, traces its routes to the U.S. Defense Department's DARPA project. The indirect role is in regulation and taxation. Lower capital gains taxes or other regulations that allow firms to keep more of what they make can allow them to spend more on innovation. Other regulations, such as the strict requirements for FDA certification of drugs, can be a blessing in disguise as they are one reason why U.S. firms are better global competitors.

Turbulent Environment

A firm's ability to recognize the potential of an innovation is also a function of the rate of change of its competitive environment. In industries where the rate of change of technology is high, firms are more likely to be on the lookout for new ways to offer new products. The rate of innovation in semiconductors is higher than that in soft drinks. If customer expectations and taste also change rapidly, there is likely to be more innovation as firms try to meet new customer demand.

TYPE OF TECHNOLOGICAL CHANGE

The last component that determines the ability of a firm to recognize the potential of an innovation is the innovation itself—how incremental or radical, knowledge based or bulk processing. How a firm collects and processes information on a technological change is a function not only of its dominant logic, but also of the type of change. If the change is incremental in that the knowledge required to exploit it builds on existing knowledge and capabilities, the firm's dominant logic is an asset since it guides the firm to the right information sources and the right problem-solving strategies. If, however, the change is radical in that the knowledge required to exploit it is drastically different from existing knowledge, the firm's dominant logic may not only be useless, it may actually be a handicap. This is because such knowledge is likely to require different information channels, filters, and processing mechanisms from those that existing dominant logic reinforces.

Bulk-processing products do not pose as much a problem as knowledge-based products. It is easier to tell what the potential of a new aluminum can will be than it is to tell what the potential of a new drug earmarked for reducing cholesterol levels would be. The drug may end up being a medicine for reducing heart attacks.

APPLICATION CASES

NCR's experience with EPOSs (electronic point of sale systems), DEC's with RISC technology, and Microsoft's with the World Wide Web serve as very good examples of the problems that firms face in recognizing the potential of innovations.

NCR and Cash Registers

EPOSs are what help get customers through the checkout line in retail stores quickly. They constitute a major part of most retailers' arsenal in the retail world. They are used to scan the bar code on products and to provide customers with a list of the items they have bought. They are also a critical component of the store manager's inventory management system as they can instantaneously provide store managers with what is being sold and how much is left, and they will automatically place orders for some types of inventory.

In the mid-1960s retailers had electromechanical cash registers to check out customers. These machines were very primitive compared to today's EPOSs. A sales clerk had to push a button for each digit of the price of a good and then pull down a lever to indicate the end of the entry process for the price. The checkout process was very long and customer receipts did not list the items bought. The machines could not give the store manager updates on store inventory. As primitive as the electromechanical cash register sounds today, it was a novel machine in the 1960s, when NCR was king and commanded over 80 percent of the market. The technological knowledge underlying electromechanical cash registers consisted largely of knowledge of mechanical components such as ratchets and gears and how they are linked to produce addition.

The idea of using transistors and other electronic components, instead of gears, ratchets, pulleys, and chains, to build cash registers surfaced in the late 1960s, and NCR just did not "get it." In the late 1960s Singer Sewing Machine needed a different kind of cash register, one that would allow it to collect data automatically and send them to its computers. They turned to NCR,[37] who told Singer's buyers that they were looking for something that was not feasible, technologically or economically. Singer turned to Friden, its subsidiary, for an electronic cash register. Friden produced the first electronic cash register, which it called modular data transaction system (MDTS), in 1969. On June 17, 1971, while NCR was still struggling with the idea of electronic cash registers, Friden won a five-year contract to supply Sears, then the United States' largest retailer, with electronic cash registers as well as with computers and data communications equipment.

Singer was not the only one whose efforts to convince NCR were rebuffed. Complained a customer:[38]

We would go to them [NCR] and describe exactly the kind of computerized system [point-of-sale system] that we need. Their people would listen politely and tell us what a great machine the Class V [improved mechanical] cash register was.

DEC and RISC Technology

In the late 1970s DEC designed a new computer called the VAX, which would go on to be very popular and profitable. Right in the middle of the popularity of the VAX, some computer industry "renegades" started preaching the virtues of a computer innovation called RISC. They claimed that the innovation would improve the speed of computers dramatically.[39] The prospect of increasing the speed of a computer was welcome by DEC and other computer companies. It was the rationale behind how it was going to be done that troubled DEC. The technology called for going in the opposite direction from the existing design rationale. In RISC, instructions—the mnemonic that computers read and execute—were simpler[40] than those in existing computers. This was difficult for some industry experts to understand, given that popular computer architectures at the time had been designed using complex instructions, not the simpler ones. They had used so-called CISC[41] (complex instruction set machine) technology. DEC had designed its VAX doing exactly the opposite of what RISC evangelists were advocating. It had used complex instructions, each of which performed the job that would normally be performed by many simpler ones. Commented two DEC top-level managers:[42]

Anecdotal accounts of *irrational* implementations are certainly interesting. Is it typical, however, that composite instructions run more slowly than equivalent sequences of simple instructions? [Author's emphasis added.]

They did not understand how using simpler instructions could result in faster computers. Several years later, in May 1987, responding to what he thought about competitors' allegations that DEC was unenthusiastic about parallel processing because the VAX was not suited to it architecturally, DEC's CEO commented:[43]

We have one very serious problem with RISC reduced instruction set computing and parallel processing: Anything we come up with has to be better than the VAX. We've made one parallel processor, and we put a lot of money and time into it. But we've downgraded it from being a product to a development project. We tried, and we're still trying, but our enthusiasm has dropped off.

Although the anti-RISC forces at DEC dominated, there were some dissenters whose opinions met with no sympathy. The Titan project at DEC's Western Research Center in Palo Alto near Stanford University headed by Forest Baskett and the PRISM project headed by Dave Cutler in Seattle, Washington, were two RISC projects initiated as "R&D efforts," but not given much thought by top management.

Microsoft Corporation and the Web

Like DEC when its CISC machines were invaded by RISC, like NCR when its electromechanical cash registers were invaded by electronic cash registers, Microsoft was very profitable when the first Netscape browser was introduced in September 1994. It dominated the market for software for personal computers—software for stand-alone tasks such as word processing that require only the information on the computer on which the software is running. The World Wide Web (or just the Web) lets a user anywhere in the world jump from one Internet (net) computer to another just by clicking on a highlighted word. While on the computer, clicking on another highlighted word can access and display graphics and photos with great precision. It was invented by Berners-Lee while working as a consulting software engineer for CERN, the European particle physics laboratory, and made available on the internet in the summer of 1991.[44] It started gaining some momentum around 1993, but its potential was still not clear. "I wouldn't say it was clear that it was going to explode over the next couple of years. If you'd asked me then if most television ads will have URL [Web addresses] in them, I would have laughed." Bill Gates, Microsoft's CEO, would later say.[45]

One of the first firms to exploit the Web was Netscape Communications Corporation, which was founded on April 4, 1994. On September 12 it introduced its first product, a Web browser. Browsers are software that allows people on the Web to navigate it—to browse through different documents throughout the World Wide Web.

The Web represents a different platform than the stand-alone personal computer. It also represented a different technology and way of doing business for Microsoft's management. However, Bill Gates, Microsoft's CEO, and his top management were receptive to the idea of the Web and gave it the full attention that it deserved. "[I]t caught my attention. I thought, 'that's a good thing' " Gates would later say.[46] In August 1995 Microsoft shipped its Windows 95 operating system with Microsoft Network (MSN) and its own browser, the Internet Explorer. Both Netscape and Microsoft have since then introduced many products for the Web market. Microsoft has also invested a lot in the Web, acquiring many startups in challenging Netscape for Web supremacy.

SUMMARY

The goal of this chapter was to explore why firms have such difficulties recognizing the technological and market rationale behind an innovation and its applications. We suggested that there are two sources for these difficulties: the firm itself, especially the way it collects and processes information, and uncertainty. Concentrating on this first reason, we suggested that where a firm turns to for new ideas, how much information it collects, and how it evaluates the information are functions of several factors: its dominant logic, its local environment, the type of innovation in question, and the firm's strategies, organizational structure, systems, and people. We then explored how each of these factors might affect a firm's effectiveness in understanding the rationale behind a new product and what its possible applications are.

KEY TERMS

Differentiation and integration   *Local environment*
Dominant logic   *Matrix structure*

Functional structure	*Not-invented-here (NIH) syndrome*
I already know it (IAKI)	*Organic and mechanistic structures*
Information channels	*Problem-solving strategies*
Information filters	*Project structure*
Information processing	*Prove it to me (PITM)*
Innovation strategy	*Sticky information*
Lead user	*Strategy, structure, systems, and people*

QUESTIONS AND EXERCISES

1. What do we mean by recognizing the potential of an innovation?
2. Given the definition of managerial dominant logic, do you think that there may exist organizational and industry logic? What is the relationship between the three?
3. "Not-invented-here (NIH) syndrome," "I already know it (IAKI)," "Prove it to me (PITM)," and "how on earth could my firm possibly do that" have been said to be innovation's worst enemies. Do you agree? Why or why not?
4. It has been suggested that the United States is more innovative than Europe. Do you agree or disagree? What is behind the United States' (or Europe's) innovativeness?
5. Why was Microsoft able to recognize the potential of the Web faster than DEC recognized the potential of RISC technology?

NOTES

1. Gross, N., P. Coy, and O. Port. "The technology paradox." *Business Week,* p. 78, March 6, 1995.
2. Since many opportunities are never recognized, we may never know whether Xerox blew the most chances. The only reason we know of its blunders is because someone else eventually exploited them. If no one had, it would be difficult to tell whether these were, indeed, opportunities.
3. Smith, C. M., and P. L. Alexander. *Fumbling the Future.* New York: William Morrow, 1988.
4. As of 1997, the alliance formed by Apple, IBM, and Motorola to promote the PowerPC RISC chip as a standard has not been very successful in displacing Intel's microprocessors in the PC market.
5. French, M. J. *The US Tire Industry: A History.* Boston: Twayne, 1991.
6. Christensen, C. M., and J. L. Bower. "Customer power, strategic investment and failure of leading firms." *Strategic Management Journal* **17:**197–218, 1996.
7. Agence France Presse, September 15, 1995.
8. Arrow (1974) uses the terminology *information channels* and filters. Hambrick and Mason (1984) use *field of vision* and *selective perception,* respectively. See Arrow, K. J. *The Limits of Organizations.* New York: Norton, 1974. Hambrick, D. C., and P. Mason. "Upper echelons: The organization as a reflection of its top managers." *Academy of Management Review* **9:**193–206, 1984.

9. von Hippel, E. " 'Sticky information' " and the locus of problem solving: Implications for innovation." *Management Science* **40** (4):429–39, 1994.

10. Cohen, W. M., and D. A. Levinthal. "Innovation and learning: The two faces of R&D." *The Economic Journal* **99:**569–96, 1989.

11. Hamel, G. M., and C. K. Prahalad. *Competing for the Future.* Boston: Harvard Business School Press, 1994. Bettis, R. A., and C. K. Prahalad. "The dominant logic: Retrospective and extension." *Strategic Management Journal* **16:** 5–14, 1995.

12. Hambrick, D. C., M. A. Geletkanycz, and J. W. Fredrickson. "Top executive commitment to the status quo: Some tests of its determinants." *Strategic Management Journal* **14:**401–18, 1993.

13. March, J. G., and H. Simon. *Organizations.* New York: John Wiley, 1958.

14. Hamel, G. M., and C. K. Prahalad. *Competing for the Future* (1994).

15. Afuah, A. N. "Maintaining a competitive advantage in the face of a radical technological change: The role of strategic leadership and dominant logic." Working Paper #9602–14, University of Michigan Business School, July 1996.

16. There is some element of serendipity in the discovery of RISC. John Cocke and his colleagues did not start out looking for a method to design processors that is radically different from CISC.

17. Galbraith, J. R. "Designing the innovating organization." *Organizational Dynamics* **10:**5–25, 1982. Galbraith, J. R. "Organization design: An information process view." *Interfaces* **4:**28–36, May 1974.

18. Freeman, C. *The Economics of Industrial Innovation.* Cambridge, MA: MIT Press, 1982.

19. Cohen, W. M., and D. A. Levinthal. "Innovation and learning: The two faces of R&D" (1989).

20. Hammer, M., and J. Champy. *Reengineering the Corporation. A Manifesto for Business Revolution.* New York: HarperBusiness, 1993.

21. Lawrence, P. R., and J. W. Lorsch. *Organization and Environments: Managing Differentiation and Integration.* Homewood, IL: Irwin, 1967.

22. Clark, K. B., and S. C. Wheelwright. *Managing New Product and Process Development.* New York: Free Press, 1994.

23. Iansiti, M. "Real-world R&D. Jumping the product generation gap." *Harvard Business Review* 138–47, May–June 1993.

24. Allen, T. *Managing the Flow of Technology.* Cambridge, MA: MIT Press, 1984.

25. See, for example, Burns, T., and G. M. Stalker. *The Management of Innovation.* London: Tavistock, 1961. Robbins, S. P. *Organizational Theory: Structure, Design and Applications.* Englewook Cliffs, NJ: Prentice Hall, 1987.

26. Hill, C. W. L., and G. R. Jones. *Strategic Management: An Integrated Approach.* Boston: Houghton Mifflin, 1995, p. 352.

27. The General Mills, HP, and 3M examples are based on a homecoming speech given by General Mill's CEO Steve Sanger at the University of Michigan Business School on October 26, 1995. Hickman, S. "General Mills delivers success story." *The Monroe Street Journal,* October 30, 1995. Labich, K. "The innovators." *Fortune,* p. 49, June 6, 1988. Mitchell, R. "Masters of innovation." *Business Week,* p. 58, April 10, 1989. Kelly, K. "3M run scared? Forget about it." *Business Week* 59–62, September 16, 1991. Loeb, M., and T. J. Martin. "Ten commandments for managing creative people." *Fortune,* January 16, 1995.

28. Schlender, B., and S. Solo. "How Sony keeps the magic going." *Fortune,* February 24, 1992.

29. Allen, T. *Managing the Flow of Technology* (1984).

30. Howell J. M., and C. A. Higgins. "Champions of technological innovation." *Administrative Science Quarterly* **35:**317–41, 1990.

31. Uttal, B., and J. Fierman. "The corporate culture vultures." *Fortune,* October 17, 1983. For a detailed discussion on culture, see, for example, Schein, E. *Organizational Culture and Leadership.* San Francisco, CA: Jossey-Bass, 1990.

32. Schlender, B., and S. Solo. "How Sony keeps the magic going" (1992).

33. Schlender, B., and S. Solo. "How Sony keeps the magic going" (1992).

34. Farrell, C., et al. "The boon in IPOs." *Business Week,* p. 64, December 18, 1995.

35. "Please dare to fail." *The Economist,* September 28, 1996.

36. Ward, M., and D. Dranove. "The vertical chain of research and development in the pharmaceutical industry." Mimeo, Northwestern University, 1991.

37. The story of Singer's invention of the electronic cash register is based on "The rebuilding job at National Cash Register. How Singer got the jump on the industry's top supplier." *Business Week,* May 26, 1973.

38. Seneker, H. "Leading NCR out of the wilderness." *Forbes,* February 18, 1980.

39. Afuah, A. N. "Strategic adoption of innovation: The case of RISC (reduced instruction set computer) technology." Unpublished Ph.D. Dissertation, MIT, 1994.

40. Simpler instructions mean that less chip space will be used to build them. And less chip space means two things. First, since the chips occupy less space, electrical currents have shorter distances to travel, making the chips run faster. Second, the chip space saved can be used to add other computer architectural innovations to speed up the whole chip.

41. Although the term CISC (complex instruction set computer) is used to describe the architectures that were prevalent before RISC, the acronym CISC was coined only after Professor David Patterson of the University of California at Berkeley had already coined RISC.

42. Clark, D., and W. D. Strecker. "Comments on 'the case for the reduced instruction set computer.' " *Computer Architecture News* **8**(6):34–38, 1980.

43. *Computer & Communications Decisions,* May 1987.

44. "The web maestro: An interview with Tim Berners-Lee." *Technology Review,* July 1996.

45. Rebellow, K. "Inside Microsoft. The untold story of how the Internet forced Bill Gates to reverse course." *Business Week,* July 15, 1996.

46. Rebellow, K. "Inside Microsoft. The untold story of how the Internet forced Bill Gates to reverse course" (1996).

6

REDUCING UNCERTAINTY: THE ROLE OF TECHNOLOGICAL TRENDS, MARKET REGULARITIES, AND INNOVATION STRATEGY

"There is no reason anyone would want a computer in their home."
— *Ken Olson, president, chairman, and founder of Digital Equipment Corporation, 1977.*

"The wireless music box has no imaginable commercial value. Who would pay for a message sent to nobody in particular?"
— *David Sarnoff's associates in response to his urgings for investment in the radio in the 1920s.*

In Chapter 5 we suggested that firms face two major problems in recognizing the potential of an innovation. First, their ability to collect and evaluate relevant information to determine the value of an innovation is limited. We explored this problem, suggesting that a firm's strategy, structure, systems, people, local environment, and managerial dominant logic, as well as the type of innovation all play a major part in the ability of a firm to recognize the potential of an innovation. Second, there is often technological, market, and business uncertainty associated with innovation.[1] Our goal in this chapter is to explore how these uncertainties can be reduced. We argue that while uncertainty will always plague the process of innovation, there are certain market and technological trends that can, together with a firm's innovation strategy, considerably reduce it.

The chapter is organized as follows. First, we define uncertainty and clarify what we mean by reducing uncertainty. Then we show how technological and market regularities can help reduce technological uncertainty. We then examine the role of innovation strategies in reducing both technological and market uncertainties. Finally, we conclude that success lies in balancing all three.

UNCERTAINTY

In Chapter 2 we defined innovation as the use of new knowledge to offer a new product or service that customers want. The new knowledge can be technological or market. Technological knowledge is knowledge of components, linkages between components, methods, processes, and techniques that go into a product or service. Market knowledge is knowledge of distribution channels, product applications, and customer expectations, preferences, needs, and wants. An important question that arises from this definition of innovation, also discussed in Chapter 2, is, how *new* is the new knowledge and how *much* of it is required to offer the new product? One way of exploring this question is to view innovation as a problem-formulating and problem-solving process, in which a firm collects and processes information (new knowledge) on different sets of variables and the relationships among them. How much more of this information a firm needs to offer the new product is the uncertainty associated with the innovation.[2] That is, the more of these variables and the relationships among them are not yet known, the more uncertainty there is.[3]

An innovator faces three kinds of uncertainty: *technological, market, and business.*[4] Technological uncertainty is the additional information on the components, relationships among them, methods, and techniques that go into making the new product or service work according to some specification that must also be determined. It is "how to make a new product and how to make it work."[5] For example, in the mid-1970s when the personal computer was in its infancy, it was not clear just what type of operating system, memory management system, or peripherals it would have, and how these would interact. It was not very clear what was to be expected of a personal computer either. In fact, Bill Gates, Microsoft's CEO, was sure that "640K [of main memory] ought to be enough for anybody."

Market uncertainty is the additional information on who the customers are, what their needs and expectations are, how to get them to buy the product, and how to get it to them. It is "how to sell the new product and make it a commercial success."[6] In the PC example it was not very clear in the late 1970s just what the personal computer would be used for, which may explain Ken Olson's skepticism about why anyone would need a computer in the home. Of course, technological and market uncertainty are very related. The more a firm knows about what customers want, the better off it would be in making decisions on what should go into the product.[7] Business uncertainty refers to the general economic climate that is largely influenced by such macroeconomic features as interest rates and government policies and that can be diversified away. In this chapter we will focus only on technological and market uncertainties.

Reducing Uncertainty

Given these uncertainties, the question becomes, is there anything that a firm can do about them? Experimentation, trial, error, and correction such as prototyping, beta site testing, and test marketing can reduce some of these uncertainties.[8] But well before experimentation can begin, especially in the face of a radical techno-

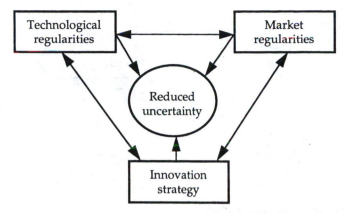

FIGURE 6.1. Reducing technological and market uncertainties.

logical change, a firm must answer several critical questions. For example, is it appropriate to abandon an existing technology and embrace the new one? Where should the firm place its R&D bets? Such critical questions are not easily answered by experimentation, trial, error, and the correction process, at least not alone. We argue that three factors help reduce uncertainty: (1) technological trajectories, in particular, sibling S curves; (2) market regularities; and (3) the firm's innovation strategy (Figure 6.1). The underlying theme in exploring these factors is echoed by Arrow:[9]

> Whenever there is uncertainty, there is usually the possibility of reducing it by the acquisition of *information*. Indeed, information is merely the negative of uncertainty, so to speak.

That is, the three factors shown in Figure 6.1 provide information that reduces the uncertainty. We will explore these factors in the context of two important questions: (1) if and when a firm should embrace a technological discontinuity, and (2) how to allocate resources once a firm has embraced the discontinuity.

TECHNOLOGICAL REGULARITIES

Technology life cycle models suggest that a technology usually evolves in a relatively predictable manner.[10] One of these models is the S curve.

S Curve

As we saw in Chapter 2,[11] various authors have suggested that a firm can predict when it has reached the limit of its technology life cycle using knowledge of the

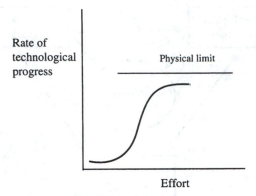

FIGURE 6.2. Foster's S curve.

technology's physical limits.[12] Foster, for example, argued that the rate of advance of a technology is a function of the amount of effort put into it, and he follows the S curve shown in Figure 6.2.[13] Technological progress starts off slowly, then increases very rapidly, and then diminishes as the physical limits of the technology are approached. Eventually the return on effort becomes extremely small. A new technology whose underlying physical properties allow it to overcome the physical limit of the old technology must be used. Supercomputers serve as a good example. For years they were designed using single-processor architectures until their ability to compute started approaching a physical limit—the speed of light. Multiprocessor architectures such as massively parallel processors give rise to a new S curve, as shown in Figure 6.3, with the new physical limit now being the communications bottlenecks from the many processors whose actions must be coordinated. According to Foster, computer makers should have been able to foresee the end of the single-processor architectures by looking at the diminishing returns on efforts put into improving single-processor designs.

As a predictor of whether and when to adopt a radical innovation, however, the

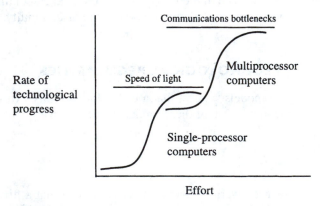

FIGURE 6.3. Supercomputer S curves.

S curve has some shortcomings.[14] First, unexpected changes in user needs, advances in complementary and component technologies, or incremental or architectural innovations can prolong the life of a technology that appeared to be on its way out, and a firm that follows the S curve too strictly may find that it switched prematurely. Second, and most important, waiting to reach the physical limit of a technology before moving on to a new one may deprive a firm of an entirely new advantage of the new technology (e.g., a new application), which has very little to do with the physical limit of the old technology. That is, reaching the physical limit is not always a necessary condition for switching. For example, the major advantage in moving from electromechanical cash registers to electronic ones is not so much the speed of the calculations or the size of the product—the attributes whose physical limits had been reached—as it is the fact that it can give customers printouts of their purchases and, more importantly, help manage inventory. Third, reaching the physical limit is not a sufficient condition to switch either. Electromechanical cash registers had reached their physical calculation limit during the vacuum tube era, yet the switch to electronic cash registers came only with integrated circuits. Fourth, it is difficult to measure effort. Is it a firm's own R&D spending or that of the whole industry, since it benefits from the industry's spillovers? Is effort measured as shipments from the industry or the firm's own shipments of products? Finally, it is also difficult to measure progress. Is it measured by profits or by some product parameter? Even apparently quantifiable performance parameters such as computer performance are difficult to agree upon. The MIP (million instructions per second) became a joke with some computer designers, who renamed it "meaningless indicator of performance."

Sibling S Curves

One solution to the problems encountered in using the S curve as a predictor of whether or when to adopt a discontinuous change is to use what we will call sibling S curves (Figure 6.4). The rationale behind the use of sibling S curves is that the core technology that underpins a product or industry often underpins other products or industries as well. Thus by paying attention to these other industries, and not just its own industry, a firm can better tell when to embrace a technological change—and this can be well before the old technology has reached its physical limit. We will explore this question of when and whether to switch to a new technological trajectory by looking at three examples: the transition from electromechanics to electronics, from the complex instruction set computer (CISC) to reduced instruction set computers (RISC), and the introduction of digital image processing in the movie industry.

Electromechanical to Electronic Transitions

At one time or another, computers, calculators, cash registers, and watches used some combination of mechanical gears, ratchets, belts, springs, motors, and levers to perform calculations. These products were very limited in their ability to com-

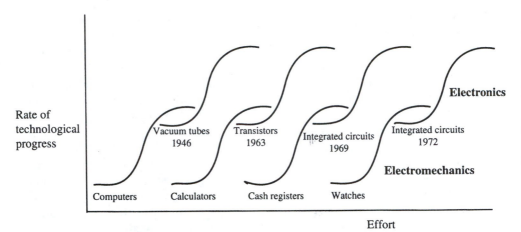

FIGURE 6.4. Sibling S curves.

pute, and they were often very bulky and unreliable. The switch to electronics came at different times for each of these industries (see Figure 6.4).

Computers were first to go electronic. The first general-purpose electronic computer, the electronic numerical integrator and calculator (ENIAC), was publicly revealed in 1946.[15] It had been funded by the U.S. Army and used during World War II for computing artillery firing tables. It used vacuum tubes and was 100 feet long, 8[h] feet high, and several feet wide. Although it was orders of magnitude larger and slower than today's computers, it was a vast improvement over electromechanical ones. These were speed improvements that the electromechanical calculator could have used, but it stayed electromechanical.

Electronics itself then experienced several technological discontinuities, as shown in Figure 6.5. Transistors displaced vacuum tubes, allowing smaller,

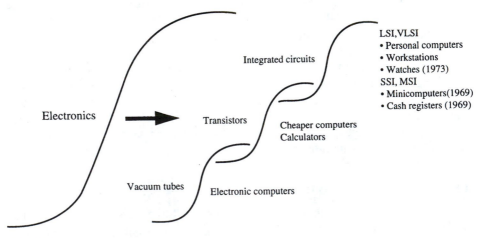

FIGURE 6.5. Discontinuities within electronics.

cheaper, and faster computers to be built. The cheaper and smaller transistors also made it possible for the first electronic calculator to be built in 1963. Integrated circuits, in turn, took over from discrete transistors. The first of these circuits, called small-scale integration (SSI) and medium-scale integration (MSI), not only enabled even cheaper computers and calculators to be built, they also ushered in an era of completely new products such as cash registers, personal computers, and watches.

By studying what was going on in related industries—computers and then calculators—makers of electromechanical cash registers and watches could have benefited from two happenings. First, it should have been no surprise to either industry when electronic cash registers and watches invaded their industries, given that electromechanical computers and calculators had been invaded by electronic ones years earlier. Second, the main advantage of switching from electromechanical cash registers to electronic ones was not overcoming the physical limits of size and calculation speeds, but the ability of electronic machines to give customers printouts of their purchases and to better manage inventory. Monitoring the physical limits of their products would not have permitted the industries to benefit from these advantages.

RISC Technology

The case of RISC technology illustrates the difficulties associated with knowing just when the physical limit of a technology has been reached. It illustrates how misreading the limit can deprive a firm of taking advantage of an architectural innovation that not only extends the physical limit of the existing technology, but also extends the physical limit of the invading technology. As we hinted in the example of the supercomputer, the single-processor architecture used to design computers was fast approaching a physical limit—the speed of light—as far as computer speed is concerned. This suggested a move to multiprocessors, where two or more processors take on the job that used to be performed by one processor (see Figure 6.3). In minicomputers, for example, DEC used its symmetric multiprocessing technology—an implementation of multiprocessor technology—to offer better performing new products.

Meanwhile an architectural innovation called RISC was invading the CISC technology that had been at the core of single-processor architectures (Figure 6.6). RISC is an innovation in designing the central processing unit (CPU)[16] of a computer, which speeds up the processor considerably. It uses simpler instructions, which take up less chip real estate, all else being equal. This simplicity, coupled with the space saved, allows designers to take advantage of incremental innovations in computer design to build RISC processors that are faster than their CISC predecessors.

RISC technology was quickly adopted for workstations. This should have been a signal to makers of minicomputers, mainframes, and personal computers that RISC could be on its way to invade their markets.[17] Equally significant is the fact that RISC technology would be useful not only in single processor architectures, but also in multiprocessing (Figure 6.6).

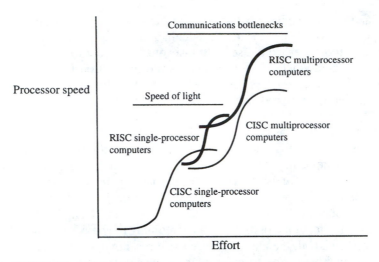

FIGURE 6.6. CISC to RISC discontinuities in single- and multiprocessor computing.

Film Industry and Digital Image Processing

The case of digital image processing in the movie industry illustrates better why depending on the physical limit can deprive a firm of critical features from a new technology. An important part of cinematography is to make scenes appear as real as possible to viewers, to make sure moviegoers are fooled into believing that they have, for example, seen dinosaurs eat human beings. For years such "reality" was created using special cinematographic effects, largely mechanical props and manual manipulation of objects. But there was only so much that audiences could be fooled with. That is, the physical limit of manual special effects was being approached. But then came digital image processing, making it possible to offer special effects that are more real. Witness *Jurassic Park,* movie that was made using digital image processing. Digital image processing also has many other advantages that moviemakers would have missed if all they had depended on for producing special effects were their existing technology. First, images of acted scenes, landscapes, and scenery can be stored on disks and used later for other movies in years to come. Second, images, scenes, and objects can be added or taken out of movies. Even parts of people can be taken out of or added to movies. True editing is possible: one can add to or cut just about anything from the movie after it has been made. Images of Brandon Lee were digitally added to scenes after he had died during the shooting of *The Crow,* allowing the producers to complete the movie. Finishing a movie after such a tragedy would have been near impossible without digital image processing. Third, shooting a scene over and over may now just mean playing with a computer mouse.

Thus waiting for the physical limits of existing special effects technology to be reached before moving to digital image processing would be foregoing all the editing, storage, retrieval, reuse, and processing advantages.

MARKET REGULARITIES

We started this chapter with a quote from an innovator who did not foresee a "home" computer. The question is, is there anything about the market for innovations that would make one more cautious about one's presumptions about future markets for products? We offer three regularities about markets that can reduce the uncertainty associated with new markets for innovation.

From Business to Home to Portable to Car: Market S Curves

Many of the major products in the home today started out in factories or businesses and then gradually found their way into the home. From the home some have found their way into cars. But before the car, portable versions to "take along" were also offered. Table 6.1 shows some of these products. Take the radio, for example. The radio was first used in telephony to transmit information from one place to the other, and by the military to receive signals in battle. Then a version to be used in the home was introduced (see second quote at the beginning of this chapter). It utilized vacuum tubes, generated a lot of heat, and occupied a lot of space. Following

TABLE 6.1. Migration of innovations from business to home to portable to car.

Product	Innovation migration trend
Air conditioners	From business to home to car. Is this a mature market?
Audio tape recorders	From sound studio to home to car to portable; being invaded by CDs.
Calculators	From office to home to portable to personal computers.
Central office switches	Used by phone companies to connect calls. To private business as private branch exchanges (PBX). Where to next? Home or car?
Computers	From government to business or factory to home to notebook to car.
Electric generators	From utility companies to business to home to portable.
Electric motors	From electric train to business to home to portable.
Fax machines	From business to home to computer.
Medical diagnostic equipment	From hospital to home?
Microprocessors	From office desktop or factory floor to home to car to portable.
Movie cameras	From TV studio to home to portable to Internet clients.
Movies	From theater to home.
Radios	From post office to home to portable to car.
Retailing	From street market to mall to home.
Satellite systems	From defense applications to business to home. Where to next? Car and individual?
Still picture cameras	From studio to portable. To notebook PC?
Telephones	From business to home to portable to car. To notebook PC?
VCRs	From TV recording studio to home to portable.

the invention of the transistor, Sony introduced the so-called transistor radio, a portable version that people could carry with them to the beach and other outdoor activities. Most cars now have one.

Perhaps one of the most chronicled is the VCR. The first commercial VCR was developed by Ampex of California in 1956. It was used largely by television broad-casters to record programs and play them back later. It also came in black and white, no color. The arrival of the integrated circuit allowed engineers to design im-proved versions with reduced size, and to add other features such as color. Sony, JVC, and Matsushita introduced some of the first home versions. Another interest-ing example is satellite systems. They were built largely for U.S. government de-fense use. As defense needs decreased and the underlying technology got cheaper, versions for the home became possible. Now some automakers vow that by the year 2010, all cars will have navigational systems.

The products are not always directly "visible" to the customer. They can come embedded in other products. The electric motor is an example. The first electric motors were used to power electric railcars. Then they found their way into facto-ries to power the conveyor belts that transport materials from one section of the factory to the other, or to power elevators and factory fans. As incremental product innovations made the motor smaller, it found its way into the home in vacuum cleaners, washers, dryers, refrigerators, and dishwashers. As it got yet smaller, it found its way into portable products such as record players, razors, toys, hair dry-ers, and compact discs. Now some cars have as many as 80 electric motors in them.

While these examples may sound trivial, the point is that such trends can help point to what the next markets are likely to be. The trend is simple, yet very in-formative: products are introduced first for use in the factory or business. Then they find their way into the home. With more innovation, portable versions are intro-duced. Eventually, some of the products end up in cars. Thus although products are often depicted as having one (market) product life cycle, some of them may actu-ally have a product life cycle that is made up of smaller life cycles, one for the busi-ness, another for the home, and one for portable versions or cars, as illustrated in Figure 6.7.

If It Is Useful to Me, It Must Be Useful to Someone Else

Observing the trend from business to home to car is not the only way to reduce market uncertainty and ambiguity. HP's product strategy, very early in its life, serves as one example of how to deal with market uncertainty. The company's en-gineers who designed electrical measurement instruments also needed for them-selves electrical instrumentation equipment to perform their jobs.[18] Thus any prod-ucts that they invented to help them do their job better often found a home at other firms with similar engineering needs. Thus HP was inventor and lead user in some products. This principle of "if it is useful to me it must be to someone else like me" is not limited to high technology. Club Mediterranée was founded in 1950 as a non-profit organization by a group of friends who liked sports and vacations in scenic

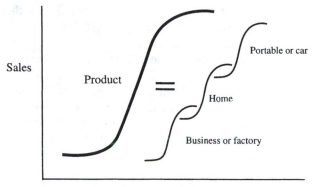

Time, effort, and advances in technology

FIGURE 6.7. Many products have several life cycles—business, home, car, and portable.

seaside locations.[19] However, because they were on tight budgets, they could not afford the full cost of such entertainment and therefore took turns cooking and slept in sleeping bags in Army surplus tents. As their number grew, "the Club" needed someone to inject some structure in the organization and its leader, Gerald Blitz, invited one of its members, Gilbert Trigano, to run it. Trigano quickly saw that there were other people like them on tight budgets (or who did not want to pay the full cost) who also liked sports and vacations in scenic locations and who could make do with spartan lodging. He went on to turn Club Mediterranée into a successful business.

Not many firms have been able to take advantage of such opportunities. In the 1980s DEC had what was arguably the largest private computer network in the world. Each site had a local area network that was tied into other sites worldwide. Using computer terminals, each employee could send and receive messages from anybody in the firm's offices worldwide. Employees could also write or read information on electronic bulletin boards. DEC's network was what many firms are now finding out that they cannot do without—an intranet. DEC developed and used three kinds of services or products that many firms now find very useful. First, there was the ethernet-based hardware that DEC produced for its own use. The company was one of the first to embrace and implement the ethernet protocol. Then there were the e-mail and on-line systems America Online and other on-line service providers would later capitalize on. Finally, there was the idea of sharing information in some computer memory working space, called Notes at DEC, which Lotus would later capitalize on, calling it Lotus Notes.

Customer Preferences: Space, Time, and Mass

While some customer preferences can be difficult to determine, others are not. For example, there are certain things that customers cannot get enough of. Space is one of them. People would prefer more square footage per dollar in their home or offices. The more memory a computer can have, the better it is for programmers and users. So it should come as no surprise that, more often than not, people would prefer more computer memory space than less. Users and software developers want more and more of it.

Customers would prefer faster lines, faster computers, and faster planes. The faster, the better. Thus for a service firm, for example, any technology that reduces the time for waiting on line may be worth exploring. "Less" can also be better. One common thing about the products that moved from office to home to car is that they got smaller with each transition. Computers do not only have to be faster, they also have to be smaller. For a given product or service, customers would prefer to pay less. The fewer the number of times that a drug has to be taken, the better.

Product Life Cycle

The market regularities we have discussed so far have been about the emergence of new markets (business, home, portable, or other). Once the market has emerged and a firm has decided to enter, it must still contend with uncertainties in the products in the market. The marketing literature offers a parallel to the technology life cycle: the product life cycle.[20] A product has four predictable stages with distinctive characteristics, marketing objectives, and strategies. The *introduction* stage starts when the new product is launched. Sales are low, costs per customer are high, profits are negative, customers are largely lead users, and competitors are few. In the *growth* stage, sales rise rapidly, costs per customer start to drop, profits start rising, and the number of customers also increases. In the *maturity* stage, sales peak, costs per customer are low, profits are high, and the number of competitors is stable. In the *decline* stage, sales start to decline, costs per customer increase, profits are declining, and the number of competitors is also declining. These characteristics call for specific strategies. For example, in the introduction stage, a firm's objective is to create product awareness, and product strategy is to offer a basic product. As shown in Figure 6.8, the demand in each market is fulfilled by a series of different generations of products (P1, P2, and P3), with the first one introduced at the emergence of the market.

The main drawback in using the product life cycle to reduce uncertainty is that the number of stages and the duration of each vary from product to product. It is also difficult to tell when a stage starts and ends. In any case, they provide some regularities to help a firm know when and what to invest in an innovation.

INNOVATION STRATEGY

In our discussion of the role of market and technological trends in reducing uncertainty, we have taken these trends as being exogenous to the firm. That is, we have viewed each trend as something over which the firm has no control. But a firm's innovation strategy can play a critical role in shaping these trends. As we saw in Chapters 2 and 5, a firm can have one of several innovation strategies: offensive,

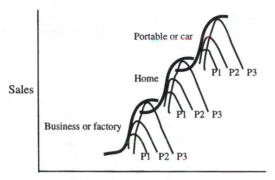

Sales

Portable or car

Home

Business or factory

P1 P2 P3

P1 P2 P3

P1 P2 P3

Time, effort, and advances in technology

FIGURE 6.8. Each market (business, home, and portable) is made up of different product generations. P1, P2, and P3.

defensive, imitative, dependent, traditional, or opportunistic. A firm with an offensive strategy, for example, is the first to introduce new products while one with a defensive strategy waits for a competitor with an offensive strategy to introduce a product first and resolve some of the uncertainties confronting the innovation. The defensive firm then introduces its own product, correcting any mistakes that the pioneer may have made. These strategies may be viewed as ways of reducing uncertainties. The offensive firm, in throwing its resources behind a technology, can help move it faster up the S curve, establishing not only a market but also a standard for the product. The VCR offers a good example. Although integrated circuits were at the heart of the transition of the VCR from studio to home, it was the determination of Sony and Matsushita to bring the VCR to the home that was largely responsible for it at that time.[21] Left to Ampex, the inventor of the larger VCRs used in television studios, there might be no VCR in the home today.

Thus a firm's innovation strategy can have a huge impact on how it resolves uncertainty. The offensive strategy means lots of uncertainty for a firm. But it also means that the firm can charter its own course. An imitative strategy means that the firm can wait until market and technological uncertainties have been resolved by pioneers, but it risks missing out on first-mover advantages.

CONFLUENCE OF FACTORS

What we have seen so far suggests that there is a strong relationship between all three factors. In many of the transitions from business to home to portable to car there has been an underlying technological change, and in some cases there was a firm that was determined to introduce the new product. Advances in integrated circuits and magnetic materials were instrumental to the migration of VCRs from the television studio to the home. So was Sony's determination to keep investing in its VCR program and working toward getting the machine to the home. The transistor was at the root of portable radios. And so was Sony's determination to offer the

TABLE 6.2. Confluence of technological and market trends.

Product	Technologies	Role of technology
Audio tape recorders	Electric motors, magnetic materials	Reduced cost, provide continuous motion
Calculators	Integrated circuits	Lower cost, miniaturization
Central office switches	Telecommunications, integrated circuits	Lower cost, added features
Computers	Integrated circuits	Improved speed, miniaturization, less power consumption, lower cost
Electric motors	Electromechanics	Miniaturization, higher efficiency, lower cost
Fax machines	Integrated circuits, materials, imaging	Faster transmission, higher quality, lower cost
Medical diagnostic equipment	Imaging technologies, materials	Improved images, less invasive surgery
Microprocessors	Integrated circuits, instruction set design	Faster, lower power consumption, more functions, portability
Movie cameras	Optics, integrated circuits, imaging	Miniaturization, precision
Movies	Digital imaging, fiber optics	Flexible inputs, distribution
Radios	Transistors, integrated circuits, communications, miniaturization	Lower cost, portability, better quality
Retailing	Buildings, fiber optics, cars	Malls, virtual shopping
Satellite systems	Communications, integrated circuits, materials	Miniaturization, lower cost
Telephones	Integrated circuits, telecommunications	More features, lower cost
VCRs	Integrated circuits, materials	Quality, miniaturization

transistor radio. Electronic cash registers were possible because of the transistor. But it was Singer's determination to build cash registers to manage its inventory better that led to the first electronic cash register.[22]

It is important to note that other factors can also help reduce uncertainty. Increasing incomes facilitate the movement of products from factory to home as people have more purchasing power. For example, some VCRs in the late 1970s cost as much as $1000, and only families with high disposable incomes could afford such products then. Table 6.2 gives some examples of the role that different technologies have played in the migration of products from factory to home to portable.

SUMMARY

The goal of this chapter was to explore how market and technological uncertainties that usually plague innovation can be reduced. We suggested that three factors help reduce uncertainty: technological trends, market regularities, and the firm's innovation strategy. We then explored the three factors in the context of two key questions: if and when a firm should seek and embrace an innovation, and how to allocate resources once the firm has embraced the innovation. First, we argued that since the technology that underpins an industry sometimes underpins other industries, a firm can better decide on when to switch to a new technology by monitoring the activities in these related industries. In particular, rather than monitor only its own S-curve, a firm may be better off monitoring sibling S curves—the S curves of related industries. Relying only on one's own S curve can be misleading. For example, at one point electromechanics underpinned computers, cash registers, calculators, and watches. Thus it should have come as no surprise to makers of electromechanical cash registers and Swiss watchmakers when electronics invaded their industries. Moreover, electromechanical cash register makers did not have to wait until the physical limit for the product's parameters had been reached. By switching before the limit, they could add such features as printouts of customer purchases and better inventory management—features that would not have been anticipated by monitoring the S curve of electromechanical cash registers. Once a firm has embraced the new technology, it can use the regularities of technology life cycles to allocate the resources needed to profit from the innovation.

Second, we also argued that regularities in markets can help reduce market uncertainty. For example, many of the major products in the American home today were first used in factories or businesses, then moved on to the home, and later some moved to the car or became portable. Thus when we talk of a product life cycle, we may really be talking about three or more different cycles, one for the factory or business, the other for the home, and yet another for the car.

Third, we suggested that a firm's innovation strategy can also help reduce both technological and market uncertainties. A firm with an offensive strategy can help charter its own course and therefore determine a market and the technology to serve it. An imitative strategy, however, lets other firms reduce most of the market and technological uncertainties at the expence of first-mover advantages.

Finally, we argued that although each of these factors, alone, reduces uncertainty, it is the confluence of all three that is best. For example, the migration of the VCR to the home was driven by the integrated circuit as well as by JVC's and Sony's determination to bring the VCR to the home.

While uncertainty will always plague innovation, careful monitoring of the firm's own and sibling S curves and of technology life cycles can help reduce some of the technological uncertainties. Monitoring market regularities can also help reduce market uncertainties. So can a firm's own strategic decisions. The confluence of all three or some subset of these factors reduces uncertainty the most.

For the practicing manager, carefully monitoring such trends can help him or her avoid such statements as: "There is no reason anyone would want a computer in their home" or "640K [of main memory] ought to be enough for anybody."

KEY TERMS

Ambiguity   *S curve*
Market uncertainty   *Sibling S curve*

Physical limit   *Strategic intent*
Rate of technological progress   *Technological trajectory*
Risk   *Technological uncertainty*

QUESTIONS AND EXERCISES

1. What are the differences between uncertainty, risk, and ambiguity?
2. Pick an industry that has experienced a discontinuity. How do you measure technological progress in this industry?
3. What industry has the (a) least market uncertainty, (b) least technological uncertainty, (c) most market uncertainty, and (d) most technological uncertainty? In each case, explicitly explain why.
4. What really is "effort" in the S curve? Is it time? Amount of money invested? Or what? For each of the products (or industries) listed in column 1 of Table 6.1, what do you believe will be the next "killer" product?
5. Can you think of other products (or industries) that should be added to Table 6.1?
6. Apart from using an S curve, how else would you predict the demise of an existing technology?

NOTES

1. Freeman, C. *The Economics of Industrial Innovation,* 2d ed. Cambridge, MA: MIT Press, 1982.
2. This definition is also in keeping with Galbraith (1974), who defined uncertainty as the difference between the information that an organization has and the information that it needs. It is also echoed by Duncan (1972), who defined uncertainty as "(1) the lack of information regarding environmental factors associated with a given decision-making situation, (2) not knowing the outcome of a specific decision in terms of how much the organization would lose if the decision were incorrect, (3) inability to assign probabilities with any degree of confidence with regard to how environmental factors are going to affect the success or failure of the decision unit in performing its function." See Galbraith, J. R. "Organization design: An information process view." *Interfaces* **4:**28–36, May 1974. Duncan, R. B. "Characteristics of organizational environments and perceived environmental uncertainty." *Administrative Science Quarterly* **17**, 313–27, 1972. See also Arrow, K. J. *The Limits of Organizations.* New York: Norton, 1974.
3. Hart (1986) offers a "state-of-knowledge" spectrum of *certainty—risk—uncertainty—ambiguity,* in which there is *certainty* if the variables and relationships among them are known; *risk* if the variables are known but the relationships among them can only be estimated—the probabilities are known; *uncertainty* if all the variables are known but some cannot be measured and the relationships among others is unknown; and *ambiguity* if all the relevant variables have yet to be identified. Shrader, Riggs, and Smith (1993) distinguish between uncertainty and ambiguity. See Hart, S. "Steering the path between ambiguity and overload:

Planning as strategic social process." In *Interdisciplinary Planning: Perspectives for the Future;* M. Dluhy and K. Chen (Eds.). Rutgers, NJ: Center for Urban Policy, 1986. Shrader, S., W. M. Riggs, and R. P. Smith. "Choice over uncertainty and ambiguity in technical problem solving." *Journal of Engineering and Technology Management* **10:**73–99, 1933.

4. Freeman, C. *The Economics of Industrial Innovation* (1982, p. 149).

5. Geroski, P. "Markets for technology: Knowledge, innovation and appropriability." In *Handbook of Economics of Innovation and Technological Change;* P. Stoneman (Ed.). Oxford, UK: Blackwell, 1995, p. 92.

6. Geroski, P. "Markets for technology: Knowledge, innovation and appropriability" (1995, p. 92).

7. Rothwell, R., C. Freeman, A. Horsley, V. T. P. Jervis, A. B. Robertson, and J. Townsend. "SAPPHO updated—Project SAPPHO phase II." *Research Policy* **3:**258–91, 1974. Cooper, R. G., and E. J. Kleinschmidt. "New products: What separates winners and losers?" *Journal of New Product Management* **4**(3):169–84, 1987.

8. Freeman, C. *The Economics of Industrial Innovation* (1982). Thomke, S. H. "The economics of experimentation in the design of new product and processes." Unpublished Ph.D. Dissertation, MIT, 1995.

9. Arrow, K. J. *The Economics of Information.* Cambridge, MA: Belknap Press of Harvard University Press, 1984, p. 138.

10. See, for example, Utterback, J. M. *Mastering the Dynamics of Innovation.* Cambridge, MA: Harvard Business School Press, 1994. Sahal, D. "Technological guideposts and innovation avenues." *Research Policy* **14:**61–82, 1985.

11. For consistency, this paragraph is largely a repeat of what we saw in Chapter 2.

12. See, for example, Ehrnberg, E. "Technological discontinuities and industrial dynamics." Ph.D. Dissertation, Chalmers University of Technology, Goteborg, Sweden, 1996.

13. Foster, R. *Innovation: The Attacker's Advantage.* New York: Summit Books, 1986.

14. Christensen, C. M. "Exploring the limits of the technology s-curve: Part I: Component technologies; Part II: Architectural technologies." *Production and Operations Management* **1:**334–57, 1992. Henderson, R. M. "Of life cycles real and imaginary: The unexpectedly long old age of optical lithography." *Research Policy* **24:**631–43, 1994.

15. The first commercial general-purpose computer, the UNIVAC I, was delivered in June 1951 by Remington-Rand. See Hennessy, J., and D. Patterson. *Computer Architecture: A Quantitative Approach.* Menlo Park, CA: Morgan Kaufman, 1990.

16. The CPU is sometimes referred to as the brain of the computer because it does all the calculations and controls all the electrical signals of the computer. For a detailed explanation of RISC technology, see Afuah, A. N. "Strategic adoption of innovation: The case of RISC (reduced instruction set computer) technology." Unpublished Ph.D. Dissertation, MIT, 1994.

17. There are two reasons why workstations were first to adopt RISC. (1) The price versus performance demanded by workstation customers made the faster and cheaper RISC technology a more viable technology than the slower and more expensive CISC. Moreover, workstations did not have as large an installed base of CISC as, for example, the personal computer with its millions of Intel-based CISC systems. (2) The strategic architecture and intent of Sun Microsystems, the leader in the workstation industry, was in keeping with adopting RISC early.

18. Packard, D. *The HP Way.* New York: HarperBusiness. 1995.

19. Hart, C. W. L. "Club Med (A)." Harvard Business School, Case #9–687-046, 1986.

20. See, for example, Kotler, P. *Marketing Management.* Englewood Cliffs, NJ: Prentice Hall, 1994.

21. Cusumano, M. A., Y. Mylonadis, and R. S. Rosenbloom. "Strategic maneuvering and mass-market dynamics: The triumph of VHS over Beta." Working Paper #91–048, Harvard Business School, 1991. Morone, J. *Winning in High-Tech Markets: The Role of General Management.* Boston: Harvard Business School Press, 1993.

22. "The rebuilding job at National Cash Register: How Singer got the jump on the industry's top supplier." *Business Week,* May 26, 1973.

C H A P T E R

7

CHOOSING A PROFIT SITE:
DYNAMIC COMPETITIVE ANALYSIS

Suppose a firm has recognized the potential of an innovation. For example, in the 1970s, a firm knows that the personal computer or the one-day delivery service will be very successful in the 1980s and 1990s. How can it profit from either innovation? Should it exploit the innovation as a supplier, manufacturer, customer, or complementary innovator? In other words, where in the innovation value-added chain (ecosystem) should the firm position itself? What profit site is best for the firm? In this chapter we argue that three factors determine the profitability of a site for a firm.[1] The first is industry attractiveness, where an industry is attractive if the pressures from Porter's five forces are low.[2] The firm would be interested in knowing which of the industries in the innovation value-added chain is attractive. In the example of the personal computer one would be interested in knowing whether supplying components for the personal computer, making the personal computers, writing software for them, distributing them, or using them for, say, desktop publishing is attractive. In the one-day delivery service example, the firm would like to know which is best: providing the service itself or being a supplier of planes, sorting equipment, logistics gear, or airport hubs. The second is the firm's capabilities. A profit site is attractive to a firm if the firm possesses the capabilities that are required to offer low-cost or differentiated products or services at that site, or if it can build such capabilities very quickly. The third is the innovation cycle. Since the industry structure and the capabilities required to succeed in an industry change with the industrial innovation cycle, the attractiveness of a profit site must also depend on the state of evolution of the underlying innovation. That is, the strength of Porter's five forces and the extent to which a firm's capabilities can be used to exploit an innovation are a function of industry structure and therefore of the phase in which the innovation is in its life cycle. Thus a firm's analysis to determine what profit site to choose consists of (1) determining industry attractiveness, (2) determining the extent to which the firm's capabilities match those that are required to exploit the innovation, and (3) performing (1) and (2) at each phase of the innovation life cycle.

The chapter is organized as follows. First, we briefly review the role of industry attractiveness and a firm's capabilities on profitability and the effect that indus-

133

try evolution has on them. We then explore the pressures exerted by Porter's five forces at each phase of the industrial innovation cycle. Next we examine the capabilities that are needed to offer products at each phase of the cycle and the extent to which each firm's unique capabilities allow it to offer these products, and we provide some caution in using the proposed model. Finally, we use the example of the personal computer to illustrate the concepts developed.

INDUSTRY ATTRACTIVENESS

A firm's success is a function of the structure of the industry in which it operates and the product market position it chooses.[3] Competition varies from industry to industry, and so do the opportunities for sustained profitability. For each industry, five competitive forces combine to erode the long-term profitability of any industry or segment of it: the threat of new entrants, the threat of substitute products or services, the bargaining power of suppliers, the bargaining power of buyers, and the rivalry among existing competitors. The stronger these forces in an industry, the lower its profitability. New entrants increase competition and therefore drive down profit margins. Availability of close substitutes makes it more difficult for the manufacturer to raise its prices without driving customers to waiting substitutes. Powerful suppliers can increase manufacturers' costs while powerful customers can bargain away profit margins. Rivalry among competitors results in an erosion of profit margins in the form of lower prices for customers and increased cost of sales. The strength of each of the five forces is a function of the industry's structure. For example, the threat of entry is a function of entry barriers such as the history of retaliation of incumbents, brand loyalty, or economies of scale (more on this in Chapter 10). Some industries, by their nature, offer more attractive opportunities for sustainable profits than others.

CAPABILITIES OF A FIRM

Even in attractive industries, not all firms make money. In fact, in unattractive industries, there may still be some firms that make money. In other words, within each industry, some firms are going to have a competitive advantage. They are going to, on average, be more profitable than their rivals or have the potential to do so. One reason for these differences in firm profitability is the fact that, as argued in Chapter 3, a firm can offer lower cost or more differentiated products than its rivals can if it has capabilities that are not easy to imitate or trade. For example, in the 1990s, Intel's capabilities in microprocessor design, installed base of microprocessors, copyrights protected by law, and semiconductor manufacturing enabled it to offer differentiated microprocessors to its customers. Underlying a firm's capabilities are technological and market knowledge. In the Intel example, its knowledge in logic design, circuit design, semiconductor processes, computer architecture, and layout design was critical to its performance. A firm's ability to exploit an innovation, then, is a function of the extent to which it owns or can build scarce, difficult to imitate capabilities that are central to its value configuration (value chain, value network, or value shop).

ONE PROBLEM WITH INDUSTRY ANALYSIS

A major problem with determining a profit site is that industry attractiveness and the type of capabilities needed to offer products in the industry all change. Why? Since profits rest on capabilities which, in turn, rest on technological and market knowledge, the profit picture can change when structural changes such as deregulation or regulation, changing customer expectations, or technological discontinuities change the underlying knowledge. For example, Los Angeles's air quality requirements suggest the use of electric cars in the future, which require different technological competences than their internal combustion engine counterparts. This allows firms with competences in electric car technology, or who can build them quickly, to enter the industry, changing the market structure. Thus barriers to entry, the nature and sources of substitutes, and the number and kinds of rivals, suppliers, and customers often change, making what is an attractive industry and a profitable product-market position today not so attractive tomorrow.

One way to incorporate industry dynamism into competitiveness analysis is to take an evolutionary perspective.[4] This perspective suggests that an innovation evolves as the firms exploiting it interact with their environments. As it evolves, so do industry structure, attractiveness, and critical success factors. The evolution determines what kinds of products (low cost, niche, or differentiated) can be offered at each of the phases of evolution. To offer any of these products (and therefore survive), a firm needs certain kinds of strategies and capabilities. The firms that don't have these capabilities, and therefore cannot offer the specific products of the particular stage, are forced to exit. Thus an industry's attractiveness and the kinds of capabilities that a firm needs to succeed also vary from one stage of the evolution to the other. A firm's heterogeneous capability in the latter part of the evolution depends on its strategies, capabilities, and market positioning early in the life of the innovation.

A SOLUTION

We draw on the Utterback–Abernathy dynamic model of innovation and the Tushman–Rosenkopf technology life cycle model discussed in Chapter 2 to define a framework that can be used to perform competitive analysis. According to these models, at the onset of an innovation, in the *fluid* phase (era of ferment) there is a lot of product and market uncertainty. Manufacturers may not be quite sure what should go into the product. Customers may not know what they want in the product either. There is competition between new and old technologies as well as between different designs using the new technology. Manufacturers interact with their local environments of suppliers, customers, complementary innovators, and competitors to resolve both technological and market uncertainties.

The evolution enters the *transitional* (dominant design) phase when some standardization of components, market needs, and product design features takes place, and a dominant design emerges, signaling a substantial reduction in uncertainty, experimentation, and major design changes. A dominant design is one whose major components and underlying core concepts do not vary substantially from one product model to the other, and the design commands a high percentage of the market share. The rate of major product innovations decreases and emphasis shifts to process innovation and incremental innovation. Materials become more specialized and equipment more specialized and expensive. Competition is based on differentiated products.

In the *specific* phase (era of incremental change) products built around the dominant design proliferate, and there is more and more emphasis on process innovation, with product innovations being largely incremental. Products are highly defined, with differences between competitors' products often fewer than similarities. The pattern described here repeats itself when a new technology with the potential to render the old one noncompetitive is introduced, often by a competitor from outside the established industry. This results in a *discontinuity,* plunging the innovation cycle back to the fluid phase (era of ferment), with another wave of entering firms.

This dynamic process also has a direct effect on industry structure.[5] Competition in an industry is a reflection of the changes in products and processes stemming from technological evolution. In the fluid phase, where product and market requirements are still ambiguous, there is expected to be rapid entry of firms with very few or no failures. Following the emergence of a dominant design, the rate of exits increases, rapidly decreasing the number of competitors. If the standard is open, however, the number of entries may actually rise, increasing the total number of competitors. When IBM entered the personal computer market and its PC quickly emerged as the dominant design, many firms entered since the company made the design open. Eventually the market reaches a point of stability, corresponding to the specific state in which there are only a few firms, having standardized or slightly differentiated products and relatively stable sales and market shares.

Figure 7.1 shows how the structure of an industry can change over the life of the underlying technology. It illustrates the case of the supercomputer industry, where until the 1980s Cray Research and Control Data Corporation (CDC) dominated the market. In the early 1980s new firms entered using minisupercomputer technology. In the mid-1980s others entered with massively parallel processor (MPP) technology. In the 1990s more firms are failing.[6]

It is evident that industry structure, the types of products that can be offered, as well as the nature of competences and endowments that a firm needs to be profitable vary from one phase of the industrial innovation cycle to the other. The attractiveness of an industry to a firm is therefore a function not only of the forces being exerted in the present phase, but of the competences of the firm and the actions it took in the previous phase(s).

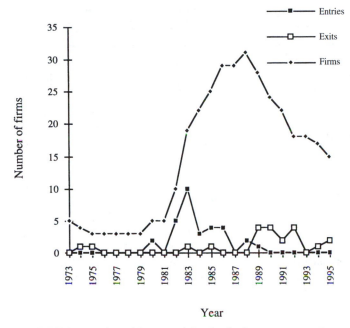

FIGURE 7.1. Number of firms participating in the super-computer industry.

A PROFIT SITE ATTRACTIVENESS MODEL

We suggest, and outline here, a three-step dynamic competitive analysis process. First, at each of the three phases of the industrial innovation cycle, the firm analyzes the pressures being exerted by Porter's five forces to determine the industry's attractiveness. This is illustrated in Figure 7.2. Second, the firm evaluates the extent to which its competences and endowments meet the levels and quality needed to be successful at each phase. Finally, at each phase the firm takes strategic steps that also anticipate the nature of the next phase(s). We explore industry attractiveness first and then the capabilities required to provide the necessary products.

Industry Attractiveness

Fluid Phase (Era of Ferment)

Since early-phase products are highly differentiated and serve niche markets, *rivalry* among existing competitors is expected to be not as high as in later phases. As more new firms enter, however, even the niches may become crowded, increasing rivalry. If the technological discontinuity that ushered in the fluid phase destroys the competences and endowments that incumbents had accumulated in the specific phase, the *threat of new entrants* is very high. Given early-stage techno-

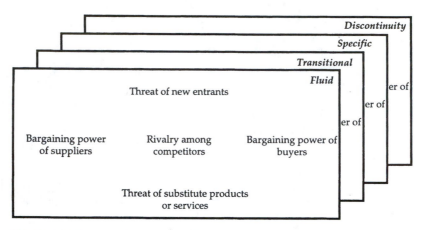

FIGURE 7.2. Dynamic industry attractivess.
Source: Reprinted with the permission of The Free Press, a division of Simon & Schuster from *Competitive Strategy: Techniques for Analyzing Industries and Competitors* by Michael E. Porter. Copyright © 1980 by The Free Press.

logical and market uncertainties, incumbents cannot take some of the measures that they would take in more stable conditions to keep out new entrants. For example, making irreversible commitments in capacity or staking out product-market positions is more difficult since uncertainty about what markets to serve or products to develop still looms large. The *bargaining power of suppliers* is low since materials and equipment are general purpose. The *bargaining power of customers* is also moderately high since the products they buy are highly differentiated and many customers may be lead users. The *threat of substitutes* comes largely from the old technology that is being replaced by the new. As Utterback and Kim have shown, some of the best innovations in the older technology may come when the threat of the invading technology is becoming a reality.[7]

Strategies. To some extent the type of strategy pursued is a function of the firm's innovation strategy: whether it is offensive or defensive. In anticipation of the transitional phase in which a dominant design or standard may be expected to emerge, a leader can invest in helping its own design emerge as the dominant design.[8] Such efforts are particularly useful for products for which network externalities are important. For example, Sun Microsystems' easy licensing of its SPARC technology to anyone who wanted it may have helped its position in the RISC workstation business.[9] Rather than compete to win the dominant design, a follower or fast second may concentrate on building its complementary assets to take advantage of the dominant design when it eventually emerges.

Transitional Phase (Dominant Design)

With the emergence of a dominant design, many of the product and market uncertainties of the fluid phase are reduced. This results in more *rivalry* among existing competitors as the "winners" of the dominant design scramble to win new customers with a product that is less differentiated than at the fluid phase. With product innovation giving way to process innovation, firms scramble to invest in capacity in R&D, in advertising, and in other measures designed to signal commitment to specific market positions in preparation for entering the specific phases with concomittant higher volumes of production. The *threat of new entrants* depends on whether the dominant design is proprietary or open. It is high if the design is open, and low if proprietary since product and market uncertainties have been reduced with the emergence of a dominant design and better defined markets. The *bargaining power of suppliers* increases (compared to the fluid phase) since equipment and materials are now more specialized. Since the emergence of a dominant design allows for differentiated but not unique products, the *bargaining power of customers* increases. An open design also increases the bargaining power of suppliers and customers. The *threat of substitutes* becomes higher since the products being sold are less niche oriented than earlier.

Strategies. Strategic alliances or licensing policies could help the firm win or consolidate the dominant design. The firm can start preparing for providing low-cost products in the specific state by making irreversible investments in capacity, process R&D, and advertising to establish brand name recognition. It can also locate and acquire intellectual property rights or enter special contracts with suppliers for key factors of production.

Specific Phase

In the specific phase competition is oligopolistic, with a few firms that produce commodity products from a dominant design. *Rivalry* among these firms is high, given the commodity nature of the products they sell. It is even higher if the design is open. Competition uses such tools as incremental product or process innovations. For example, some automobile makers have used such incremental product innovations as electronic fuel injection, antilock brakes, all-wheel drive, and air bags to try to gain an advantage. The rate of such innovations, and therefore of the amount of rivalry, is also a function of such environmental factors as how demanding customers or government regulators are.[10] An incumbent can also stake out a product-market position by making irreversible investments in capacity or advertising, thus signaling to rivals that any entry into its product-market space will be met with retaliation.[11] For example, a computer memory chipmaker who invests $1.3 billion to build a manufacturing facility signals to its competitors that it will fight to stay in the memory chip business.

Several factors reduce the *threat of new entrants* who want to use the prevailing technology to enter.[12] In the first place, incumbents may have certain advantages over new entrants. For example, they may have licenses and patents that give them exclusive access to complementary technologies, supplies, or special distribution channels. They may also be further along the technology learning curve or have established brand names and reputations through prior advertising and performance. In the second place, incumbents may exhibit certain characteristics that signal to new entrants that they will fight entry by, say, lowering their prices. For example, incumbents with high irreversible investments in capabilities, excess capacity, or a reputation for retaliating against new entrants are likely to keep new entrants from entering their markets. If an incumbent has high exit costs, it is also more likely to fight to stay in the industry than one without. The biggest threat, therefore, comes from new entrants who are using an invading technology that can render incumbent competences and firm- or technology-specific assets obsolete. For example, electronic cash registers rendered NCR's competences and irreversible investments in capacity and service centers obsolete. This allowed Singer to use electronic cash registers to invade the electromechanical cash register market.

The *threat of substitutes* is mostly from new technologies, although in some cases it may be from so-called generics when, for example, an incumbent's patent has expired. On the other hand, the *bargaining power of suppliers* may be higher since they supply specialized equipment and materials and are a major source of innovations. The *bargaining power of customers* may also be higher since products are more or less a commodity. In both cases the bargaining power may be reduced by collusion or other strategic measures on the part of rivals.

Strategies. A firm can pursue several strategies. It could maintain a low-cost strategy given that the products being sold are largely undifferentiated commodities and most innovations are process innovations earmarked for cost reduction. Some product differentiation is possible, but more a matter of positioning. For example, Honda positioned the Acura brand cars in a more luxury bracket than the Honda brand. Mass customization can also give a firm an advantage.[13] The firm can also make irreversible investments in capacity or build a reputation for retaliation to signal to rivals and new entrants alike to stay out of its product-market positions. Since the biggest threat is that of an invading technology that will take the industry into a more turbulent period, the firm can scan sibling technologies to better detect the arrival and potential of a viable discontinuity.

Discontinuities

A technological discontinuity sometimes renders the old technology noncompetitive, and many of the barriers that firms have erected around them in the specific phase may become useless. Irreversible investments in plant capacity and R&D, special licenses, or contracts for special materials or services may become obsolete. For example, the arrival of electronic cash registers destroyed a lot of the barriers to entry such as specialized plants, excellent service networks, and investments in R&D for electromechanics, patents, and other intellectual property that NCR had accumulated in exploiting electromechanical cash registers. Technological discontinuities normally level the playing ground since incumbent existing capabilities may be rendered obsolete.

The *threat of new entrants* is high since the playing ground has been leveled and incumbent existing capabilities may not only be useless, but may actually become a handicap. The *threat of substitutes* from the new technology is now very high. *Rivalry* among incumbents gets higher as the new technology invades the old, and incumbents who have not switched to the new technology are increasingly squeezed. As manufacturers leave the specialized materials and equipment of the specific phase to turn to the general-purpose equipment of the emergent fluid phase, the *bargaining power of suppliers* drops. The impending discontinuity further increases the *bargaining power of customers.*

Strategies. Leaders may want to cannibalize their own products and quickly embrace the new technology. Where network externalities are important, a manufacturer may want to ensure that the new product is compatible with the older ones. For example, in developing its user-friendly Windows operating system, Microsoft made sure that it was compatible with the character-based DOS operating system. A firm can also identify lead users that will be helpful in the product development of the fluid phase and try to work out joint developments.

Capabilities

The capabilities that a firm needs to be successful also vary from one phase to the other. Thus, following the determination of industry attractiveness as outlined earlier, the strategy process consists of (1) determining what kinds of assets and competences are necessary to stake out a profitable market position for that particular industry at each phase of the industrial innovation cycle, (2) examining the firm's own assets and competences to see to what extent they can allow the firm to compete in the industry at the phase in question, and (3) since unique capabilities take time to build, establishing strategies at each phase to build assets and competences for that phase and the next one(s).

Fluid Phase

Given the high technological and market uncertainty of the fluid state, a firm needs the ability to make some sense out of chaos, communicate well with customers to help them identify their needs, and work with lead users. Since the fluid phase is often ushered in by a competence-destroying technological change that requires completely new knowledge, there may be some problems unique to incumbents. An incumbent's history—especially the capabilities acquired in the specific phase of the previous technology—plays a vital role in where it will search for the new technological information and the kinds of decisions it will make. Thus an incumbent's perception of the attractiveness of an industry may be greatly biased by its history. For example, NCR saw the invading cash registers as only a faster way of adding numbers. It did not see them as a new tool for its customers to better manage their inventories and supplier relations. Incumbents may have to unlearn most of what made them so successful in the specific state of the previous technology.[14]

The ability to decipher customer needs and translate them into products, for example, is a good competence, while skilled personnel and good relationships with suppliers and lead users are valuable assets.

Strategies. For a firm with an offensive strategy, the focus is in building the capabilities that will enable it to win the dominant design. These can include building a stock of patents to use as a bargaining chip in establishing alliances. For the firm with a defensive strategy, the focus could be on building the absorptive capacity so that it can quickly imitate the dominant design when it emerges.

Transitional Phase

The emergence of a dominant design greatly reduces both product and market uncertainties and suggests the need for competences that are different from those of the fluid phase. Whereas, in the fluid phase, the focus was on those capabilities that allow one to determine what features to include in the product, in the transitional phase attention shifts to how to improve the values of those features. There is a shift from major product innovations to process innovations and a corresponding shift in skills. As materials and equipment become more specialized, the need for supplier-focused competences increases. As products are no longer niche but differentiated, the need for customer-focused competences also increases.

A strong reputation in related technologies or products and strategic alliances can help win the dominat design. For example, IBM's reputation in mainframes and minicomputers was instrumental in making its PC the standard.

Strategies. Prior to the emergence of the dominant design, strategic maneuvering such as detailed by Cusumano, Mylonadis, and Rosenbloom in the case of VHS emerging as the standard for video tape recording can take advantage of existing capabilities.[15] Building customer and supplier-focused competences may also be valuable, given the switch from using generic supplies to using more specialized ones.

Specific Phase

Since products are largely commodity in the specific phase, emphasis is on those assets and competences that allow a firm to produce at low cost. Low costs are attained largely through process and incremental product innovations. Special licenses or patents that give a firm unique access to low-cost processes can give a firm a competitive advantage. The source of process innovations is often major suppliers of specialized equipment who, in this phase, have high bargaining power. Special contracts, unique supplier relations, or special skills in dealing with such suppliers can be important. Close supplier relations that allow for codevelopment of components or close monitoring of incremental innovations from suppliers can be assets in the specific phase. Low cost and some product differentiation can also come from incremental product innovations. Such incremental innovations, by definition, require skills that build on existing capabilities. This gives incumbents an advantage since they already have the capabilities to build on for incremental innovations. As we saw in Chapter 2, some innovations that masquerade as being incremental, however, may actually be architectural and can present firms that view them as incremental with problems.

Given that the bargaining power of customers and the rivalry among existing competitors are high, a firm's customer-focused capabilities can be particularly valuable. For example, a firm's brand names, reputation for high-quality products, networks of service centers, distribution channels, user networks, and ability to synthesize customer needs into product attributes, as well as a language that product developers can implement technologically, are invaluable.

Strategies. Since all these acquired assets and competencies can become handicaps in the face of a competence-destroying technological discontinuity, one of the biggest challenges to a firm in the specific phase is balancing the act of exploiting the old technology while getting ready for the inevitable arrival of the new one.[16] Strategies in this phase are focused on preparing for the discontinuity and fluid states.

Discontinuities

A technological discontinuity can be competence enhancing if the capabilities required to exploit it build on those used to exploit the previous technology.[17] Such a discontinuity would tend to perpetuate the oligopolies of the specific state. If, however, the technology is competence destroying in that the capabilities required to exploit it are significantly different from existing ones, then a firm's accumulated competences and endowments may not only be useless, they may actually constitute a handicap for the firm.[18]

The technological change may not make obsolete all of an incumbent's capabilities to exploit it. For example, if a discontinuity renders obsolete technological capabilities leaving market ones intact, incumbents can have an advantage if such market capabilities are important and difficult to establish. Similarly, if supplier-focused capabilities are left intact in industries where supplier relations are important, incumbents may also have an advantage. Thus a firm's ability to recognize just which of its capabilities will be rendered obsolete by the arrival of a technological discontinuity and to build those capabilities while taking advantage of those capabilities that are not impacted by the technology can also be an asset.

Strategy. It is important to focus on recognizing the potential of the threats and opportunities that the discontinuity presents. In addition, for incumbents the primary focus is on unlearning the old knowledge so that it may not be a handicap in exploiting the new. In anticipation of the fluid phase, a firm may also start acquiring the skills that it needs to cope with the rapid rate of product innovations of the phase.

SOME CAUTIONS ABOUT THE MODEL

It is important to remember that the profit site attractiveness model detailed in this chapter is just that—a model. This means that it is only as useful, in any situation, as the underlying assumptions of the model apply to that situation. This model has several assumptions. The first is that innovation evolves in a predictable way, with the boundaries between the different phases—fluid, transitional, and specific—distinguishable. These boundaries are, at best, fuzzy. The duration of each phase also varies from product to product. For example, the emergence of a dominant design for automobiles took much longer than that for DRAMs (dynamic random access memories). Sometimes it is difficult to tell whether the dominant design has emerged or not, and what it is exactly. The second assumption is that major process innovation only comes after product innovation. That is not always the case. For example, early in its life Intel bet its future on a process technology called MOS (metal oxide semiconductor), well before most of its pioneering semiconductor product innovations.[19] A case can be made for the fact that although a product technology may exist at a firm before the arrival of product innovations, major process-specific innovations may take place only after a product has been introduced and some feedback received from customers. For example, Intel eventually had to change its process technology to CMOS to meet customer power consumption requirements. The third is that a dominant design does not always emerge. Fourth, it is not always easy to tell which innovation is process and which is product.

Finally, and most important of all, in using Porter's five forces to evaluate how attractive an industry is, we have implied that suppliers, customers, and competitors are out to increase our cost, pay us low prices, or take away our market share. But as we saw in Chapter 4 and will see in Chapter 8, they are also the sources of innovations and assets. Moreover, if a Porter's five forces analysis shows that an industry or market is unattractive, that does not mean that one cannot make money in the industry. One can still make money using the right strategies—strategies that give one a competitive advantage in the industry.

An important thing to remember from this model is that any analysis to determine the suitability of a profit site must incorporate dynamic elements. This evolutionary approach is just one such approach. We now explore the case of personal computers to highlight some of the key points in this chapter.

PRACTICE CASE: THE CASE OF THE PERSONAL COMPUTER INNOVATION

Before the Internet, no single innovation in recent memory had created more millionaires so quickly than the personal computer. These millions have come not only from making the personal computers, but also from supplying the chips that go into them, from supplying the software that is needed to run them, and from buying them to improve productivity—that is, they have come from all over the innovation value-added chain of Figure 7.3. Manufacturers are firms such as Compaq, Apple, Dell, and HP, who make personal computers. Suppliers are firms such as Intel, Cyrix, AMD, Micron Technology, NEC, Toshiba, and numerous others, who supply chips, disk drives, and other components that go into the personal computer. Complementary innovators are firms such as Microsoft, IBM, Novell, and Lotus, who supply software, but over whom personal computer makers have very little or no control. Value-added retailers (VARs) are firms that take personal computers

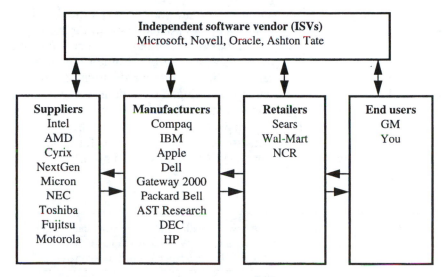

FIGURE 7.3. Personal computer innovation value-added chain.

and add some value to them before retailing them. They range from stores such as Sears or Wal-Mart, whose value addition is a convenient shopping location, to others who buy the personal computers and customize them for lawyers (e.g., add special software). End customers are lawyers, firms such as GE, or individuals who use the presonal computers at home.

One very interesting thing about the personal computer is that some of those who have profited the most from it do not make it. In 1994 alone, Intel, the top supplier of microprocessor chips for the personal computer, made $2.288 billion in profits on revenues of $11.521 billion, and Microsoft, the maker of personal computer software, earned $1.146 billion on revenues of $4.649 billion. On the other hand, Compaq, the top personal computer maker, made only $239 million on sales of $4.099 billion. Using the cases of these three companies, we argue that what matters in making profits is not so much where a firm is located in the innovation value-added chain as the kinds of capabilities it has. We also explore how some of these firms built their capabilities during the evolution of the personal computer.

Microsoft

Microsoft was founded by Bill Gates and Paul Allen in 1975. Their first successful products were personal computer versions of compilers for the computer programming languages BASIC, COBOL, and FORTRAN, which programmers used to write software. Their biggest break may have come in 1980, when IBM decided to enter the personal computer market and went to Microsoft for help. It wanted Microsoft to develop the programming languages BASIC, FORTRAN, and COBOL for the upcoming PC. In a meeting to see how they were going to meet their commitments to IBM and what else they could sell to Big Blue, Bill Gates, Paul Allen,

Steve Balmer, and Kay Nishi had an even more important question to discuss: whether they should commit to developing an operating system for the new machine. Knowing that Paul Allen was in the process of buying an operating system called Q-DOS (quick and dirty operating system) from Seattle Computer, Nishi, their Japanese partner, insisted that they agree to provide IBM with the operating system. Bill Gates would later recall Nishi saying, "got to do it, got to do it."[20] So they offered to develop the operating system for IBM. In fact, when they promised to license Q-DOS to IBM, the deal with Seattle Computer had not been closed yet. Microsoft paid $50,000 for it, turned around, and sold it to IBM for $186,000. But it was the terms of the contract with IBM that Microsoft is most proud of. As Bill Gates would later recall,

---

We didn't get paid that much—the total was something like $186,000—but we knew that there were going to be clones of the IBM PC. We structured that original contract to allow them [the cloners] to buy from us. It was a key point in our negotiations.[21]

Bill Gates knew that good IBM products were usually cloned and was sure that the PC would be one of those. So in the contract selling MS-DOS to IBM, Microsoft made sure that IBM had the right to sell its own PCs with the modified Q-DOS in them, *but not* the right to license DOS to other makers of personal computers. That right belonged to Microsoft.[22]

As it turned out, Microsoft was right. Many firms decided to clone the IBM PC and Microsoft could sell its operating system to them. However, Microsoft still had one problem: CP/M-86. This was a competing operating system, which, on the August 1981 announcement of the IBM PC, had been offered as an alternative operating system for the PC and was considered, by some, superior in performance, given its memory management and other features. Although CP/M-86 was late (released in the spring of 1982), it was the strategic actions taken by Microsoft and IBM that helped DOS triumph over it. First, Microsoft was the leading producer of languages such as BASIC, COBOL, and FORTRAN for PCs. These languages ran on DOS but not on CP/M-86, and Microsoft was not about to drop everything and develop the languages for the competing CP/M-86. When it did get to delivering such languages for CP/M-86, Microsoft priced them 50 percent higher than comparable languages running on its DOS. The version of BASIC that Microsoft sold for CP/M-86 was also an inferior one, with the graphics having been stripped.[23] Since these languages were the major tools that software firms used in the development of applications software for the PC, their absence from CP/M-86 meant fewer applications being developed for the platform. For a computer operating system to emerge as a standard, applications software is critical.

Second was IBM's pricing. DOS on the PC came with two advanced versions of BASIC, ran all the applications software available on the machine, and was priced at $40. When CP/M-86 eventually came out in the spring of 1982, it was priced at $240, even though it ran almost no applications software and did not include BASIC.[24] Third, Microsoft went aggressively after firms such as Compaq that wanted to build IBM PC clones. It gave them a 50 percent discount over the listed price of $95,000, which was very low for an operating system to begin with, and for an operating system that, unlike CP/M-86, was already deliverable and had many applications running on it.[25]

With all of this going for Microsoft, its DOS quickly emerged as the standard for personal computer operating systems (and the standard for the IBM PC compatibles) and the major source of its profits. What it now had to do was keep exploiting it, and it did just that. It actually started laying the groundwork for exploiting the standard back in 1981, shortly after the announcement of the IBM PC, when it started negotiations with Apple Computer to provide applications software for Apple's Macintosh. Like most computer enthusiasts, Gates knew that the "look and feel" of the Macintosh, which was superior to that of the DOS-based IBM PC and compatibles,[26] was critical to future computing. The PC had a so-called character-based interface in that all the users see are numbers and letters. They must communicate with the computer by typing commands, which they have to remember every time. The Macintosh used a so-called graphical user interface (GUI). With today's GUI, users see not only characters but pictures, or *icons*. With the use of a *mouse,* they can click on these self-explanatory icons to invoke programs instead of having to remember the exact file name and typing it correctly. Moreover, once a user has learned to use a GUI-based applications program, it becomes very easy to learn other applications without a manual.

One reason for Microsoft's commitment to developing the applications programs for the Macintosh was its belief that the future of computing (and therefore of Microsoft[27]) was in GUI, and the earlier it started developing the capabilities to exploit it, the better. It hired Charles Simonyi from Xerox's Palo Alto Research Center (PARC), where GUI had been invented. In January 1984, when Apple introduced the Macintosh, Microsoft offered Multiplan, BASIC, and Word 1.0 (a word-processing program). A year later, Microsoft announced Microsoft Excel, a spread sheet for Macintosh.

Developing the applications programs for the Macintosh gave Microsoft an opportunity to understand the GUI technology and the relationship between it and how applications programs interface with it. Microsoft used these competences to develop its Microsoft Windows operating system, a GUI-based operating system that is compatible with DOS and, therefore, the huge installed base of personal computers and applications that run on them. The first two versions of the program, introduced in 1985 and 1987, had problems that the firm rectified in the very successful 1990 version. Using the same GUI capabilities, Microsoft quickly developed versions of its Microsoft Word and Excel for the PC, and later the popular Microsoft Windows 95. Having laid the groundwork, we can now conclude by answering the question: why has being a complementary innovator been a good profit site for Microsoft? We answer this question using the framework of Figure 7.4, which is an application of Figure 3.8. Microsoft offers differentiated products such as DOS, Windows 95, Word, and Excel. While its ability to exploit standards, negotiate contracts, and recognize winning ideas cannot be questioned, it is its installed base of PCs, which use its DOS and Windows software, and its copyrights on these programs that allow the firm to offer products differentiated from those of its competitors. Competitors cannot legally copy these products because they are copyrighted and protected by U.S. copyright laws. The millions of people who

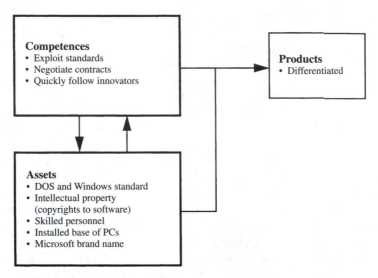

FIGURE 7.4. Sample of Microsoft's competences and assets.

have learned to use these programs or who have developed their own programs to run on Windows or DOS do not want to switch to another supplier of software.

Compaq Computers

Compaq was the first to offer an IBM-compatible PC—a personal computer that ran all the software that the IBM PC ran. In founding the company, Rod Canion was banking on one thing: since IBM had "legitimized" the personal computer, there might be more demand than a sluggish IBM could satisfy. A cloner could make money by offering the product at lower cost than Big Blue's overhead would allow it to or by maintaining compatibility while offering some unique features. Rod Canion opted for the latter, offering a portable personal computer that could run all the software that IBM machines could. In a survey of users, the innovative Canion had found that the feature that they wanted most in a personal computer was portability.[28] Users wanted to be able to work in the office and take the computer home to keep working if they wanted to. In 1982 Compaq introduced its IBM-compatible portable personal computer. Compaq knew that being different, even as a clone, was important, and in that spirit it also introduced the first PC that used Intel's 80386 microprocessor in September 1986, some six months before IBM did. Such innovative moves made Compaq a huge success. Its profits shot from $3 million in 1983, when it went public, to $455 million in 1990. It made the Fortune 500 list in the shortest time ever.

Unfortunately for Compaq, however, it neither controlled any standard nor possessed any core copyrights like Microsoft. Moreover, the competences it had used to introduce the first portable and the first 80386-based PC were neither unique nor inimitable. It had utilized its capabilities in logic design, circuit design, miniaturization, component assembly, and testing, all of which hundreds of other computer companies already had or could quickly put together. What is more is that semiconductor manufacturers such as Intel, which controls the brain of the PC, also had these skills and could integrate vertically any time they wanted. In October 1990, when Compaq launched its 80386SX-based notebook, several competitors had already launched better performing notebooks. In 1994, when competitors such as Packard Bell were selling consumer PCs made using Intel's latest chip, the Pentium, Compaq was still trying to peddle PCs that used the old 486 microprocessor. Compaq lost considerable market share to Packard Bell.[29] The reason for Packard Bell's sudden capability in introducing PCs with the latest Intel chips: Intel's decision to integrate vertically and increase the rate of diffusion of its Pentium. (Chapter 10 details this side of Intel's strategy.) Compaq was bought by HP in 2002.

Intel Corporation

Like Microsoft, Intel controlled a standard and had copyrights that were protected by law. These core endowments, together with its competences in circuit design, logic design, semiconductor physics, and semiconductor process manufacturing, gave Intel what it took to profit from supplying microprocessors to PC makers. It invented the microprocessor in 1972 and thereafter made numerous incremental innovations to it. In 1980 IBM decided to use Intel's 8088 microprocessor as the brain of its PC. As more firms cloned the PC and it emerged as the dominant design, Intel's microprocessor also emerged as the microprocessor PC standard. Chapter 10 provides a more detailed look at Intel.

These three cases illustrate one key point. A firm does not have to manufacture an innovation in order to profit from it. What is important is that the firm recognizes the potential of the innovation, has a strategy for exploiting the innovation, and either has the capabilities to exploit the innovation or is able to build them quickly as the innovation evolves. We will return to the strategy part in Chapter 10.

SUMMARY

Once a firm has recognized the potential of an innovation, the next step is to decide whether to exploit it as a supplier, manufacturer, complementary innovator, distributor, or customer. To do so, it must explore the attractiveness of the industry as well as the extent to which its competences match those that are required to offer the product. One problem with such an analysis is that industry attractiveness and the type of capabilities that are needed to offer products in the industry change. Capabilities that once were useful in exploiting certain markets may be rendered obsolete by structural changes such as deregulation or regulation, changing customer expectations, or technological discontinuities. One way to incorporate industry dynamism into competitiveness analysis is to take an evolutionary perspective, which suggests that an innovation evolves as the firms exploiting it interact with their environments to resolve uncertainties. As it evolves, so do industry structure, attractiveness, and the capabilities needed to exploit it.

We suggested a three-step process for determining the attractiveness of a profit site. First, at each of the four phases of the innovation cycle and for each of the supplier, manufacturer, complementary innovator, distributor, and customer industries, the firm analyzes the pressures being exerted by Porter's five forces to determine the industry's attractiveness. These forces must be balanced against benefits such as the innovations that come from suppliers, customers, and competitors. Second, the firm determines the capabilities that are needed to supply the product or service at each phase of the cycle. Third, the firm evaluates the extent to which its existing competences and endowments meet the levels and quality needed to offer products successfully at each phase and how quickly it can build them if it does not already have them.

We used the cases of Intel, Compaq, and Microsoft to illustrate the concepts of the chapter, especially the fact that a firm does not have to be the manufacturer of an innovation to profit from it. What is important is having the right strategies or capabilities, or the ability to build these capabilities quickly.

KEY TERMS

Bargaining power of buyers
Bargaining power of customers
Bargaining power of suppliers
Dynamic analysis
Industry attractiveness
Profit site

Rivalry among existing competitors
Static analysis
Technological discontinuity
Threat of new entrants
Threat of substitute products

QUESTIONS AND EXERCISES

1. As an analysis tool in determining a profit site, what are the shortcomings of Porter's five forces?
2. What are the shortcomings of the dynamic competitiveness model? How would you improve this model?
3. Pick an industry of your choice and perform a dynamic competitiveness analysis on it. Why are the industry leaders at each level of the innovation value-added chain performing as well as they do?

NOTES

1. This chapter draws heavily on a paper that the author of this book wrote with Professor James M. Utterback. See Afuah, A. N., and J. M. Utterback. "Responding to structural industry changes: A technological evolution perspective." *Industrial and Corporate Change* **6**: 183–202, 1997.
2. Porter, M. E. *Competitive Strategy: Techniques for Analyzing Industries and Competitors.* New York: Free Press, 1980.

3. Porter, M. E. *Competitive Strategy: Techniques for Analyzing Industries and Competitors* (1980). Porter, M. E. "Towards a dynamic theory of strategy." *Strategic Management Journal* **12:** 95–117, 1991.

4. Utterback, J. M. *Mastering the Dynamics of Innovation.* Cambridge, MA: Harvard Business School Press, 1994.

5. See, for example, Klepper, S., and K. L. Simmons. "Technological change and industry shakeouts." Unpublished Manuscript, Department of Social and Decision Sciences, Carnegie-Mellon University, 1993. Utterback, J. M. *Mastering the Dynamics of Innovation* (1994). Utterback, J. M., and F. F. Suarez. "Innovation, competition, and industry structure." *Research Policy* **22:** 1–21, 1993.

6. Afuah, A. N., and J. M. Utterback. "The emergence of a new supercomputer architecture." *Technology Forecasting and Social Change* **40:** 315–28, 1991.

7. Utterback, J. M., and L. Kim. "Invasion of a stable business by radical innovation." In *The Management of Productivity and Technology in Manufacturing*; P. R. Kleindorfer (Ed.). Cambridge, MA: Plenum Press, 1986.

8. Hariharan, S., and C. K. Prahalad. "Strategic windows in the structuring of industries: Compatibility standards and industry evolution." In *Building the Strategically-Responsive Organizations*; H. Thomas, D. O'Neil, R. White, and D. Hurst (Eds.). New York: John Wiley, 1994.

9. Khazam, J., and D. Mowery. "Commercialization of RISC: Strategies for the creating of dominant designs." *Research Policy* **23:** 89–102, 1994.

10. Thomas, L. G. "Spare the rod and spoil the industry: Vigorous competition and vigorous regulation promote global competitive advantage: A ten nation study of government industrial policies and corporate pharmaceutical advantage." Working Paper, Columbia Business School, 1989.

11. Ghemawat, P. *Commitment: The Dynamics of Strategy.* New York: Free Press, 1991.

12. Oster, S. *Modern Competitive Analysis.* Oxford: Oxford University Press, 1994.

13. Pine, J. *Mass Customization: The Next Frontier of Business Competition.* Boston, Harvard Business School Press, 1993.

14. Bettis, R. A., and C. K. Prahalad. "The dominant logic: Retrospective and extension." *Strategic Management Journal* **16:** 5–14, 1995.

15. Cusumano, M. A., Y. Mylonadis, and R. Rosenbloom. "Strategic maneuvering and mass-market dynamics: The triumph of VHS over Beta." *Business History Review* **66:** 51–94, 1992.

16. Tyre, M. J., and O. Hauptman. "Effectiveness of organizational responses to technological change in the production process." *Organizational Science* **3** (3), 1992.

17. Tushman, M. L., and P. Anderson. "Technological discontinuities and organizational environments." *Administrative Science Quarterly* **31:** 439–65, 1986.

18. Leonard-Barton, D. "Core capabilities and core rigidities: A paradox in managing new product development." *Strategic Management Journal* **13:** 111–26, 1992.

19. Moore, G. E. "Intel—Memories and the microprocessor." *Daedalus, Journal of the American Academy of Arts and Sciences* 55–80, Spring 1996.

20. Goldblatt, H. "How we did it: Paul Allen and Bill Gates." *Fortune,* October 2, 1995.

21. Goldblatt, H. "How we did it: Paul Allen and Bill Gates" (1995).

22. Their experience in marketing one of these products, BASIC, would prove very valuable later. They signed a contract with MITS, a pioneer PC maker, giving MITS an exclusive worldwide license to their BASIC. MITS also had the exclusive right to sublicense the prod-

uct to third parties (Manes and Andrews, 1993), promising to make "best efforts" to sell it (Goldblatt, 1995). MITS later reneged on its promise and Microsoft had to go to litigation. Needless to say, Bill Gates and Paul Allen were mad (Goldblatt, 1995). See Manes, S., and P. Andrews. *Gates: How Microsoft's Mogul Reinvented an Industry—and Made Himself the Richest Man in America.* New York: Touchstone, 1993. Goldblatt, H. "How we did it: Paul Allen and Bill Gates" (1995).

23. Cusumano, M. A., and R. W. Selby. *Microsoft Secrets.* New York: Free Press, 1995, p. 142. Manes, S., and P. Andrews. *Gates: How Microsoft's Mogul Reinvented an Industry—and Made Himself the Richest Man in America* (1993, pp. 192–193).

24. Manes, S., and P. Andrews. *Gates: How Microsoft's Mogul Reinvented an Industry—and Made Himself the Richest Man in America.* (1993).

25. Manes, S., and P. Andrews. *Gates: How Microsoft's Mogul Reinvented an Industry—and Made Himself the Richest Man in America* (1993).

26. From now on, when this book refers to the "PC" it is referring to the IBM PC and its clones.

27. Cusumano, M. A., and R. W. Selby. *Microsoft Secrets.* New York: Free Press, 1995, p. 142.

28. Daniel, I., and S. Knepper. *The Making of Microsoft.* Rockland, CA: Prima, 1993.

29. Burrows, P. "Where Compaq's kingdom is weak." *Business Week*, May 8, 1995.

8

STRATEGIC CHOICE OR
ENVIRONMENTAL DETERMINISM

In Chapters 3, 4, and 7 we saw that while a firm's local environment can be a good source of innovations, it can also exert pressures that can quickly sap profits from innovation. This raises a simple but important question: can a firm control its environment in such a way that it benefits from the flow of innovations and knowledge from it while not yielding to the pressures that can drain entrepreneurial rents? In this chapter we argue that a firm can, through strategic choices, influence or even determine the environment in which it operates. We use the cases of Wal-Mart from the retail industry and of Sun Microsystems from computer workstations to explore the question.

The chapter is organized as follows. First, we review the role of each member of a firm's local environment and the strategic measures that the firm can take to influence that role. We then show how Wal-Mart took such strategic decisions to control its environment. Its decisions on where to locate its stores and what technologies to use have had a significant impact on its competitors and the bargaining power of its suppliers. Following that, we explore the cases of Sun Microsystems and DEC, which had rather contrasting strategies in their pursuit of excellence in the workstation industry, with very different results. In particular, we show how Sun's use of universities as the primary source of its technologies, its treatment of universities as preferred customers, and its pursuit of "open" standards allowed it not only to prosper in stable industry conditions, but also to overcome the discontinuity problems brought by the arrival of RISC (reduced instruction set computer) technology. DEC did not quite achieve the same results. Finally, we conclude that Wal-Mart's and Sun's strategic choices since their inception have been instrumental in influencing their local environments and are partly responsible for their performance advantage over competitors.

BACKGROUND AND FRAMEWORK

Manufacturer—Environment Quasi Equilibrium?

At any time a firm can be thought of as interacting with its local environment as shown in Figure 8.1. Suppliers have developed certain capabilities to supply labor, components, and equipment and also constitute a source of innovations for the manufacturer as well as of opportunism and bargaining power. Complementary innovators have also developed a certain level of capabilities to allow them to supply not only complementary products but also innovations. They also constitute a source of opportunism and threat of entry. Universities and scientific laboratories are sources of skilled personnel, innovations, inventions, and knowledge, not only for manufacturers but also for their competitors, suppliers, and complementary innovators. Customers have some knowledge of how to use a manufacturer's products and have developed a certain level of expectations and preferences. They also constitute a source of innovations and possess some level of bargaining power. Competitors also want to innovate and therefore want everything that the manufacturer wants.

INFLUENCING THE LOCAL ENVIRONMENT

Given the critical role that a firm's environment plays in its ability to innovate, the question is whether there are any strategic actions that the firm could take so that,

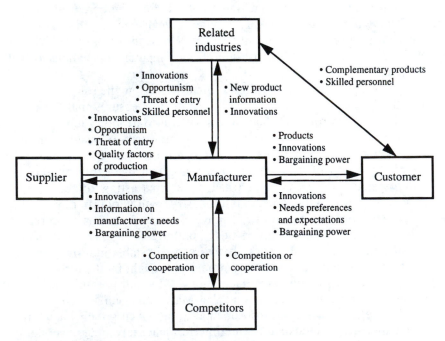

FIGURE 8.1. A firm and its local environment.

for example, it could receive the best components and equipment from its suppliers without any opportunistic behavior from them, or be the first to have insights into an upcoming innovation from suppliers, related industries, or customers.[1] More importantly, the question is whether such actions can allow a firm to take better advantage of such threats as deregulation or regulation, changing customer preferences, and technological discontinuities. The framework, whose key elements are summarized in Figure 8.2 and discussed later, is designed to help in the exploration of such questions.

Suppliers of Materials and Equipment

In making supplier-related strategic choices, a manufacturer must be concerned about three factors: reducing relationship-specific idiosyncrasies in order to limit opportunism, insuring a high rate of flow of innovations from suppliers, and ensuring the on-time flow of quality factors of production from suppliers while limiting

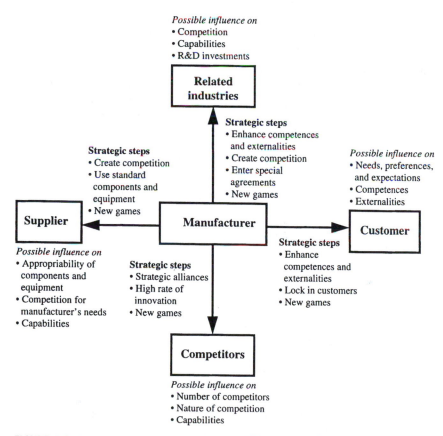

FIGURE 8.2. Strategic measures that a firm can take and what the measures can influence.

their bargaining power. Very specialized components or equipment from a single supplier can lead to opportunism on the part of the supplier,[2] reduce the rate of innovation, and increase the bargaining power of the supplier. For example, PC makers have very little bargaining power when it comes to dealing with Intel, the supplier of microprocessors for their PCs. To avoid such problems, the manufacturer can take two measures. First, it can ensure that it has more than one supplier since the more suppliers there are, the higher the rate of innovations from them, and the less likely any of them is going to hold the manufacturer hostage. In the 1970s and 1980s IBM required its suppliers of microchips to have second sources. Second, the manufacturer can use the same standard components and equipment that other manufacturers use. That way, since manufacturers can be a source of innovations for suppliers, the supplier can be a conduit for pooling innovations from different manufacturers. Maintaining a credible threat of backward vertical integration can be a good strategic vehicle for achieving all these. For example, one reason IBM was very successful at convincing its suppliers to find second sources for their products was because of the threat of backward integration that it posed, given its size and capabilities in semiconductors. Table 8.1 summarizes these arguments.

Customers

As Table 8.2 details, a manufacturer is concerned not only about meeting the changing needs, preferences, and expectations of customers, but also about having access to the innovations that often come from customers, and about coping with customers' bargaining power and threat of entry. There are certain measures that a firm can take to exploit these threats and opportunities. First, there is the much-talked-about being close to the customer. This can mean visiting customers often,

TABLE 8.I. Possible impact of a manufacturer's strategic actions on suppliers.

Manufacturer sees suppliers as:
    Source of innovations
    Source of on-time, high-quality factors of production
    Source of opportunism and bargaining power
    Potential competitor

Manufacturer can influence:
    Appropriability of components and equipment
    Competition at supplier level
    Supplier's capabilities

Strategic actions that manufacturer can take:
    Create multiple sources
    Use standard components that are also used by other manufacturers
    Adopt innovations that are competence enhancing to suppliers
    Maintain a credible threat of vertical integration

TABLE 8.2. Possible impact of a manufacturer's strategic actions on customers.

Manufacturer sees customer as:
   Source of innovations for new products
   Source of information on customer needs and preferences
   Source of revenues (in exchange for products or services)
   Bargaining power
   Potential competitor

Manufacturer can influence:
   Changing needs, preferences, and expectations of customers
   Capabilities

Strategic actions that manufacturer can take:
   Track customer changing needs, preferences, and expectations
   Lock in customers where learning and externalities are important
   Give away some products early in the life of the innovation
   Introduce competence- and externalities-enhancing products
   Advertise to boost its reputation and brand name recognition

---

listening to them, observing them, and helping them discern or, sometimes, "discover" their needs. The rationale here is that since market knowledge can be tacit, it is best transferred in person. Being close to a customer can also mean joint product development. For example, GE's plastics unit and BMW jointly developed the first body panels made with thermoplastics for the automaker's Z1 two-seater car.[3] Second, getting to many customers early is very important, especially for products that exhibit network externalities and that require a certain level of training prior to use. Customers who buy these products and learn how to use them can get locked in. Moreover, as detailed in Appendix 1, moving first can be a contributing factor to winning a standard. Third, it is important to make sure that new products do not unduly render the competences of customers obsolete. Fourth, the firm can advertise or perform any other activity that can boost its brand name recognition.

Related Industries

Like suppliers, complementary innovators can be a source of opportunism. For example, it may be in Microsoft's interest to spend more time on versions of its word processing software that runs on Pentium PCs than on Apple's RISC PowerPC personal computers. Without applications software that take advantage of the speed of RISC processors, customers may not see the full intended benefits of buying Apple PowerPC (Macintosh) machines and therefore will buy Pentium machines, which run many more Microsoft products than does the Macintosh. Thus a manufacturer may have to ensure that it has multisources for major complementary products or enters long-term agreements with complementary innovators. Here again, there are certain strategic steps that a manufacturer can take. First, when it introduces prod-

TABLE 8.3. Possible impact of a manufacturer's strategic actions
on complementary innovators.

Manufacturer sees complementary innovators, universities, and labs as:
  Providers of complementary products
  Source of scientific and technological knowledge, inventions, and innovations
  Source of opportunism
  Source of skilled labor for customers, manufacturers, and complementary innovators
Manufacturer can influence:
  Competition at the complementary innovator level
  Investments in complementary products
  What universities and research laboratories learn
Strategic action that a manufacturer can take:
  Introduce products that are competence and externalities enhancing to complementary innovators
  Enter special agreements with complementary innovators, universities, and public laboratories
      for research results
  Increase expected network size
  Advertise to boost its reputation and brand name recognition
  Give away products

---

ucts it can make sure that they are not capabilities obsoleting for complementary
innovators. Second, the firm can enter long-term agreements with complementary
innovators to assure itself of sources of complementary products. Third, the manufacturer can encourage competition at the complementary innovator level by, for
example, giving away complementary technologies. Table 8.3 lists impacts a manufacturer can have on complementary innovators.

Universities, research laboratories, and other generators and incubators of
ideas constitute a source of scientific and technological knowledge, inventions, and
innovations. They also constitute a source of skilled labor for the manufacturer as
well as for customers and complementary innovators. By giving away equipment
to these universities and laboratories, a manufacturer can also get them to lock into
its products. Since these are sources of skilled labor, personnel from there who go
on to work for customers and complementary innovators would prefer products
from the manufacturer whose products they have used in the past and built competences in. These also ensure that related innovations are likely to be related to this
manufacturer's products.

Competitors

A firm's competitors may be the most difficult part of its local environment to influence. The goal of competitors is simple: to exploit innovations too. The strategic
steps that a firm can take to "control" competitors are detailed in Chapter 10 but
summarized in Table 8.4. Briefly, however, a firm can block entry so that it can earn

TABLE 8.4. Possible impact of a manufacturer's strategic actions on competitors.

Manufacturer sees competitors as:
    A drain for its competitive advantage
    Allies

Manufacturer can influence:
    Number of competitors
    Nature of competition (mutualism or competition)

Manufacturer can take strategic actions to:
    Prevent entry
    Encourage entry and ally
    Maintain high rate of product innovation
    Take advantage of any unique capabilities

---

monopoly rents, encourage entry so as to win a standard, or keep introducing new products faster than its competitors.

THE ROLE OF STRATEGY AND CAPABILITIES

Whether and when a firm takes any of these strategic actions is a function of not only its environment, but also its strategy and capabilities (Figure 8.3). We will explore this in more detail in Chapter 10. Briefly, however, a firm with an offensive innovation strategy, by definition, is more likely to be the one to try to shape its environment than one with a defensive strategy. A firm's capabilities also play a sig-

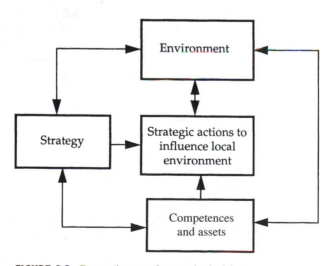

FIGURE 8.3. Determinants of strategic decisions.

nificant role in its ability to shape its local environment. IBM's share size and reputation in the computer world were instrumental to its PC being adopted as a standard. The faster the environment changes (and therefore the higher the uncertainty), the more likely a firm's decisions are to have little effect on its environment.

PRACTICE CASES

We now explore how two very different firms, Wal-Mart and Sun Microsystems, in very different industries, have through strategic decisions, taken early in their lives, been able to influence their environments in very different ways with rather similar results.

WAL-MART

Over the past two decades no major retailer has recorded the kinds of profits and growth that Wal-Mart has. It has continuously outperformed arch rivals J. C. Penney, Kmart, and Sears. One reason for this phenomenal performance has been the firm's ability to influence its local environment of suppliers, customers, and competitors.

The Environment Wal-Mart Faced

In the 1950s Sam Walton owned a series of Benjamin Franklin variety retail franchises that were very successful. But he also sensed that discount retail posed a threat to his variety stores and decided to preempt the threat by entering the discount retail business. However, he faced two major potential impediments to success in the discount retail business. First, he faced in both Kmart and J. C. Penney incumbents who enjoyed first-mover advantages such as brand name recognition and established relationships with suppliers. Second, the manufacturers who supplied goods to retailers were king. They decided which customer got what goods and at what prices, and in many cases, actually decided what the end customer buying from the retailer had to pay for the good.

Controlling the Environment

Wal-Mart solved both problems with several strategic measures: (1) it located its first stores in small towns previously shunned by larger retailers, (2) it saturated whole new areas with stores before moving on to the next, (3) it built a Wal-Mart "culture" that has been difficult for other firms to replicate, and (4) it made extensive use of information technology, integrating it into the way it buys, distributes, and sells goods.

Competition

In his market research, Sam Walton had found out that Kmart and J. C. Penney had avoided small towns and concentrated on urban centers. So when he established his store in 1962, he decided to concentrate on areas with populations of 25,000 or less.[4] By moving into these "little one-horse towns which everybody else was ignoring"[5] that had been shunted by incumbents, it avoided early head-on confrontation. This also gave it some economies of small town operations. According to Sidney McKnight, a Wal-Mart official, "occupancy fees, advertising costs, payroll, and taxes are all lower than in the big cities. You get a work force that is likely to be more stable and the instant identity of being the biggest store around."[6] Such economies, while beneficial to Wal-Mart, would also attract competitors. So Wal-Mart took several more steps to keep competitors out or behind. First, once it entered a small town, it proceeded to saturate the surrounding area with stores before moving to the next. Having a high concentration of stores in an area allowed Wal-Mart to build its own warehouses and distribution to serve its stores, giving the firm some economies of scale advantages.

Second, in its stores Wal-Mart established what is now sometimes referred to as the Wal-Mart culture. It "empowered" employees, letting them participate in the management of the store through contributions such as suggestions. Giving employees such empowerment was Sam Walton's own idea. As Sam Glass, Wal-Mart's CEO, recalled, "I was talking with Sam the other day, and he was remarking about how 99 percent of the best ideas we ever had came from our employees."[7] The Wal-Mart culture has been difficult to duplicate by competitors, given its tacit nature. The company also went on to cement its relationship with local communities, offering scholarships to students, stocking its stores with a certain percentage of goods from the community, and making the community feel like it is part of Wal-Mart. Competitors who tried to move into the small towns or areas that Wal-Mart had saturated with stores have had a difficult time duplicating the Wal-Mart culture and sense of community. All of this, coupled with Wal-Mart's use of information technology and an innovation called cross-docking, have enabled the firm to keep offering low prices. Chapter 10 provides more details on these innovations.

Suppliers

Being a new entrant in the retail business at a time when the manufacturers who supplied the goods to be sold commanded a tremendous amount of bargaining power was bad enough, and being from a small Arkansas town made things particularly difficult for Wal-Mart when dealing with its suppliers—a retailer's lifeline. As Sam Walton would later recall, "Sometimes it was difficult getting the bigger companies—the Procter & Gambles, Eastman Kodaks, whoever—to call on us at all, and when they did, they would dictate to us how much they would sell us and at what price."[8] Once Sam started saturating whole new areas with stores and built central distribution warehouses to serve these stores, it also centralized buying. At suppliers, Wal-Mart presented a united front that gave it more power than earlier. As the number of stores and the volume of goods it bought increased, so did Wal-Mart's power. In 1987 Procter and Gamble, which once wouldn't talk to Wal-Mart, proposed setting up a "partnership" with Wal-Mart. The two firms installed an electronic data interchange (EDI) link between them to share information. Through the link, Procter & Gamble instantaneously receives sales information on the hundreds of different items that it sells to Wal-Mart. This allows P&G to better tailor its production to meet Wal-Mart's demand.[9] The company has since established similar information links with its other suppliers. In some cases Wal-Mart has taken the relationship further. For example, Gitano, maker of fashionable jeans, is responsible for the inventory in a specific area of Wal-Mart warehouse space, but Wal-Mart does not "buy" the merchandise until it is moved into the store. In return, Wal-Mart tells Gitano the rate and prices at which it is selling the jeans.[10]

Thus by moving to small towns first, saturating whole areas with stores, and building distribution centers to match, Wal-Mart has been able to use its size to command the type of bargaining power that once belonged to suppliers.

SUN AND DEC

Ever since Sun and DEC entered the computer workstation business in 1982 and 1985, respectively, the former has consistently outperformed the latter (using workstation market share as the performance measure). In what follows, we argue that one reason for the difference in the performance of the two firms is the rather different approaches they have taken in influencing their local competitive environments. Before discussing the cases, it is worthwhile to define briefly what the environment is in this context. It consists of suppliers, customers, independent software vendors (complementary innovators), competitors, and repositories of technological knowledge such as universities and research laboratories. Suppliers include firms such as Motorola and Intel, which supply components such as microprocessors and memory chips, all of which require a considerable amount of skill and knowledge to develop and manufacture. Customers include both firms such as General Motors and individuals such as university professors, who must also learn how to use the workstations. In particular, they must learn the operating system, the program that manages all the other programs on the computer. Independent software vendors (ISVs) are firms such as Microsoft, which develop software and sell directly to customers, and over whom workstation makers have little or no control. They must also acquire programming and other computer science skills to be able to develop the applications software that is critical to the viability of workstations.

SUN MICROSYSTEMS

By many measures, Sun Microsystems' performance in the ten years after entering the computer workstation market in 1982 was phenomenal. Table 8.5 shows its

TABLE 8.5. Market share between 1982 and 1992 for Sun and DEC.

Year	Share %	
	Sun	*DEC*
1984	35.6	4.9
1985	26.2	11.0
1986	30.9	8.2
1987	27.2	19.1
1988	34.0	20.4
1989	34.5	22.9
1990	38.3	16.8
1991	39.3	13.7
1992	38.3	12.5

Source: Data from IDC, company financial statements.

market share over some of those years. One reason for this performance has been the company's ability to influence its environment through strategic decisions it took early in the workstation technology life cycle and maintained during the evolution. In particular, three strategies have enabled the company to influence the capabilities of its suppliers, customers, independent software vendors, and competitors: (1) the use of universities as a primary source of some of its major technologies, (2) treatment of universities as preferred customers, and (3) the pursuit of "open" standards.

Universities as an Important Source of Technologies

From its inception, Sun has looked to universities for more than college graduates to join its ranks. It has seen these institutions as a source of technologies to capitalize on. When Khosla founded the company, rather than design a workstation from scratch, he went to Stanford University, where a Ph.D. student, Andy Bechtolsheim, had already designed a computer workstation using standard microchips that were readily available from semiconductor manufacturers (more on this later). In fact, SUN (from which the name Sun Microsystems is derived) stands for Stanford University Network. The workstation still needed software, especially the operating system—the program that manages all the activities of the computer. Unlike workstation pioneer Apollo, which had developed its own proprietary operating system from scratch, Sun Microsystems opted to adopt the widely and publicly available UNIX operating system from the University of California at Berkeley. The significance of this decision is best understood by briefly looking at the history of UNIX. It was invented by AT&T, which allowed the University of California at Berkeley to develop a version of it that it made freely available to anyone who wanted it. The fact that it was free and could also be easily ported to different computers made it popular, especially at college campuses. Electrical engineering and computer science departments of major universities such as MIT, University of California at Berkeley, Stanford, Carnegie Mellon University, University of Michigan, UCLA, and Caltech adopted UNIX. Most of the students graduating from these universities learned how to use this complex operating system and familiarized themselves with some of its idiosyncrasies. This is important when considering how difficult it is to master an operating system. Thus choosing an operating system that many universities had already adopted gave Sun several advantages. In the first place, until the early 1990s[11] most workstations were used for technical applications, used by the same engineers and scientists trained at universities where they are likely to have learned UNIX. In the second place, the schools themselves used workstations and were therefore more likely to buy UNIX workstations than those with proprietary operating systems like Apollo's. In the third place, the engineers that Sun recruited from universities already had learned UNIX and did not have to learn an operating system from scratch.

The operating system helps manage software and other activities of the workstation. But to interface with the workstation, users need another piece of software, the graphical user interface (GUI). This is a more sophisticated predecessor of the Microsoft Windows available on most IBM PC compatibles today. X-Windows, developed by MIT and made available free of charge, was also very popular. Sun, after initially trying to develop its own GUI, eventually adopted derivatives of X-Windows. Adopting X-Windows gave Sun advantages similar to those it received from adopting UNIX.

The UNIX operating system and GUI, although the most important of all the software, are only two of hundreds that workstation users need. The others are developed by ISVs over whom a workstation maker like Sun has little or no direct control. But these ISVs also need to understand the operating system of the computers for which they develop software. They too recruited scientists and engineers from those schools where UNIX was being learned, again making it more likely that they would develop software for Sun's systems.

The way Sun adopted UNIX is also important. Instead of just sending for its own free copy, it went to the University of California at Berkeley and recruited Bill Joy, the UNIX guru behind the development and proliferation of the Berkeley version of UNIX. This sent a signal to UNIX users and developers of software for UNIX systems that Sun was committed to UNIX. Moreover, he could bring the knowledge he had accumulated on UNIX with him.

To summarize, although Sun had in universities a source of cheap and readily available technologies, its biggest advantage may have come from using this source as a means to influence its local environment. By choosing UNIX and X-Windows, very popular products at major universities, it was not only able to get to the market early, it either enhanced or at least maintained the competences of its customers, independent software vendors, and new employees. In using Andy Bechtolsheim's design, Sun was able to enter the market early, while reducing the chances of opportunism by suppliers since the system used standard off-the-shelf components. We will see later that when RISC technology invaded CISC, Sun again turned to universities for help, and this again paid off by letting it enter the market early. According to a manager at DEC, Sun's nemesis, this early entry was the "killer."

Constant Pursuit of "Open" Standards

In choosing the microprocessor, operating system, graphical user interface, and RISC technology, Sun pushed for open industry standards. That is, it pushed to keep its technology nonproprietary. At the heart of the workstation is the microprocessor. It is the source and driver of most of the innovations that have led to better workstation price and performance, and the choice of one presents the workstation maker with a dilemma. On the one hand, integrating vertically into microprocessors gives the workstation maker control over this critical component, drastically reducing the risk of opportunism. But since customers are also a source of innovations, such integration can limit microprocessor innovation unless the workstation maker decides to sell the processor in the open market. On the other hand, buying a processor from the open market exposes the workstation maker to opportunism by the microprocessor maker. Sun chose to use a microprocessor from Motorola in its first series of workstations. This assured Sun access to innovations from other workstations via Motorola's microprocessors. The risk of opportunism was also greatly reduced by the fact that Motorola had several second sources for the component.

Universities as Preferred Customers

Although computer makers have traditionally given preference to institutions of higher education, Sun took it a little further. It not only used them as beta sites,[12] it offered them huge discounts. When it first entered the workstation market, it saw in universities and research laboratories customers who were willing to try new machines. It also saw in universities the training ground for the same engineers and scientists who would go on to work for its customers and independent software vendors. It therefore made sure that universities were the first to obtain each new generation of its workstations for extensive testing and feedback. It also offered them huge discounts. For example, in 1989 when Sun's workstations were selling very well, it still offered universities discounts. Its least costly SPARC workstation was priced at $8995, but with discounts, universities could obtain it for close to $5000.[13] On the Web in 1995 Sun made Java freely available for research, education, or evaluation purposes, while site licenses cost businesses as much as $125,000.[14]

DEC

In many ways DEC's strategy in influencing its environment has been very different from Sun's. When the company entered the workstation market in 1985, it designed its own workstation instead of going to a university to obtain a design, as had Sun. While the other major workstation vendors used microprocessors from Motorola or Intel in their workstation designs, DEC used its own proprietary microprocessor, the microVAX.[15] While this gave it control over its supply of microprocessors, it limited the number of innovations the product could see from workstation makers since DEC was the only one using the processors to design workstations. Its strategy in choosing an operating system was also different from Sun's. It offered potential customers two kinds of workstations: one with its VAX/VMS[16] proprietary operating system and the other with ULTRIX, the firm's version of UNIX. At first an overwhelming majority of its installed base of customers (80 percent) chose VAX/VMS over UNIX since these customers did not have to learn a new operating system and DEC had many VAX/VMS applications programs that customers could use, but not enough on the UNIX platform. New customers without an installed base or experience in VAX/VMS, however, were attracted more and more to the low cost of UNIX systems and to Sun in particular. The other reason why they chose Sun was because, looking to the future to what kind of network size they could expect, many customers did not see DEC as committed to UNIX. DEC officials did not do much to lessen these fears. When asked at a press conference in 1988 about what he thought of UNIX, a DEC official answered: "It's like selling the Brooklyn Bridge—it's absolutely snake oil."[17]

Such statements were not very comforting to customers, who wanted to be assured of continued support for UNIX in the future.[18] The statement caused a furor in the UNIX press, and competitors like Sun took advantage of it, pointing out to customers that Sun, unlike DEC, had a history of being fully committed to UNIX and industry open standards in general.

ENVIRONMENTAL CHANGE:
THE ARRIVAL OF RISC

We have seen how Sun's strategies helped it manage its environment during the early part of the evolution of the workstation industry. The question now is whether the same strategies can help it exploit a technological discontinuity such as RISC. Before exploring this question, we define RISC and outline its impact on its competitive environment.

What Is RISC?

RISC is an innovation in the instruction set architecture of a computer, a method of designing the central processing unit (CPU)[19] of the computer. An instruction set is a menu of commands that the CPU understands. Before RISC, there was CISC[20] (complex instruction set computer). In the design of CISC computers, a primary goal in instruction set design was to have so-called semantically rich instructions—instructions that get the hardware of the CPU to do as much as possible per instruction, moving as much of the burden of programming as possible from software to hardware. RISC technology calls for the opposite—simple instructions that get the hardware to do less per instruction, thereby moving the programming burden from hardware back to software. With their simpler instructions, RISC microprocessors take up less chip real estate, all else being equal. This simplicity, coupled with the space saved, allows designers to take advantage of incremental innovations to build RISC processors that are faster than their CISC predecessors.[21]

The faster RISC microprocessor and the change in relationship between software and hardware presented CISC incumbent workstation makers such as DEC and Sun with architectural innovation problems.[22] They failed to understand the implications of RISC for the linkages between the microprocessor and other components of the workstation, such as the memory system, I/O, graphics subsystems, and software. Therefore either they failed to recognize the potential of RISC or, when they did, they did not quite know how to exploit it fully.

Sun Microsystems and RISC

As Table 8.5 shows, Sun's market share increased every year from its adoption of RISC in 1987 to 1992. In this section we argue that Sun's strategies of looking to universities for major technologies, treatment of universities as preferred customers, and the pursuit of "open" standards were instrumental to its successful adoption of RISC technology. The timing of its decision to adopt RISC, its implementation of the decision, and the outcome were all greatly influenced by its strategic thrust.

As was discussed earlier, when Sun Microsystems entered the workstation market in 1982, it decided, like Apollo, to use Motorola's 680X0 CISC microprocessors to power its workstations. In 1985, when Sun was seriously considering adopting RISC technology for its workstations, Motorola was having problems accepting the rationale behind RISC and recognizing the threat that RISC posed to its microprocessor business. Like DEC, Intel, and other CISC microprocessor makers, Motorola found the concepts of RISC difficult to accept. Its 680X0 family of CISC microprocessors was the microprocessor architecture of choice for most workstation makers. The idea that such a successful design, which had made so much use of semantically rich instructions, should be abandoned for simple instructions sounded ludicrous to Motorola. Motorola was not about to adopt RISC.[23] Sun had to turn to someone else for RISC microprocessors. The only firm developing RISC microprocessors for the merchant market at the time (1985) was MIPS Computers, founded a year earlier. MIPS's "strange" strategy worried both Apollo and Sun. MIPS planned to design microprocessors, but instead of manufacturing them, it would license the designs to semiconductor companies. It would then buy the microprocessors from the semiconductor manufacturers and build workstations to compete with Sun and Apollo.

Sun decided to design its own microprocessors. But rather than develop design competence from scratch, it once again turned to a university. It adopted the RISC and SOAR architectures developed by RISC pioneer Professor David Patterson and his students at the University of California at Berkeley. Sun engineers added extensions[24] to the Berkeley design and named it SPARC (scalable processor architecture).

Now Sun had a microprocessor architecture of its own. It will be recalled that there are two primary concerns about the supply of a key component such as microprocessors: the fear of opportunism and the concern about the rate of innovations. Sun solved both problems. It licensed its SPARC design to several semiconductor manufacturers who could also design and manufacture future generations of the architecture and sell to anyone they liked. Thus any firm, including Sun, that used SPARC microprocessors in their workstations were assured of several second sources, greatly reducing the chances for opportunism on the part of a supplier. SPARC microprocessor vendors, in turn, could sell to many computer makers—the sources of many innovations. That took care of the supplier end of the local environment. Now we turn to rivalry (competitors), complementary innovators, and customers.

In adopting RISC, Sun knew that other firms, especially new entrants, would use the new superior technology to enter the workstation market, increasing rivalry. To influence the nature of rivalry, it turned to an old strategy: the pursuit of "open" standards. In 1987, when it introduced its first RISC (SPARC) workstation, Sun also announced that it would license SPARC to anyone who wanted to use it to build workstations. Shortly thereafter it lowered the licensing fee to $99 and in 1989 formed SPARC International, a separate organization with responsibilities that included making sure that so-called Sun clones were actually compatible with Sun machines. The number of computer makers who belonged to SPARC International in 1993 is shown in Table 8.6. In making its technology nonproprietary and attracting other computer makers to join its camp, Sun was able to exploit two factors. In the first place, by building a larger RISC camp, Sun was able to increase the survival chances of its RISC niche compared to other RISC niches. The different RISC camps as of 1993 are shown in Table 8.7. In the second place, the larger RISC camp serves as a source of network externalities. The more firms there are in that network, the more likely independent software vendors are to commit to developing software for SPARC products and the more customers can share in soft-

TABLE 8.6. Some members of SPARC International in March 1993.

SPARC International (Founded February 1989)		
AFE Displays	Hal Computer Systems	Seiko
Amdahl	Hyundai	Sidus Systems Inc. (Canada)
Aries Research	ICL Inc.	Siemens
AT&T	Kubota	Solborne Computer Inc.
Auspex Systems	Marner International Inc.	Sony
Axil Workstations (Hyundai)	Matsushita Electric Industrial	Star Technologies Inc.
CDC	Meiko	Stone Systems (Hong Kong)
Computer Systems Engineering	Mobius Computer Corp.	Sun
Cray Research Superservers	NEC	Tadpole
Daishin Electric	Open Concept International	Tatung Technologies Inc.
Datatech Enterprises Co. Ltd.	Opus	Tecnologia Del Grupo
EOS Technologies	Panatek Computer GmbH	Tera Microsystems
Ericsson Telecom	Philips	TI
Fujitsu Microelectronics	Prime	Toshiba Corp.
Goldstar Corp.	Prisma	TriGem Computer Inc. (Korea)
GSP Electronics	Samsung	

Source: SPARC International Inc.

TABLE 8.7. The other RISC consortia (see Table 8.6 for SPARC International).

88Open (Apr. 88)	*MIPS* (Jul. 90)	*MASS860* (Sep. 90)	*PRO* (Mar. 92)	*ALPHA* (1992)	*PowerOpen* (Mar. 93)
BBN	AT&T Federal Systems	Alliant	Convex	Cray Research	Apple
DG	Concurrent	IBM	Hitachi	**DEC**	Bull
Encore	Control Data Systems	**Intel**	**HP**	Encore	Harris
Modcomp	Convex	Oki Electric	Hughes	Kubota Pacific	**IBM**
Motorola	Kubota	Olivetti	Mitsubishi	Olivetti	Motorola
NCR	NEC	Samsung	Oki	Raytheon	Tadpole Tech
Sanyo	Olivetti	Stratus	Prime		Thomson CSF
Stratus	Pellucid		Samsung		Wang
Unysis	Pyramid		Sequoia		
	Siemens-Nix		Stratus		
	Silicon Graphics		Windbond		
	Sony Microsystems		Yokogawa		
	Tandem Computers				
	TIS				
	Toshiba				

ware and other complementary products. Thus members of the group are better off than if each had its own proprietary architecture.

When Sun introduced its RISC workstations, it took three measures to conserve the competence and network externalities of its customers and independent software vendors. In the first place, it was able to maintain the same operating system and GUI in moving from CISC to RISC, so that its installed base of customers and ISVs did not have to learn a new operating system or GUI. In the second place, Sun made sure that the RISC workstations were forward compatible with CISC ones, that is, all the applications software that ran on its CISC workstations could also run on the new RISC machines. In hindsight, these decisions may look rather very obvious and expected. But as we see next, DEC did not see them as obvious when it adopted its first RISC technology.

DEC and RISC

DEC actually has two RISC stories: one for RISC workstations using microprocessors from MIPS Computers, and the other for workstations using DEC's own technology called ALPHA. In the early 1980s, when RISC advocates were evangelizing the virtues of the new technology, DEC was a major force in workstations and minicomputers, all of which used its very CISCy and successful VAX instruction set architecture. It did not see the opportunities and threats that RISC posed to its business. But in 1989, when it saw its workstation market share being eroded by Sun's RISC technology, DEC decided to do something about RISC. By this time a workstation group within the company had, unknown to management, been designing a workstation using microprocessors from MIPS Computers. DEC decided to adopt MIPS's RISC technology and promptly acquired a 15 percent stake in the company.

Since MIPS's microprocessors were being manufactured by many suppliers, DEC did not have to fear any opportunistic behavior from MIPS. Moreover, the 15 percent stake in MIPS could be increased if need be. MIPS microprocessors, as Table 8.7 shows, were being used by other computer makers and therefore could benefit from innovations with origin at the customer level.

From a competition point of view, things at DEC were very different from those at Sun. Although many firms were using MIPS's microprocessors, their workstations, unlike those of the members of SPARC International, were not compatible. Their versions of UNIX were largely different and their applications software was not easily interchangeable. Thus instead of one MIPS group fighting other RISC niches for survival, the group was actually a group of niches fighting among themselves and with everyone else.[25]

Even within the MIPS group, DEC was not the formidable competitor that one would expect. Why? In building the MIPS-based workstation, DEC had two operating systems to choose from: its proprietary VAX/VMS operating system and ULTRIX, its version of UNIX. VMS had some idiosyncrasies that made it more difficult to port to MIPS's microprocessors, especially given the nature of the processor, the time DEC had to ship the product, and the need to attain the best price versus performance in order to compete with Sun Microsystems.[26] Moreover, its huge installed base of VAX/VMS applications software could not run on the new workstations. Thus VMS users who wanted the superior performance of a RISC workstation had two options: switch to DEC's ULTRIX-based workstations or to another vendor's UNIX-based system like Sun's. These customers used two primary criteria in their choice of RISC workstation: (1) the number of applications software packages available for each RISC workstation platform and (2) the number of applications written for the UNIX version and a commitment to UNIX, all else being equal. ULTRIX had very few applications software packages that ran on it. Programs written for other versions of the UNIX operating system would not run on DEC's ULTRIX without major modifications. Sun Microsystems, on the other hand, had many applications that ran on its RISC workstations.

The lack of applications software for DEC's RISC workstations might have been alleviated if many ISVs had undertaken to write software for DEC. However, ISVs are more likely to commit resources to develop software for a workstation maker if it already has a strong market position. As an engineer at View Logic, in explaining why the firm chose to develop CAE (computer-aided engineering) software for Sun workstations, put it: "It's a catch 22. We need them to have volume for us to start development, and they need our software in order to do well in the market." ISVs would rather develop software for Sun or any other hardware vendor who already has a compatible installed base than for DEC's new RISC workstations.

Even as DEC was shipping MIPS microprocessor-based workstations, it was developing its own RISC technology called ALPHA. It designed and manufactured its own chips and at first kept the technology proprietary, as it had done with its CISC technology. It did, however, realize the need to preserve the competence and applications software of its customer base. In 1992 the firm introduced ALPHA workstations that came with both VAX/VMS and ULTRIX. For DEC's customers and independent software vendors this was not competence destroying. ALPHA could also run the huge installed base of VAX/VMS applications that DEC's customers had accumulated over the years. This preserved the competence as well as the network externalities of its customers and complementary innovators and provided ALPHA with large demand-side economies of scale.

Summary

The importance of the interacting nature of Sun's strategies cannot be overemphasized. Each of them alone is not sufficient to give a firm a competitive advantage. For example, it is often suggested that Sun's pursuit of open standards is what enabled its SPARC RISC technology to excel in the workstation market for so many years. But it would be remembered that Motorola's 88Open RISC camp was also very committed to open standards. In fact, SPARC International, in many ways, was mimicking 88Open management. Motorola's 88Open, however, failed. Sun had the edge in that it had, earlier in the life of the workstation industry, started building an installed base of workstations that used standard components and UNIX. But that too was not a sufficient condition. If Sun had developed its own operating system and made it "open," it would have been hard pressed, given its size and no reputation at entry, to find takers. It was the fact that it turned to universities, which were already using UNIX and that trained the lead users of workstations, that gave the firm the extra edge. By the time RISC came along and Sun decided to make its RISC technology public, it had built an installed base and reputation that could attract other firms to join its RISC camp. And within the camp, as we will see in Chapter 10, its reputation, strong distribution channels, and other capabilities helped it thrive within the SPARC camp.

SUMMARY

The goal of this chapter was to explore the extent to which a firm's discretionary choices can influence its local environment of suppliers, competitors, customers, and complementary innovators. By creating competition at the supplier level or using standard components, for example, a manufacturer can increase the level of supplier-sourced innovations while reducing potential opportunism on the part of the supplier. Similar measures can be taken at the complementary innovator level. For products that require high levels of learning by customers and that exhibit network externalities, the manufacturer can lock in customers by giving away products or pricing low early in the life cycle of the innovation and by introducing products that are competence enhancing to customers. Through strategic alliances and a high rate of innovation, a firm can control the number of competitors that it has and the nature of the competition it faces.

Using the cases of Wal-Mart and Sun Microsystems, we showed how strategic decisions made by a firm early in its life, or the life of an innovation, can help control its local environment. By moving to small towns first, saturating whole areas with stores, and building distribution centers to match, Wal-Mart has been able to take advantage of economies of scale to keep its prices low enough to keep competitors out and keep customers coming. The large size has also allowed the firm to command tremendous bargaining power with its suppliers. Sun's use of universities as the primary source of its technologies, treatment of universities as preferred customers, and the pursuit of "open" standards enabled it to enter markets earlier than DEC, enhance the competences and externalities of its customers better than DEC, and have a bigger influence on its competitors when adopting RISC technology. It used similar strategies to pursue the World Wide Web.

KEY TERMS

Environmental determination   *Strategic choice*
Opportunism

QUESTIONS AND EXERCISES

1. How would a technological discontinuity impact the "quasi equilibrium" of Figure 8.1?
2. The role of financial institutions in a local environment is not explored in this chapter. Is the role of such institutions important in innovation?
3. Can there be another Wal-Mart in retail?
4. How successful do you think Sun's Java strategy will be? Why?

NOTES

1. von Hippel, E. *The Sources of Innovation*. New York: Oxford Unviersity Press, 1988.
2. Williamson, O. E. *The Economic Institutions of Capitalism*. New York: Free Press, 1985.
3. Ehrle, C. "GE and BMW's 'major breakthrough.' " *Chemical Week,* October 7, 1987.
4. "Wal-Mart: A discounter sinks deep roots in small town, U.S.A." *Business Week*, November 5, 1979.
5. Walton, S., and J. Huey. *Made in America: My Story*. New York: Doubleday, 1992.
6. "Wal-Mart: A discounter sinks deep roots in small town, U.S.A." (1979).
7. Saporito, B., and S. Kirsch. "Is Wal-Mart unstoppable?" *Fortune*, May 6, 1991.
8. "Change at the check-out: A survey in retailing." *The Economist*, March 4, 1995.
9. "Change at the check-out: A survey in retailing." (1995).
10. Saporito, B., and S. Kirsch. "Is Wal-Mart unstoppable?" (1991).
11. In the late 1980s, financial analysts, with the help of Sun, discovered the multiwindow, multitasking, high performance of workstations. These features allowed the analysts to, say, watch stock or futures fluctuations in one window, read electronic mail in another window, while analyzing stock portfolios in yet another window. Other computers did not offer that at the time.
12. Beta sites are companies or individuals who are given the first products to perform extensive tests on and provide manufacturers with feedback on product performance, reliability, and customer preferences.

13. *The Wall Street Journal*, February 5, 1989.

14. Cortese, A., et al. "The software revolution." Cover Story, *Business Week*, p. 86, December 5, 1995.

15. VAX stands for *v*irtual *a*ddress e*x*tension.

16. VAX/VMS, a trademark of DEC, stands for *v*irtual *a*ddress e*x*tension/*v*irtual *m*emory *s*ystem.

17. *Digital Review*, March 21, 1988.

18. What the DEC official actually meant was that UNIX was not really a standard since each vendor had its own version, some of which could be as different from others as VAX/VMS is from UNIX. This author holds the DEC official in very high esteem.

19. The CPU is sometimes referred to as the brain of the computer because it performs most of the calculations and controls most of the electrical signals of the computer.

20. Although so-called complex instruction computers existed long before RISC, the acronym *CISC* was coined by Professor David Patterson of the University of California at Berkeley and his students *after* they had already coined the term *RISC*.

21. Such innovations included superpipelining and superscalaring.

22. Henderson, R., and K. B. Clark. "Architectural innovation: The reconfiguration of existing product technologies and the failure of established firms." *Administrative Science Quarterly* **35**:9–30, 1990.

23. Eventually, in 1988 Motorola announced that it was entering the RISC microprocessor business with its 88000 microprocessors. The chips, first delivered in 1989, were never very successful, despite an excellent campaign. Motorola would later abandon the 88000 RISC architecture for an alliance with Apple and IBM that developed the PowerPC, a RISC processor based on IBM's POWER (RS/6000) architecture.

24. Specifically, the extensions were to accommodate multiprocessors, floating point, and tightly coupled coprocessors.

25. MIPS eventually tried unsuccessfully to resolve this problem by forming the MIPS ABI alliance which, unlike SPARC International, 88Open, or PowerOpen, did not have an independent body charged with administering compliance to compatibility.

26. DEC's declared reason for building the MIPS microprocessor-based RISC workstations was to "fight" Sun, whose RISC machines were already selling very well. DEC called its RISC workstations "SUN killers."

C H A P T E R

CO-OPETITORS

Suppose your firm has recognized the potential of an innovation and determined a profit site that is attractive enough for you to exploit. There is a good chance that other firms have also recognized the potential of the innovation and would like to profit from it too. We will call these other firms your *co-opetitors*[1]—the suppliers, customers, competitors, and complementary innovators who are also interested in profiting from the innovation and with whom you must collaborate or compete in order to succeed. An important part of a firm's strategy for exploiting an innovation is knowing who these potential co-opetitors are. Our goal in this chapter is to explore how to find out who they are. We will first explore where co-opetitors are likely to come from. Then we will examine when a firm would want to collaborate or compete. Finally, we explore when incumbents, established entrants, or start-ups are likely to be co-opetitors.

SOURCES OF CO-OPETITORS

The first step in predicting co-opetitors is to explore where they are likely to come from. One obvious place to look is the sources of innovation. As we saw in Chapter 4, suppliers, customers, competitors, related industries, universities, public research laboratories, and the firm's internal value chain are all sources of innovation and therefore good places to look for potential co-opetitors (Figure 9.1).

Customers

As we saw in Chapter 4, lead users are users whose needs are similar to those of other customers, except that they have these needs months or years before the bulk of the marketplace does, and they stand to benefit significantly by fulfilling these needs earlier than the rest of the customers.[2] If their suppliers cannot provide these needs, these customers may find ways to fulfill them—they may become manufacturers. For example, in the late 1960s, during the reign of the electromechanical cash register, Singer Sewing Machine Company wanted a different kind of cash register—an electronic cash register—that could record data (sales) for its retail

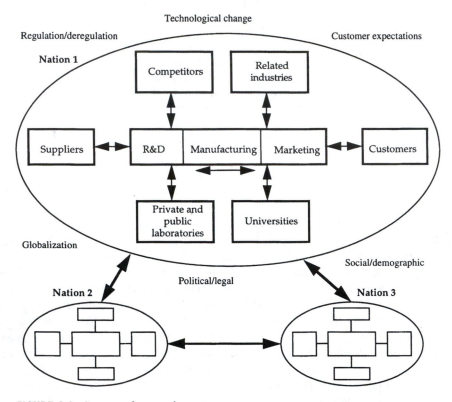

FIGURE 9.1. Sources of co-opetitors.

stores and send them directly to computers, thereby simplifying its inventory management. It wanted to get rid of intermediate steps such as manually punching
cards, taking them to a computer somewhere, and reading them into the computer.[3]
Singer's attempts to convince entrenched electromechanical cash register makers
such as NCR were rebuffed. NCR told Singer that such a machine was neither technologically nor economically feasible. Singer decided to build an electronic cash
register itself and turned to Friden, its subsidiary with capabilities in making calculators and electronics.

Suppliers

A firm with an offensive innovation strategy may be seen as a kind of *lead supplier*
in that it stands to benefit by being the first to offer products, before its competitors
do. There may be times when customers are not quite ready for products from such
a lead supplier, and it may have to play the role of its customer, the manufacturer.
For example, when Intel was ready to sell its Pentium, some of the PC makers who
use the chip in their PCs were not ready to buy. So the firm integrated forward into
making the PC motherboards that contain the key components that go into a PC, in-

cluding the Pentium chip. This helped accelerate the pace at which PC makers switched over from earlier processors.

A supplier of critical components may see a radical innovation at the manufacturer level as an opportunity to enter and take advantage of the new market or to ensure a downstream market for components or equipment. For example, when electronic calculators invaded electromechanical calculators, microchip makers such as National Semiconductor were quick to start making calculators using the chips they produced. Massively parallel processor technology rendered many of the capabilities that incumbents such as Cray Research had used to exploit single-processor von Neuman architecture obsolete.[4] This gave a chip maker such as Intel the opportunity to move into the supercomputer business, building massively parallel supercomputers that use its microprocessor chips.

Present Competitors

Potential co-opetitors can come from any of the functions of your present competitor's value chain, although very often from the R&D group. Many so-called renegades leave their employers to found start-up companies. They are normally those who do not hold the dominant managerial logic of the firm, and are therefore more likely to recognize the potential of a radical innovation.[5] Examples of these renegades abound, especially in the semiconductor and computer industries. For example, Gordon Moore and Robert Noyce left Fairchild Semiconductor to found Intel and to exploit the emerging technology of the metal oxide semiconductor (MOS) while Fairchild stuck with bipolar technology. Jeff Kalb left DEC to found MasPar and exploit the technology of massively parallel processors, whereas DEC stayed with minicomputers. Start-ups to exploit new technologies are full of such renegades. They can be identified by the papers they publish or deliver at conferences on the new technology or by their capabilities at their old jobs. For example, Jim Clark, chairman of Netscape, came from Silicon Graphics Inc. (SGI), a computer workstation maker one of whose core competences is the ability to develop very high-resolution graphics workstations—which were used to make movies such as *Jurassic Park*. Offering workstations also entails competences in computer networks. These two competences are important in exploiting the World Wide Web. Thus in founding Netscape and developing its successful Web browser—Navigator—Jim Clark was able to use his competences in networking and graphics, especially graphical user interfaces (GUI), both of which were developed or honed at SGI.

Related Industries

A complementary innovator is likely to enter for two reasons: to make money as a new entrant manufacturer or to ensure that its complementary products can be sold, or both. In the 1970s, when electromechanical cash registers were giving way to electronic cash registers, IBM's computers were very popular with retailers, who used them to process manually entered data from sales. IBM saw the radical change from electromechanical to electronic as an opportunity to enter the cash register business and consolidate its stronghold on retail computers. Moreover, the electronic competences needed to build the new registers built on IBM's competences in building electronic computers.

Firms from related industries may also have capabilities that underpin the innovation, but which had been developed for an entirely different product. For example, in delivering electricity and water to homes, many utility companies acquire the right-of-way to homes. With deregulation of telecommunications, the right-of-way is an endowment that these utilities could use to offer local phone service to homes and businesses. Moreover, some electric utility firms built their own phone infrastructures in order to reach their remote locations, which even the phone monopolies could not reach. Thus although they were never in the phone service innovation value-added chain, these electric companies may have capabilities that can be used to enter the phone service business, making them potential co-opetitors.

Sometimes industries are related by the technology that underpins the products offered in their different industries. For example, as we detailed in Chapter 6, at some point computers, calculators, cash registers, and watches were mechanical. So during the change from mechanical to electronic technology, makers of calculators could be expected to enter the watchmaking industry. Indeed, National Semiconductor and Mostek, makers of calculators, also entered the watch market.

Universities and Public Research Laboratories

Another type of potential new entrant is the researcher from a university or a public research laboratory who understands the rationale behind the innovation and its potential and wants to exploit it. Such professors and researchers have played key roles in commercializing new technologies. John Hennessy took a leave of absence from Stanford University to found MIPS Computers and exploit the technology of RISC. Numerous biotechnology firms were started by these renegades from basic research institutions or universities.

Internal Value Chain

Since a firm's value chain is also a source of innovations, it can expect some of its own employees to be potential co-opetitors. Semiconductors and computers have many examples.

International

Other nations can be the source of co-opetitors in two ways. First, since some nations are more conducive to certain types of innovations than others, a firm can expect competitors to come from such nations in the face of such innovations. For example, U.S. firms trying to exploit innovations in consumer electronics can expect competition from Japanese and Korean firms. These foreign countries can also be the sources of potential allies. Second, makers of positive-feedback goods can benefit from international economies of scale by extending their activities to other nations.

COMPETITOR OR COLLABORATOR

Which of these co-opetitors a firm decides to collaborate or compete with is a function of four factors: (1) the type of technology and market, (2) the timing and cost of the innovation, (3) co-opetitors' capabilities, and (4) complementarity of capabilities. The bottom line is to collaborate if doing so increases the size of the pie, and then compete for your share of the pie.[6] If collaboration does not increase the size of the pie or get you in early, compete. It is important to note that the payoff from collaborating does not have to be right away. As we will see in the case of Intel in Chapter 10, the payoff may come years later, following other strategic actions.

Type of Technology and Market

By their nature, certain technologies are more likely to require collaboration than others. Take positive-feedback technologies, for example. First, their up-front costs are very high, but per-unit production costs thereafter are very low. Thus it may take more than one firm to afford the high cost of development. The collaboration between Toshiba, IBM, and Siemens to develop a 256M DRAM was partly due to the high cost of developing such a chip. Second, positive-feedback products also exhibit network effects in that the more people who use these products, the more valuable they become. Collaboration with other firms to create a larger network can make the product more attractive for customers and makers of complementary products. Third, where a standard is important, collaboration may help win such a standard.

As we will see in Chapter 12, if an innovation is competence destroying to a firm, it may want to collaborate rather than compete. This gives the firm time to unlearn the old knowledge and absorb the new one.

Timing

For several reasons, collaboration may be important early in the life of some innovations. First, as suggested earlier, if a standard is important, a firm may want to collaborate with others early in the life of the innovation in an effort to win the standard. Second, firms that want to enter a new business right away but do not have the patience to develop the capabilities from scratch may also want to collaborate.

TABLE 9.1. The VIDE criteria.

Customer *Value*	Does the capability make an unusually high contribution to the value that customers perceive?
*I*mitability	How quickly and to what extent can other firms duplicate or substitute the capability?
Competitor *Differentiation*	Is the type or level of the capability unique to the firm?
Extendability	Can it be used in more than one product area?

Co-opetitors' Capabilities: The VIDE Analysis

To collaborate with co-opetitors, a firm must have something to bring to the table. It must have some competences or endowments that will help make the innovation pie larger. In Chapter 3 we saw that capabilities are more valuable when they meet the three criteria of coreness—competitor differentiation, customer value, and extendibility—and are difficult to imitate. Thus in evaluating what it is that a firm has to bring to the collaboration table, one can analyze the four criteria listed in Table 9.1. We call this process the VIDE analysis. For each stage of the value chain for the innovation, a firm can determine what the key capabilities are and evaluate each of them using the VIDE criteria.

Customer *Value*

In the end, customers must find some *value* in an innovation if it is going to be successful. This value comes in the form of low-cost or differentiated products or services as perceived by customers. A critical question in evaluating capabilities, then, is just what it is about the capability that clearly impacts the value that customers perceive. Intel's microcode copyrights directly impact the kind of differentiated microprocessor that customers can buy. With the microcode, firms can keep running the installed base of software that they have built over the years. Honda's ability to design efficient and reliable engines is important to customers who buy its cars. Thus somewhere in the value chain of a firm that hopes to perform well, there should be some capability that makes an unusually high contribution to the value that customers perceive. If a firm is going to collaborate with co-opetitors, it must have one of these capabilities to offer. Co-opetitors must also have something of value to bring to the table.

*I*mitability

If the capability adds customer value, the next question is, how long can such a capability last before it can be duplicated or substituted, that is, what is its *imitability*? Take Caterpillar, a maker of earth-moving equipment, in the 1970s and the early 1980s. One of its endowments was its worldwide service and supplier networks, which allowed the firm to deliver any part, for any of its equipment, to any part of the world, in two days or less. For customers who are usually on remote construction sites and must meet tight completion schedules, this is a very valuable capability.[7] To duplicate such an endowment would take a competitor like Komatsu years and a lot of effort. It may be even too expensive. A firm can, however, substitute for this capability with some other capability. And that is what Komatsu did. It built reliable machines that did not need as much service and therefore no need for the type of service and supplier network that Caterpillar had. Thus in trying to exploit an innovation in the earth-moving equipment industry, a service and supplier network would be a valuable capability. A firm would want to know how long such a capability would last before it is duplicated or substituted.

Co-opetitor *Differentiation* (Rareness)

For a co-opetitor to stand out with a valuable capability, it must be the only one with the capability, or its level of the capability must be higher than that of co-opetitors. This is sometimes referred to as the rareness or uniqueness property *(differentiation)*.[8] Microsoft is the only one with a copyright to its DOS operating system, making the copyright unique. On the other hand, many firms have engine and drive train design capability, but the level of Honda's is higher than that of its competitors. In evaluating co-opetitors, it is important to determine how unique or how much better (compared to competitor's) the capability is. One reason why Caterpillar's service and supplier network was so valuable was because Caterpillar was the only company that had such a network.

Extendability

The last criterion for VIDE is *extendability*—the extent to which a capability can underpin other products. A popular example is Honda's engine capability, which is used not only to offer cars, but also to offer portable generators, marine vehicles, lawn mowers, and motorcycles.[9] The more extendable a capability, the larger a choice of co-opetitors the owner of the capability would have.

Using these criteria, a firm can decide just how valuable its capabilities and those of its co-opetitors are. This is useful information in deciding whether to collaborate or compete; and if to collaborate, with whom.

Complementarity of Capabilities

The final factor that influences the choice of a co-opetitor is complementarity—the extent to which a firm's capabilities will be complemented by the co-opetitor's capabilities. Let us consider the simple question: what type of co-opetitor should an inventor or a firm with the technology seek? As we have suggested on several occasions, most firms adopt new technologies because they want to profit from them. And, as we saw in the Teece model of Chapter 2, profitability from a new technology is a function of the imitability of the new technology and of the importance and availability of complementary assets. Thus, the type of co-opetitor that a firm seeks should be a function of the imitability of the technology in question and of the importance and availability of complementary assets. Recall from the Teece model that when a technology is easy to imitate or substitute and complementary assets are unimportant or freely available, the inventor does not stand to make much money. Thus a firm that develops such a technology first may want to find a co-opetitor who is a low cost producer or who has an offensive strategy (Figure 9.2, cell I). The technology can be licensed to a low cost producer who can use its low cost capabilities to offer products or services at lower cost than imitators. The firm can also license to or team up with a co-opetitor that has an offensive strategy. Since such a co-opetitor prefers to offer new products before rivals have had a change to imitate it, it is likely to entertain the offer to team up so that it can take advantage of the new technology.

If imitability of the technology is high but complementary assets are important and not easily available, the firm with the technology may want to team up with a co-opetitor that has the complementary assets (cell II of Figure 9.2). The question here is, why should a co-opetitor with the complementary assets bother to team up when it knows that the technology is easy to imitate? Why not just wait and imitate the technology? Of course, the co-opetitor can wait but it may not always be in its interest to do so. It is the responsibility of the firm with the technology to explain to the co-opetitor why it should team up. No matter how easy a technology is, it still takes a finite amount of time to imitate it. Therefore the firm with the invention should approach the co-opetitor for whom time is of the essence. For example, a co-opetitor that has an offensive strategy might want the technology in order to be first, while one with a defensive strategy may want the technology to prevent others from having it or to be better prepared when it finally decides to enter.

If imitability of the technology is low and complementary assets are important and not easily available, the inventor may still need co-opetitors if it does not have the complementary assets (Figure 9.2, cell III). If imitability of the technology is low and complementary assets are freely available or unimportant, the inventor does not need any co-opetitors (Figure 9.2, cell IV).

| | | **Complementary assets** | |
		Freely available or unimportant	Tightly held and important
Imitability	High	**I** Low cost producer or co-opetitor with offensive strategy	**II** Co-opetitor with complementary assets
	Low	**IV** No need for co-opetitor	**III** Co-opetitor with complementary assets if inventor does not have them

FIGURE 9.2. What type of co-opetitor should a firm pursue?

INCUMBENTS OR NEW ENTRANTS AND INCREMENTAL VERSUS RADICAL

One method for narrowing down the number of co-opetitors on whom a firm has to perform an analysis in order to determine whether to collaborate or to compete with them is to make use of some of the concepts discussed in Chapter 2: the type of firm that is most likely to introduce and exploit an innovation is a function of the type of innovation in question. Figure 9.3 summarizes the discussion that follows. The figure is the usual two-by-two matrix, but with a contingency on how important and difficult to establish the capabilities (competences and endowments) are.

Area I

If an innovation is incremental from both a technological and market point of view (area I of Figure 9.3) in that all the capabilities needed to offer the product build on existing ones or do not change at all, incumbent positions are likely to be unassailable, all else being equal. For example, Intel's offering of its 486 DX microprocessor was an incremental innovation over the 486 SX. A math co-processor was built into the DX. This and other changes made to the SX were an incremental innovation since all of the capabilities Intel needed either never really changed, or, if they did, they built on existing ones. Thus if the competences and assets required to ex-

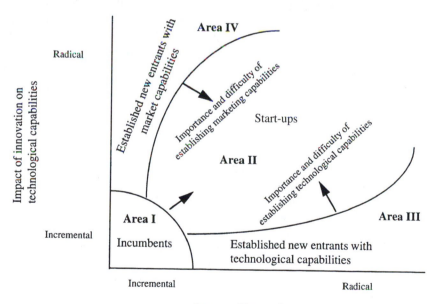

FIGURE 9.3. Who is most likely to be a co-opetitor is a function of the type of innovation.

ploit an innovation build on existing technological and market capabilities, incumbents are likely to dominate, all else being equal, leaving little room for entry.

Area II

If, as shown in area II, both existing technological and marketing capabilities are rendered obsolete by the innovation, new entrants have a better chance of toppling incumbents and are therefore very likely to enter. The rationale here is that incumbent capabilities are not only useless, but may actually be a handicap in building the new ones. Why? In the first place, incumbents must first successfully unlearn the old ways of doing things since old capabilities can be a handicap in building new ones.[10] In the second place, it takes time to acquire the capabilities.[11] Thus potential co-opetitors are likely to be new entrants. These include, as we saw earlier, renegades from existing competitors, researchers from universities and research laboratories, lead users, and lead suppliers.

Area III

An innovation can be competence enhancing to technological capabilities but not to marketing capabilities. That would be the case, for example, when an incumbent is so blinded by the needs of its existing customers that it does not see the needs of potential new customers; needs that can be satisfied using the firm's existing technological skills. The makers of 8-inch disk drives used in minicomputers when 5.25-inch drives came along are an example. These disk manufacturers were so interested in satisfying the needs of their minicomputer customers that they were late in recognizing the potential of 5.25-inch drives.

Area IV

If, as shown in area IV, technological capabilities are destroyed but market capabilities left intact, then firms with existing market capabilities are more likely to enter. If these market capabilities are important and difficult to establish, incumbents have time to make product development mistakes and to correct them before new entrants have had a chance to establish the kinds of distribution channels or reputation that it takes to succeed in the market. For example, in the technological changes from X rays to CAT scans to MRI medical diagnostics equipment, the change was competence destroying to technological capabilities but not to marketing capabilities. Thus firms such as GE with strong marketing competences and distribution channels were usually very successful in exploiting the changes, even when embracing them late.[12] Thus firms with strong marketing capabilities are likely to be potential co-opetitors. This includes established firms that have produced different products but served the same markets that the innovation is addressing. For example, IBM already had strong distribution channels and a reputation to match when it entered the electric typewriter market by buying Electrostatic Typewriters during the transition from purely mechanical typewriters to electro-mechanical ones. It quickly became the market share leader in typewriters.[13]

THE INNOVATION VALUE-ADDED CHAIN

We said earlier that an incumbent's position is likely to be unassailable when an innovation is incremental since exploiting the innovation utilizes existing incumbent capabilities. Some of these capabilities are focused on suppliers, customers, and complementary innovators. Well-established supplier relations in automobiles, good client relations in financial services, and strong distribution channels are examples. A key assumption in the earlier discussion is that the innovation only impacts the capabilities of the manufacturer, and not those of its suppliers, customers, and complementary innovators. If, for example, it renders the capabilities of a customer useless, any customer-specific capabilities that may have given a manufacturer an advantage may actually become a disadvantage. One way of putting this is that we have focused on what the innovation does to the capabilities of a manufacturer, and not on what it does to the capabilities of the firm's existing co-opetitors. As pointed out in Chapter 2, an innovation that is incremental to a manufacturer may not be to its suppliers or customers. For example, the Dvorak keyboard was an incremental innovation to manufacturers of typewriters, but a radical innovation to customers who had to relearn how to type. The electric car renders obsolete not only the technological capabilities of incumbent internal combustion engine automobile makers such as Ford, but also those of suppliers of auto parts such as Bendix as well as those of gas station owners. Thus incumbents may be faced with new entrants when they least expect it—when the core technological and marketing knowledge that underlies the firm's capabilities remains relatively unchanged. As an example, take the moviemaking business, which we will explore in greater detail soon. The replacement of the copper wiring that had been laid by AT&T to residential and commercial buildings by fiber optics does not directly affect the technological bases on which moviemaking rests. But it does make moviemaking more vulnerable to entry. If a moviemaker's primary endowment were its relationships with movie theaters or movie renters, then this endowment would quickly disappear when people can watch any movie they want without going to the theater or the movie renter since all they have to do is click on a mouse at home and view the movie from any moviemaker they like.

PRACTICE CASE: THE MOVIE INDUSTRY

Thanks to digital image processing and computer workstations, the dominant position that firms such as Disney and Warner Brothers once enjoyed in moviemaking is now being challenged.[14] This case briefly describes the old as well as the current moviemaking technologies and uses the framework developed earlier to predict the likely sources of new entrants into the moviemaking businesses.

The Technology

Traditionally live-action movies are made by actors or actresses playing their parts in front of an optical camera in sometimes exotic locations with expensive props, and the images of the scenes are recorded on a 35-millimeter film. When the movie team has finished shooting, the producer edits the film by cutting out the parts that she or he does not want and rearranging the sequence of scenes the way she or he wants them. The final film is processed and replicated for distribution. This is demonstrated pictorially in Figure 9.4(a). Digital image processing brings several advantages to moviemaking. First, images of acted scenes, landscapes, and scenery can be stored on disks and used later for other movies. Second, images, scenes, or objects can be added to or taken out of movies. Even parts of people can be taken out or added. True editing is possible: one can add to or cut just about anything from the movie after it has been made. Third, shooting a scene over and over may now just mean playing with a computer mouse. Thus with the arrival of digital image processing (packaged in workstations by the likes of Silicon Graphics), moviemakers can make two kinds of movies: a mixture of human and digitally processed images, and digitally processed image movies. An example of the first type is *Jurassic Park,* where dinosaurs were digitally created and then digitally added to recorded images of actors and actresses. Images of Brandon Lee were also digitally added to scenes after he had died during the shooting of *The Crow,* allowing the producers to complete the movie. Finishing a movie after such a tragedy would have been near impossible without digital image processing. Like the traditional movies, scenes can be cut off or their sequences rearranged. This is depicted in Figure 9.4(b), and from now on we will call this arrangement with-human-partly-digitized (WHPD). The second type of movie is the no-human-fully-digitized (NHFD) one, where all the characters are created digitally. That is, full motion movies are made without human beings in them. This is shown in Figure 9.4(c). In either case, digital image processing not only allows a firm to offer new

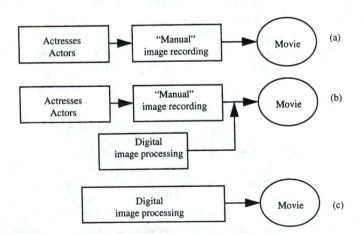

FIGURE 9.4. Innovation in moviemaking technologies.

features in films, but can greatly reduce the cost of making movies as filming in exotic locations can be avoided, old images reused, and the bargaining power of suppliers greatly reduced.

Impact on the Capabilities of Movie Studios

Digital image processing has both positive and negative impacts on moviemakers. First, it can replace actors, actresses, and other suppliers to moviemakers. This increases the bargaining power of moviemakers over actors and actresses, as well as over the unions that normally provide the personnel for production. That is the good news for incumbent movie studios. The bad news is that any relationships that they had with famous actors or actresses or unions are rendered obsolete, encouraging entry by firms who would have been prevented from entry by such relationships. It also means that more firms than before do not have to go to Hollywood to make movies. A computer workstation and artistic creativity may be all that a firm needs to enter the moviemaking business.

In animation, where the role of actors and actresses as well as of unions as not as substantial as in full motion movies, digital image processing plays an even more important role. The ability of computers to replicate and increment suggests that there could not be a movie task more suitable for digital image processing than animation, where characters are replicated images with alterations here and there to produce movement. Traditionally artists drew literally hundreds of pictures of their characters, props, and sets with small variations shot to depict motion and action. With computers, digital characters, sets, props, and even scenes are stored in computer memory. Since they are stored in computer memory, they can be reproduced at any time and adapted infinitely in film. They are also designs ready to be used for toys, T-shirts, CD-ROM games, and the bases for many more products. This means that any hand-made props or characters that incumbents such as Disney used in their old animation products are rendered obsolete by digital image processing. (These can be digitized and stored for reuse.) Thus many new entrants can now enter the animation moviemaking business. Pixar, Digital Domain, Industrial Light and Magic, DreamWorks SKG, and R/GA Digital Studio have done just that. Steve Jobs, a founder of Pixar, came in with competences in graphical user interfaces (GUIs), having overseen the development of the Macintosh and having founded NeXt Computers, a workstation maker. Industrial Light and Magic belongs to Lucas, who has be very interested in special effects since his making of *Star Wars* in 1977. Steven Spielberg, a cofounder of DreamWorks, has also been interested in special effects for a long time.

Fiber Optics and Information Superhighway

One advantage that these incumbents have is their deep pockets and distribution channels—the relationships with movie theaters, TV networks, and video stores, which movie studios have built over the years. In fact, some of the movie studios

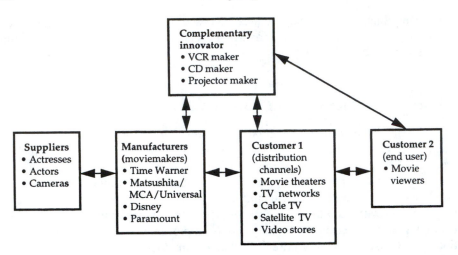

FIGURE 9.5. The moviemaking innovation value-added chain.

are vertically integrated downstream into movie theaters. Such relationships are difficult to establish, and once established, can be important endowments. In fact, it is because of such difficulties to penetrate distribution channels and Disney's foresight that Pixar had to team up with Disney to offer *Toy Story,* an animation movie that was very successful. Fiber optics may, however, decrease the advantage that incumbents have in their relationships with distributors. With fiber cables being laid to homes, whoever makes movies does not have to pass through customer 1 of Figure 9.5. All the moviemaker has to do is find a carrier to deliver the images to the homes or businesses. These carriers would be phone companies, cable companies, utility firms, or any other new entrants in the information delivery business. Both new entrants and incumbents would have to establish new relationships with these carriers from scratch. In that case, firms with GUI competences and artistic moviemaking skills would stand to benefit.

SUMMARY

In the face of an innovation, a firm would like to know who its potential competitors and allies are likely to be. Two methods of identifying them are proposed. In the first, a firm starts by making the basic assumption that co-opetitors are likely to come from the sources of innovation. That is, the same existing suppliers, customers, competitors, related industries, universities, public research laboratories, and the firm's internal value chain that are the sources of innovation are also the places where co-opetitors are most likely to come from. The firm then determines what capabilities are needed to exploit the innovation. Then using a VIDE analysis, it determines who from the sources of innovation has appropriate capabilities to be a potential ally or competitor. The second method rests on the findings that the firms that are likely to perform well in exploiting the innovation are those for whom the innovation is competence enhancing. If, for example, the technological capabilities needed to exploit the innovation are radically different from existing ones, while marketing capabilities are the same, incumbents or established new entrants with such marketing capabilites are likely to enter.

KEY TERMS

Co-opetitors

Customer differentiation

Customer value

Established new entrants

Extendibility

Imitability

Market capabilities

Technological capabilities

VIDE analysis

QUESTIONS AND EXERCISES

1. Pick an industry that currently faces a technological discontinuity. Who are likely to be the losers and winners? [Suggestions: (a) deregulation of telecommunications in Japan and Germany, (b) fiber optics to the home in the United States.]

2. In which country do you think that utility companies (water, electricity, and gas) have a real chance at profiting from the telecommunications revolution and why?

NOTES

1. The term *co-opetitors* was coined by Brandenburger and Nalebuff (1996). These are the firms in a manufacturer's local environment—suppliers, competitors, customers, and complementary innovators—with whom it collaborates or competes in the process of exploiting an innovation. Brandenburger, A., and B. Nalebuff. *Co-opetition.* New York: Doubleday, 1996. Afuah, A. N. 2000. "Do your co-opetitors' capabilities matter in the face of a technological change?" *Strategic Management Journal* **21(3)**: 387–404.

2. von Hippel, E. *The Sources of Innovation.* New York: Oxford Unviersity Press, 1988.

3. "The rebuilding job at National Cash Register. How Singer got the jump on the industry's top supplier." *Business Week,* May 26, 1973.

4. Afuah, A. N., and J. M. Utterback. "Responding to structural industry changes: A technological evolution perspective." *Industrial and Corporate Change* 6:183–202. 1997.

5. Afuah, A. N. "Maintaining a competitive advantage in the face of a radical technological change: The role of strategic leadership and dominant logic." Working Paper #9602–14, University of Michigan Business School, July 1996.

6. Gomes-Casseres, B. "MIPS computer systems (A) and (B)." Teaching Note, Harvard Business School Case #5-794-020, August 2, 1993.

7. Rangan, U. S., and C. A. Bartlett. "Caterpillar Tractor Co." Harvard Business School Case #9-385-276, 1985.

8. For more on this property and an analysis similar to VIDE (called the VRIO analysis), see Barney, J. B. *Gaining and Sustaining Competititve Advantage.* Reading, MA: Addison-Wesley, 1997.

9. Prahalad, C. K., and G. Hamel. "The core competences of the corporation." *Harvard Business Review* 79–91, May–June 1990.

10. Leonard-Barton, D. "Core capabilities and core rigidities: A paradox in managing new product development." *Strategic Management Journal* **13:**111–26, 1992.

11. See, for example, Henderson, R., and K. B. Clark. "Architectural innovation: The reconfiguration of existing product technologies and the failure of established firms." *Administrative Science Quarterly* **35:**9–30, 1990.

12. Mitchell, W. "Whether and when? Probability and timing of incumbents' entry into emerging industrial sub fields." *Administrative Science Quarterly* **34:**208–30, 1989. Morone, J. *Winning in High-Tech Markets: The Role of General Management.* Boston: Harvard Business School Press, 1993.

13. Utterback, J. M. *Mastering the Dynamics of Innovation.* Cambridge, MA: Harvard Business School Press, 1994.

14. Christensen, C. M., and J. L. Bower. "Customer power, strategic investment and failure of leading firms." *Strategic Management Journal* **17:**197–218, 1996.

15. This section draws on "The virtual studio." *The Economist,* December 24, 1994–January 6, 1995. Schlender, B. "Steve Jobs' amazing movie adventure; Disney is betting on computerdom's ex-boy wonder to deliver this year's." *Fortune,* September 18, 1995. Coy, P., and R. Hof. "3-D computing." *Business Week,* September 4, 1995. Farrell, C., et al. "The boon in IPOs." *Business Week,* p. 64, December 18, 1995.

10

STRATEGIES FOR

SUSTAINING PROFITS

If the worker with such a loom is now in a position to produce six times as much as a hand worker in a day, it is obvious that the business must yield a surplus over costs. . . . But now comes the second act of the drama. The spell is broken and new businesses are continually arising under that impulse of the alluring profit. Consequently, the surplus of the entrepreneur and his immediate followers disappears. Not at once, but as a rule only after a longer or shorter period of progressive diminution. Nevertheless, the surplus is realized . . . and constitutes a definite amount of net returns, even though only temporary. Now, to whom does it fall? The profit will fall to those individuals whose achievement it is to introduce the looms. What have these individuals contributed? Only the will and action.
    —*Schumpeter.*[1]

So far, this book has been about how to recognize the potential of an innovation and exploit it to earn profits. The problem is that a firm's profits from an innovation are usually only temporary. They last only until other firms realize how profitable the innovation is and imitate it, or until such discontinuities as radical technological change, government deregulation or regulation, and changing customer preferences and expectations come along and render the innovator's existing core competences and assets obsolete. However, as an incumbent or even a new entrant, there are certain things that an innovator can do to prolong the time over which it can keep making profits. The goal of this chapter is to explore just what it is that an innovator can do to maintain the flow of profits. Building on the fact that competition is not only at the end-product level, but also at all the other stages of the value chain, we argue that it takes combinations of *block, run*, and *team-up* strategies at different stages of the value chain and at different phases of the evolution of a product to maintain profitability. In the block strategy a firm prevents entry by, for example, protecting its intellectual property, brand name, or distribution channels. In the run strategy the firm keeps innovating, often rendering some of its own capabilities obsolete and cannibalizing its existing products. Running can also mean

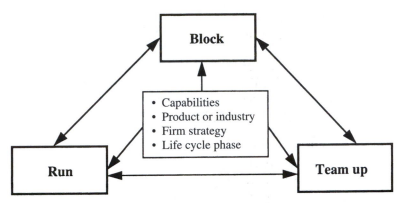

FIGURE 10.1. It takes a combination of block, run, and team up to profit from an innovation.

building a stock of technological and market knowledge as well as new competences and assets for later use. In the team-up strategy a firm invites entry by, for example, licensing its patents, copyrights, or trademarks to competitors or allowing the cloning of its products. The choice of block, run, or team up at any stage of the value chain is a function of several factors: the firm's capabilities, its strategy, the type of product or service, and the phase of evolution of the innovation (Figure 10.1).

BLOCK

Suppose a firm is presently profiting from an innovation. One strategy to stay profitable is to prevent entry by competitors. It can do so in two ways. On the one hand, if its capabilities at each stage of the value chain are unique and inimitable, the firm can limit access to them, thereby keeping out competitors. On the other hand, if all firms are equally capable of performing these activities, incumbents may still be able to prevent entry by signaling that post-entry prices will be low. Such signals can prevent profit-motivated potential entrants from entry. We now explore each of the blocking schemes.

Unique Capabilities as Block

The effectiveness of a firm in blocking entry to any stage of the value chain is a function of how unique and inimitable its competences and assets are at that stage. At the development level, for example, intellectual property protection can make it very difficult for new entrants to offer designs that are comparable to those of incumbents. Take Apple's Macintosh. Apple was able to keep the design of its Macintosh proprietary because of two things. First, its intellectual property rights made it difficult for other firms to copy its microcode without legal repercussions. Second, it is not easy to imitate[2] the "look and feel" of the Macintosh. Microsoft's efforts to offer a similar system resulted in Windows 95 in the summer of 1995, which, by some estimates, just matches Macintosh's 1987 operating system.

At the research stage, close relationships with universities can provide fast access to scientific research findings. If such relationships are difficult to establish, incumbents can have an advantage. Moreover, their experience in performing such research may also give them an advantage over new entrants since it takes knowledge to absorb knowledge, and incumbents have stocks of it. At the manufacturing stage there are several endowments that a firm can use to prevent entry. It may hold contracts that give it exclusive access to certain inputs, or licenses that allow it to manufacture its products at lower cost or with higher quality than new entrants. It may also have built plants that are critical to manufacturing but that entrants may not be able to afford.

Low Post-Entry Price Signals as Block

Now suppose all firms are equally capable of performing the activities of each stage of the value chain and have equal access to the underlying technological and market knowledge. Is there anything that an innovator can do to deter entry? The answer to this question has been the subject of research in economics.[3] We very briefly summarize some of it later. The underlying assumption here is that potential entrants will enter the market only if they believe that they will make profits by entering, and an important piece of information in deciding whether or not to enter is the post-entry price. Given the market uncertainty usually associated with innovation, it is often difficult to obtain this information. By observing incumbents, however, new entrants can pick up signals that provide some information on the nature of post-entry prices. If the signals suggest that post-entry prices will be low, potential entrants will not enter. We discuss several such signals next.[4]

Management's Commitment to Existing Technology

If the management of a firm is committed to its existing technology or is emotionally attached to it, the firm is not likely to take entry lightly, especially if the technology constitutes a major source of revenue for the firm. An important part of fighting to stay in the business may be lowering its prices. For example, one reason that Intel took a long time to decide to get out of the DRAM business, a product it had invented, was the emotional attachment of some of its managers to the product.[5] Such a commitment to the technology should signal to potential entrants that post-entry prices might not be very attractive.

Technology Drivers, Coshared Resources

In the face of the introduction of an innovation in a market, an incumbent is likely to stay and fight (by reducing its prices) if its existing technology also serves as a technology driver for its other products. A product is a technology driver if its development and manufacture enable a firm to acquire competences and assets that the firm can also use to develop and produce other products. If a product is a technology driver, incumbents can afford to lower post-entry prices if, for example, the firm's profits come from other products and its primary reasons for offering the technology driver is to learn. For example, if new entrants threaten Honda's market in lawn mowers, it may decide to lower its prices if it believes that what it learns from lawn mower engines can help it in its search for an even smaller fuel-efficient automobile engine. Many firms stayed in the DRAM business longer than they needed because it was a technology driver.

History of Retaliation

If an incumbent has a history of retaliating against firms that have ventured into its product-market space, that may be a signal that it will lower its prices with entry. Such a reputation would alert new entrants to the fact that they may be in for a big fight upon entry. For example, if entry into a route dominated by an airline carrier has been followed by drastic fare cuts by the carrier, it is likely that it will cut its prices on other routes if another airline enters. Start-up airlines would think twice before venturing into the carrier's routes, unless their cost structures or other reasons suggest that they would still make money offering low prices.

Idiosyncratic Assets

An asset is idiosyncratic to a market if it is of little value in another market. For example, an aluminum smelter built in a remote area next to a cheap source of electricity and close to bauxite deposits is an idiosyncratic asset since it is of little value for other purposes. If an incumbent invests in such assets, it is sending a signal to potential entrants that it can lower its prices post entry. Thus a chipmaker with a $1 billion semiconductor facility in a small town in Utah is likely to fight by lowering its prices when faced with new entrants in the DRAM chip business. It may be more difficult for it selling such a specialized plant than lowering its prices for a while. If this plant has empty capacity, the threat of lowering post-entry prices is even higher.

Minimum Efficient Scale for Industry Is High

As a firm produces more of a particular product, the cost per unit of the product usually falls. Beyond a certain volume, however, the decrease in unit cost stops. This volume is called the minimum efficient scale (MES). That is the minimum volume that a firm has to produce in order to attain the minimum per-unit cost possible in the industry. This means that an entrant must produce at least at this volume if its costs are going to be competitive. But producing that much means adding so much product to the market. The larger the MES and therefore the more of the product that a new entrant would have to bring into the market, the lower the prices would be. Thus if the MES is large, entrants are less likely to enter since they can expect prices to drop considerably, given how much they have to add to the industry's capacity.

Thus a firm can effectively block entry if it has unique inimitable capabilities, or if it can make certain commitments that send signals to potential entrants that post-entry prices will be too low for any new entrant to make profits.

RUN

The blocking strategy works only as long as competences and assets are unique and inimitable, or industry barriers to entry last. But competitors can circumvent patents or copyrights or keep challenging them in court until they fall. Moreover, such capabilities last only until such discontinuities as deregulation or regulation, changing customer preferences and expectations, and radical technological change render them obsolete. The run strategy admits that blockades to entry, no matter how formidable they may appear, are often penetrable or eventually will fall. Sitting behind these blockades only gives competitors time to catch up or leapfrog the innovator. The innovator must run. That is, it must be innovative enough to build new capabilities and introduce new products rapidly and do so well ahead of competitors. It must be able to render its own capabilities obsolete and cannibalize its products before competitors do. Running can give a firm many first-mover advantages including, as we saw in Chapter 9, the ability to control parts of its own environment.

We can classify runs as a function of their impact on the capabilities of the firm in question and the extent to which the run cannibalizes existing products (Figure 10.2). For expositionary reasons, we have labeled them as types I, II, III, and IV, and will limit our illustration to the development stage of the value chain. In the

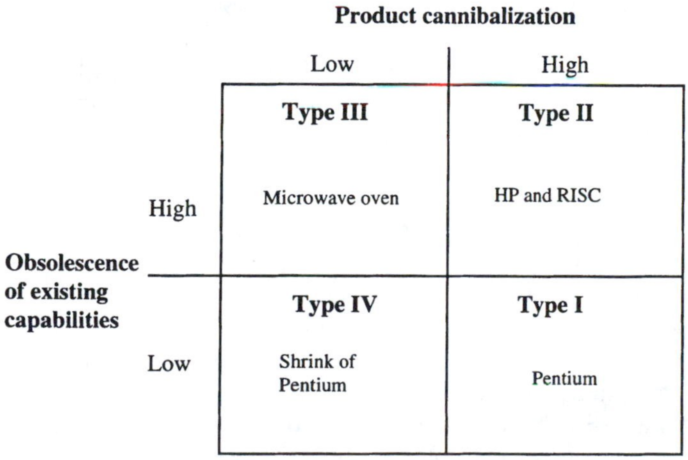

Product cannibalization

		Low	High
Obsolescence of existing capabilities	High	**Type III** Microwave oven	**Type II** HP and RISC
	Low	**Type IV** Shrink of Pentium	**Type I** Pentium

FIGURE 10.2. Examples of different runs.

type I run, the innovator introduces a new product that cannibalizes existing ones, but the capabilities required to develop it build on the firm's existing capabilities. For example, when Intel introduces a new generation of microprocessors, older generations are cannibalized. However, the capabilities that it needs to offer these new generations build on its existing capabilities. Its copyrights and its accumulated competences in circuit design, semiconductor device physics, and process technology serve it well in offering the new products. In Chapter 2 we said such an innovation is radical in the economic sense but incremental in the organizational sense. Since the technological knowledge needed to carry out such runs builds on existing stocks of knowledge, roadblocks to runs would come from the fear of cannibalization or erosion of organizational political power.

In the type II run, the capabilities required to offer the product are different from existing ones, and the product creates new markets, while rendering existing products noncompetitive. Transistors replacing vacuum tubes and electronic point-of-sale registers replacing electromechanical ones are both examples of type II runs. Apple's introduction of the Macintosh is a close example. The Mac's look and feel and its easy-to-use interface, in many ways, required very different competences from those that Apple had used to design the Apple II. The computer also greatly expanded the use of personal computers to such markets as desktop publishing. In many ways, a type II run is a much more difficult run to make than a type I, but when successful, it can be very rewarding. As we saw in Chapter 5, it is difficult to recognize the opportunities that such runs offer. Even after the opportunities have been recognized, there is still the fear of cannibalization, the fear of the loss of political power, and the unwillingness to detach emotionally from existing capabilities, and they all make adoption difficult. Moreover, existing capabilities may not only be useless in making the run, they may actually be a handicap. But the advantages can be very rewarding.

In type III, the run requires new technological and market knowledge, but leaves existing products competitive. The microwave oven offers a good example. In type IV, changes in capabilities are negligible, and the new product is no threat to existing ones.

Finally, the reader may be wondering if there is any relationship between a *run* strategy and innovation strategies such as *offensive* and *defensive,* which we saw in earlier chapters. Yes, there is. Offensive and defensive strategies are different degrees of run.

TEAM UP

In a team-up strategy, a firm formally cooperates with others to allow it to keep profiting from innovation. This cooperation can be in the form of a strategic alliance, venture capital, or acquisition, where strategic alliances can be joint ventures, licensing, distribution agreements, co-marketing agreement, technology agreements, design agreements, manufacturing agreements, or other agreements to cooperate in adding value in the firm's value-creating activities. Note that these forms of cooperation have a formal element to them whose intent is normally expressed in the form of some kind of formal agreement. This contrasts with informal know-how trading between engineers and other developers of intellectual capital that takes place even when firms are pursuing a block or run strategy.[6] In all the cases, the firm has to bring something to the table and hopefully get something from the partner that complements or reinforces what the firm brought to the table if the team up is going to be successful. In a joint venture, for example, the firm pools its capabilities with those of a partner to create a separate legal entity. By bringing together complementary capabilities under the roof of the joint venture, the partners can exploit innovations in ways that each one alone could not. In other strategic alliances such as licensing, distribution, co-marketing, technology, design, manufacturing, or other agreements, the degree of cooperation varies with the terms of the agreement usually expressed in writing. In venture capital, the firm invests in a start-up and can learn from the start-up as it grows. In acquisition, the firm buys its team-up and owns it. The firm can also offer itself to be bought by another.

In a team-up strategy, then, a firm sometimes encourages entry rather than discouraging it. The question is, why would a firm want to give away its technology? There are five reasons why a firm might want to do so: to win a standard or dominant design, to increase downstream demand, to build capabilities, to exploit the second source effect, and to access a market that would otherwise be inaccessible.

Win the Standard (Dominant Design)

Early in the life of a product, different designs compete for a standard (or the dominant design). For some products that exhibit network externalities,[7] making a design open can improve its chances of emerging as the de facto standard or dominant design. Why? Making a design open invites other firms to enter the market using it. This increases the number of manufacturers of the design, and the more people that manufacture it, the more complementary innovators that will commit to developing complementary products for it. The more manufacturers and complementary innovators that support a particular design, the more likely customers would choose it. And the more customers, the more makers of complementary products that will sign up. This type of positive-feedback effect can lead to a dominant design. The case of VHF's triumph over Beta as detailed by Rosenbloom and Cusumano[8] is an example.

Increase Upstream Demand

A firm can give away a technology downstream if that is going to increase demand for its products upstream.[9] For example, to accelerate the diffusion of its faster microprocessors for multimedia applications, Intel may develop multimedia software and give it away to PC end users. If this results in more firms buying more personal computers, that would mean more sales for Intel's microprocessors.

Build Capabilities

Very often a firm has to license its innovation to competitors so that it can build competences in an area in which it lacks such capabilities. Take the case of pharmaceutical drugs. To get a drug approved in the United States requires coordinating clinical tests, which are run at different medical centers by different physicians, and filing the results, together with many other documents, with the FDA for examination. This can take a long time. But for some drugs, each day spent waiting for the approval process means a loss of millions of dollars in revenues and time for imitators to try to circumvent the underlying patents. Many foreign pharmaceutical firms or small U.S. start-ups do not have the capabilities to successfully get their drugs through the FDA approval process as quickly as incumbents can. Consequently, some of them form alliances with established U.S. firms with these capabilities and hope to learn. Selling pharmaceutical drugs in foreign countries is another area where some firms may have to license their drugs to local firms and use them as a vehicle to learn more about the local markets or to establish brand identity.

Second-Source Effect

Some customers are reluctant to incorporate a component in their systems unless they are sure that compatible generations of the component will be forthcoming when they need them. This is particularly true of products such as airplanes and computers, where there is a lot of learning by using and product compatibility is important. In fact, in some industries buyers insist on having second sources for the components that they use in their systems. For example, in semiconductors some large buyers often insist on second sources for the components they buy. Encouraging other firms to adopt one's technology assures such customers of many second sources and may increase the number of customers who are willing to adopt the innovation.

Access to International Markets

Sometimes a firm may have to team up with a firm in a foreign country so as to enter that market. This may be because the government of the country mandates it, or because the best way to obtain local market knowledge is through an alliance.

RELATIONSHIP BETWEEN
THE THREE STRATEGIES

As it can be expected, the three strategies are related. If a firm keeps its design proprietary by, for example, rigorously prosecuting anyone who tries to infringe on its copyrights, potential entrants have to spend time and resources trying to circumvent the copyright. While they are doing that, the innovator can concentrate on developing and introducing another generation of products. That is, as competitors struggle through blockades that an innovator has erected, it can run further away. On the other hand, the fact that an innovator can introduce designs faster than new entrants may discourage potential entrants from attempting entry. That is, a run can substitute for a block. There is also a relationship between run and team up. A firm's ability to introduce new designs every so often makes it easier for it to attract takers when it offers to make its design open. With type II runs, where a firm's capabilities are rendered obsolete or where winning the dominant design is important, a firm may want to team up. Sometimes, in order to find worthwhile partners to team up with, a firm may have to prove itself by the way it runs or with the capabilities that it has built. The three strategies can be reinforcing and corroborating. As shown in Figure 10.1, they all rest on competences and endowments as well as on the underlying technological and market knowledge. A firm's ability to joggle all three in the face of technological change, deregulation or regulation, changing customer preferences and expectations, and global competition is critical to maintaining entrepreneurial rents.

DYNAMICS OF STRATEGIES

As suggested earlier, each of these strategies alone may not be enough for maintaining profitability. In this section we explore why, when, and what.

Why Combinations

Block, and Run or Team Up

There are two reasons why maintaining tight appropriability of a technology alone may not result in long-term profitability. First, as we have already suggested, the fast pace of technological change suggests that competitors can quickly circumvent patents and copyrights, or leapfrog a firm that depends only on blocking entry into its existing technology space. The firm may also have to run. That is, while fighting imitation of its innovations, a firm can keep developing new product generations to cannibalize existing products before competitors circumvent its intellectual property protection. Second, advantages secured through blocking last only until such discontinuities as deregulation or regulation, changing customer preferences and expectations, and radical technological change render them obsolete. In the face of such discontinuities, the firm may be better off teaming up in order to exploit technologies and markets that are unfamiliar to the firm.[10]

Team Up, and Block or Run

As we suggested, one reason why a firm may want to team up is to improve its chances of gaining a standard. If its alliance wins the standard, the firm must still do something distinctive that allows it to perform better than members of its team if it is going to have a competitive advantage. It must block or run somewhere else in its value chain or product life cycle time line. For example, one reason why the IBM PC became the standard was because IBM "gave away" the technology by making the architecture nonproprietary. Within the PC standard, however, each firm has had to distinguish itself somehow. For example, early in its life, Compaq had a run strategy, introducing personal computers with the latest generation of Intel microprocessors well before anyone else did. What has allowed IBM to stay in the market so far has been its brand name reputation and its distribution channels. In the cases that follow we will show how Intel and Sun used the combinations of team up and block or run strategies successfully.

Run, and Team Up or Block

There are several reasons why a run may need to be complemented by team up or block. First, where the run involves radically different technological and market knowledge, and the firm is unfamiliar with them, it may need to form alliances. Second, in some industries new product development can be very expensive. Thus by fighting entry, a firm can slow down competitors enough so that it does not have to introduce products as quickly as it would otherwise. Third, a firm may not have the competences to depend on new product introductions alone. By fighting entry, it may be able to slow the rate of imitation enough to allow it time to introduce new products at its own pace, and still stay ahead of the race. Finally, as a technological trajectory evolves, there may be a time when costs are so high that a firm can no longer develop products alone. It may have to team up. For example, many DRAM makers have had to form alliances in order to be able to afford the cost of building a manufacturing plant.

When

Having provided some reasons why combinations of strategies, not a single strategy, are conducive to sustained profitability, the question becomes, when should a firm pursue these combinations?

Combinations along the Value Chain

A firm would successfully run or block only at those stages of its value chain where it has the capabilities that underpin each strategy. For example, a firm in the semiconductor industry can exercise block and run strategies only if it has the intellectual property and the competences in circuit and logic design that are critical to introducing new products. At any one time a firm can pursue different strategies along its value chain, as shown in Figure 10.3. The innovator can license its design to any firm that wants to imitate the design so as, for example, to help the design emerge as the standard. At the same time, however, the firm protects its idea generation and development capabilities. Thus although competitors can offer compati-

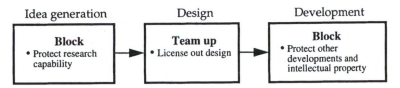

FIGURE 10.3. Strategies along the value chain at a point in time.

ble designs, they may not have the capabilities to offer products as often as the innovator. The Sun Microsystems case that follows illustrates this.

Combinations over Innovation Life Cycle

As illustrated in Figure 10.4, the strategies that a firm pursues over the life cycle of a technology can also vary. Prior to the emergence of a dominant design, an innovator may want to team up to improve its chances of winning the dominant design. Following the emergence of the dominant design, the firm may want to introduce versions of the design more frequently (run) than its competitors. It may also want to defend its intellectual property or brand name reputation (block). At a discontinuity, the type of strategy pursued depends on the nature of the discontinuity. If the discontinuity is competence enhancing, the firm may pursue a run or block strategy, or both, since the capabilities required build on existing ones. If it is competence destroying, it may require a team-up strategy.

Type of Technology and Nature of Complementary Assets

The type of strategy that a firm pursues at any point in time—for example, at each phase of a technology life cycle—is also a function of the imitability of the technology and nature of complementary assets needed to profit from the technology at the point in time. In cell I of Figure 10.5, where imitability of the technology is high, a firm can pursue a run strategy. That is, since its technology can be easily imitated, the firm keeps innovating so that by the time competitors catch up with yes-

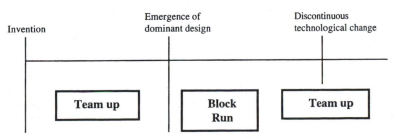

FIGURE 10.4. Sample strategies along the evolutionary path of an innovation.

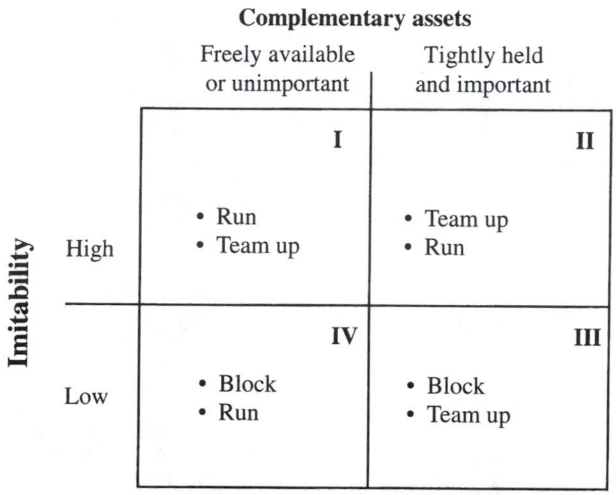

Complementary assets

FIGURE 10.5. Strategies as a function of imitability and complementary assets

terday's technology, it has moved on to tomorrow's technology. Sometimes, a run strategy alone may not be enough in this cell. A firm may need to team up in order to run. For example, running may be too expensive for one firm to run alone. The dynamic random access memory (DRAM) technology offers a very good example. It is easy to imitate but so expensive to develop that firms often have to team up to share development costs. As we will explore later, a firm may need to team up because it is not familiar with the new technology. In cell II, where although complementary assets are tight and important the technology is easy to imitate, the firm must develop the complementary assets internally or get them by teaming up with someone else. Either way, a critical factor here is timing. If the firm decides to build internally, it has to do so before competitors with complementary assets have had a chance to copy the technology. If the firm is going to team up, it must do so while it still has something to bring to the table—while potential partners have not yet imitated the technology. Teaming up means forming some kind of partnership with a firm that has the important complementary assets. This partnership can be a joint venture, strategic alliance, or acquisition. It can also mean that the firm offers itself for acquisition by a firm with the complementary assets. In any case, the firm must still think of pursuing the run strategy since, sooner or later, its technology is going to be imitated.

In cell III, a firm can pursue one of two strategies: block or team up. If it has both the technology and complementary assets, it can protect both. The danger here is that, sooner or later, most technologies are imitated or become obsolete. Imitation or obsolescence moves the firm from cell III to cell II, where it can use its complementary assets to team up with someone who has the new technology. In a world where technology is difficult to imitate but complementary assets are easy to come by (cell IV), a firm would depend on protecting that technology if it is going to make money. That is, a firm can pursue a block strategy. Very few firms are in cell IV. A firm in the cell could also pursue a run strategy to allow it to stay ahead of its competitors so that if they ever caught up, they would be catching up with yesterday's technology while the firm is already exploiting today's technology.

Internal Development or External Sourcing

Firms that pursue a team up strategy go outside their boundaries for some of the capabilities that they need to exploit the technology. Whether a firm decides to develop a technology internally or go outside for help is also a function of two factors: (1) the firm's familiarity with the new technology and market and (2) transaction costs.

Familiarity of the New Technology and Market

Since a firm's ability to profit from an innovation is also a function of the extent to which the capabilities required to exploit the innovation build on the firm's existing capabilities, the firm would be better off adopting an innovation that is capabilities enhancing—one with which it is familiar. But breakthrough innovations that offer significant gains in profits often destroy both technological and market capabilities. The firm is thus faced with what Roberts calls the innovation dilemma:[11]

> The further that any company seeks to innovate, as measured by the degrees of change from its base markets and technologies, the greater the likelihood that its innovation efforts will fail. And yet, the less that a firm seeks to innovate, across the board, the greater the likelihood that the corporation itself will fail.

That is, the more the technological and market capabilities needed to exploit an innovation differ from a firm's existing capabilities, the more likely the firm will fail in trying to exploit the innovation. But staying away from such radical innovations means earning fewer and fewer entrepreneurial rents. Roberts and Berry offered a solution to this dilemma that we will build on to explore when and whether a firm should develop an innovation internally using its internal capabilites or go outside for them.[12]

To be successful with a new technology, a firm needs capabilities that allow it to gain or reinforce a competitive advantage using the new technology. The more unfamiliar the technology and market are to a firm, however, the more unlikely the firm is to have the capabilities or absorptive capacity required to exploit the innovation. Since building these capabilities from scratch is often difficult and takes time, a firm may be better off teaming up with another firm that has them. Such cooperation allows the firm to learn from its partner and develop its own capabilities or codevelop capabilities for joint use. In other words, the mechanism that a firm uses to obtain the capabilities to exploit a new technology is a function of the extent to which the firm is familiar with the underlying technological and market knowledge.[13] Figure 10.6 shows which mechanism might be best to pursue in adopting a technological change. When the new technology and the market served by products from the technology are familiar to the firm and the firm has the capabilities to exploit the new technology, it has two options for profiting from the new technology: internal development and acquistion (cell IV of Figure 10.6). In internal development, the firm develops the capabilities it needs internally and uses them to exploit the new technology. For example, it may build its own R&D and design groups and use them to develop its products. Internal development is preferred in three cases: (1) when the technological change is competence enhancing or incremental in the organizational sense and the firm's task is largely one of building on its existing capabilities, and (2) when the firm is not in a rush, and (3) when the firm wants to protect its technology. Acquistion of a firm that has already developed the technology may be preferred in those situations where the firm needs the new technology quickly. Since the firm is familiar with the new technology, it has the absorptive capacity to assess and assimilate what it buys.

If the new technology is familiar to the firm but the market that it serves is unfamiliar, the firm has three options for obtaining the capabilities it needs: joint venture, acquisition, or strategic alliance (cell I of Figure 10.6). In a joint venture, firms form a separate legal entity that they jointly own. Preferably, each firm brings to the table what the other firm does not have—that is, their capabilities complement each other. Since the firm is familiar with the new technology but not with the market, it can find a partner that is familiar with the market. That way, the firm brings technological capabilities to the table while the partner brings market capabilities and both companies can form a joint venture to exploit the new technology. If each firm brings core capabilities to the table, the joint venture can be very successful. Sometimes, some other form of strategic alliance short of a joint venture is also appropriate. For example, Pfizer struck a strategic alliance with Warner Lam-

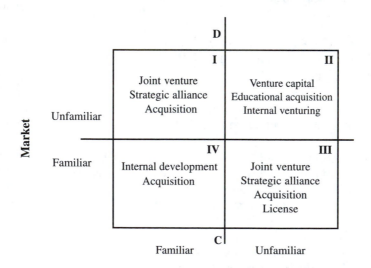

New Technology

FIGURE 10.6. Internal development or external sourcing?

bert centered on a new cholesterol drug called Lipitor that was based on a new technology called statins. This new technology was new and unfamiliar to Pfizer. Although Warner Lambert had marketing and sales capabilities in pharmaceuticals, it lacked the type of formidable capabilities in sales and marketing that Pfizer had, especially in cardiovascular drugs, the market into which statin drugs were sold. This alliance resulted in a formidable combination of complementary capabilities that were one of the reasons why Lipitor quickly captured the largest market share despite the fact that the drug was the fifth in the statin technology family in an industry where the fifth drug usually does not do well. Instead of forming a joint venture or other form of strategic alliance, a firm that is familiar with the new technology but is not familiar with the market can also buy or be bought by one that is familiar with the market. Such an acquisition will also result in the right combination of complementary capabilities. In fact, Pfizer ended buying Warner Lambert so that it could have Lipitor and the statin technology capabilities that underpin the product and potential new products.

In cell II of Figure 10.6, both the new technology and the market are unfamiliar to the firm. Innovations in this cell require capabilities that are very different from the firm's existing capabilities. They are often the ones that offer order of magnitude improvements in product or service costs and features. Sometimes, they offer completely new features or open up new markets, and with them, the possibilities for more profits. However, since they are likely to be competence destroying, the likelihood of failure is highest when a firm adopts such innovations. To increase its chances of succeeding with these technologies, a firm might want to pursue one of three options: venture capital, educational acquisition, and internal venturing. The rational behind these strategies is that the firm's existing capabilities are likely to be a handicap in the face of the new technology and market since the technology is capabilities obsoleting. Venture capital, educational aquisition, and internal venturing all allow a firm to learn and build new capabilities while not being handicapped by existing ones. In venture capital, a firm makes an investment in a start-up that has the capabilities, usually technological, required to exploit the innovation. By taking this close interest in the firm, the investing firm obtains a window on the technology and markets and can learn. In educational acquisition, a firm buys another one not to keep it as a subsidiary, but for the sole purpose of learning from it. It is the reverse engineering of an organization—buy, open up, and learn from it. A firm that faces a new technology and market that it is not familiar with may want to pursue an educational acquisition strategy. Ferguson suggests that, in the 1960s, 1970s, and 1980s, Japanese firms used venture capital and educational acquisitions successfully as strategies for obtaining American technologies.[14] Internal venturing can also be pursued by a firm to build capabilities in a new and unfamiliar technology and market. In an internal venture a firm forms a separate entity within it to develop the new technology and serve the market. The idea here is to give the new group the type of independence that separate legal entities such as start-ups have so as to attract the right talent and keep existing groups and capabilities from handicapping the development of the new capabilities.

Sometimes, as in cell III, the technology is new and unfamiliar but the market is familiar. This is the mirror image of cell I with one difference: in cell III, a firm that faces an unfamiliar new technology but has the market capabilities can license the technology from another firm. An important precaution in licensing a technology from another firm is to make sure that the licensee has the absorptive capacity to successfully transfer the technology. Pfizer offers another example. Its best-selling drug for treating high blood pressure was licensed from Bayer, AG.

Mistakes Are OK, Too

The rationale for using cautious methods to adopt an innovation is to decrease the chances of failure. Thus in the face of a radical innovation, a joint venture, rather than internal development, would allow one to learn slowly without the painful experience or threat of failure. But failure is not always bad. In fact, at 3M failure is sometimes rewarded.[15] According to Gordon F. Brunner, a P&G senior vice president in 1988, "virtually every success was a failure somewhere along the line."[16] As we saw in Chapter 3, an important implication of multilevel, multistage competition is that a failed product launch for a firm may not really constitute "failure" since the firm may have built a stock of competences and assets as well as technological and market knowledge that can be used to offer other products or services. Two examples from General Mills and Microsoft illustrate this.

Some Learners

General Mills

After the U.S. gymnastics team won a gold medal in the 1996 Olympics, one of the biggest winners was General Mills. It sold hundreds of thousands of boxes of its Wheaties cereal with a picture of the team on the cover, some of the boxes to first-time and potential would-be long-term Wheaties customers. Having the picture of a celebrity or team on the cover of a Wheaties box is actually an innovation that started out as a burst. A General Mills's vice president, who would become CEO of the firm, wanted to improve the packaging of Wheaties. His idea: have customers vote for a local sports hero by sending Wheaties box tops in to General Mills. The picture of the winner would then appear on the cover of the package. The first winner was a high-school football player in a small Ohio town. That first product failed. The idea was resurrected years later, but this time with pictures of national sports celebrities such as Michael Jordan or winning teams like the Boston Celtics. As General Mills's CEO Steve Sanger would later say, "you don't always hit it the first time, but that idea may have a cousin."[17]

Microsoft

The first company that Bill Gates and Paul Allen, founders of Microsoft, founded was Traf-O-Data.[18] They used Intel's 8008 microprocessor to develop a system that performed traffic volume count for municipalities. In 1972/1973, they earned some $20,000 in revenues from clients as far away as the state of Maryland and the

Canadian province of British Columbia. When the U.S. federal government decided to offer the same service free of charge, Traf-O-Data failed. But Bill Gates and Paul Allen had learned a lot from their experience with the failed company. Recalled Paul Allen years later, "Even though Traf-O-Data wasn't a roaring success, it was seminal in preparing us to make Microsoft's first product a couple of years later. We taught ourselves to simulate how microprocessors work using DEC computers, so we could develop software even before our machine was built."[19] The capabilities acquired in Traf-O-Data came in handy when the founders had to write quickly the programming language BASIC for MITS's personal computer.

What Bill Gates and Paul Allen learned was not limited to technological failures. Their experience in marketing their BASIC to MITS would prove very valuable later. In their eagerness to sell the BASIC, they signed a contract with MITS, giving it an exclusive worldwide license to their product. MITS also had the exclusive right to sublicense the product to third parties,[20] promising to make "best efforts" to sell it.[21] MITS later reneged on its promise and Microsoft had to go to litigation. So when, as detailed in Chapter 7, Microsoft had to negotiate a contract to supply IBM with an operating system for its personal computer in 1980, Microsoft made sure that it maintained the right to sell its operating system to cloners of the PC. It did not give that right to IBM[22] and could therefore sell to all the clone makers, building the huge installed base of computer PCs that is now its primary asset.

These examples suggest that there may be other reasons—largely strategic—that would make a firm decide to develop a technology internally, even when the technological knowledge and the market knowledge are unfamiliar. The firm may do so to build its absorptive capacity and competences. It may also do so to signal to its rivals that it is committed to that particular business.

Transaction Costs

Transaction cost theory suggests that whether a firm organizes activities internally or externally is a function of the cost of carrying out the activity in either mode.[23] These costs depend on four factors: (1) the amount of uncertainty, (2) how opportunistic the parties are, (3) the asset specificity of any assets used in the activity, and (4) the frequency of the transactions. The theory rests on the assumption that individuals and organizations are boundedly rational. That is, they are cognitively limited and cannot collect and process all the information that they need to make all decisions. Since for cognitively limited individuals or organizations it is difficult to foresee all the possible contingencies in a transaction, writing, monitoring, and enforcing complete contracts for the transactions can be prohibitively costly. Without such contracts, the parties must negotiate the terms of their relationship as the relationship develops, which presents room for *opportunism*. A party is opportunistic if it takes advantage of an information asymmetry and cheats in pursuing its own ends.[24] The more uncertainty—that is, the more information that is needed—the more difficult it is to draw the contract and the more room for information asymmetry and opportunism. The chances to exercise opportunism are also a function of *asset specificity*. Asset specificity refers to how idiosyncratic an asset in a relationship becomes as the relationship develops. For example, if a supplier develops an operating system (OS) for a manufacturer's computer and the manufacturer builds many applications software packages that can run only on the OS, then the OS is highly *asset specific* to the relationship between the supplier and the manufacturer. Using the software example, the owner of the OS may decide to hold back information on a new revision of it from developers of applications software so as to get a headstart on its own applications software development. Frequency of transactions is how often the transaction between the parties must take place. The higher the asset specificity and the frequency of transactions, the more chances there are for opportunism.

Opportunism is not the only source of transaction costs. Since individuals are cognitively limited, a party to a transaction may not be able to articulate the information it has, especially if the information is sticky. (Information is sticky if, because of its tacitness or shear volume, it is difficult to articulate, absorb, or process, making its transfer very costly.[25]) And even if the party could articulate it, the other party may not be able to understand all of it. This means that for certain types of information, transaction costs may still be high, even when the parties have no intentions of being opportunistic.[26]

Radical innovation has the qualities that would suggest internalization to minimize transaction costs. It is full of uncertainty, making the specification of future states of the world very difficult and leaving a lot of room for opportunism. Because of the tacit nature or shear volume of some of the information, it may be difficult to specify in contracts what it is that is expected of each party. Innovation often requires specialized plants or individuals, again increasing the chances for opportunism.

PRACTICE CASES: INTEL, SUN, AND WAL-MART

Intel

Intel's success and, to some extent, the United States' success in the semiconductor industry can be attributed to a series of strategic decisions that the firm has been making since it invented the microprocessor.[27] It has erected and defended blockades to entry by vigorously protecting its intellectual property (copyright, trademark, patents, and trade secret), accelerated the rate at which it introduces new generations of its microprocessors (self-cannibalization), and advertised to increase its brand name recognition.

Early Alliances

In the late 1970s Intel licensed out its 1972 invention—the microprocessor—to several semiconductor and computer companies, including Mostek, AMD, and NEC. Together these firms built an alliance that assured customers of future supplies of microprocessors and of the systems support that is a vital part of designing a microprocessor architecture into a new system. Together they also developed the many complementary chips that are critical to the success of a microprocessor. In

1980, when IBM needed a microprocessor for its personal computer, it chose Intel's, partly because of the availability of these many complementary chips at low prices, thanks to the firm's efforts and to the alliances the firm had forged.[28]

Protecting Intellectual Property

As the Intel architecture emerged as the dominant design in microprocessors, Intel decided to keep newer versions of the chip proprietary, prosecuting any firm that violated its intellectual property. In keeping with this decision, it filed a suit against NEC, claiming that NEC had violated the copyright on the microcode[29] for its 8088 and 8086 microprocessors. In 1986 Judge Ingram ruled that NEC had violated Intel's 8088 and 8086 microcode copyright. Until then it was not clear whether microcode was copyrightable or not. Software was copyrightable, but hardware was not. And since microcode is somewhere between the two, it was for the courts to decide. This decision—that microcode was copyrightable—was a landmark case. NEC appealed because Judge Ingram belonged to an investment club that owned $80 worth of Intel stock in his name. When the case was retried in 1989, Judge William Gray ruled again that NEC had violated Intel's 8088 and 8086 microcode, that is, microcode is copyrightable. The ruling meant that the microcode for the next generations of Intel microprocessors was copyrightable, and therefore the firms to which Intel had licensed earlier versions of its microprocessors could not build later generations without new licenses. Intel was not about to give anyone any new licenses.

Fighting NEC in court sent the message to the microchip community that Intel would use legal means to protect its intellectual property. Intel made this threat even more credible when it subsequently filed a lawsuit against AMD and won. Table 10.1 highlights Intel's legal fights to protect its intellectual property.

Despite Intel's success in defending its intellectual property, some firms entered the Intel microprocessor architecture market. AMD, Cyrix, NextGen, IBM,

TABLE 10.1. Chronology of Intel's legal fight to protect its intellectual property.

Year	Event
1980	IBM elects to use Intel's microprocessor in all its personal computers.
1982	Intel files a law suit against NEC alleging violation of its microcode copyright on the 8088 and 8086.
1983	Law suit between NEC and Intel is settled in a secret agreement.
1984	Relations between Intel and NEC flare up again. Intel goes back to court.
1986	Judge William Ingram rules that microcode is copyrightable.
1989	Case comes back to court, and Judge Gray rules that Intel's microcode for its 8086 and 8088 is protectable under U.S. laws. Effectively, chip makers can copyright microcode.
1990	Intel files a law suit against AMD alleging violation of its trademark when AMD used the numbers 386 in the naming of its part AM386.
1991	Intel files a law suit against AMD claiming two transgressions: AMD had violated the copyright for its 386 microcode as well as for the control program in 386's PLA.

and Chips & Technologies at one time or another produced Intel-compatible microprocessors. Consequently, in addition to protecting its intellectual property, Intel had to seek other ways to protect its profits from these entrants. In 1985 it got out of the DRAM business to concentrate on microprocessors.[30] With the focus on microprocessors, the firm was able to develop new generations of microprocessors with dramatically higher complexity (as measured by the number of transistors in each chip) and mind-boggling increase in performance (as measured by the number of instructions that the microprocessor executes per second[31]). What is of more significance is that Intel was able to introduce these more complex and better performing processors at the slimmer and at the same rate as slower earlier generations (Table 10.2). Some generations of microprocessors were introduced before sales of the earlier generation had peaked (Table 10.2).

Intel has also been working hard to establish a brand name identity. Although the microprocessor has been responsible for most of the performance improvements in personal computers, this processor has been buried in the black box that is the personal computer, and with it, Intel's identity. That is, until 1991, when Intel went directly to end users, advertising heavily and promoting its *Intel Inside* logo in numerous technical and business magazines and on national television. It also promoted its logo by offering personal computer makers discounts on chips if they displayed the logo on the personal computers they sold.

Another fact that Intel has had going for it is the high cost of a semiconductor plant, which at $1.5 billion in 1995[32] constituted a barrier to entry for many firms. The fact that Intel has already built these plants, has concentrated on microprocessors ever since dropping out of memory chips in the 1980s, and has a war chest[33] of

TABLE 10.2. Intel's rapid introduction of new generations of microprocessors.

Processor	Descrip- tion	Clock frequency	Number of transistors	Design start	Formal introduction	Volume ship- ments	Peak sales	Initial speed (MIPS‡)
286*	16-bit	5.0 MHz	130,000	1978	Feb. 1982	1983	1989	1
386	32-bit	16.0 MHz	275,000	1982	Oct. 1985	1986	1992	5
486	32-bit	25 MHz	1.2 million	1986	April, 1989	1990	1995†	20
Pentium (586)	32-bit	60.0 MHz	3.1 million	1989	March 1993	1994	1997†	100
Pentium II (686)	32-bit	300 MHz	7.5 million		May 1997	TBD	TBD	300
Itanium (Merced) (786)	64-bit	1000.0 MHz	TBD		2000	TBD	TBD	TBD

*This is actually the 80286, but usually just called the 286. The 80386 and 80486 are similarly abbreviated.
†Estimate.
‡MIPS stands for million instructions per second.

Sources: Intel Annual Reports and product briefs; *Business Week* (Feb. 20, 1995). http://www.intel.com/pressroom/kits/quickrefyr.htm.

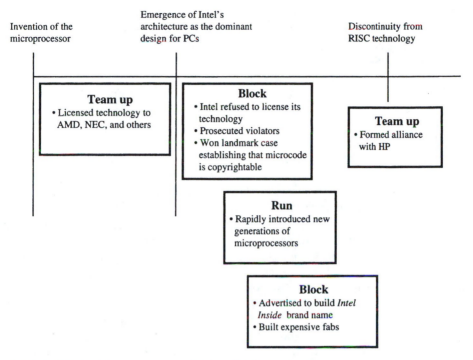

FIGURE 10.7. Intel's strategies over the life cycle of its microprocessors.

about $10 billion dollars sends a signal to potential entrants that any entry attempts will be fought.

The landmark ruling by Judges Ingram and Gray that microcode is copyrightable practically prevents competitors from imitating Intel's designs. This makes it very difficult for competitors to design a microprocessor that can run all the software that PC users have accumulated over the years, and which only runs on an Intel architecture, of which its microcode is a critical part. Customer switching costs to another machine are high. Because microprocessor design is very complex, trying to circumvent the microcode makes the task of designing it even more formidable. With the protection of its copyright and continued generational product innovations, Intel does not have to depend on its manufacturing competence—a competence that is usually critical following the emergence of a dominant design. That is, although Intel has invested heavily in manufacturing and does very well in it, its competence in manufacturing alone is not sufficient to give it a competitive advantage. Figure 10.7 summarizes these Intel strategies.

Sun Microsystems

The case of Sun Microsystems illustrates how a firm can "give" away its design technology but still be able to make money through run and block strategies elsewhere in its value chain. In 1987, when Sun Microsystems introduced the first workstation using its SPARC[34] RISC technology, it also announced that it would license the technology to anyone who wanted it. It was literally giving away the technology it had developed, instead of using its intellectual property protection rights as a barrier to entry. It backed this promise in 1989 with the formation of SPARC International Inc., an independent corporation with responsibility for supporting any firm that wanted to produce Sun workstation clones. On the surface, the offer was too good for potential entrants to resist. For one thing, SPARC was compatible with the largest installed base of workstations that ran the largest number of applications software in the workstation market. Entering such a market meant access to the large installed base of customers. For the other, the workstation market was the fastest growing computer market at the time. Surely, it appeared, it would be easy for new entrants to come in and make money. Many firms took advantage of the "free" entry and offered SPARC workstation clones. We will come back to their fate shortly. For the moment, let us see what the decision to encourage entry meant to Sun. Figure 10.8 summarizes Sun's strategies.

For several reasons, giving away its SPARC technology was an important strategic move for Sun. First, in making their decisions today about what network to join, users of products that exhibit network externalities (and computers do) care about what the size of the network will be tomorrow.[35] That is, future network size is important to users. By making its SPARC standard open, Sun was sending a signal to customers that there would be many firms offering SPARC workstations and therefore a large user network. Such a large network would give customers the benefits of network externalities: computers they could share and more software. Second, Sun was sending a signal to independent software vendors (ISVs), the firms that develop software for computers, that the size of the network of SPARC customers would be large, and therefore these ISVs could commit their scarce resources to developing software for SPARC. Third, some workstation users were developing a bitter taste for RISC technology, given what had happened to a giant called IBM. IBM had introduced a RISC workstation in 1986, and it had failed woefully. By providing a united front behind SPARC, Sun hoped customers would be more willing to give RISC technology another chance. Finally, there were other RISC technologies, albeit on the drawing board, that would be competing for supremacy in the workstation market. Cooperating with computer makers in its RISC camp would be better than fighting against them from other RISC camps. The more

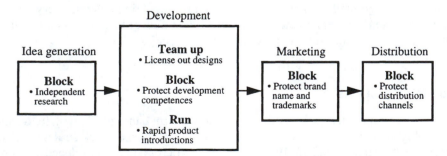

FIGURE 10.8. Sun's strategies along its value chain.

such firms in its camp, the better the chances for SPARC emerging as the dominant design, especially since it already had the largest installed base of compatible workstations and software running on it.

As Table 10.3 shows, Sun's strategy may have paid off for the SPARC camp as the technology captured a substantial share of the RISC workstation market. The more important question for Sun, though, is how well it has done within the SPARC camp. For that, we turn to Table 10.4. It is clear that Sun has maintained a very high share of the SPARC market. Its strategy of encouraging entry has allowed the SPARC camp to maintain a large market share, and within the camp Sun has managed to maintain an extremely high market share. The question is, why has Sun done so well while the cloners have not? To understand why, we need to look at what it did on the entire value chain, not just at the design level. Sun allowed other firms to clone its workstation design. But downstream along the value chain, it protected its brand name reputation and distribution channels. Some customers were not willing to forgo Sun's reputation and brand name for the expected lower prices of cloners (which turned out not to be very low compared to Sun's). Commented a Sun customer when asked why his company had not switched to clones: "I am loyal to Sun".[36] Sun also offered excellent service, which cloners could not.

Cloners also found out that it was not easy to convince Sun's distributors to carry their workstations, as Sun took advantage of the relationships that it had forged with its distribution channels and customers prior to licensing out is technology. Asked a Sun manager, "Why should another vendor, whose products compete directly with Sun's, be allowed to step in and leverage Sun's investment in its reseller partners to their benefit and Sun's expense?"[37] Upstream in R&D, Sun still slugged it alone, being able to make advances that some cloners could not. Moreover, copying a firm's design is one thing, but imitating the competences that allow the firm to offer the design at lower cost or to introduce new generations more frequently is another. Sun was often the first to introduce newer generations of work-

TABLE 10.3. Workstation and workstation server shipments by RISC technology.

RISC technology	*Market share (%)*			
	1989	*1990*	*1991*	*1992*
SPARC	56.36	63.74	62.75	51.93
MIPS	19.75	18.19	15.20	18.16
PA-RISC	0.81	0.00	6.23	15.31
IBM	4.53	7.56	8.37	9.18
Clipper	15.93	6.67	4.98	3.52
MC88X00	1.66	2.99	2.17	1.25
Alpha	0.00	0.00	0.00	0.47
i860	0.00	0.00	0.18	0.12
Other	0.97	0.86	0.13	0.07
Total	100.00	100.00	100.00	100.00

Source: Data from IDC, company reports.

TABLE 10.4. Workstation market share for SPARC
open standard.

	Market share within SPARC camp (%)			
	1989	*1990*	*1991*	*1992*
Sun	98.90	97.70	93.68	92.18
Tatung	0.00	0.75	1.39	1.67
Fujitsu	0.00	0.00	0.00	1.57
CompuAdd	0.00	0.00	1.00	1.07
Axil Workstation	0.00	0.00	0.00	0.85
DTK Computer	0.00	0.00	0.00	0.64
Aries Research	0.00	0.04	0.05	0.37
Solbourne	0.89	0.95	2.49	0.31
Opus Systems	0.00	0.36	1.00	0.21
Others*	0.21	0.21	0.39	1.13
Total	100.00	100.00	100.00	100.00

*Others include Matsushita, Solflower Computer, Integrix,
Twinhead, CMS Computing, Mobius Computing, Vertos Technology, and Samo America.

Source: Data from IDC, company reports.

stations and did so more often than the cloners.[38] Sun was also able to offer discounts to customers that cloners could not always match.

Wal-Mart

Wal-Mart has also used block and run strategies in its very successful ride to the
top of the retail world, although in different ways than Sun and Intel, who were
very interested in standards and team up early in the evolution of their innovations.
The story of Wal-Mart starts with Sam Walton, who is credited with most of the
success of the company. In the 1950s Mr. Walton, who owned several Ben Franklin
variety stores, realized that the variety store was being invaded by two innovations:
the supermarket and the discount store.[39] He decided to adapt, but not by following
the lead of large discounters such as Kmart, who located their stores only in large
population centers. He decided to take on small towns. As he would later recall, he
believed that "if we offered prices as good or better than stores in cities that were
four hours away by car, people would shop at home. It was just that simple."[40] So
he built his first Wal-Mart discount store in Rogers, Arkansas, in 1962. As detailed
in Chapter 9, he also started what is now known as the Wal-Mart culture, giving
employees a lot of latitude to participate in the management of the firm before the
word *empowerment* became popular in the management literature. Being the first
to open large discount stores in small towns offered several advantages: lower real
estate prices, lower advertising fees, a more stable workforce, and the "brand

name" that comes from being the biggest store in town. But Wal-Mart would have to do a lot more if it were going to offer the low prices that would make people stay and shop "at home,"[41] and, above all, if it were going to prevent incumbent giants such as Kmart from moving in. Wal-Mart turned to three innovations whose combined[42] effect has been instrumental to its success. The first was its aggressive expansion into neighboring small towns, opening 276 stores in 11 southwestern states of the United States by 1979. Saturating small towns was only the first step toward the kind of economies of scale that it needed to be able to offer the low prices that the firm believed would make customers shop at home. Wal-Mart needed more, and so it turned to its second innovation: cross-docking.[43] In cross-docking most of the goods for all the stores within a certain radius are ordered centrally and then delivered to different distribution centers, each covering a certain geographic region with many stores. At these distribution centers the merchandise is sorted and loaded into waiting trucks to be delivered to the individual stores. Finally, there was the use of information and communications technologies—their integration with such retail functions as logistics, purchasing, and inventory management. Wal-Mart put electronic point-of-sale (EPOS) systems in all its stores to manage store inventory better and to collect information on customer buying trends well before its competitors. This information is then relayed by satellite communications systems to distribution warehouses. At the distribution centers the data are consolidated and used to order merchandise as well as to sort and direct merchandise to the right trucks, which will deliver the needed goods to the stores within their distribution zones. On the way back to the distribution centers some of these trucks also pick up merchandise from manufacturers.

When, in 1991, Wal-Mart decided to go international, it sought partners or bought subsidiaries. In Mexico it formed a joint-venture partnership with CIFRA S.A. de C.V. In 1994 it purchased 122 stores in Canada from Woolworth, Inc., of New York. In 1995 it expanded into Argentina (with a wholly owned company) and Brazil (with joint-venture partner Lojas Americanas). Table 10.5 presents a chronology of some of Wal-Mart's moves.

Like Intel's decision to introduce the Pentium, Sam Walton's move from variety to discount retail was an example of the run strategy. It was cannibalizing its successful Benjamin Franklin variety retail franchise. Sam knew that if he did not cannibalize his variety stores with discount retail, someone else would. For several reasons, the combined effect of offering discount retail in small towns that had been shunned by large discounters, its saturation of entire areas, and its use of cross-docking and information technology amounted to what can be seen as a block. In the first place, with stores in small towns clustered in an area of the southern United States and with large investments in warehouses, computers, and even satellite systems it was sending a signal to any potential new entrants that it would fight entry in that part of the world. In the second place, these investments may also have raised the MES for successfully operating in an already saturated area. That is, to offer the kinds of low prices that Wal-Mart was offering, an entrant would have to build as many stores, warehouses, and logistics. With that much added capacity, prices would have to be too low for anyone to make money. In the third place, as a large buyer, Wal-Mart stood to enjoy certain size advantages. For ex-

TABLE 10.5. Chronology of Wal-Mart's moves.

Date	Event
1950s	Sam Walton owns some Benjamin Franklin variety stores, but is also aware of the invasion by supermarkets and discount retailing.
1962	Sam Walton and his brother Bud open the first Wal-Mart discount store in Rogers, Arkansas.
1979	Wal-Mart has 276 stores in 11 southern states in the United States, mostly in towns with populations of less than 25,000.
1985	Wal-Mart opens its first SAM'S Club in Midwest City, Oklahoma.
1988	Wal-Mart opens its first Wal-Mart Supercenter that combines a full-line grocery store and general Wal-Mart merchandise in Washington, Missouri.
1980s	Wal-Mart adds 1126 stores.
1990	Bud's Warehouse Outlet opens its first store in Franklin, Tennessee. Bud's carries name-brand home appliances and a variety of goods from manufacturers' closeouts, discounted models, and factory overstocks.
1991	Wal-Mart goes international for the first time, opening Club Aurrera (now SAM'S Clubs), and Wal-Mart Supercenters in Mexico sought a joint-venture partnership with CIFRA S.A. de C.V.
1994	Wal-Mart purchases 122 stores in Canada from Woolworth, Inc., of New York.
	Wal-Mart announces that it will expand into Argentina (with a wholly owned company) and Brazil (with joint-venture partner Lojas Americanas).
	First Wal-Mart co-owned Value Club opens in Hong Kong.
1995	Wal-Mart stock is approved and listed on the Toronto Stock Exchange.

Source: Wal-Mart company brochures and annual financial statements.

ample, as discussed in Chapter 8, Wal-Mart enjoyed certain scale economies, including a huge bargaining power with suppliers, as well as other informational benefits. In 1991 alone, for example, it saved over $720 million in distribution costs.[44] With lower costs it could offer customers the low prices that can keep out new entrants.

Finally, even if a new entrant could overcome all these scale advantages, there is no guarantee that it would be able to replicate the kind of organizational culture (e.g., its policy of empowering its employees) or competences in integrating information technology on the one hand and inventory management, logistics, purchasing, and marketing on the other, that Wal-Mart has built as an incumbent. In fact, Kmart did move into some of the smaller towns to compete with Wal-Mart but has never been able to catch up with, let alone overtake, Wal-Mart. In 1995, while Kmart's very future as a discounter was being questioned,[45] Wal-Mart was the largest retailer in the world and growing. Above all, it was still leading in such critical retail measures as sales per square foot ($379 versus $185 for Kmart and $282 for Target), 49 percent of shoppers drive past Kmart to go to Wal-Mart, and 46 percent of Wal-Mart customers are loyal to the chain compared to 19 percent for Kmart.[46] Finally, at 15.8 percent, Wal-Mart's costs (selling, general, and administrative), as a percentage of sales, were the lowest in the industry (compared to 22.2 percent for Kmart and 33.3 percent for Federated Department Stores).[47] In 2002, Kmart declared bankruptcy.

Conclusion

These cases demonstrate how a firm can use the block, team-up, and run strategies at different times to protect its profits. Early in the life of its microprocessor, Intel formed several alliances, allowing many semiconductor and computer companies to design, produce, and sell its microprocessor under license. After its design emerged as the dominant microprocessor design, its approach to protecting its profits from microprocessors has been multipronged. It has erected and defended blockades to entry by vigorously protecting its intellectual property (copyright, trademark, patents, and trade secret), accelerated the rate at which it introduces new generations of its microprocessors, and advertised to increase its brand name recognition. This approach has, so far, successfully limited entry, while at the same time preventing the few entrants from making any substantial dents into its profits.

Sun's approach has been somewhat different. Its first workstation designs were proprietary, although it used standard components. When it adopted RISC, however, it decided to allow other firms to clone its workstations, but it held unto its brand name, distribution channels, and service networks. Now it is giving away its Java software in an effort to win a standard in the growing Web.

Wal-Mart, a discount retailer, started out by blocking when it moved into "one-horse" towns, which had been shunned by large retailers such as Kmart, and saturating whole areas with its "good-size" stores. It looked for partners only when it decided to go global.

SUMMARY

In this chapter we have seen that protecting one's entrepreneurial rents goes beyond erecting and defending entry barriers. Since these barriers nearly always leak and, sooner or later, crumble under the weight of global competition, radical technological change, or changing customer preferences and expectations, sitting behind them may not be enough to protect entrepreneurial rents. Moreover, for certain products, and at certain phases of an innovation's evolution, encouraging entry has benefits that outweigh erecting barriers—even when (although rarely) such barriers are ironclad. A combination of three strategies—block, run, and team up—is suggested. They vary from one stage of the value chain to the other, and from one phase of the innovation life cycle to the other, as well as with the type of capabilities that a firm possesses.

In the block strategy a firm keeps the innovation proprietary by limiting access to its competences and assets if such capabilities are unique and inimitable. If they are not unique or easy to copy, an incumbent may still be able to limit entry by sending signals to profit-motivated potential entrants that post-entry prices will be low. In the run strategy the firm keeps innovating, often obsoleting its own capabilities and cannibalizing its existing products as it builds new ones. In the team-up strategy a firm forms alliances with others or licenses out its innovation. Teaming up is especially useful when a firm wants to win a dominant design or standard, build new capabilities, have access to downstream markets, gain access to foreign markets, or enjoy the second-source effect.

The three strategies are related and often complement and corroborate each other. For example, if a firm protects its patents and other firms want to imitate its products, they must circumvent these patents. Doing so takes time—time that will allow the firm to run further away. A firm's reputation for running can also be a deterrent to entry since potential entrants know that they may never catch up. Sometimes a firm must team up in order to run, especially when such a run is taking advantage of an innovation that renders a firm's competences obsolete.

Competing for entrepreneurial rents should be considered a race where a firm builds and defends blockades to prevent entry or slow down entrants but, at the

TABLE 10.6. Chapter summary.

Block	Limit access to unique, inimitable capabilities.
	Signal to entrants that expected post-entry prices will be lower:
	Management is committed to technology.
	Products are technology drivers.
	Firm has history of retaliating against new entrants.
	Firm has invested in idiosyncratic assets.
	Industry's minimum efficient scale is large.
	But can blind a firm from many opportunities and threats of discontinuities.
Run	Introduce new products or services before competitors do, to:
	Keep competitors behind.
	Deter entry.
	Build new capabilities.
	Prove worthiness as partner.
	But can obsolete capabilities and cannibalize existing products.
Team up	Form alliance or other partnerships with co-opetitors, to:
	Improve chances of winning a standard or dominant design.
	Increase upstream demand.
	Build capabilities.
	Access foreign markets.
	Exploit second-source effects.
Intel	Teamed up earlier in the evolution of its microprocessor to win dominant design.
	After dominant design, it has been blocking by protecting its intellectual property, and running by introducing newer microprocessor generations even before existing ones have peaked in sales.
	It is building new endowments by advertising and promoting its *Intel Inside* brand.
Sun Microsystems	Teamed up when it adopted RISC in order to win the standard.
	Blocked at the brand and distribution levels.
	Teaming up in the early stages of the Web.
Wal-Mart	Ran when Sam Walton moved from variety retail store to discount retail.
	Blocked early by moving into "one-horse" towns and saturating whole areas with "good-size" stores.
	Ran and blocked when it integrated its cross-docking innovation and information technology to leverage and consolidate its economies of scale.
	Teaming up as it goes global.

same time, must keep running. Sometimes, especially early in the life of certain technologies, it may take a team to run the race. In that case the firm may need to invite entry. Sometimes a firm may need to block or run well enough to prove that it is worth partnering with. In any case, while running, a firm must be careful that its momentum does not carry it into a crevasse created by technological changes, global competition, deregulation, changing government policies, or changing customer tastes and preferences. Hiding behind barriers may also be dangerous if they crumble and the firm finds out that it cannot run.

Table 10.6 summarizes the examples presented in this chapter.

KEY TERMS

Block
Commitment
Copyright
Entrepreneurial rents
Idiosyncratic assets
Intellectual property

Minimum efficient scale (MES)
Run
Second source
Team up
Trade secret

QUESTIONS AND EXERCISES

1. Why is it so difficult to maintain the profit flow from an existing product while ushering in a radical innovation? What is your solution to this problem?

2. What really is Intel's secret to profitability?

3. In combining run, block, and team-up strategies, what are the drivers, to the extent to which each of them can be emphasized?

NOTES

1. Schumpeter, J. A. *The Theory of Economic Development.* Boston: Harvard, 1934. (A translation of the German version, *Theorie der wirtschaftlichen Entwicklung.* Leipzig: Duncker & Humboldt, 1912.). Oster, S. *Modern Competitive Analysis.* Oxford: Oxford University Press, 1994.

2. Chapter 2 provides some of the reasons why the Macintosh's look and feel is difficult to imitate.

3. See, for example, Oster, S. *Modern Competitive Analysis* (1994). Tirole, J. *The Theory of Industrial Organization.* Cambridge, MA: MIT Press, 1988.

4. Pricing in the face of potential competitors is a popular topic in strategy, economics, and marketing. See, for example, Oster, S. *Modern Competitive Analysis* (1994). Tirole, J. *The Theory of Industrial Organization* (1988).

5. For a detailed description and analysis of how Intel got out of the DRAM business, see Burgelman, R. A. "Fading memories: The process theory of strategic business exit in dynamic environments." *Administrative Science Quarterly* **39**:24–56, 1994.

6. Schrader, S. "Information technology transfer between firms: Cooperation through information trading." *Research Policy* **20:**153–70, 1991.

7. A technology is said to exhibit network externalities if the more people that use it, the more valuable it is to the users.

8. Rosenbloom, R. S., and M. A. Cusumano. "Technological pioneering and competitive advantage: The birth of the VCR industry." In *Readings in Management of Innovation,* M. Tushman and W. Moore (eds.). Cambridge, MA: Ballinger, 1988.

9. Harhoff, D. "Strategic spillover production, vertical integration, and incentives for research and development." Unpublished Ph.D. Dissertation, MIT, 1991.

10. Roberts, E. B., and C. A. Berry. "Entering new businesses: Selecting strategies for success." *Sloan Management Review* **26**(3):3–17, 1985.

11. This section draws on notes that the author took in Professor Ed Roberts course (15.369: Corporate Strategies for Managing Research, Development and Engineering) while a student at the Massachusetts Institute of Technology.

12. Johnson, S. C., and C. Jones. "How to organize for new products." *Harvard Business Review* 49–62, 1957. Roberts, E. B., and C. A. Berry. "Entering new businesses: Selecting strategies for success." *Sloan Management Review* **26**(3):3–17, 1985.

13. Roberts, E. B., and C. A. Berry. "Entering new businesses: Selecting strategies for success" (1985). See also Meyer, M. H., and E. B. Roberts. "New product strategy in small technology-based firms: A pilot study." *Management Science* **32**(7):806–21, 1986.

14. Ferguson, C. H. "Technological development, strategic behavior and government policy in information technology industries." Unpublished Ph.D. Dissertation, MIT, 1989.

15. *Fortune*, March 28, 1988.

16. Labich, K. "The innovators." *Fortune*, p. 49, June 6, 1988.

17. The General Mills example is from a talk that CEO Steve Sanger gave at the University of Michigan Business School on October 26, 1995.

18. Goldblatt, H. "How we did it: Paul Allen and Bill Gates." *Fortune*, October 2, 1995.

19. Goldblatt, H. "How we did it: Paul Allen and Bill Gates" (1995).

20. Manes, S., and P. Andrews. *Gates: How Microsoft's Mogul Reinvented an Industry—and Made Himself the Richest Man in America.* New York: Touchstone, 1993, pp. 82–83. Cusumano, M. A., and R. W. Selby. *Microsoft Secrets.* New York: Free Press, 1995, p. 158.

21. Goldblatt, H. "How we did it: Paul Allen and Bill Gates" (1995).

22. Goldblatt, H. "How we did it: Paul Allen and Bill Gates" (1995).

23. Coase, R. "The nature of the firm," *Econometrica* **4:**386–405, 1937. Williamson, O. E. *The Economic Institutions of Capitalism.* New York: Free Press, 1985.

24. Oster, S. *Modern Competitive Analysis.* Oxford: Oxford University Press, 1994.

25. von Hippel, E. " 'Sticky information' and the locus of problem solving: Implications for innovation." *Management Science* **40**(4):429–39, 1994.

26. This is the argument advanced in Conner, K., and C. K. Prahalad. "A resource-based theory of the firm: Knowledge versus opportunism." *Organization Science* **7**(5):477–501, 1996.

27. Intel's success has been attributed to its decision to get out of the DRAM business and concentrate on the microprocessor. While the firm's focus on microprocessors may have helped its generic rent-protecting strategies, it was not, in and of itself, enough to give the firm the dominant and near monopoly position that it held, in 1997, in microprocessors for personal computers. It has also been suggested that it was an infusion of $400 million from IBM (through an equity stake that IBM acquired in Intel) that made the firm's success possible.

Such an infusion from DEC to MIPS did not save the pioneer RISC microprocessor maker. If a single incident had to be chosen as the key point in the firm's history, it would either be IBM's choice of the Intel microprocessor architecture for its PC or the landmark ruling by judges Ingram and Gray that microcode is copyrightable. See "The pizzazz factor." *The Economist,* September 16, 1995.

28. One reason often given for IBM choosing the Intel design is the fact that Intel had a version of its 16-bit design (the 8088) that could use the older and cheaper 8-bit complementary chips. Since IBM wanted a low-cost PC, it chose Intel's 8088. See Afuah, A. N., and N. Bahram. "The hypercube of innovation." *Research Policy* **24:**51–76, 1995.

29. This is a layer of instructions that helps execute instructions from a computer's instruction set. It is a bunch of "ones" and "zeros" imbedded in the microprocessor's hardware.

30. Burgelman, R. A. "Fading memories: The process theory of strategic business exit in dynamic environments" (1994).

31. This is usually measured in MIPS (million instructions per second), a unit of performance that one design manager and former colleague of the author jokingly called "meaningless indicator of performance."

32. *The Wall Street Journal,* October 17, 1995.

33. Intel's profits for 1995, estimated at more than $3.5 billion, while inviting entry, also suggest that it has even more money to fight entry by, for example, building the very expensive plants.

34. SPARC (scalable processor architecture) is Sun's RISC technology.

35. Katz, M. L., and C. Shapiro. "Network externalities, competition and compatibility." *American Economic Review* **75**(3):424–40, 1985.

36. Ould, A. "SPARC clone market is on the rocks." *PC Week,* July 22, 1991.

37. *UNIXWorld,* October 1991.

38. An exception is Solbourne, which, on several occasions, was the first to introduce some key innovations. For example, it was the first to introduce multiprocessor workstations.

39. This section draws on several references: Gemawat, P. "Wal-Mart stores' discount operations." Harvard Business School Case #9–387-018, 1986. "Wal-Mart: A discounter sinks deep roots in small town, U.S.A." *Business Week,* November 5, 1979. Vlasic, W., and K. Naughton. "Kmart: Who's in charge here?" *Business Week,* p. 104, December 4, 1995. "Change at the check-out: A survey in retailing." *The Economist,* March 4, 1995.

40. "Wal-Mart: A discounter sinks deep roots in small town, U.S.A." (1979).

41. Note that "home" here means "own town" as opposed to "virtual reality," shopping when a customer takes advantage of fiber optics, visualization, and communications technologies to browse through shops from his or her bedroom.

42. The term *combined* is important because each of these innovations alone may not be sufficient.

43. "Change at the check-out: A survey in retailing" (1995).

44. "Change at the check-out: A survey in retailing." (1995).

45. Vlasic, W., and K. Naughton. "Kmart: Who's in charge here?" (1995).

46. Vlasic, W., and K. Naughton. "Kmart: Who's in charge here?" (1995).

47. Kuntz, M., et al. "Re-inventing the store." *Business Week,* November 27, 1995.

P A R T

IMPLEMENTATION

11

FINANCING ENTREPRENEURIAL ACTIVITY

So far in this book we have made the same important assumption that most research in innovation makes—that there is money to finance the innovation. Unfortunately it is not always the case that an entrepreneur or a firm can find the money that it needs to generate new ideas and turn them into products that customers want. Recognizing the potential of an innovation, locating the right profit site, putting together a good team, and developing and implementing the right strategies are one thing. Finding the money to undertake all these activities is another. There are three roadblocks to finding the necessary financing. First, the innovation may be so full of uncertainty that even the manager or entrepreneur cannot fully understand the future benefits of the innovation and may therefore be reluctant to commit internal (or personal) funds to it. Second, if the manager or entrepreneur seeks external financing, the financier may be reluctant to finance the innovation because of the information asymmetry that exists between the manager and the financier. If the financier knows very little about the innovation, it is difficult for him or her to tell whether the manager is telling the truth about it. This may result in financiers being reluctant to invest in radical innovation, and therefore there will be less innovation in general. Third, there is the monitoring problem. If the financier invested in an innovation that he or she thought was not very risky, the manager may decide to use the money to sponsor a much more risky innovation. The goal of this chapter is to explore all three problems. We will start by listing the sources of financing that are available for entrepreneurial activity. We will then explore the problems we have just listed. Finally, we discuss some solutions to these problems.

SOURCES OF FINANCING

The first thing that comes to many people's mind when they think of financing an innovation is the bank—obtaining a loan from the bank. Debt is just one of many instruments for financing an innovation, and a bank is only one of many places to obtain debt financing. Four sources of financing entrepreneurial activity are internal assets, equity, debt, and complementary assets from co-opetitors.

Internal Sources

There are several sources internal to the firm that it can turn to for financing an innovation. First, the firm or entrepreneur can use its retained earnings to finance the innovation. As shown in Figure 11.1, retained earnings come from the profits that a firm makes, net of any dividends that the firm pays out to shareholders. Thus a very profitable firm does not have to seek outside financing.[1] As we will see in Chapter 15, a cut in corporate income taxes by the government, tariffs, quotas, and subsidies increases profits after tax, making more money available to firms for financing innovation. Most start-ups do not have any earnings.

Second, the firm can use existing assets, originally earmarked for another project, for the innovation. Chrysler's need for outside financing of its blockbuster minivan was reduced because it already had a front-wheel-drive engine and transmission, critical components in the minivan, that were used in its Dodge Omni and Plymouth Horizon cars.[2] Entrepreneurs often use personal assets. HP and Apple were started in garages in the Silicon Valley. Third, the firm can find a way to delay

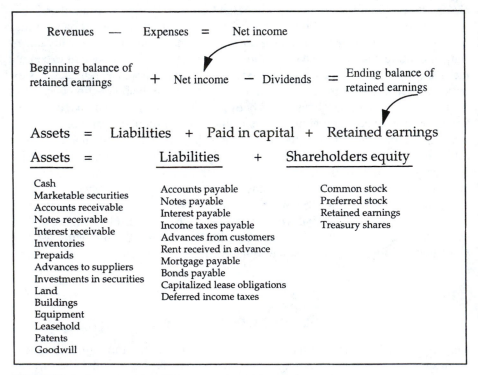

FIGURE 11.1. Sources of financing—the Balance sheet context.

payment of any payables that are due. By not using any available cash to pay interest, taxes, bonds, notes payable, or interests on old loans, the firm can use the money to finance the innovation. Fourth, a firm can also accelerate the rate at which it collects accounts receivables.

Equity

The entrepreneur or firm can issue equity. That is, the firm can sell shares of its company to investors in return for the money that it needs. Figure 11.2 provides some elements of the equity market. Equity can be issued to the public via a stock exchange such as NASDAQ or the London Stock Exchange. This can be in the form of an initial public offering (IPO) in which, for the first time, a firm offers its shares to the public for purchase. A firm with outstanding shares can also issue more shares to the public to raise more money. For start-ups without proven products or some private firms, the most likely buyer of their equity is a private equity firm. Private equity can be venture or nonventure. Venture equity is issued by start-ups (new ventures) in the early or later stages of their life cycle. For part ownership of the start-up, a venture capital firm or other financier can finance the start-up. Sometimes the financing is in the form of debt that is convertible to equity. The money that venture capital firms use to finance the ventures can be theirs or that of limited partners (more on this later). They sometimes also provide management expertise to the start-up. Their primary motivation is the anticipation of cashing in during the IPO, which eventually comes when the start-up has proven itself enough to go public. In the United States, venture capital can also come from small business investment companies (SBICs). These are private corporations that have been

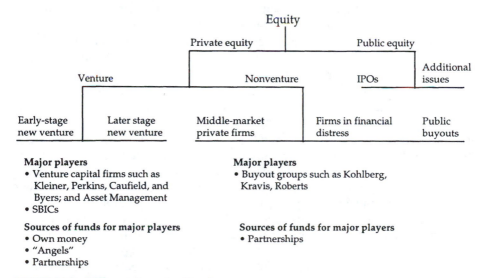

FIGURE 11.2. Different elements of equity.

licensed by the Small Business Administration to provide financing to risky companies. To encourage them to undertake these risky loans, the government gave SBICs tax breaks and Small Business Administration (SBA) loans.

Nonventure equity is usually issued by private firms that want to raise money but want to remain private, by firms experiencing financial difficulties, or by groups that want to buy out other firms. Major players in this area include buyout groups such as Kohlberg, Kravis, Roberts (KKR). The money they use is largely from partnerships.

Debt

A firm or entrepreneur can also borrow money from a money-lending institution such as a bank, or sell bonds or notes, that is, it can acquire debt. The problem with borrowing is that the financier usually wants some physical assets or a reputation as collateral—something that most start-ups usually do not have. Their assets are often their brains and willpower, which may not be enough for some banks. The drawback in borrowing is that interest payments may drain off profits, which could have been ploughed back into the business or paid out as dividends to investors.

Complementary Assets from Co-opetitors

Some of the money that firms raise goes to finance the acquisition of complementary assets—the brand, complementary technologies, manufacturing, distribution channels, installed base, and so on that, as we argued in Chapter 2, are critical to profiting from innovation. The question then is, rather than find money to buy such complementary assets, is there some other way that a firm can obtain them? Teaming up with a co-opetitor can be a solution. By teaming up with a firm that has the complementary assets that a firm wants, it can avoid having to raise money to purchase the complementary assets. The firm is effectively financing its activities through teaming up with owners of complementary assets. A biotech firm that teams up with a traditional pharmaceutical company to give it access to a sales force and the assets that are needed to get a drug through clinical testing and FDA approval can considerably reduce the need for equity, venture, or debt financing. Two questions are relevant in pursuing these forms of financing: (1) Who is likely to have the complementary assets, and (2) What will the firm looking for financing bring to the bargaining table to convince the owner of the complementary assets to team up? In the face of a technological change in an industry, established incumbents in the industry are usually the ones that have complementary assets. While some of these complementary assets can be a handicap to profiting from the new technology, many of them are usually useful in exploiting the new technology. If a new entrant has built the technological capabilities, it can use them to bargain with an incumbent that wants the technological know-how. In the biotech example, the biotech start-up has built technological capabilities in biotechnology while established pharmaceutical companies have the complementary assets. It is important for the start-up to understand that incumbents may be impedded by their dominant logic and capabilities in the old technology. Therefore, the start-up may have to work very hard at articulating what it is that the new technology will do for the incumbent. If the incumbent is interested enough in the technology, it may not only want to team up, but may actually want to invest cash in the start-up to finance further development of the technological capabilities.

Complementors

Recall that a start-up's complementors are the firms that offer products whose sales go up with the sale of the start-up's products. They are therefore very interested in the start-up doing very well and can invest in it. Start-ups that develop software and other applications that facilitate the use of fast microprocessors and complementors to Intel. In the late 1990s, Intel had a new ventures group that sorted out and invested in such ventures with the goal of increasing sales of microprocessors. It is also important for the start-up to be able to articulate just what it is that the complementor will get out of the its invention or technological capability.

PROBLEMS WITH OBTAINING FINANCING

Now that we know something about what the sources of financing an innovation are, we can turn to why it is so difficult to obtain financing for some kinds of innovations. For a manager or entrepreneur to commit any funds to an innovation, she must somehow convince herself or show her top management that the project will be profitable enough to cover the cash outlays. One problem here is that, given the amount of technological and market uncertainty that underpins many innovations, it is difficult to determine just what the expected cash flows and outlays are. We will call this the *uncertainty problem*. If, after the analysis, the manager decides that the innovation is worth pursuing, she must determine how to finance it: whether to use existing assets or seek external financing (e.g., issue equity or debt). Seeking external financing has two problems associated with it. First, even though the manager faces a lot of uncertainty about the innovation, she still has more information about it than the financier. What is to say that the financier can obtain (from the manager) all of the information about the innovation that he needs in order to make a sound investment decision? We will call this the *ex ante* information asymmetry problem, since these problems occur before the financing is obtained. Second, once the manager gets the money, what is to say that she will not use it for a more risky project than the financier would like? How does the financier make sure that the manager's actions are in his best interest? We will call this the *ex post* information asymmetry problem, since it occurs after the manager has obtained the financing.

MANAGER'S UNCERTAINTY PROBLEM

A popular method for determining if it is worthwhile to undertake an innovation is to perform a net present value (NPV) analysis. First, the present value of the stream of outlays that are required to invent and commercialize the innovation is calculated. Next, the present value of the expected stream of profits that the innovation will generate is also calculated. If the difference between the second and the first— the NPV—is positive, the manager can go ahead and invest in the project.[3]

Discounted Cash Flows

One method of performing these NPV analyses is to use the discounted cash flow (DCF) model represented by Equation (1). Expected profits $E[X_t]$, for each period t are discounted back to the present using the appropriate discount rate r_t at each period for a specific duration T:

$$PV = \sum_{t=1}^{t=T} \frac{E[X_t]}{(1 + r_t)^r} \tag{1}$$

This discounting reflects the fact that money has a higher value today than it does tomorrow. The discount rate, r_t is the opportunity cost of capital for the project in question. It is the expected rate of return that could be earned from an investment of similar risk. It reflects the systematic risk that is specific to the project and therefore undiversifiable. This can be estimated using a model such as the capital asset pricing model (CAPM):

$$r_t = r_f + \beta_i(r_m - r_f). \tag{2}$$

That is, the discount rate is equal to r_f, the risk-free rate, such as the interest rate on treasury bills, plus a risk premium. This risk premium is equal to the sysematic risk β_i of the project, and the excess return over the market return rm. The β (beta) of similar projects (within or outside the firm) is used. Often, however, the β of a specific project is difficult to measure, making it difficult to estimate the discount rate. Sometimes the discount rate is approximated with the weighted cost of capital (WACC)—a good approximation if the company's projects have similar betas.

Shortcomings of the DCF as an Innovation Tool

For many reasons, DCF is not a good tool for estimating whether to undertake a radical innovation or not. First, by definition, a radical innovation often has no existing or past projects whose betas can be used as a proxy for estimating the systematic risk.[4] What was a good beta for electronic point of sale cash registers in 1969 when they were invading mechanical cash registers? WACC is not a substitute given that a radical innovation may be nothing like any of the projects that a firm has pursued before. For very long-term planning, distant years (five years and beyond) tend to be considered speculative and are heavily discounted in DCF analysis. Since the risk associated with the project is constantly changing as uncertainty decreases, the discount rate for the project is also changing. But DCF assumes a constant discount rate. Second, the competences and knowledge that a firm accumulates during the process of innovation are not considered. How does a firm incorporate in a DCF analysis the competences and assets that a firm has accumulated in designing internal combustion engines for cars, given that these capabilities can be used to build engines for lawn mowers, marine engines, and portable generators? Third, DCF does not take into consideration the consequences of not pursuing the innovation. If I give up research on galium arsenide (GaAs) technology today because it does not meet my DCF criteria for producing supercomputers, what happens down the line if other applications such as telecommunications suddenly need GaAs because of their speed and low power consumption needs? Will I have the competences and absorptive capacity to compete in the new market? Fourth, DCF assumes that investments are reversible, and if irreversible, the decision to invest is a now or never decision.[5] Fifth, the terminal value—the value of assets upon commercialization—is assumed to be zero. Finally, DCF does not take into consideration the immense role that management plays in making strategic decisions as an innovation evolves and the uncertainty underlying it decreases.

Brealey and Myers suggest that one reason why DCF valuation is so inappropriate for radical innovations is because it was designed for an entirely different purpose.[6] It was developed for bonds and stocks. Investors in these securities are passive since there is rarely much that they can do to improve the interest rate that they get on bonds or the dividends that they get on stocks. Thus applying DCF to an asset assumes that firms hold it passively. As Brealey and Myers further note, DCF does not reflect the value of management. Managers for radical innovations are anything but passive. They are constantly making decisions as technological and market uncertainties decrease. They take advantage of the various options that come up as the uncertainty decreases. They may decide, for example, following the emergence of a dominant design, that they lost, to abandon their own design and adopt the dominant design, as Sony did when it abandoned the beta format and adopted the VHS.

Options

Options evaluation methods are a better alternative to evaluating radical innovation projects than DCF. Investors who hold options are given the right to make a decision. They can exercise that right to either profit or cut their losses. The process of innovation has many options embedded in it, which management can exercise as the uncertainty in the innovation decreases. It can, as Sony did, bail out of its proprietary design to a standard, cutting its losses.

Before exploring how options valuation methods can better help a manager determine whether or not to invest in an innovation, it is important for us to understand just what we mean by options. We will concentrate on the *call* option since it is the most relevant for our purposes. Now suppose that you have somehow found out that Intel's stock, which presently sells for $50, will be selling for $100 five months from today. If you have the money to buy the stock, you can buy tons of them and double your money in only five months. The other thing you could do is buy a *call* option on the stock. That is, for a specific amount of money, you can obtain the right to buy a specific number of shares of Intel stock at a specific price on a specific date (five months in this example). If at that specific date the market price of the stock is $100, as you hoped it would, or just greater than the $50 price specified in the contract, you can *exercise* the contract by buying the stock at the strike price of $50 and then sell it right away for $100. If, for some reason, you were wrong in thinking that Intel's stock would perform very well and its market value instead dropped below the $50 strike price, you can allow the contract to *expire* and limit your losses to just the amount that you had originally paid for the right to buy the stock.

An important question in finance, and one that we will find useful shortly, is how to value an option. That is, how much should you pay today for the right to buy Intel stock five months from now? Some of the elements in valuing options are shown in Figure 11.3. At $t = 0$, the option purchase date, you pay a price—the *contract* or *option price*—and in return, you get the right to buy shares at the exercise price P_e on the exercise date ($t = 1$). The value of the stock can take any path from $t = 0$ to $t = 1$. Three of these possible paths are shown in Figure 11.3. If the price of

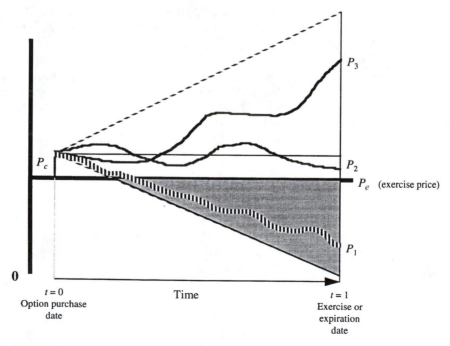

FIGURE 11.3. Some elements of a call option.

the stock is below the exercise price, as is the case with P_1, you may not want to buy the stock since it is worth less than the exercise price, the price you contracted to buy at. The area that has been shaded indicates the area in which exercising the right to buy is not worthwhile since it falls below the exercise price. If it came in at P_3, however, you want to buy since it is worth more than the exercise price and you can make money, even after taking into consideration what you paid originally for the right to buy the stock. If the market value of the stock is P_2, a firm may still want to invest, even though the price is less than the sum of the exercise price and the contract price. The rationale is that the contract price is a bygone. And bygones are bygones. If you decide not to exercise the contract, you are losing out on $P_2 - P_e$.

In general, the value of a call option depends on several factors.[7] First, the higher the price of the stock, the higher the price that one has to pay for the right to buy the stock later. Second, the higher the exercise price, the lower the price of the call option. That is, if you are going to pay more for the stock five months from now, the right to buy the stock should cost you less. Third, the higher the interest rate, the higher the price of the call option. Buying a call option is like making a down payment on something. The higher the interest rate, the higher the down payment one can expect to make. Fourth, the further out the exercise date is from the option purchase date, the higher the valuation of the call option. Finally, the more volatile the stock price, the higher the valuation of the option.

Now the question is, what has a call option to do with innovation? A lot. The process of innovation usually consists of many steps, and the outcome of each is uncertain. Idea generation, R&D, the emergence of a dominant design, manufacturing, and advertising often have uncertain outcomes and sometimes open up opportunities that were not available at the beginning. For example, in the process of developing a drug earmarked for hypertension, a firm can find out that an option for the drug is to use it as a treatment for baldness. Sometimes projects have to be abandoned well before the first product ever gets out of the door. A manager can invest in the first stage of a project. At the end of that first stage, when some of the uncertainties surrounding the innovation are resolved, the manager has a better idea as to whether it is worthwhile continuing with the project or not, and better still, whether other options have opened up as a result of the activities undertaken in that first stage. If she decides to continue, she can then invest in the second stage.

Investing in the first stage can therefore be viewed as buying a call option that gives a manager the right to invest in the second stage. The beginning of that first stage can be seen as the option purchase date and the investment, the option price. Purchasing the call option (investing in the first stage) gives the manager the right to any options that emerge during the activities of the stage: the technical possibilities, the market applications, and competitors' strategies. Effectively, the investment creates more options for the manager. At the end of the stage, the manager can decide whether to invest in the next stage or not. More importantly, she can decide in which of the different opportunities that have opened up to invest. Investing in that next stage is tantamount to exercising the *call option* that was bought by investing in stage 1. Not investing is letting the *call expire*. Investing in the second stage is like buying a call option for the right to invest in the third stage. At the end of that second stage, management can then determine whether to invest in the third, and so on. The downside is limited to the costs incurred in the previous stage(s).

Options versus DCF as an Innovation Tool

Most of the characteristics of innovation suggest that options valuation methods would be preferred to DCF analysis. Innovation is often full of uncertainty. DCF "punishes" uncertainty by using very high discount rates, with the result that NPVs are lower, suggesting that the more the uncertainty, the less a firm should invest in it.[8] Options see uncertainty as an opportunity to create more value, and the more uncertainty, the more the options, and therefore the more one should think about investing. Innovation requires attention from management and decision making at the various stages of the strategic innovation process. The options approach incorporates that. DCF does not. Many investments in innovation are not reversible—R&D expenses, investment in a steel plant, or advertising for a particular drug. DCF assumes they are.[9] The options approach does not.

As we will see in Chapter 12, the competences and assets that one accumulates during the innovation process, even "failed" innovations, can be very useful in subsequent innovations. DCF does not take these into consideration. The options approach allows managers to capture the competence and asset "value" of different stages of the innovation process. If after invention, for example, a manager discovers that it will cost too much to commercialize it, she may decide not to invest in the commercialization. But the firm would have acquired some competences during the invention that it could use later in other inventions. Thus a pharmaceutical firm that discovers a new chemical compound with some therapeutic value, but decides not to pursue FDA approval for the drug, may not have wasted the investment in the discovery. It has learned more about drug discovery. It has also taken a patent that it can license out to other firms. It may also turn out that the compound has some other therapeutic value that was not anticipated at the beginning of the discovery. DCF would not capture such effects, since it calculates NPV by looking only at cash flows.

Example to Illustrate the Differences between DCF and Options

We will use an example to illustrate some of the differences between the DCF and options approaches to evaluating innovation projects.[10] Consider a project to discover and market a drug for reducing cholesterol levels. There is a lot of uncertainty about whether a chemical compound that reduces cholesterol levels will be found. There is also a lot of uncertainty about how safe it will be, whether the U.S. government will approve it for marketing, whether to advertise or not, how much of a market share it will have, how much of the firm's existing product it will cannibalize, and so on. The decision tree of Figure 11.4 shows some of the stages of the innovation process for the drug and the associated outcomes. In this very simplified example, the firm initially has the choice of investing in the R&D or not pro-

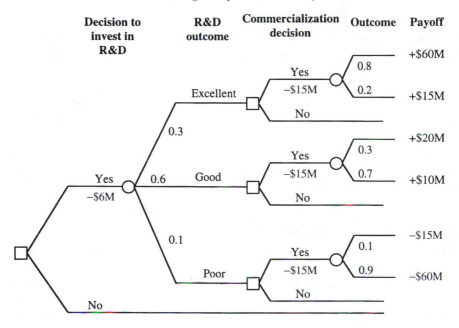

	Decision to invest in R&D	R&D outcome	Commercialization decision	Outcome	Payoff

FIGURE 11.4. The cholesterol drug project.
Source: Adapted from Faulkner, T. W. "Applying 'options thinking' to R&D valuation."
Research Technology Management **39**(3): 50–56, 1996.

Valuation method	NPV (million)	1993	1994	1995
Method A: DCF using most likely scenario	−$11.4	— 6	$-\dfrac{15}{1.12}+$	$\dfrac{10}{1.12^2}$
Method B: DCF with only market uncertainties included	−$9.0	— 6	$-\dfrac{15}{1.12}+$	$\dfrac{0.3(20)+0.7(10)}{1.12^2}$
Method C: Options	+$2.2	— 6	$-\dfrac{0.3(15)}{1.12}+$	$\dfrac{0.3[0.8(60)+.2(15)]}{1.12^2}$

ceeding with the project. If the firm decides to invest in the project, the initial investment in the R&D process will be $6 million. With this investment, there is a 30 percent chance of an "excellent" outcome in that it will discover a chemical compound that is safe, reduces cholesterol levels, and that the FDA is likely to approve. It also has a 60 percent chance of a good outcome—that is, that a safe compound that reduces cholesterol levels somewhat and that might be approved by the FDA will be discovered. There is a 10 percent chance that no safe compound that reduces cholesterol levels will be found. Following the R&D process, the drug must be commercialized. Commercialization requires an investment of $15 million. Depending on the outcome of the commercialization process, the payoffs can be anywhere from $60 million to −$60 million, as shown in Figure 11.4.

The results of determining the NPV using both DCF and options approaches to this problem are also summarized in Figure 11.4. A DCF analysis may consider just the most likely outcome at each stage, given the previous stage. That means the firm can expect a "good" outcome at the end of the first year and $10 million as the payoff at the end of commercialization in the second year. Thus using a 12 percent discount rate, the net present value is −$11.4 million, as shown in row 1 of the table. A DCF analysis can also take into consideration market uncertainties, with the assumption that once the decision to invest in R&D has been made, the firm must commercialize the product. As shown in row 2 of the illustration, the NPV is −$9 million. Not shown is the NPV when both technological and market uncertainties have been taken into consideration. The reader may verify that this is −$5.4 million.

In the options approach the firm sees the investment in R&D only as a call option that allows it to see what its alternatives at the end of that stage are. If a new compound is found, and preliminary testing suggests that the drug is safe and does indeed lower cholesterol levels, and that it can pass FDA testing, the firm can proceed with the commercialization. That is, the firm can proceed only if the outcome is "excellent." No money is invested in commercialization until the outcome of R&D is known. Thus the "excellent" path in Figure 11.4 is taken. There is a 80 percent chance of a $60 million payoff, given that the outcome is excellent. This gives an NPV of +$2.2 million.

EX ANTE AND EX POST INFORMATION
ASYMMETRY PROBLEMS

Suppose a manager has determined, using DCF or options, that an innovation is worth pursuing but must raise money externally. How easy is it to obtain the financing?

Adverse Selection

For a financier to decide whether or not to invest in an innovation, he needs information to help him determine whether the innovation is going to be profitable enough for the investment to be repaid. For several reasons, however, he may not be able to obtain this information. First, because of the uncertainty inherent in many innovations, the manager may not know enough about the innovation to provide the financier with the information he needs. Moreover, the information is likely to change as the innovator interacts with its local environment and learns more about what goes into the product and what customers want. Second, the manager may be opportunistic and hold back some of the information from the financier. Third, given that individuals and organizations are boundedly rational, the manager may not be able to articulate accurately what she knows about the innovation. Moreover, even if she could articulate all the information, the financier may not be able to understand all of it.[11] Finally, the entrepreneur may be afraid of giving away her ideas to a financier, who may turn out to be a thief of ideas. The result of all these is that the financier ends up not having the same information that the entrepreneur has. This information asymmetry can lead to the financier financing "bums," firms that are not good at innovation, but can exploit the information asymmetry to give the financier the impression that they are. Such firms can selectively give the financier information that makes investments look less risky, or they may just be better at articulating what little information that is known about a radical innovation than other firms, which may actually be better at innovation. This amounts to the *adverse selection* problem, where either one or both of two events can happen: only those firms or entrepreneurs who are no good at innovation would go for outside financing, or firms go for outside financing because they know that the innovation is too much of a risk for them to use their own money and would rather use someone else's. They could not obtain financing elsewhere.

Moral Hazard

Suppose a financier has decided to acquire equity in a firm and become an owner. What prevents the manager or entrepreneur from turning around and using the money for a much more risky venture? And even if she uses the money for the planned project, what prevents the manager from being lazy and not living up to the specifications set in the application to sell equity in the project? Moreover, the manager may just be overwhelmed with the new information that she has to process. The owner is not likely to be around looking over the shoulder of the entrepreneur. Even if he were, there is a good chance that he may not be able to tell if the manager is doing the right thing or not until it is too late, given the uncertainty associated with innovation and the tacitness of the knowledge that underpins it. This situation, where a manager or an entrepreneur, knowing that he already has someone else's money to spend, behaves differently is the *moral hazard* problem that can occur in a *principal–agent* relationship. The principal (financier owner) employs an agent (the manager or entrepreneur) to undertake the process of innovation, but the agent would rather be doing what is best for him, which may not be the best thing for the financier.

Solutions

Several solutions have been proposed for the adverse selection and moral hazard problems. For adverse selection, one solution is for the financier to look for firms that rely more on debt than on equity, as they are less likely to be bums.[12] The other is to finance only firms with a reputation in the type of innovation in question. The problem with these solutions is that most start-up firms do not have any capital structures to show how much debt they already have. They do not have a reputation either. Even if they did, a superb job in one innovation may actually be a handicap in a radical one.

For moral hazard, the solutions include monitoring the activities of the manager, providing managers with the right compensation packages, and designing the right capital structure.[13] Again, radical innovation, by its nature, makes implementation of these solutions difficult. For example, how can a banker monitor the activities of a start-up biotechnology firm? For radical innovations, where the outcomes are unpredictable, how much and how should managers be paid when their products are still years away? All of these make start-up firms undertaking radical innovations very risky and likely to have a lot of difficulties finding loans. Private equity markets may be the solution.

Private Equity Market

The relationship between issuers of private equity, investors, and intermediaries that make up the organized private equity market is shown in Figure 11.5. Issuers are largely firms that are not likely to be able to obtain financing in the debt or public equity market, given the riskiness of their projects.[14] They do not have the collateral assets, reputation, or cash flow that lenders usually want. They are variously called ventures, start-ups, and new ventures. These include firms that are undertaking radical innovations and are in the early or later stages of their venture lives and to whom banks are not likely to listen. Apple, DEC, and many biotech firms at one time or another issued private equity. Issuers are not limited to new ventures. Private companies that want to expand, change their capital structure, or change ownership also issue private equity. Public firms that want to go private can issue private equity to finance their leveraged or management buyouts.

Investors are largely organizations that have diversified investment portfolios and therefore can afford to invest part of their portfolios in very risky ventures. These include both public and private pension funds, foundations, investment banks, insurance companies, and wealthy families and individuals. Because these investors are often not very conversant with the knowledge that underpins the innovations they are backing, they usually depend on intermediaries.

Intermediaries are the investors' limited partners. They have the expertise in a specific area or industry that allows them to avoid the pitfalls of adverse selection and moral hazard that a less knowledgeable investor who deals directly with issuers is likely to fall in. They provide the expertise while investors provide the money. They manage investments pooled from different investors. Their experience in managing high-risk investments provides them with the expertise and reputation that are critical in convincing investors to entrust them with their money. In their limited partnership role with investors, intermediaries serve as general partners responsible for managing the partnership's investments. They contribute about 1 percent of the total capital while investors provide the rest. As general partners, intermediaries have unlimited liability. Investors, on the other hand, have limited liability and therefore, at worst, they lose their investment.

A partnership between investors and intermediaries means that investors bring in the money that is so sorely needed while the intermediaries bring in the expertise to select the best investments, and they monitor and control the post-investment activities of the issuer. The adverse selection problem is solved in the way intermediaries, as general partners, select investments. They have large networks that provide leads to investment opportunities, sources of technological and market knowl-

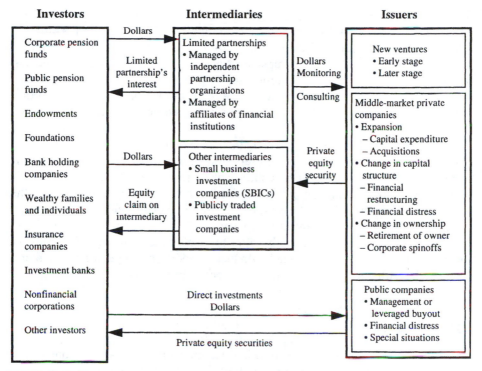

Investors	Intermediaries	Issuers

FIGURE 11.5. Organized private equity market.
Source: Adapted from Fenn, G. W., N. Liang, and S. Prowse. "The economics of private equity."
Board of Governors of the Federal Reserve System. Washington, DC. December 1995.

edge to help in evaluating the investments, and sources of more money. They specialize by industry, market, location, type of investments, and, sometimes, the type of technology that underpins the innovation. Proposals or business plans are first screened using the partner's internal predetermined criteria. Those that survive this first phase undergo more screening. This includes archival computer searches for information on the investment, consultation with industry experts, and visits to the firm to interview key personnel. For certain innovations, interviews with the key personnel are critical. If a startup is counting on an invention by two inventors, it is important to try to have some idea not only about the rationale behind the innovation and its potential, but also of how the inventors get along. It is important to know how management gets along and its dedication toward the project. General partners also interview suppliers, customers, and complementary innovators.

The moral hazard problem is tackled via managerial incentives, which try to align management interests with those of investors, and control mechanisms that further protect investors' interest. Several managerial incentives are typical.[15] First, the managers of the firm not only own a significant share of common stocks of the firm, a good share of the manager's compensation is in common shares. Many firms have an "earn out" arrangement, whereby management can increase its share of stocks as the firm meets certain performance measures. Second, investors are issued convertible preferred stock. Since, in the event of liquidation, preferred stock holders are paid before common stock holders, management (which owns common stock) is likely to work harder to make sure that the firm stays liquid. Third, employment contracts also provide provisions for penalizing poor performance. Stock ownership incentives look at the upside of performance and may encourage very risky undertakings. Providing a provision to penalize poor performance guards against that. Management can, for example, be replaced under certain conditions and their stocks bought back at some low price if their performance drops below a certain level.

Several control measures can also alleviate the moral hazard problem.[16] First, the partnership ensures that it is well represented at the boards of directors of the firms it finances. Second, partners control access to additional capital. This can be done by making sure that any promised funds are not released at once, but rather distributed over the life of the venture. Ventures usually get their financing in rounds, and partners can control when and how each round is released. Third, covenants can also give partners the right to inspect the company's facilities and records, and also to receive timely financial reports and operating statements. Fourth, the partners try to maintain voting control of the firm.

Other Financing

In exploring the solutions to the adverse selection and moral hazard problems, we focused on an extreme case: we explored the case of a start-up firm that is pursuing a radical innovation where information asymmetry problems are most severe and the risk is highest. With no physical collateral assets or reputation, such firms have more difficulties obtaining debt financing. For them, the private equity market is the solution. The other extreme would be an established firm with lots of physical assets and a reputation that is undertaking an incremental innovation. Such a firm would have an easier time obtaining debt financing. It may also be earning enough from an existing innovation not to want external financing. Somewhere between these two extremes are other firms with different risks and different solutions to the adverse solution and moral hazard problems.

The Government

Innovation plays a critical role in a country's economy. However, because of the uncertainty and the adverse selection and moral hazard problems, there may not be enough investors to sponsor certain innovations. This is where the government can play a role. Chapter 15 provides a more detailed version of this role of the government.

SUMMARY

A firm can finance its innovations by using its own existing cash and other assets, or by raising money from the outside through debt or equity. In obtaining financing for an innovation, a firm faces three problems: uncertainty, adverse selection, and moral hazard. To commit funds to an innovation, management usually has to show that the innovation will be profitable enough to cover the cash outlays. But given the amount of technological and market uncertainty that underpins many innovations, it is difficult to determine just what the expected cash flows and outlays are. The use of discounted cash flows (DCF) to determine whether a radical innovation is worth investing in has many flaws. For many innovations, an options-oriented methodology is better.

If the innovator wants to issue debt or equity, the financier does not have as much information about the innovation and the innovator's capabilities as the innovator does. This can result in the adverse selection problem, where only those innovators who are no good at innovation would go for outside financing, or they go for outside financing because they know that the innovation is too much of a risk for them to use their own money. There is another problem. When the financier has provided the innovator with the money, the innovator may decide to take it easy or use the money for more risky activities. Given the information asymmetry between financier and innovator, it may be difficult to tell if the innovator is shirking. This is the moral hazard problem.

Where the innovation uncertainty is high, such as with start-ups, specialized financiers such as venture capital firms develop the expertise to minimize the adverse selection and moral hazard problems. They have the unique competences and assets to select the right investments. They also provide managerial incentives that align management interests with the financiers' and control mechanisms to monitor the innovator's actions without cramping creativity.

KEY TERMS

Adverse selection
Agency problem
Angels
Beta
Call option
Discounted cash flows (DCF)
Early-stage venture
Exercise price
Initial public offering (IPO)

Moral hazard
Option purchase date
Principal–agent
Private equity
Strike price
Uncertainty problem
Venture capital
Venture partnership

QUESTIONS

1. Do you believe that the sources of financing for highly risky products are a major factor in the United States, lead in entrepreneurial activity? Is the United States really the leader?

2. Can the same screening and monitoring methods and skills that U.S. venture

capital firms use to select and monitor U.S. start-ups be used in France? Germany? Why and why not?

3. What is the role of a national government in financing entrepreneurial activity?

NOTES

1. Just what type of financing is best for a firm and how the firm should go about obtaining that financing are very important topics in corporate finance. See, for example, Brealey, R. A., and S. C. Myers. *Principles of Corporate Finance.* New York: McGraw-Hill, 1995.

2. Taylor III, A., and J. E. Davis. "Iacocca's minivan: How Chrysler succeeded in creating the most profitable products of the decade." *Fortune,* May 30, 1994.

3. Net present value (NPV) estimations feature prominently in many finance texts. See, for example, Brealey R. A., and S. C. Myers. *Principles of Corporate Finance* (1995).

4. The disadvantages of DCF outlined here are further explored in Dixit, A. K., and R. S. Pindyck. *Investment under Uncertainty.* Princeton, NJ: Princeton University Press, 1994. Brealey, R. A., and S. C. Myers. *Principles of Corporate Finance* (1995). Naj, A. K. "Manager's journal: In R&D, the next best thing to a gut feeling." *Wall Street Journal,* May 21, 1990.

5. Dixit, A. K., and R. S. Pindyck. *Investment under Uncertainty* (1994).

6. Brealey, R. A., and S. C. Myers. *Principles of Corporate Finance* (1995).

7. Brealey, R. A., and S. C. Myers. *Principles of Corporate Finance* (1995).

8. Dixit, A. K., and R. S. Pindyck. *Investment under Uncertainty* (1994).

9. Dixit, A. K., and R. S. Pindyck. *Investment under Uncertainty* (1994).

10. Faulkner, T. W. "Appying 'options thinking' to R&D valuation." *Research Technology Management* **39** (3):50–56, 1996. Morris, P., E. Teisberg, and A. L. Kolbe. "When choosing R&D projects, go with long shots." *Research Technology Management,* p. 3540, January–February 1991.

11. Conner, K., and C. K. Prahalad. "A resource-based theory of the firm: Knowledge versus opportunism." *Organizational Science* **7:**477–501, 1996.

12. Leland, H., and D. Pyle. "Information asymmetries, financial structure, and financial intermediation." *Journal of Finance* **32:**863–78, 1977. Ross, S. A. "The determination of financial structure: The incentive signalling approach." *Bell Journal of Economic* **8:**23–40, 1977.

13. Jensen, M. C. "Theory of the firm: Managerial behavior, agency costs, and ownership structure." *Journal of Financial Economics* **3:**305–60, 1976. Diamond, D. W. "Monitoring and reputation: The choice between bank loans and directly placed debt." *Journal of Political Economy* **99:**689–721, 1991.

14. For an outstanding treatment of the private equity market, see Fenn, G. W., N. Liang, and S. Prowse. "The economics of private equity." Board of Governors of the Federal Reserve System, Washington, DC, December 1995.

15. Fenn, G. W., N. Liang, and S. Prowse. "The economics of private equity" (1995).

16. Fenn, G. W., N. Liang, and S. Prowse. "The economics of private equity." (1995).

12

IMPLEMENTATION OF THE
DECISION TO ADOPT

Suppose a firm has recognized the potential of an innovation; determined that it has the capabilities to exploit the innovation either as a supplier, manufacturer, customer, or complementary innovator; and has decided to adopt it. Now it must implement the decision to adopt. Innovation means change, and many organizations are likely to resist it, especially when it is radical. In this chapter we examine what the roadblocks to implementing the decision to adopt are, and what strategies, organizational structures, systems, and people can be used to minimize these roadblocks.

ROADBLOCKS TO IMPLEMENTATION

As defined in Chapter 2, innovation is the use of new technological or market knowledge to offer a new product or service that customers want. The word *new* here implies some change for the firm, which can be economic or organizational. This implies that the firm is likely to face both economic and organizational roadblocks (Figure 12.1).

Economic

If an innovation is radical in the economic sense in that it renders the firm's existing products noncompetitive, these products are said to be cannibalized. For example, Intel is said to have cannibalized its 486 microprocessor when it introduced the very successful and much more powerful Pentium. The prospect that existing products may be cannibalized can lead to four potential roadblocks to implementation of the decision to adopt an innovation: fear of the loss of revenues, lack of incentive to invest in the innovation, fear of being stranded in a smaller network, and large exit costs.

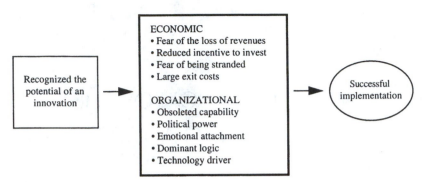

FIGURE 12.1. Roadblocks to adopting an innovation.

Fear of Loss of Revenues

If a firm's innovation renders its existing products or services noncompetitive, the firm loses the revenues from the old product. Since a firm's stock value usually depends on expected earnings, such a loss in revenues and accompanying profits may result in a drop in a firm's value. The fear of such a loss may result in the firm being reluctant to adopt the invading innovation. Such a loss in revenues can also have organizational consequences. As we see shortly, if the source of power for the most powerful in the firm is the revenues from the old product, the political coalition may impede implementation.

Reduced Incentive to Invest

The fear of the loss of revenues can reduce a firm's incentive to invest in a drastic (radical in the economic sense) innovation. If a firm holds a near monopoly position in a product market, and knows that by investing in a drastic innovation it will accelerate the introduction time of the innovation, it may not want to invest, all else being equal. The incentive changes if the firm knows that by not investing in the innovation, someone else would. For example, Intel's Pentium was a drastic innovation since it rendered the 486, for the most part, noncompetitive. If Intel had not introduced the Pentium, there is a good chance that its competitors would have introduced a comparable product.

Fear of Being Stranded

If an innovation exhibits network externalities in that the more people who use it, the more valuable it is, firms would prefer to be in large networks. Thus if an innovation is incompatible with existing products, a firm may be reluctant to adopt it for fear of being the only one to adopt it and therefore being stranded in a small network. For example, some firms were reluctant to start building RISC workstations until Sun Microsystems did. When it offered to license its RISC technology to anyone who wanted it, many firms entered because entry gave them instant access to Sun's large installed base of compatible workstations.

Large Exit Costs

Getting rid of an old technology can be very costly. For example, a change from nuclear power generation to gas-powered generation may require expensive disposal of the nuclear power plant. Important customers who are not quick to see the usefulness of an innovation may be upset over a manufacturer's decision to adopt the innovation. The fear of such costs of disposing of old plants or of upsetting key customers may retard the switch to an innovation.

Organizational

If an innovation is radical in the organizational sense in that the capabilities required to exploit it are very different from existing capabilities, implementation of the decision to adopt may be hampered by several factors: obsolescence of existing capabilities, the firm's dominant logic, political power coalitions, emotional attachment to the old innovation, and fear of losing a competence builder in the old technology.

Obsolescence of Capabilities

The first problem with a radical innovation is that it renders some of a firm's competences and assets obsolete. What is more is that these capabilities are not only useless, they may actually be a handicap to acquiring the new ones, which the firm so desperately needs.[1]

Political Power

So far we have talked of a firm as if it were some homogeneous entity with congruent goals, whose employees' primary interest is to pursue these goals. Often, however, top management does not share a common purpose, and the interest of the firm may not be the primary consideration in every manager's decision. As such, firms can be thought of as being made up of political coalitions formed to protect and enhance their vested interests.[2] The extent to which each of these coalitions can influence a firm's decisions is a measure of how much power it has. (Power is defined here as the ability to have one's preferences or inclinations reflected in any actions taken in the firm or organization.[3]) A coalition whose interests are often reflected in a firm's decisions is said to be a dominant coalition. Each of these coalitions acts in its own interests. One can expect a firm to be more likely to adopt an innovation if the innovation is power enhancing to its dominant coalition. Thus if an innovation is going to destroy the power of the power elite in a firm, the elite may work hard to make sure that the technology is not adopted.[4]

Emotional Attachment

The success of some firms can usually be attributed to a product, service, or technology. Also, some top decision makers reach their top positions because of the valuable contributions that they made in the invention and commercialization of an existing technology. In either case, these managers may, in the face of an innovation that will replace the product that made them what they are, have such strong emotional attachments to it that they may delay the adoption of the innovation. For example, some of Intel's managers were reluctant to get out of the DRAM business and concentrate on microprocessors.[5] They were emotionally attached to DRAMs. Intel invented the DRAM, and for a while it was a good source of revenues.

Dominant Logic

As detailed in Chapter 5, management's beliefs—from its experiences with existing products, technology, and environment—about how a business should be run can have a huge effect on the firm's ability to recognize the potential of an innovation. The same managerial dominant logic can also have an impact on a firm's decision to adopt and how it allocates resources. This can be manifested in many ways. Take the firm's hurdle rate for projects, the rate of return that must be met before the firm funds any project. The assumptions that a firm makes in calculating such rates are a function of the firm's dominant managerial logic. If management is still blinded by the existing ways of doing things, it may not give the advantages of the innovation the kinds of weighting that they deserve in the analysis. This can slow down, if not stall, implementation.

Technology Driver

A product is a technology driver if it has two properties: (1) if the technological knowledge that underpins the product can be used to offer other products, and (2) if the activities that underlie the offering of the product are performed so often that the firm can learn a lot from them. In semiconductors, for example, firms can perfect their production processes by producing large quantities of memory chips and then use the same process to produce, say, microprocessor chips, or vice versa. A firm may be reluctant to adopt an innovation if doing so means having to part with a technology driver.

Combined Economic and Organizational Effects

Both economic and organizational roadblocks can be reenforcing and difficult to separate. For example, managers may rise to top management positions through outstanding performance in the development and marketing of the firm's existing products or services. In doing so they may develop some emotional attachment to the products. Moreover, maintaining their power may also depend on the revenues that come from the existing product. What is more is that over the years of success with the existing technology, they have developed a managerial logic that is deeply rooted in their success with existing products. In the face of a radical innovation, such a firm is likely to have difficulties adopting the innovation. This example is not farfetched. IBM's reluctance to enthusiastically embrace RISC technology and personal computer software has been attributed to the firm's power elite being composed mostly of former mainframe sales or marketing managers.[6] It can also be argued that their experience with mainframes may have blinded them from understanding the potential of RISC technology, and that these managers may have entertained the idea of RISC more if the sustenance of their power did not depend that much on mainframe revenues.

When to Expect Each Effect

When can a firm expect to see which of these roadblocks? It depends on the impact of the innovation on the firm's capabilities and the competitiveness of its existing products. Figure 12.2 illustrates when the roadblocks can be expected. If the innovation is incremental in the economic sense in that existing products remain competitive, there are likely to be no economic roadblocks. The revenues from old products keep flowing, managers who derive their power from these revenues have no fear of losing it, and there is no fear of having to exit. If the innovation is radical in that it renders existing products noncompetitive, then the fear of losing revenues and power, and of being stranded in a smaller network, sets in. If the innovation is

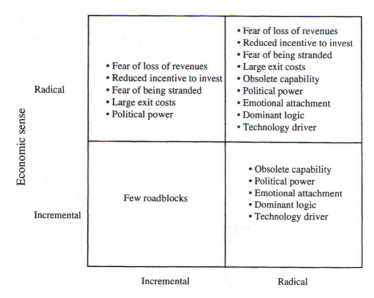

FIGURE 12.2. The number of roadblocks depends on the impact of the innovation on the firm's existing capabilities and products.

incremental in the organizational sense in that the capabilities required to exploit it build on existing capabilities, the firm has few organizational roadblocks. However, if it is radical in that the capabilities needed are radically different from existing ones, then managerial dominant logic, the handicap from old capabilities, fear of the loss of political power, and emotional attachment to old technologies come into effect.

The rather different definitions of radical innovation suggest that an innovation that is radical in the organizational sense can be incremental in the economic sense and vice versa. Diet cola is an example of an innovation that is incremental in the economic sense but somewhat radical in the organizational sense.

OVERCOMING THE ROADBLOCKS: STRATEGY, STRUCTURE, SYSTEMS, AND PEOPLE (S³P)

Overcoming these roadblocks and successfully implementing the decision to adopt an innovation is a function of the firm's strategy, structure, processes and systems, people, and environment and how all five fit together (Figure 12.3).

STRATEGY

A firm's strategy is its theory on how to compete successfully—[7] how it plans to piece together the activities and underpinning capabilities of its value configuration so as to create and offer better value to its customers than its rivals. An important goal in pursuing a strategy is to gain and maintain a competitive advantage. As we saw in Chapter 10, maintaining a competitive advantage entails pursuing one of three generic strategies: block, run, and team up. Which of these strategies is pur-

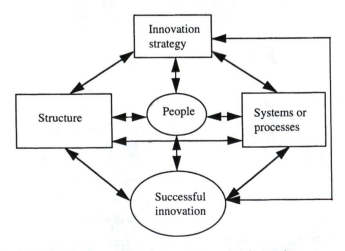

FIGURE 12.3. Successful implementation of an innovation.

sued is a function of the imitability of the new technology and the importance and availability of complementary assets. We also saw in that chapter that whether a firm develops an innovation using internal capabilities or goes to the outside for the appropriate capabilities is a function of the imitability of the technology, the nature of complementary assets, and how familiar the firm is with the new technology and the markets for which products from the new technology are earmarked.

Implementing the Strategies

How should a firm implement its strategy? Using the PC example, suppose you are IBM in 1980. You have just decided to enter the personal computer market, and you would prefer to develop it internally. The question is, how should you implement this decision? In adopting an innovation, a firm faces two major problems. First, it must locate and transfer information to where it is needed. For example, to design a product, a firm needs both technological and market information, not only from internal functions such as manufacturing and marketing, but also from co-opetitors. It must find ways to get this information on time. Second, the information must be processed correctly in order to make the right decisions. These are problems largely because of the cognitive limitations of the firm and of the uncertainty that is inherent in most innovations. We explore what it is about a firm's organizational structure, systems and processes, and people that can facilitate the sourcing, transfer, and processing of this information. Many of the same structures, systems, and kinds of people that we saw in Chapter 5 as being conducive to recognizing the potential of innovation also bear well with the implementation of innovation strategies.

STRUCTURE

Fast and reliable information sourcing, transfer, and processing depend on (1) how tasks are organized; (2) how people are organized in order to tackle the tasks, that is, who reports to whom and how; and (3) how much and what type of communication needs to take place.

Task Organization for *Low* Uncertainty Situations

How and when each of the tasks that underpin an innovation is performed can have an impact on the cost, development time, and quality of the final product.

Improve Each Step

Figure 12.4 (a) shows several stages of a simplified product development process. Each step begins after the previous stage has been completed. Thus prototyping (phase 2) begins only after the design (phase 1) is done. One way to improve the

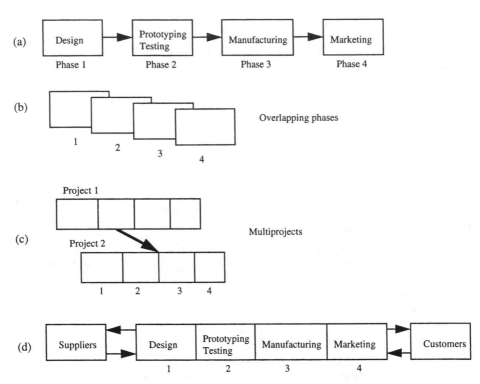

FIGURE 12.4. Improving the product development process.

performance of the process is to improve each individual step. Take, for example, the use of computer-aided design (CAD) tools in product design.[8] First CAD tools allow engineers to reuse modules from previous successful designs, thereby shortening design time and reducing the number of errors. Second, they can be used to simulate the prototyping process, thereby shortening development times. For example, in 1996 Chrysler estimated its engineering expenses to be 2.7 percent of its revenues compared to 5.9 percent for Ford, 5.5 percent for General Motors, and 5 percent for Toyota.[9] One reason for this cost advantage is the firm's use of CAD tools to simulate prototyping rather than actual models. Such CAD simulations allowed the firm to build only one real prototype of its new 2.7-liter aluminum engine instead of the usual five real models. Such simulations also save development times. Third, they provide an electronic log of each engineer's work. This allows an engineer working on one design to receive outputs from another engineer and use them as inputs in his or her own design. It also allows engineers in, for example, Israel and the Silicon Valley to work continuously on one design, with one group taking over the design when the other group goes home to sleep.

Overlapping

In addition to or instead of improving each step of the development process in an effort to improve performance, a firm can overlap the phases, as shown in Figure

12.4(b). The idea is that while, for example, the design of the product is still going on, prototyping can start. And while prototyping is going on, process development for manufacturing can start. This contrasts with waiting until upstream steps are completed before any work on downstream activities is started, as we saw in Figure 12.4(a). By performing some activities in parallel, the overall development time can be shortened. It also allows, for example, results from prototyping to be fed back to design while the design process is still going on and can incorporate changes more easily. Overlapping production processes and product design and development are one reason Chrysler's cost and development times in 1996 were lower than those of its competitors.[10]

Multiprojects

More often than not a firm has more than one project going on at the same time. The question is, can design modules, test results, or other knowledge from one project be useful in improving the performance of another project and therefore the overall performance of the firm? This is the question explored by Nobeoka and Cusumano.[11] In their study of the automobile industry they found that firms with the least transfer of knowledge between projects were very slow in introducing new products. Product introduction rates were improved when technology was transferred sequentially, that is, from one completed project to one just starting. Firms with the fastest product introduction rates transferred the technology from one project while it was still going on, to another one that was running concurrently (see Figure 12.4(c)). In particular, firms that transferred the technology rapidly from one project to the other were the most efficient in terms of the number of engineering hours spent on development. In 1996 Chrysler attributed its reduced development times to the fact that its platform teams for different projects shared technologies.[12]

Preplanning

One other way to improve the development process is to preplan. Preplanning can eliminate extra steps in determining what sequences are best for what activities, and what type of phase overlap makes sense.[13] It provides a common road map that everyone can follow. Thus each team member knows his or her responsibility and that of other members of the team, and as such they can monitor and help each other. The road map reduces misunderstandings. It also allows a firm to locate and train the right personnel for the different positions that will be needed down the line in the development process. It gives a chance for participants to get to know each other before they start. Finally, it allows participants to learn more about the project and be in a better position to articulate a vision of it to outsiders, who may be critical to the success of the product. All of these improve the speed and productivity of the development process as well as the quality of the final product. However, more recent research suggests that preplanning is not as good for product development in industries where the rate of technological and market change is high. In fact, in such fast-paced industries, preplanning may actually hurt.[14] Rather, firms in industries that perform well are the ones that resort to more experimentation, testing, and product probes to better determine customer needs and better ways to resolve technological and market uncertainty.

Use Co-opetitors

Since co-opetitors can be the source of a lot of the technological and market knowledge that goes into the development process, getting them involved in it can improve it. By working with lead users, for example, a firm can better incorporate customer needs into the design. The manufacturer and the customer can codevelop the product, increasing the chances of incorporating more customer needs. For several reasons cooperation with suppliers can also improve product development performance. First, suppliers know a lot about their components, including how they are used. A manufacturer can therefore delegate some of the development tasks to the suppliers who may not only do a better job, but also free the manufacturer to perform other development tasks. Second, such close interaction allows firms to better share the tacit knowledge that goes into the product. Third, early involvement of suppliers makes it easier to catch mispecifications or unrealistic technical demands on components and fix them before the development process has gone too far. Thus involving suppliers in the development process can improve it. In the automobile industry, for example, it has been shown that delegating some of the development tasks to suppliers can reduce development times and costs while also improving quality.[15]

Task Organization for *High* Uncertainty Situations

Eisenhardt and Tabrizi argue that preplanning, task overlapping, and task delegation to suppliers are most effective only in the face of low uncertainty where, for example, it can be assumed that product development is a series of predictable steps.[16] If these steps are predictable, a firm can preplan who will carry out which steps and which parts can be overlapped. When uncertainty is high, however, these measures are not appropriate. Instead, experimentation, trial, error, correction, and learning, which help resolve uncertainties, come into play. In particular, frequent iterations of product designs, extensive testing of the designs, and short times between project reviews are more appropriate.[17]

Frequent Iterations

For some radical innovations there can be competing technologies, and within each technology there can be different competing designs. Early in the life of an innovation it is not quite clear which of these technologies or designs is best. By experimenting with various designs within each technology and interacting with co-opetitors, developers can better understand which design or technology might best serve their needs. With each design iteration, designers learn more about not only the technology and the design, but also their capabilities to exploit each one. Each design also tells customers more about just which of their needs can be satisfied, and suppliers about the types of components they need to supply.

Extensive Testing

A critical part of the experimentation, trial, error, correction, and learning process is testing. Testing is desirable not only at the end of each design iteration, but also at various phases of the design process. The earlier testing can be done during this process, the more likely errors can be discovered before the design has progressed too far. And the earlier errors can be caught, the faster they can be corrected with the least rework, and the more likely the final design will be error free. The more testing, the better. Some of this testing should be done by lead users who can provide feedback on just what other customers would want in the product. Following the options theory argument of Chapter 11, the time and resources invested in each phase of the design process can be viewed as a call option that gives the firm the right to invest in the next stage of the project. After each test, the firm can exercise its right to invest in the next stage or to let the option expire.

Short Times between Project Reviews

During the design process there are usually review sessions in which project participants meet to review the progress and needs of the project. Given the tacit nature of the knowledge that is gained in the design iterations and testing, the more often participants meet to review and share what each has learned in the process, the better off the group can be. The reviews are an opportunity for participants to interpret the results of the testing and their view of what next. Like frequent testing or design iterations, frequent reviews also give the participants a chance to change direction, in case of any problems, before it's too late. For fast-changing markets and technologies, the review gives firms a chance to review where the project is vis-à-vis competitors and the market. Again, the review can be viewed as an exercise date, when the team decides whether to exercise the option to invest in the next stage of the project or to let it expire.

Team Tenure

Team tenure or how long members of a team have been together also has an impact on team performance.[18] Early in the life of the team, members are not likely to have developed the appropriate information collection and sharing patterns or to have learned how to get along. This can hurt performance. As time goes on, however, they overcome these handicaps and perform at their best. Teams that have been together too long become too focused on internal communications and neglect external communication, which can be critical, especially in fast-changing industries or in projects where information from co-opetitors is critical. This degrades performance.

Project or Functional

Now that we have seen how tasks can be organized, the question becomes, how should people be organized in order to better carry out these tasks? We focus on the functional and project organizational structures.[19] The primary constraint in designing an organizational structure for effective implementation of innovation strategies is in balancing differentiation and integration. That is, balancing the need to maintain separate functional units because each one necessarily has to specialize in what it does in order keep building the stock of knowledge that underpins its activities, and the need for these different functions to interact in order to develop and build the products that need inputs from all these functions. Development of a car, for example, is more successful if designers, marketers, manufacturing, sales, component makers, and suppliers all work together, and if each of these functions also has detailed knowledge of its function.[20] It will be recalled that in the functional organization, people are grouped according to the activities that they perform in the value chain and the capabilities and knowledge that underpin these activities. In the project organization, employees are organized by the project they are working on. That is, employees from, say, marketing, design, and manufacturing are assigned to a project and work for the project's manager. Which structure is best is a function of several factors: (1) the type of performance being sort, (2) the type of technology that underpins the innovation, (3) the project duration, and (4) the degree of interdependence of the components.

Type of Performance

Various studies have been undertaken to explore what structure is best for what type of performance. One study found that functional organizational structures tend to be more effective at achieving high technical performance, whereas project structures tend to be better at attaining low cost and lead time targets.[21] A second study found that when the performance measures are cost, meeting schedules, and technical performance, project-oriented teams performed better than function-oriented ones.[22] A third one found that, overall, performance is higher when organizational activities are centered around the project manager while technical matters are centered around the functional manager. The fact that the first study attributes better technical performance to the project structure while the second study attributes it to the functional form suggests that some other contingency variables may be missing. Some of these variables were explored by Allen in his model, which we discussed in Chapter 5.[23] He suggested that the type of structure (project or functional) that a firm chooses for an activity is a function of the duration of the activity, the rate of change of the underlying technology, and the complexity of the activity.

Type of Technology, Project Duration, and Complexity

If the project is very long and the rate of change of the technological knowledge that underpins different functions is also changing very fast, the firm may want to stay with the functional structure (Figure 12.5). This allows employees to stay in their functional groups where, through interaction with functional colleagues, they can keep updating their stock of functional knowledge. If the product or service development is of short duration and the rate of change of knowledge that underlies

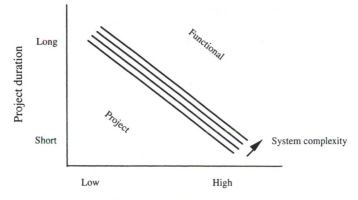

Rate of change of underlying technology

FIGURE 12.5. Choosing between functional and project structures. *Source:* Adapted from Allen. *T. Managing the Flow of Technology.* Cambridge. MA: MIT Press. 1984.

functional areas does not change much, the firm is better off with a project structure. The choice of structure is also a function of how much coordination of intraproject activities is needed and how frequently. These coordination demands are a function of the complexity of the product or service. For example, assembling an airplane requires more coordination than assembling a two-piece aluminum can, given the complexity of the components of a plane compared to that of a can's components. The more of this coordination that is needed, the more a firm may want to use the project structure. When the project duration is long but the rate of change of the underlying knowledge is low, the matrix organization is appropriate. In the matrix organization, individuals from different functional areas are assigned to a project, but rather than reporting only to the project manager, they report to both their functional managers and the project manager.

Communications

Frequent and continuous communications, both within and outside the team and firm, are critical to the success of the development process.[24] The rationale is that since individuals and firms are cognitively limited and the knowledge that underpins innovation is often tacit, knowledge transfer often requires personal and frequent interaction. The more frequent the communications, the more information can be transferred. Moreover, because of the uncertainty often associated with these projects, different types of information may be needed as more uncertainties are resolved and different options open up. Thus communications should not only be frequent, they should also be continuous over the life of the project, not just at the beginning and the end. Internal communications also build group cohesion.

Frequent and continuous external communications also keep in touch with changes in technological knowledge as well as input from suppliers and customers.

The amount of communications is not the only thing that counts; the type also matters. While most of the communications are about the technological and market knowledge that goes into the development efforts, some also go into seeking senior management support, lobbying for resources, and maintaining a good image of the project.[25]

SYSTEMS

How the performance of employees is evaluated and rewarded also matters. If the goal is to finish the development on time, performance evaluations and rewards can be focused on how quickly tasks are performed rather than on product attributes. Human resources practices also play an important role. For example, since team performance drops with very long tenure, the human resources group can continuously bring in new members for its teams.

Information systems are of major importance. Firms can leave project information on an electronics bulletin board for everyone involved in the project to access. A firm's problems/solutions bulletin board can also serve as a good clearing house for routine design problems to which new employees have not been exposed. This can help increase the performance of early-tenure project members. Access to "cell" libraries of ongoing and past projects can increase the speed of new product introductions.

PEOPLE

The successful implementation of a strategy also depends on people. As we saw in Chapter 5, it depends on the extent to which employees share common goals, how knowledgeable they are, their organizational culture, and what motivates them. It also depends on the types of key roles that individuals in the organization play. In Chapters 2 and 5 we discussed how idea generators, gatekeepers, boundary scanners, and innovation champions can help a firm's efforts in recognizing the potential of an innovation. In the development of the product or service these individuals also play a critical role. Gatekeepers and boundary spanners act as interfirm and intrafirm information transducers, respectively. The champion continues to communicate his or her vision of the potential of the innovation to the firm, especially to different functional groups and customers, even as the innovation makes its way from design through prototype and testing to manufacturing and launch. The sponsor is still the "sugar daddy" of the project. The most important function at this point, though, is that of the project manager, which we discuss after taking a look at the product champion.

Champions

As we saw in Chapter 5, champions are individuals who take an idea (theirs or that of an idea generator) for a new product or service and do all they can within their power to ensure the success of the innovation. By actively promoting the idea, communicating and inspiring others with their vision of the potential of the innovation, champions can help their organizations realize the potential of an innovation. But recognizing the potential of an innovation does not mean that a firm is going to adopt the innovation. In fact, recognizing the potential of an innovation may actually make the political coalitions that more determined to block its adoption since they can better see how their political power will be diminished with the innovation. This is where the champion's power and prestige in the organization come in. He or she can use this power to fight any coalitions that may want to block the development process.

Project Manager

The project manager is to meeting schedules what the innovation champion is to communicating his or her vision of the potential of the innovation to others. She or he is the "one-stop shop" for decision making, questions, and information on the project. An important question is, how much authority should a project manager have? Should he or she just collect information on the progress of the project and give it to those who want it, or should she or he have some decision-making authority? Clark and Fujimoto's research in the automobile industry provides some guidance. They classified product managers as heavyweight or lightweight, based on the manager's span of control.[26] A heavyweight product manager is one with extensive authority and responsibility for the product from concept creation through design to manufacturing. The lightweight product manager's authority and responsibilities are not as extensive, being limited only to engineering functions, with no authority or responsibility over concept creation and other market-related aspects of the product. Clark and Fujimoto found that the use of heavyweight product managers helped reduce lead times, total engineering hours (and therefore cost, all else being equal), and improved design quality.

It is important to note that the research done on heavyweight project managers was in automobiles, which do not have the kinds of high uncertainties that pharmaceuticals or semiconductors have.

S³PE Fit?

A firm's innovation strategy, the way the firm organizes its tasks, the type of reward systems in place, and the kinds of people that can best perform the tasks are all interdependent. Figure 12.6 provides an example. A firm whose strategy is to introduce new products rapidly in an environment with a high rate of technological change and fluctuating customer tastes needs to organize its development tasks differently from one with a less rapid rate of product introduction. It not only needs to have multiprojects going on simultaneously, it also needs many design iterations, frequent testing, and numerous project reviews. In such an environment the firm needs project managers who are more champions than heavyweight, that is, people

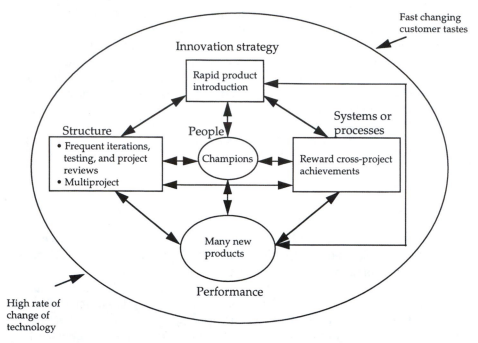

FIGURE 12.6. The S³PE fit.

who can better articulate a vision of market needs and technological potential and convince the team to change direction when the need arises. It needs people who can better cope with uncertainty. Performance evaluation and reward systems place emphasis on the ability to deal with uncertainty and use information from the firm's other products. In a more stable environment with less uncertainty, firm strategy, structure, systems, and people would be different.

IMPLEMENTATION AND CONTRADICTING DEMANDS

Choosing a combination of the generic strategies is one thing. Successfully implementing them is another. The major difficulties that a firm faces in implementing these strategies arise from the somewhat contradictory demands put on the type of organizational structures, people, and processes that are required for successful implementation. Take a run, for example.

Run Strategy

Firms face a major problem in implementing the run strategy. They must keep the profit streams from an existing product flowing while they develop and launch the next generation of products. Maintaining the flow of revenues from an existing product may require fundamentally different organizational strategies, structures, systems, and people from those required to develop and launch the new product.[27] The magnitude of the difference is a function of whether the innovation is incremental, architectural, or radical. An existing mature product faces little technological uncertainty and emphasis in offering the product is largely on efficiency. Tasks are routine, preplanning is encouraged, interaction between functions is infrequent, information flow is hierarchical, and performance and reward systems encourage these kinds of information flows and efficiency-oriented performance. There may be no need for such individuals as gatekeepers, sponsors, boundary spanners, champions, or even project managers. Emphasis is on unidirectional giving and taking of directions, facilitated by hierarchical structures rather than exchange of information.[28] A run, especially one exploiting architectural or radical innovation, requires a very different kind of organizational structure. Tasks are organized so as to allow for the experimentation, trial, error, and correction that are critical for resolving the uncertainties of new product development. Cross-functional structures, such as the project structure, allow for the lateral communications that are critical for development. Project managers, sponsors, gatekeepers, boundary spanners, and champions are critical. Emphasis is on the exchange of information rather than unidirectional giving and taking of direction. People are valued for their expertise rather than for their position in the hierarchy and are more entrepreneurial than methodical executioners of preplanned activities. Performance and reward, as well as information systems that support these types of flexible structures and entrepreneurial people, are also critical.

Thus executing a run strategy requires an organization with contradicting demands[29]—one that can maintain the existing revenue stream while ushering in the next source of revenue. The question is, how can such contradicting demands be met by a single organization? One solution is to have each team with its own structure, systems, and people. Many firms practice this. Makers of DRAMs normally assign one group to reducing the cost of an existing generation with such goals as die shrinks and process improvements, while another group is charged with the design and development of the next generation. Sun had two groups when it switched from CISC to RISC—one to keep an eye on CISC products, while the other developed and launched RISC products. To design its PC, IBM had to form a separate group with an organizational structure, people, and physical location that were entirely different from those of mainframe computers, which were the cash cow for the company. A critical element in a firm's success in managing both kinds of activities is the firm's top management team (TMT). Its responsibility is to create the environment for both teams to coexist and thrive, that is, an environment where profits from exiting products can keep flowing while an innovation is being ushered in.

Top Management Team

A TMT is the group of upper level managers with overall responsibility for the firm.[30] The TMT's role is critical. In particular, its ability to recognize the potential of the innovation that is the next run before its competitors do and to allocate resources accordingly can be the difference between failure and success.[31] This abil-

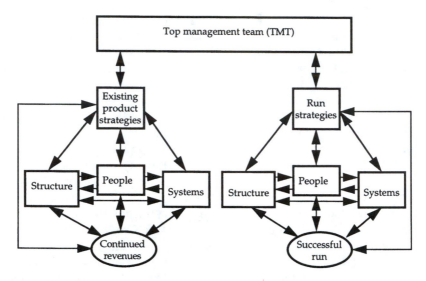

FIGURE 12.7. Balancing the contradicting demands of a run strategy.

ity is a function of the dominant managerial logic of the team, which in turn is a function of its experiences, and its organizational and industry logic. Hamel and Prahalad suggest that a firm injects a genetic mix in its TMT if it is going to solve the dominant logic problem.[32]

Recognizing the potential of the innovation and allocating the resources accordingly is just part of the story. The TMT may also have to be able to articulate its vision of the innovation to the rest of the firm. This not only provides better direction as to where the firm should be going, but also motivates some employees. One way of implementing a run strategy, then, consists of having two groups within the firm, each with its own organizational structure, systems, and people, headed by a TMT that recognizes the potential of the innovation and has a vision, which it can articulate, of where the firm should be going. Figure 12.7 summarizes this.

SUMMARY

After recognizing the potential of an innovation and deciding to adopt it, a firm must still decide how best to implement the decision to adopt. A firm faces several economic and organizational roadblocks in implementing an innovation: fear of the loss of revenues, lack of incentive to invest in the innovation, fear of being stranded in a smaller network, large exit costs, obsolescence of existing capabilities, the firm's dominant logic, political power coalitions, emotional attachment to the old innovation, and fear of losing a competence builder in the old technology. A firm's innovation strategies, organizational structure, systems and processes, and people can help overcome these problems and help the firm successfully implement the decision to adopt.

A firm's innovation strategy determines whether the firm develops the innovation internally or goes outside the firm for help from co-opetitors, and when to implement it—whether the firm leads or follows. The more an innovation renders both technological and marketing capabilities obsolete, the more the firm should think about going outside for help. There are two exceptions. A firm can develop such an innovation internally when it wants to build its own capabilities. A firm may also decide to form an alliance even when it has both the marketing and technological capabilities to undertake the implementation. That would be the case, for example, when development is too costly and the firm has complementary capabilities that it can use to exploit the jointly developed product.

Following the choice of strategy, a firm must also determine how tasks are organized; how people are organized in order to perform the tasks, that is, who reports to whom and how; and how much and what type of communication needs take place. For low uncertainty situations, preplanning of tasks, overlapping of tasks, use of knowledge and modules from other projects, and delegation of some tasks to co-opetitors can all improve development performance. For high-uncertainty situations, however, other measures such as frequent iterations, extensive testing, and frequent reviews are critical. In either case, the cross-functional teams are critical for successful development.

Whether a firm uses a project or a functional organization for an activity is a function of the activity, the rate of change of the underlying technology, and the complexity of the activity. If, for example, a project is very long and the rate of change of the technological knowledge that underpins it is also very high, a firm may want to stay with the functional structure. If the product or service development is of short duration and the rate of change of the knowledge that underlies functional areas is low, the firm is better off with a project structure. The choice of structure is also a function of how much coordination of intraproject activities is needed and how frequently.

The performance reward and information systems put in place also matter. So do the type of people in the company. In any case some kind of fit between innovation strategy, organizational structure, systems, and people can be expected for optimal performance.

KEY TERMS

Acquisitions	*Licensing*
Cannibalization	*Multiprojects*
Champions	*Overlapping processes*
Cross-functional teams	*Political power*
Dominant logic	*Product champion*
Educational acquisition	*Strategy implementation*
Familiarity matrix	*Technology driver*
Heavyweight project manager	*Transaction costs*
Internal ventures	*Venture nurturing*
Joint venture	

QUESTIONS

1. How often do you think fundamentally sound strategies have failed because they were not well implemented?

2. What are the roles of structure, systems, people, and environment (S^3PE) in the implementation of a strategy? Must there be an S^3PE fit?

3. Pick an industry that you believe faces a relatively low level of uncertainty. To what extent will overlapping, multiproject, preplanning, and the use of co-opetitors speed up and improve the quality of product development?

4. What is the role of product complexity in the S^3PE fit?

NOTES

1. Leonard-Barton, D. "Core capabilities and core rigidities: A paradox in managing new product development." *Strategic Management Journal* **13:**111–26, 1992.

2. Pfeffer, J. *Managing with Power: Politics and Influence in Organizations.* Boston: Harvard Business School Press, 1992.

3. Pfeffer, J. *Power in Organizations.* Marshfield, MA: Pitman, 1981.

4. Ferguson, C. H., and C. R. Morris. *Computer Wars: How the West Can Win in the Post-IBM World.* New York: Time Books, 1993.

5. Burgelman, R. A. "Fading memories: The process theory of strategic business exit in dynamic environments." *Administrative Science Quarterly* **39:**24–56, 1994.

6. Ferguson, C. H., and C. R. Morris. *Computer Wars: How the West Can Win in the Post-IBM World* (1993).

7. Barney, J. *Gaining and Sustaining a Competitive Advantage.* Englewood Cliffs, NJ: Prentice Hall, 2002.

8. Eisenhardt, K. M., and B. Tabrizi. "Accelerating adoptive processes: Product innovation in the global computer industry." *Administrative Science Quarterly* **40:**84–110, 1995.

9. Vlasic, W. "Can Chrysler keep it up?" *Business Week,* November 25, 1996.

10. Vlasic, W. "Can Chrysler keep it up?" (1996).

11. Nobeoka, K. "Multi-project management in automobile product development" (1993). Nobeoka, K., and M. A. Cusumano. "Multiproject strategy, design transfer, and project performance: A survey of automobile development projects in the US and Japan." *IEEE Transactions on Engineering Management* **42**(4):397–409, 1995.

12. Vlasic, W. "Can Chrysler keep it up?" (1996).

13. Cooper, R. G., and E. J. Kleinschmidt. "New products: What separates winners and losers?" *Journal of New Product Management* **4**(3):169–84, 1987. Hayes, R. H., S. C. Wheelwright, and K. B. Clark. *Dynamic Manufacturing: Creating the Learning Organization.* New York: Free Press, 1988. Zirger, B. J., and M. Maidique. "A model of new product development: An empirical test." *Management Science* **36**(7), 1990. See also the excellent review by Brown, S. L., and K. M. Eisenhardt. "Product development: Past research, present findings, and future directions." *Academy of Management Review* **20:**343–78, 1996.

14. Brown, S. L., and K. M. Eisenhardt. "The art of continuous change: Linking complexity theory and time-paced evolution in relentlessly shifting organization." *Administrative Science Quarterly* **42**(1):1–34, 1997. D'Avenir, R. A. *Hypercompetition.* New York: The Free Press, 1994.

15. In particular, Clark showed that one-third of the Japanese advantage in engineering hours and four to five months in their advantage in lead time were directly attributable to supplier involvement. See Clark, K. B., B. W. Chew, and T. Fujimoto. "Product development in the world of auto industry: Strategy, organization and performance." *Brookings Papers on Economic Activity* **3**:729–71, 1987. Clark, K. B. "Project scope and project performance: The effect of parts strategy and supplier involvement on product development." *Management Science* **35**(1):1247–63, 1989.

16. Eisenhardt, K. M., and B. Tabrizi. "Accelerating adoptive processes: Product innovation in the global computer industry" (1995).

17. Eisenhardt, K. M., and B. Tabrizi. "Accelerating adoptive processes: Product innovation in the global computer industry" (1995). Thomke, S. H. "The economics of experimentation in the design of new product and processes." Unpublished Ph.D. Dissertation, MIT, 1995.

18. Katz, R. "The effects of group longevity on project communications and performance." *Administrative Science Quarterly* **27**:81–104, 1982.

19. These different types of organizational structures are described in Appendix 2.

20. Clark, K. B., and S. C. Wheelwright. *Managing New Product and Process Development.* New York: Free Press, 1994.

21. Marquis, D. G., and D. L. Straight. "Organizational factors in project performance." Unpublished Working Paper, Sloan School of Management, MIT, 1965.

22. Larson, E. W., and D. H. Gobeli. "Organizing for product development projects." *Journal of Product Innovation Management* **5**:180–90, 1988.

23. Allen, T. *Managing the Flow of Technology.* Cambridge, MA: MIT Press, 1984.

24. Allen, T. *Managing the Flow of Technology* (1984).

25. Ancona, D. G., and D. F. Caldwell. "Bridging the boundary: External process and performance in organizational teams." *Administrative Science Quarterly* **37**:634–65, 1992. Ancona, D. G., and D. F. Caldwell. "Demography and design: Predictors of new product teams." *Organizational Science* **3**(3), August 1992.

26. Clark, K. B., and T. Fujimoto. "Lead time in automobile product development: Explaining the Japanese advantage." Harvard Business School Working Paper, 1988. Clark, K. B., and T. Fujimoto. *Product Development Performance: Strategy, Organization, and Management in the World Automobile Industry.* Boston, MA: Harvard Business School Press, 1991.

27. Tushman, M. L., P. C. Anderson, and C. O'Reilly. "Technology cycles, innovation streams, and ambidextrous organizations: Organization renewal through innovation streams and strategic change." *In Managing Strategic Innovation and Change: A Collection of Readings.* M. L. Tushman and P. C. Anderson (Eds.) New York: Oxford University Press, 1997.

28. Burns, T., and G. M. Stalker. *The Management of Innovation.* London: Tavistock, 1961.

29. This has been called an *ambidextrous organization* in Tushman, M. L., P. C. Anderson, and C. O'Reilly. "Technology cycles, innovation streams, and ambidextrous organizations: Organization renewal through innovation streams and strategic change" (1997).

30. Hambrick, D. "Top management teams: Key to strategic success." *California Management Review* **30**:88–108. 1987.

31. Hambrick, D. C., M. A. Geletkanycz, and J. W. Fredrickson. "Top executive commitment to

the status quo: Some tests of its determinants." *Strategic Management Journal* **14:**401–18. 1993. Afuah, A. N. "Maintaining a competitive advantage in the face of a radical technological change: The role of strategic leadership and dominant logic." Working Paper #9602–14, University of Michigan Business School, July 1996.

32. Hamel, G. M., and C. K. Prahalad. *Competing for the Future.* Boston: Harvard Business School Press. 1994.

GLOBALIZATION

13

GLOBALIZATION

FOR INNOVATIONS

In Chapters 2, 4, and 9 we argued that some environments are more conducive to innovation than others. For example, a nation with financial support and rewards for innovation in the form of initial public offerings (IPOs) and venture capital, a culture that tolerates failure, certain related industries, and emphasis on basic research at universities and other research institutions can be conducive to recognizing the potential of innovations and exploiting them. Thus, when possible, firms may want to locate in such environments. At the same time, certain products are best exploited when sold worldwide. For example, positive-feedback products, which have very high up-front cost but very low per-unit production costs thereafter, can take advantage of the scale that worldwide markets provide. To keep earning profits globally, firms must make sure that local needs and preferences are embodied in their products or services. Firms are thus faced with an important problem: how to take advantage of their capabilities at home and of innovation-conducive environments such as the United States' Silicon Valley, or Switzerland's Basel, and, at the same time, meet local customer needs worldwide. The question is really one of where in the globe a multinational corporation (MNC) locates each of its functions (such as R&D, engineering, manufacturing, marketing, service, finance, and human resources). Should it locate all of these functions in every nation that it serves, or have its R&D and engineering in a Silicon Valley, and marketing close to the customer? Better still, should it locate all the functions at home and export products from home? Which of these modes of organizing activities globally is the best for recognizing the potential of an innovation, for implementing the decision to adopt, and for protecting innovation rents? These are the questions that we will explore in this chapter.

The thesis of the chapter is that to be effective in recognizing the potential of innovations and exploiting them worldwide, a firm should put the right people where the uncertainties are, that is, where information collection and processing needs are greatest. For example, if a firm is in an industry where consumer tastes not only change often, but are also difficult to discern, the firm should locate its marketing function close to the customer. If these conditions are relatively stable, the marketing function can even be located back in the firm's home country. If, on the other hand, there is high uncertainty in the technological information that underpins the firm's ability to offer the product or service, the firm can locate its R&D functions in an environment that is conducive to rapidly increasing its stock of technological knowledge. For example, in semiconductors, where the rate of change of technology is very high, a firm is better off putting the R&D function in the Silicon Valley or a similar environment. We will use Bartlett and Ghoshal's typology of *multidomestic, international, global,* and *transnational* strategies to organize our discussion.[1]

We start the discussion by recapping what uncertainty is in the global context. Next we review the Bartlett and Ghoshal categorization of how firms organize their activities worldwide and use it to build a model for dealing with technological and market uncertainties. We then use the model to explore how best to organize globally in order to recognize the potential of innovations, adopt them, and protect entrepreneurial rents. In particular, we explore how complementary innovations, such as information and communications technologies (ITC), can be used to reach the delicate balance between innovating and keeping the cost of operations low. We use the case of *Ford 2000* to illustrate some of these concepts.

FRAMEWORK

Technological and Market Uncertainties

In Chapter 2 we defined innovation as the use of new technological or market knowledge to offer a new product or service that customers want. In Chapter 6 we also defined uncertainty as the amount of additional information that a firm needs to tackle the problem at hand. The ability of a firm to innovate for worldwide applications, then, is a function of how it can resolve both technological and market uncertainties, that is, of how much technological and market information it can obtain so as to be able to offer low-cost and differentiated products worldwide that meet local customer preferences and expectations.

Market Uncertainty

Market uncertainty is the additional information on distribution channels, product applications, and customer expectations, preferences, needs, and wants that a firm needs in order to offer the new products. This is a function of four factors. First, it is a function of the rate of change of customer preferences, tastes, and expectations. For example, the type of toys that children want is more likely to change from year to year than is the kind of drug that doctors would like for their heart patients. Second, it depends on the stickiness of the information. Stickiness here refers to how difficult (and therefore costly) it is to understand just what it is that customers want or prefer. It is a function of the volume of knowledge required, how tacit it is, and the transmission and absorptive capacities of the sender and receiver, respectively.

It is more difficult, for example, to discern just what it is that a customer wants in a 1998 car than its is to know what it is that a doctor is looking for in a cholesterol-lowering drug. Third, it is a function of how often local government policies change. For example, the safety and efficacy requirements that a drug must meet before the U.S. Food and Drug Administration (FDA) approves it for sale in the United States are very demanding. But they pose no large uncertainty since they have not changed drastically since the 1960s and are not likely to do so very soon. Copyright laws have not changed much either. However, in some developing countries this might not be the case. Fourth, for cultural or historical reasons, local needs for what would appear to be the same market often vary significantly. Take the popular example of laundry detergents in Europe. In northern Europe "boil washing" was the norm, while hand washing was common in Mediterranean countries in the 1980s. Water hardness and phosphate legislation also differed from region to region, leading to different requirements for a detergent in each region.[2]

Technological Uncertainty

Technological uncertainty is the amount of additional information on what goes into the product or service—the components, linkages between components, methods, processes, and techniques—that the firm needs in order to offer the products worldwide. This is a function of three factors. First, it is a function of the rate of change of the technology. For example, the rate of change of semiconductor technology is higher than that for automobile technology, and thus, all else being equal, the uncertainty in semiconductor product technology should be higher than that in automotive technology. Second, there is also the information stickiness factor where, for certain products, technological knowledge is more sticky than others. Third is the complexity of the product. The more complex a product, the more uncertainty there is in the product technology. Finally, there is the sociopolitical potentially negative impact of the technology. For example, as promising as biotechnology is to solving many of our medical problems, there is also a lot that we do not know about its negative potential. Thus, all else being equal, biotechnology has more uncertainties associated with it than do semiconductors.

Endogeneity

It is important to note that technological uncertainty is not entirely exogenous to the firm. It also depends on the firm's strategy. If a firm maintains a run strategy, as detailed in (Chapter 10,) it can influence the rate of change of the technology that underlies its innovations. Market uncertainty is not entirely exogenous to the firm either. A firm can influence market uncertainty in two ways. First, it can advertise, thereby influencing the rate of change of preferences and wants. Second, it can, through technology push, create new expectations and needs. For example, many people did not see the need to cook things very quickly until the microwave oven came along.

Some Classifications

Based on our discussion so far, we can classify products as a function of the market and technological uncertainties that offering new products worldwide entails. In the two-by-two matrix of Figure 13.1 we call a product *market information bound* if the market uncertainty needed to offer new products worldwide is high whereas the technological uncertainty is low. Branded packaged goods such as cereals would be in this category. Just what customers in different parts of the world would prefer in these goods can differ significantly, changes often, or is difficult to discern. Next, there are *technology information bound* products where offering new products involves a high level of technological uncertainty but a low level of market uncertainty. Many pharmaceutical drugs would fall in this category. It takes a lot to discover, develop, manufacture, and deliver new drugs, but their applications do not change much. Then there are products that are associated with both high technological and high market uncertainty. We say that they are *technology and market information bound*. Earth-moving equipment such as tractors fall in this category since terrain varies from region to region and the technologies that go into such equipment can be complex. Finally, McDonald's food services would be in the opposite category, where neither the technological nor the market information needed to offer them has relatively less uncertainty.

Classifying products according to the kind of information needed to offer them is but one step toward our goal of organizing so as to best recognize the potential of

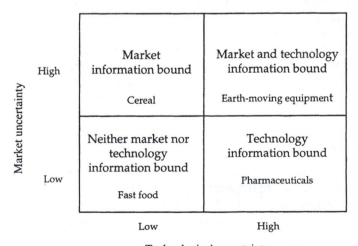

FIGURE 13.1. Technological and market information needs for successful innovations.

innovations and exploit them globally. The next step is to find strategies in a global context that can best match these information needs. For that, we turn to Bartlett and Ghoshal's model.

GENERIC STRATEGIES FOR WORLDWIDE INNOVATION

The different strategies that can be used to better meet the information requirements of different innovations are shown in Figure 13.2. The *multidomestic* strategy is appropriate for innovations that depend a lot more on understanding local customer preferences, tastes, expectations, distribution channels, and local government regulations than they do on the technological knowledge on which they rest.[3] That is, as shown in Figure 13.1, this strategy is appropriate when the need for market information is high while that for technological information is low. Makers of packaged consumer goods (detergents and cereals) such as Unilever have pursued this strategy.[4] Firms that pursue the multidomestic strategy have self-sufficient units in each country to better discern and meet local customer preferences and tastes. On the other hand, if technological information requirements are high relative to market information requirements, a firm may want to pursue a *global* strategy.[5] Firms can locate their facilities either where the environment is most suitable for technological innovations or at home where they have home endowments that give them some advantage. From there they develop products for world markets. For example, Intel has located its development facilities in the United States (especially in the Silicon Valley) and served the world from there, with some peripheral help from overseas units such as a design center in Israel. If both market and technological information demands are low, a firm can operate using the *international* arrangement. It can take advantage of whatever home capabilities it has to develop

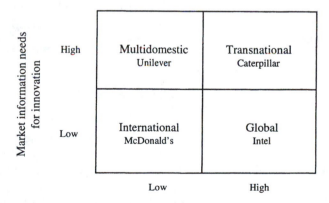

FIGURE 13.2. Strategies for innovating worldwide.

products for its home market. Once the products are successful at home, it can then transfer the capabilities and the innovation to overseas. McDonald's has used this strategy very successfully, moving into Europe and China only after "perfecting" the hamburger at home. If both market and technological information needs are high, the *transnational* arrangement is best. In this mode, firms have access to the best sources of innovation, and the technological knowledge and the market knowledge that underpin them, worldwide.

STRATEGIC CHOICE: BALANCING COST AND INNOVATION

Having outlined what strategic options are available to firms for worldwide innovation, the question becomes, what else determines a firm's choice of these strategies? We will discuss just one of these factors: cost.[6]

The costs of pursuing the different strategies vary considerably and must be balanced against the benefits of innovation. Global firms produce a standard product for the whole world and locate their R&D, manufacturing, and marketing at the most favorable locations. As such, they can take advantage of economies of scale and learning. Since they also buy many standard parts, they can command a very high bargaining power with suppliers. All of these give the global strategy the lowest costs. The most costly of the four is the multidomestic strategy. Since each national market has its own value chain and designs with their own unique parts, the multidomestic strategy is almost the opposite of the global. This duplication of facilities, effort, and designs makes it very difficult for the multidomestic organization to take advantage of economies of scale or learning. They also have less bargaining power with suppliers, compared with global firms. In the international strategy a firm locates most of its key facilities at home, but may also have marketing and manufacturing overseas. It offers limited product customization. This puts its cost somewhere between that of the global and the multidomestic. In the transnational strategy competences can be developed anywhere and flow to wherever they are needed. Its costs are somewhere above *international* costs but depend on the ease of flow of competences and information.

THE ROLE OF COMPLEMENTARY TECHNOLOGIES

Given the proliferation of ITC, the question becomes, can these complementary technologies be used to reduce the technological and market uncertainties and therefore alter the possibilities of globalization strategy? The answer, as we now show, is yes.

Without ITC, a multinational's strategic options would be as we saw earlier in Figure 13.2. With it, however, the range over which a firm can pursue a global strategy as compared to a multidomestic one increases. How? There are two ways this could happen (Figure 13.3). First, ITC helps reduce the need to be physically pres-

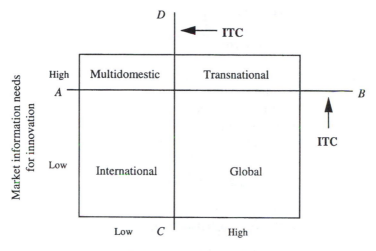

FIGURE 13.3. The role of information and communications technologies (ITC).

ent in a country in order to discern local customer needs and preferences. For example, marketers in Italy can look at the rotating image of a new car design, being developed in Detroit, on a computer workstation in Milan and suggest changes by marking up parts of the car on the Milan screen. These suggestions are instantaneously received and evaluated in Detroit. Customers all over the world can give Ford feedback on a new car design by viewing three-dimensional images of the car on the Web or test driving it via interactive virtual reality. Effectively, ITC reduces the need to be physically present in a country in order to respond to local information needs. As shown in Figure 13.3, this is tantamount to shifting the line *AB* upward and increasing the area over which the global and international strategies can be pursued. But the use of ITC increases technological uncertainty since the firm now not only has to worry about the technological knowledge that underpins the product, but also about ITC. This is reflected in Figure 13.3 by a shift of *CD* leftward. The shifts in *CD* and *AB* amount to increasing the area over which a firm can pursue a global strategy as compared to a multidomestic one. That is, the proper use of ITC can allow a firm to take advantage of the cost benefits of a global strategy while not giving up local responsiveness.

The other way ITC helps increase the range over which the global strategy can be pursued is by influencing worldwide consumer tastes. With worldwide television networks such as CNN, the World Wide Web, and networks of travelers, multinationals can influence customer tastes, preferences, and needs worldwide through advertising via these media.[7] Teenagers in many developing countries already know about McDonald's and Nike brands. By influencing what customers want, a firm is reducing the need to collect market information. This is tantamount to shifting *AB* in Figure 13.3 upward, increasing the area over which the global and international strategies can be pursued. Again, by adding ITC to the equation, the net effect is to increase technological uncertainty, effectively shifting *CD* to the left. The net effect again is to increase the area over which the global strategy can be pursued.

In summary, to innovate, a firm can choose from four strategic options: multidomestic, international, global, and transnational. A firm's choice depends on its competence, the bureaucratic costs associated with the strategy, the information needs of the products it wants to offer, and its proximate environment. The use of information and communication technologies can allow a firm to take advantage of the cost effectiveness of the global strategy while not giving up the advantages of a multidomestic strategy such as local responsiveness.

PROTECTING ENTREPRENEURIAL RENTS

We have just explored the different strategies that a firm can pursue in an effort to recognize the potential of an innovation and exploit it. The question now becomes, what is the impact of these globalization strategies on a firm's ability to protect the profits that it makes from the innovation? In Chapter 10 we showed that it takes combinations of block, run, and team-up, strategies at different stages of the value chain and at different phases of the evolution of a product to maintain profitability. In the block strategy a firm prevents entry by, for example, protecting its intellectual property, brand name, or distribution channels. In the run strategy the firm keeps innovating, often rendering some of its own capabilities obsolete and cannibalizing its existing products so as to stay ahead of its competition.

Team Up

One use of the team-up strategy, especially early in the life of an innovation, is to improve a firm's chances of winning a standard or to try to establish the credibility of an innovation. Both of these require the full backing of the innovator. A multidomestic globalization strategy is particularly unsuitable for this generic rent-protecting strategy, given how independent national units can be. The example of North American Philips (NAP) illustrates this. NAP's parent company, Philips, was a pioneer, together with Matsushita and Sony, in developing the VCR for the home. As we now know, a critical part of Matsushita's strategy to win the standard was to form alliances with other firms while mustering the support of its parent JVC and its fellow subsidiary Panasonic. Philips's product offering was the V2000 VCR format. NAP refused to adopt the V2000 (from its parent company) and opted for Matsushita's VHS format. It bought VCRs from Matsushita and put its Philips labels on them to sell on the American market. Given the number of lead users in the United States and the sheer size of the North American market, this was a big blow to the chances of Philips's format emerging as the standard. Matsushita's VHS won the standard. The global strategy would be preferred when it comes to teaming up, since in it one standard product is developed for the whole world. Given that the activities of the international mode are normally limited to the home firm early in the life of the innovation, this mode may not be particularly favorable for fully exploiting the global advantages of the team-up strategy either.

Block

What globalization strategy is best for the block strategy is not very clear. On the one hand, it can be argued that since in the global strategy a firm's capabilities are centralized, the firm can enjoy economies of scale and thus obtain more patents or copyrights, all else being equal. Moreover, since it also offers a standard product, its designs have a better chance of emerging as the standard. If it uses standard components for its products it can command a higher bargaining power with buyers than its competitors. A standard, coupled with patents or copyrights, can better allow a firm to prevent entry. On the other hand, it can be argued that locating facilities in one country deprives a firm of working with local authorities in different countries to enforce intellectual property protection. This is particularly true of positive-feedback goods such as software, which costs a lot to develop, but very little to "manufacture." Witness the problems that software firms face with some developing countries, where compact disks loaded with illegally copied software worth $20,000 can be sold for as little as $52.[8]

Run

Again, the global firm has a better chance of effectively using the run strategy. With its capabilities located at a favorable site, where it has a better chance of recognizing the rationale behind an innovation, it is in a better position to initiate an innovation. By definition, a firm that uses the multidomestic strategy has two problems when initiating a run. First, since in each country the unit is almost independent of all the others, some of them may be located in environments that are not conducive to innovation. Second, each run may only be good for the nation in which the unit is located. For example, until Ford 2000, a new version of a Ford Escort in Europe had very little to do with the Escort in the United States.

METHODS OF GLOBALIZATION

Some of the mechanisms that we outlined in Chapter 12 for acquiring new technologies can be used for globalization: acquisitions, licensing, strategic alliances, joint ventures, and internal development. Since the generic advantages and disadvantages of each mechanism were discussed in that chapter, we only explore those aspects that are unique to globalization.

Acquisitions and Mergers

Acquiring a foreign firm has the advantage that it gives the buyer control over the unit. This can be critical in the global arrangement, where the MNC needs to have high levels of control. There are, however, several drawbacks to foreign acquisitions. In some developing countries, the MNC may lose its investment if a government that is against foreign investments rises to power. Second, the mismatch between the managerial styles of the two companies may be larger than that between two firms from the same nation, given the larger cultural and language differences. Third, foreign acquisitions can be more expensive than nonforeign ones.[9]

Strategic Alliances

Global strategic alliances, of which international joint ventures are a special case, have several advantages. First, in some cases an alliance may be the only way to enter a country that will not allow other measures such as acquisitions. The firm can then use this local alliance to gradually gain more concessions. Motorola had to do just that when it entered Japan. Motorola formed an alliance with Toshiba, in which Motorola provided Toshiba with some of its 68000 microprocessor technology and, in return, Toshiba provided Motorola with some marketing personnel, including Isamu Kuru, a guru marketeer, who had worked for Toshiba for 28 years.[10] If a foreign country is very risky, a strategic alliance may be a good way to share the risk of operating in the country. The disadvantages include cultural differences, some of which, fortunately, tend to disappear after a shaky start, as we saw in the Toshiba–IBM–Siemens alliance in Chapter 4.

Licensing

Licensing one's technology out has the advantage that it can help one win a standard. For example, Sun Microsystems' licensing of its RISC workstation technology helped it win the workstation RISC standard. Licensing to some countries, however, may have additional disadvantages. Some countries' intellectual property laws may not protect the licensor, especially its other patents and copyrights that the firm may want to keep proprietary.

Internal Development

Internal "development" here refers to the case where a firm decides to use its own people to go international for the first time or to convert from one mode to another, as is the case with the Ford Motor Company, which we discuss shortly. The advantage is that the firm does not have to hire new people. But cultural differences can still be a problem. In going from multidomestic to global, for example, people from different cultures must now work together more closely than they did before.

Which Mechanism Should a Firm Use
in Innovating Abroad?

If a firm decides to exploit a technological change in another country, what mechanism should the firm use to enter the country? It depends on how familiar the firm is with the market and local conditions and the new technology. Figure 13.4 presents a model for choosing which mechanism a firm can use for entering a new country in the face of a technological change. If the model looks familiar, that is because it is the same model that we used to explore when a firm should develop a technology internally or go outside for help. If the market and local conditions in the country that a firm wants to enter and the new technology are familiar to the firm, the firm can pursue internal development or acquistion (cell IV of Figure 13.4). Since the market, local conditions, and technology are familiar to the firm, the capabilities that it needs to exploit the technology in the new country build on the firm's existing capabilities. Therefore the firm has the capabilities to build on if it decides to develop them internally. It also has the absorptive capacity to acquire a local firm. In internal development, the firm develops the primary market and technological capabilities that it needs internally. If time is of the essence or if economies of scale are important in entering that market in the country, the firm may want to consider acquiring a local firm. Local government regulation may dictate otherwise.

If the market and local conditions are unfamiliar to the firm but the technology is familiar, the firm has three options for obtaining the capabilities it needs: joint venture, acquisition, or strategic alliance (cell I of Figure 13.4). In a joint venture, partners pool their capabilities to create a separate legal entity that they own. Since the firm is familiar with the technology but not with the market or local conditions,

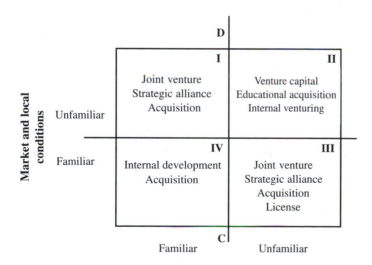

FIGURE 13.4. How to enter a new country to exploit a new technology.

it can find a local or other partner that is familiar with the market and local conditions. By so doing, the firm brings technological capabilties to the table while the partner brings local market. The joint venture between General Mills and Nestle is a good example. General Mills wanted to enter the European breakfast market but was very unfamiliar with the European market, although it had great breakfast technology. Nestle had the European distribution channels but not the technology. The firm in question may decide to pursue some form of strategic alliance other than a joint venture. In place of a joint venture or other form of strategic alliance, a firm entering another country can also buy or be bought by one that is familiar with the market and local conditions. Such an acquisition could also result in the right combination of complementary capabilities.

In cell II of Figure 13.4, the market, local conditions, and technology are unfamiliar to the firm. As such, the firm requires capabilities that are very different from its existing capabilities and is very likely to fail if it tries to do it all alone. To increase its chances of succeeding in such conditions, a firm might want to pursue one of three options to ease its way into the country: venture capital, educational acquisition, and internal venturing. Venture capital, educational acquisition, and internal venturing all allow a firm to learn and build capabilities for the new country while not being handicapped by home country capabilities. In venture capital, a firm makes an investment in a start-up that has the capabilities in local market conditions and technology. By taking this close interest in the firm, the investing firm obtains a window on how business is conducted in the country and can learn. In educational acquisition, a firm buys a local firm not to keep as a subsidiary, but to learn all it can about doing business in the local country. Internal venturing can also be pursued by a firm to build capabilities in exploiting a technology in new country. In an internal venture the firm forms a separate entity within itself to develop capabilities internally to exploit the technology in the new country. The goal in an internal venture is to give the venture group the type of independence that separate legal entities such as start-ups have so as to attract the right talent and keep existing groups and capabilities from handicapping the development of the new capabilities.

Sometimes, as in cell III, market and local conditions are familiar while the technology is not. This is the mirror image of cell I but with the important difference that in cell III, a firm that faces an unfamiliar new technology but has the local market capabilities can license the technology from another firm. Again, an important precaution in licensing a technology from another firm is to make sure that the licensee has the absorptive capacity to successfully transfer the technology.

PRACTICE CASE: FORD MOTOR COMPANY AND FORD 2000

On April 21, 1994, the Ford Motor Company announced that, effective January 1, 1995, it would merge its North American Automotive Operations, European Automotive Operations, and Automotive Components Group into a single operating unit called Ford Automotive Operations (FAO). Product development, previously undertaken independently by each operation, would be integrated into five vehicle program centers (VPCs), with each having worldwide responsibility for the design, development, and engineering of any vehicle assigned to it. Manufacturing, production purchasing, marketing, and sales operations would also be integrated worldwide. The firm was effectively moving from a multidomestic strategy, in which each of its North American and European operations independently developed products to serve its own market, to a global strategy, in which the company would have one operation that develops products for worldwide markets. The question then was, would this strategic change allow Ford to better innovate—keep using new knowledge to offer low-cost or differentiated cars that worldwide customers want?

Before Ford 2000

In 1994, when the program called *Ford 2000* was announced, Ford's financial position looked very strong. Its 1994 profits from its automotive operations were $3.8 billion. There were, however, two things wrong with the rosy picture that the figure painted. In the first place, the firm's automotive operations had *lost* $3.769 billion and $1.775 billion in 1991 and 1992, respectively. As Figure 13.5, shows, the automobile industry was in the upswing of one of its cycles, and Chrysler performed better than Ford. Could this upswing, in which everyone makes money, be hiding a less than optimal strategy? Second, and most important, market performance measures like profits, return on investment, and stock prices can hide problems that are brewing in a company, just waiting to surface later. Ford had its share of them. While Chrysler's pretax margins on automobiles were 11.6 percent, Ford's were 5.4 percent.[11] While it took Ford five years to redesign its Taurus, its Japanese com-

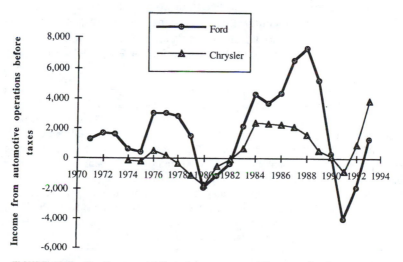

FIGURE 13.5. Cyclic automobile industry: automobile operating incomes for Ford and Chrysler from 1970 to 1993.

petitors took less than two years to introduce competing models. Toyota made 37 cars a year per worker while Ford only made 20.[12] The company's recent model, called the Mondeo in Europe and the Contour/Mystique in North America, had cost $6 billion to develop and launch. This cost was four times that of competitors' models.

Since the introduction of its Taurus in 1985, its first "home run" since the Mustang and the Thunderbird, there had been no other home runs, not even triples. The company's much-touted quality programs may not have prevented it from becoming complacent following the Taurus. Ford's attempt to make its European-designed Escort a world car that used common parts and could be assembled in different parts of the world failed. Each geographic region ended up redesigning the car, duplicating cost. In the United States, only six of the car's 5000 parts remained in common with the European Escort's; one of the six was the radiator cap.[13]

Underlying these troubling signals was an innovation-stifling organization. Ford's operations in different parts of the world—Ford of Europe (FOE), North American Automotive Operations (NAAO), and Ford Asia Pacific Automotive Operations—all developed, manufactured, and sold their products independently. Although this focus on regions allowed Ford to, theoretically, be more responsive to local customer needs, it deprived the company of the bargaining power over suppliers that only combined worldwide operations could provide. Such bargaining power would not only give a manufacturer some price advantages, but would also give it first access to critical component innovations.

Perhaps the most innovation-stifling were the hierarchical functional organizations within each regional operation that have been described as "chimneys" for their hierarchical depth. Despite abundance of evidence that product development and other innovative activities in the automotive industry are best undertaken with a lot of cooperation and interaction between functional groups or using project teams, Ford's chimneys seemed designed to discourage any such cooperation.[14] The organizational structure, incentives, and systems and processes discouraged the kind of cooperation that innovation so deeply depends on. Each function had its own goals and perspective. Donald Peterson, a former Ford CEO, put it best:[15]

You dealt only with issues that the Statements of Authorities and Responsibilities said were yours. You learned real fast to stay inside your limits. . . . There was little or no interaction and no problem solving. What's more, the financial rewards were geared to results in managing your own chimney. Top management knew this was a problem, but there were historical barriers in the way. An entire layer of people at the chimney tops . . . had come up through their respective chimneys and had enormous loyalty to their former colleagues. It was civil war at the top. The question was never, "Are we winning against the Japanese?" but rather, "Are we winning against each other?" You had to reach your objectives, even if they were in conflict with the other chimneys or in conflict with the broader objectives of the company.

Ford's Japanese competitors as well as Chrysler had already abandoned the functional structure in favor of the project one for product development.

What Was *Ford 2000?* The Strategy

With all of these problems hiding under an otherwise sound financial balance sheet, Ford's chairman and CEO, Alex Trotman, decided to pursue a different global strategy. He decided to integrate Ford's worldwide product development, manufacturing, supply, marketing, and sales activities. The company's North American Automotive Operations, European Automotive Operations, and the Automotive Components Group were merged into a single operating unit called Ford Automotive Operations (FAO). Product development, previously undertaken independently by each operation, was integrated into five VPCs with each having worldwide responsibility for the design, development, and engineering of new automobile models for a particular worldwide market segment. The VPCs included four in Detroit—large front-wheel-drive (FWD) cars, rear-wheel-drive (RWD) cars, light trucks, and commercial trucks—and one in Europe split between the Ford Research and Engineering Centers in Dunton (United Kingdom) and Merkenich (Germany) for small and medium front-wheel-drive (FWD) cars. Each VPC was made up of members from different functions, giving it a project structure. Manufacturing, supply, marketing, and sales operations now had a matrix structure as compared to the hierarchical functional structures that hindered innovative efforts before. In time, Ford Asia Pacific Automotive and other operations would follow the same consolidation.

Analysis

The question now was, would the change in strategy from multidomestic to global and in organizational structure from the functional chimneys to a project orientation allow Ford to innovate better while keeping costs low?

Strategic Change

A change from multidomestic to global offers several benefits. First, by eliminating the duplication of value chain activities, a firm saves on product development, manufacturing, and bureaucratic costs. Second, by producing a standard product for the world that uses standard parts, a firm can enjoy economies of scale. In particular, it can command more bargaining power over suppliers than before. Such bargaining power would allow Ford not only to lower its cost of components, but also to have earlier access to supplier innovations than competitors with less power. The new strategy could also permit Ford to reduce the number of suppliers and to increase their participation in the engineering design of cars. Such cooperation, as we saw in Chapter 12, not only reduces the cost of producing cars, but it also increases the quality of the resulting cars. Ford estimated that it would be able to save as much as $3 billion in cost per year by 2000, with $11 billion between 1996 and 2000.[16] With the automobile industry, like computers, depending more and more on supplier innovations, maintaining supplier relations that facilitate the flow of such innovations to manufacturers was critical. It was estimated that more than 50 percent of the content of cars would be electronic in the not too far future. Such dependence on components, whose core concepts are fundamentally different from those that underpin the traditional internal combustion engine automobile, underscored the importance of supplier relations and the need for a global approach.

Finally, by consolidating its R&D, Ford stood to benefit from the economies of scale that can come from larger scale R&D. The question was whether such cost savings and the potential increase in supplier-generated innovations were enough to overcome the main disadvantage of the global strategy—not being close enough to customers to respond to their needs quickly. By locating the VPCs in Detroit, would Ford not be too far from worldwide customers to incorporate their preferences and expectations in its new cars? The answer rests in how well the firm would be able to exploit complementary innovations, such as the Internet and CAD tools. As we saw earlier, the use of ITC reduces the negative effects (on the ability to innovate) that would otherwise result from a firm moving from a multidomestic strategy to a global one. Ford could use ITC in two ways. First, it could use CAD tools, intranets, and the Web to obtain inputs from overseas sales and marketing offices and customer feedback on new car designs, thus alleviating the need to locate locally. For example, as we suggested earlier, marketers in Italy could look at the rotating image of a new car design, being developed in Detroit, on a computer workstation in Milan and suggest changes by indicating, on the Milan screen, what they deemed necessary. Second, instead of (or in addition to) trying to capture customer preferences, Ford could influence them by advertising through the ever more popular international media for advertising.

The effect of using information technology to capture customer preferences and needs or advertising in the change from a multidomestic to a global strategy is captured in Figures 13.6 and 13.7. In the multidomestic strategy Ford was better able to respond to local customer needs (Figure 13.6). Figure 13.7 shows that the

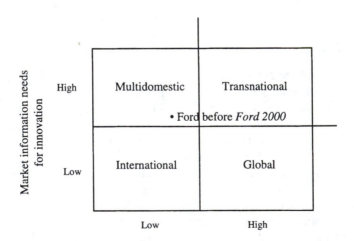

FIGURE 13.6. Ford Motor Company before *Ford 2000.*

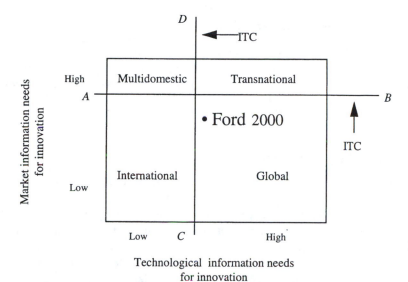

FIGURE 13.7. Inforamtion and communications technologies (ITC) allow Ford to have the benefits of a global strategy without sacrificing all the benefits of a multidomestic strategy.

need to have a value chain in each country in order to respond to local needs can be reduced by using ITC such as the Internet. This is depicted by the line *AB* moving upward. But the use of ITC increases Ford's technological information needs, as shown by the line *CD* shifting left. Effectively, then, Ford could, by using ITC, follow the global strategy without sacrificing local responsiveness.

ITC could also play another role. They could allow engineers in Japan, Germany, and the United States to work on the same car, with each group handing over the job to the next at the end of their workday, thus allowing work to be carried on almost round the clock, accelerating the time it takes to develop and launch a car.

Finally, suppose, using ITC or otherwise, Ford were able to collect all the local market information it needs to offer just what customers want. The question still is, how would it incorporate all of the information into a world car? Would the firm risk producing a McCar that customers all over the world do not want? Not necessarily. The firm could learn from what microchip makers have done so successfully in selling a type of chip called ASIC (applications-specific integrated circuits). The core product is the same for all customers. But the last stage of the manufacturing process allows the firm to tailor the product to specific needs of different customers. Ford could design cars that use the same standard components and features up to some level. Then, through flexible manufacturing and improved design tools, customization could be achieved for each local country or region. The company could take it further; it could allow individuals to specify what they want in a car, and Ford would build the car to individual tastes. This is what has been termed build-to-order.

Organizational Structure and Systems

To support its global strategy, Ford was effectively moving from its very hierarchical functional structure to two types of structures: a project structure for product development and a matrix structure for manufacturing, marketing and sales, and purchasing.

Functional to Project for Product Development

In the project structure of the VPCs, engineers with functional skills in design, engineering, manufacturing, and marketing were assigned to a vehicle design center and reported to the head of the vehicle center instead of the heads of their functional areas (Figure 13.8). The project structure allows for better interaction between team members, and has been shown to be most effective in product development. With one executive responsible for concept, design, development, and engineering, the company effectively had a so-called heavyweight project manager. And having a heavyweight project manager in automobile development can reduce lead times and total engineering hours (and therefore cost, all else being equal), and improve design quality.[17] At Ford it used to take 22 meetings and over two months to get a new-car project approved. With *Ford 2000* it took less than a month.

One disadvantage of the project structure is that by assigning employees from different functions to the project, their knowledge may become dated since they are not within their functional units, where they are more likely to keep abreast of changes in the knowledge that underpins their functions. As we saw in Chapters 5 and 12, how dated a project member's knowledge becomes is a function of the project's duration and the rate of change of the knowledge that underpins the employee's area of expertise. Since the technological knowledge that underlies the internal combustion engine automobile does not change that much but the customers' tastes change, and they do so often, a project structure would be better for car development than the functional structure that Ford had used for decades.

Functional to Matrix for Manufacturing, Marketing and Sales, and Purchasing

Ford 2000 used the matrix organizational structure for manufacturing, marketing and sales, and purchasing. In the matrix structure, managers had two bosses: one in a VPC and the other in a functional area (Figure 13.8). This structure had two primary advantages. The first was better skills upgradability. How? In innovative activities such as the design, development, manufacturing, and sale of automobiles, individuals need so-called T-skills,[18] that is, deep expertise in one discipline combined with broad enough knowledge in others to see the linkages between them. A matrix organization allows individuals to maintain these skills by staying in their

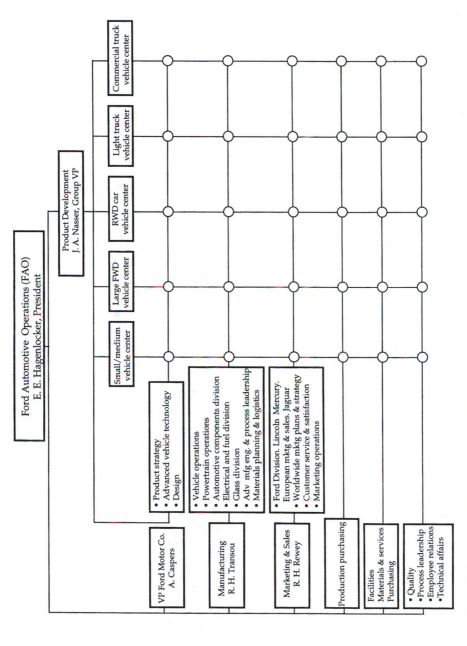

FIGURE 13.8. *Ford 2000 matrix organization.*

Source: Ford

functional areas while actively participating in product development or another project activity. The second was the sharing of expertise. The functional expertise of a particularly good individual can be used on more than one project. The drawback of the matrix organization is the dual-boss phenomenon. Not knowing who is responsible for evaluating and rewarding or punishing performance can be a problem, especially when a firm's values and goals are not shared by all managers.

Some Issues

In moving from multidomestic to global Ford was trying to follow a strategy that Honda and Toyota had pursued for years. While building cars with common platforms and peripheral local customization would be better than building an Escort whose European and American versions had completely different platforms, Ford would only amount to catching up to competitors. The question is, why stop at common platforms and local customization? Why end customization at the local level? Why not pursue a build-to-order strategy? Rather than precustomize cars for different regions, why not follow the semiconductor industry example and build cars up to some level (call it the platform) and then use vastly available technology to customize cars according to individual customer tastes? A customer could place an order from her or his home and Ford would have the car ready in ten days. Such a system would also allow the company to collect useful information on customer tastes and preferences.

Whether Ford offers product customization at the individual level or at the regional level, a critical component of the multidomestic-to-global change is the use of technology to better respond to local customer needs, harness intellectual capability, and influence customer tastes and preferences. The assumption here is that Ford will be able to integrate these technologies with its other skills. This may prove to be a major hurdle in itself.

The change from functional to matrix posed several potential problems for Ford. Many employees would have two bosses whose goals and self-interests might be vastly different. Which of these two bosses would the employee satisfy? How quickly would employees pick up the T-skills that they needed to function in these capacities? What new reward systems encourage the building of T-skills that are now critical to major firm activities such as product development and manufacturing? How would the firm measure the performance of an employee in a matrix organization who must satisfy two bosses and contribute to both project and functional activities? What reward systems foster shared values as compared to empire building?

The firm's empowerment and diversity programs, like its new strategy, had been adopted by other companies for years. Wal-Mart had been practicing empowerment since the 1960s. If Ford really wanted a competitive advantage, couldn't it pursue other organizational behavior inventions?

In general there were still many questions to be asked. How would political power be used in the firm? How could the firm keep getting the message to its employees? How would it deal with employee and union mental models of what it takes to thrive in the automobile business? Would it take another crisis such as those in 1972, 1980, and 1991—when U.S. automakers lost considerable amounts of money—to rally everyone behind the new program? Might such a crisis not, in fact, be an excuse for people to want to revert to the old multidomestic strategy? How would one change 320,000 people from different national cultures? What would it take to motivate all these people? What kinds of performance measures and reward systems were appropriate?

SUMMARY

The goal of this chapter was to explore what globalization strategies a firm should pursue in order to recognize the potential of innovations, exploit them, and protect the rents from them. We argued that an MNC's optimum strategies are a function of its information needs, that is, of the technological and market uncertainties that it faces. For market-information-bound products, such as consumer packaged goods that have little technological uncertainty, the multidomestic strategy in which overseas units have their own value chains and can better discern customer needs and translate them to local products is appropriate. If the products are technology information bound, as is the case with most semiconductors, then the firm can pursue the global strategy. In this strategy the firm locates in the most favorable location and offers standard products worldwide. Using the semiconductor example, such a location would be a place like the Silicon Valley, which is conducive to semiconductor innovation.

Some products, such as the fast foods that McDonald's offers, have low technological and market uncertainty associated with them. To exploit such innovations worldwide, an MNC can use the international strategy, where a firm develops and markets a product in its home country, and with the experience it has accumulated, it can then move on overseas to offer the product there. Finally, where both market and technological uncertainties are high, the transnational strategy is best. In it, a firm's functions are decentralized and located all over the world, taking advantage of the best that each nation can offer by way of sources of innovation and markets for the innovations.

The choice of each of these strategies must be weighed against its cost. The multidomestic strategy, while appropriate for products with high market uncertainty, is extremely expensive, given the duplication of value chains and the proliferation of unstandardized components for the products. The global strategy is the least expensive given that firms can locate facilities in the most conducive locations and its standard products give the MNC scale advantages. Fortunately, by using complementary innovations such as ITC, a firm can pursue the global strategy when one would expect it to pursue a multidomestic one.

We also argued that, in protecting profits, the global arrangement is best for the team-up, block, and run strategies, while the multidomestic is worst. Finally, we used the case of Ford Motor Company, which moved from the multidomestic strategy and the functional organizational structure to the global strategy and the matrix structure—*Ford 2000*—to illustrate some of the concepts of the chapter and concluded that the success of the change depends on the firm's use of ITC and its ability to implement the strategies given the inertia of the pre-*Ford 2000* organization.

KEY TERMS

Acquisitions and mergers
Complementary innovations
Global
Information and communications
   technologies (ITC)
Technology information bound

International
International product life cycle
Market information bound
Multidomestic
Multinational corporation (MNC)
Transnational

QUESTIONS AND EXERCISES

1. For what products would you pursue each of the following strategies: global, international, multidomestic, and transnational? How would the use of ITC change your strategies?

2. What firms have pursued the mutidomestic strategy? Should they?

3. What type of organizational structure, systems, and people would you suggest for each of global, international, multidomestic, and transnational strategies?

4. It has been suggested that some software piracy is actually good for software makers such as Microsoft. Do you agree or not? Should Microsoft stop prosecuting violations of its copyrights by foreign countries?

5. Do you believe that *Ford 2000* was a good strategy? How critical is implementation and why?

NOTES

1. Bartlett, C., and S. Ghoshal. *Managing across Borders*. Cambridge, MA: Harvard Business School Press, 1989.

2. Bartlett, C., and S. Ghoshal. *Managing across Borders* (1989, p. 20).

3. The terminology of *multidomestic, global, international,* and *transnational* was adopted from Bartlett, C., and S. Ghoshal. *Managing across Borders* (1989).

4. Bartlett, C., and S. Ghoshal. *Managing across Borders* (1989).

5. The words *global* and *international* as used in this categorization of different strategies can be confusing given their normal everyday uses. Hence these two words will be used in this chapter only in the context of being one of the four strategies.

6. Hill, C. W. L., and G. R. Jones. *Strategic Management: An Integrated Approach*. Boston: Houghton Mifflin, 1995.

7. Levitt, T. "The globalization of markets." *Harvard Business Review,* May–June 1983.

8. Smith, C. S. "Microsoft may get help in China from its Uncle Sam." *Wall Street Journal,* November 21, 1994.

9. Warner, J., J. Templeman, and R. Horn. "The world is not always your oyster: Why cross-border mergers so often come to grief." *Business Week,* October 30, 1995.

10. Hill, C. W. L., and G. R. Jones. *Strategic Management: An Integrated Approach* (1995, p. 246). "Asia becons." *The Economist,* May 30, 1992. "TI, Hitachi sign 16M DRAM pact: Plan joint development; Texas Instruments Inc." *Electronic News,* December 26, 1988. "Motorola, Toshiba cast new 16M DRAM deal." *Electronic News,* January 28, 1993.

11. Treece, J. B., K. Kerwin, and H. Dawley. "Ford." *Business Week,* April 3, 1995.

12. "The world that changed the machine." *The Economist,* March 30, 1996.

13. Pelofsky, M., and L. Schleisinger. "Transformation at Ford." Harvard Business School Case #9–390-083, revised November 15, 1991.

14. Chapter 12 provides more details.

15. Pelofsky, M., and L. Schleisinger. "Transformation at Ford" (1991, p. 11).

16. Naughton, K. "Trotman's trial." *Business Week,* April 8, 1996.

17. Clark, K. B., and T. Fujumoto. *Product Development Performance: Strategy, Organization, and Management in the World Automobile Industry.* Boston: Harvard Business School Press, 1991.

18. Iansiti, M. "Real-world R&D. Jumping the product generation gap." *Harvard Business Review* 138–47, May–June 1993.

C H A P T E R

14

INNOVATING FOR
EMERGING ECONOMIES

By the year 2015 the population of Asia is estimated to be close to 4 billion, with that of China alone estimated to be 1.3 billion. For many multinational corporations and local firms alike, such potentially large markets evoke images of huge profits to be made. Are such images justified? The goal of this chapter is to explore how local and foreign firms can profit from innovation in emerging economics. We start the chapter by exploring the different capabilities that a firm has at its disposal to use in order to enter an emerging economy. We then examine the different strategies that a firm can use to enter these foreign markets. Finally, we explore how these strategies might be implemented.

VALUE STOCK

Suppose a German firm were interested in entering an emerging Asian market such as China. The first question it may want to ask itself is, "what is it about us that will make us innovate better for China than our competitors?" One way for this firm to answer this question is to start by examining its *value stock*—the repertoire of end products, core products, capabilities, and knowledge that it has accumulated, and how this stock can allow it to serve the new market better than its competitors. Figure 14.1 shows the different elements of the value stock for automobiles using Mercedes Benz as an example. The firm has many different kinds of cars (including the SLK) that it can offer "as they are" to an emerging economy. It can also modify its cars by offering right-hand steering wheel versions to, say, Southern Africa, Hong Kong, or Australia. It can also resurrect a car that was discontinued but whose simple design and low cost may be more suitable for an emerging market, that is, it can dip into its stock of technologies, old and new.

Rather than enter with cars that have been proven elsewhere, the firm may prefer to use existing core products such as the drive train (engine, electronic fuel injection, and transmission) and add a frame that better reflects local taste. A firm can also use its competences in designing automobiles to design a car from scratch for

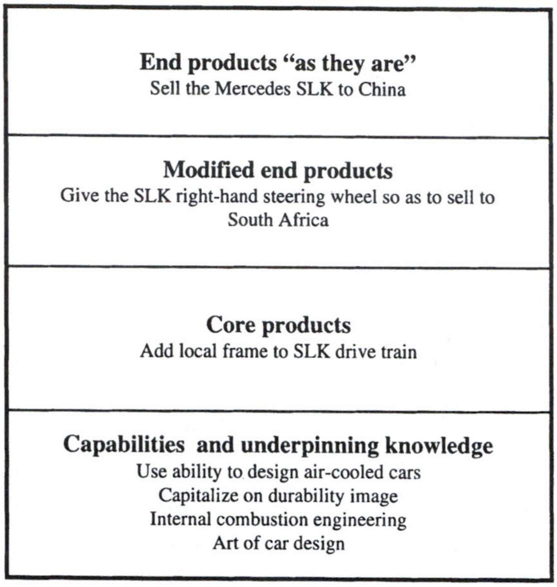

FIGURE 14.1. A firm's value stock.

the new market. These can include its ability to design air-cooled cars, cars that can take the punishment of large cities with the least emission of pollutants, or cars that can better handle dusty unpaved country roads. Finally, the firm can decide to hire engineering graduates from local universities and teach them automobile design and production using its stock of knowledge in internal combustion engineering, advanced materials, the art of design, and manufacturing.

TECHNOECONOMIC FACTORS

A firm's value stock represents different weapons that it can use to exploit an emerging market. Which level of this value stock the firm uses is a function of two factors: (1) the economic differences between the nations in which a firm's value stock has been developed and exploited and the nation that the firm wants to enter, and (2) the *specificity* of the product the firm wants to offer. Throughout this chapter we will use the word *home* to refer to the country in which a firm's value stock presently resides. So home for a Dutch firm could be the United States or Nigeria if it has value chain activities there that allow it to design, manufacture, and market products for the local market. *Foreign* country means any country outside of home.

Economic Differences

The importance of the economic differences that can exist between two countries can be seen by looking at income distribution. In Germany, where the Mercedes

SLK was developed and sold, the income per capita in 1993 was $20,980, whereas that in China was about $400.[1] So although China has over a billion people (more than ten times the population of Germany), not many of them can afford the SLK. In fact, at $35,000 in 1995, the SLK cost more than the yearly household income for more than 90 percent of the families in many emerging economies. The difference between incomes and the relative price of a product is only one economic factor. The other is the spending habits of the population. For example, in China families may prefer to invest in apartments, small businesses, and children's education rather than buying cars.[2]

Product Specificity

By product specificity we mean the extent to which the use of a product depends on local sociotechnical conditions. This is a function of the type of applications to which the product can be put, its interrelatedness to other products, the local culture, and government regulation. Cars, for example, would sell better in a large country with a good highway system, space to park cars, good credit systems, and availability of gasoline, than in one without. Such complementary conditions for selling automobiles can be taken for granted in the United States, but not in Nigeria. In some countries, air pollution standards limit the level of pollutants that a car can emit.

Baking foods requires baking ovens, which many households in many countries may not have. For example, General Foods found out the hard way that only 3 percent of the homes in Japan, where it was trying to sell a cake mix, had ovens.[3] Coca Cola had to withdraw its two-liter bottle from Spain because it found out that most homes in Spain did not have refrigerators with large enough compartments to hold the bottles.[4] Foods that require refrigeration may not do well in countries like Nigeria, where very few people have refrigerators. In the local culture there may be taboos associated with certain products. Local culture can also make some features in local products unnecessary. For example, S.C. Johnson's wax floor polish initially failed in Japan because it made the floors too slippery in a country where most people do not wear shoes in their homes.[5]

ENTRY STRATEGIES

Given product specificity and economic differences between a firm's home country, where it now operates, and the emerging economy, the question is, how can the firm use its value stock to innovate for the foreign market? As depicted in Figure 14.2, the higher the product specificity and the larger the economic differences between the home and foreign countries, the later in its product life cycle the firm may want to reach, and the deeper into its value stock a firm may want to dig for products and knowledge in order to enter the foreign country.

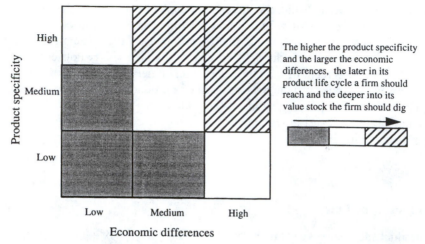

FIGURE 14.2. How deep into the value stock should a firm reach?

Reach for Later Stage of Product Life Cycle

Vernon's international product life cycle theory best describes how some firms can exploit their innovations internationally.[6] The theory argues that the starting point for innovating for other countries is innovating at *home*. This home is often an advanced country, where there is greater need for the innovation, whose citizens have the incomes to buy the products, and firms have the know-how to innovate. In the early stages of the cycle, all of the innovator's operations are at home to foster vital communications between functions such as R&D and manufacturing, as well as with suppliers and customers. Some demand at this early stage may also come from other advanced countries. This demand is filled via exports from the innovator's home.

In the mature stage, where more standardization has taken place, demand in other advanced countries picks up and may constitute an important portion of the firm's revenue streams. The firm sets up manufacturing facilities in these countries to satisfy local needs, and possibly to export to other countries. Competitors are now also interested in entering those markets.

In the final stage the product is highly standardized and competition is fierce, focusing on low cost. With its lower cost, the product can now be afforded by customers in emerging economies. To meet these needs in emerging economies and to afford the low cost dictated by the stage, the firm moves its production to the emerging economies to take advantage of low wages. The product is now produced in these emerging economies and shipped to the advanced countries.

According to this international product life cycle theory, then, a firm that wants to innovate for an emerging economy innovates for its home country first. Later in the life cycle of the innovation, when the cost has dropped and the emerging economy can afford the product, the firm can export the products to this country. Much later it can move its production activities to emerging countries. This may work for products with little or no product specificity.

Reach Deeper into the Value Stock

A firm does not have to wait until the latter part of a product life cycle when costs have dropped, in order to exploit an innovation in an emerging economy. It can, depending on the product specificity and the economic differences between the home and foreign countries, use one of the layers of its value stock to enter the emerging market. It can, for example, use its capabilities to offer low-cost products that are custom designed for the overseas market. Figure 14.3 shows when each layer of the value stock might be used to enter foreign markets.[7]

If product specificity is low and economic differences between the emerging economy and a firm's home country are low, the firm can sell its product "as it is" to the emerging country. Thus the firm does not have to do much by way of innovating from a technological point of view. It may, as we will see later, still have to innovate from a marketing point of view. Personal computer software is a good example. For English-speaking countries its product specificity is low. Thus a U.S. company such as Microsoft can export its most recent word-processing software to the United Kingdom without major modifications.

If the economic differences between the two countries are medium or average, but product specificity is low, the firm can ship mature proven products. The rationale here is that the cost of these "earlier" products has dropped to a level that these less wealthy economies can afford. In the software example, Microsoft can ship earlier versions of its software (e.g., Word 2) to South Africa. South Africa can afford these earlier versions not only because they are cheaper, but because they do not require the larger memory space that the country's older computers may not

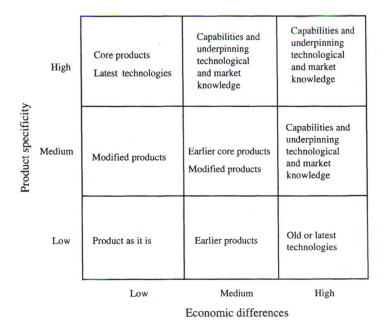

FIGURE 14.3. Entry strategies.

have. Where the economic differences are even larger, as is the case between the United States and Nigeria, earlier technologies may have to be offered to the country. For example, a pharmaceutical firm can use its rational drug synthesis skills to discover and develop inexpensive medicines for malaria for markets in the tropics.

If economic differences between the two countries are low, but there is reasonable product specificity, the firm can enter with modified versions of its most recent product. For example, Microsoft can sell the latest version of its word-processing software to France or Germany by offering French or German language versions. If product specificity is even higher, a firm may want to use core products to design end products for the new market or reach for its latest technologies to offer entirely new products.

Where both product specificity and economic differences are high, a firm may want to reach for its capabilities and underlying technological and market knowledge to develop new products for the market. For example, low-cost nutritious foods with long shelf lives in tropical climates would need the latest in capabilities in food technology and marketing.

It is important to remember that the different entry mechanisms shown in Figure 14.3 are not meant to be exhaustive. Rather, they illustrate the fact that the higher the product specificity and the larger the economic differences between home and foreign countries, the later in its product life cycle a firm should reach and the deeper into its value stock the firm should dig when entering the foreign market.

Options Approach

Because of the large uncertainty inherent in some emerging markets, a firm may decide to enter these markets in stages, as illustrated in Figure 14.4. In stage 1, for example, the firm exports its end products to the foreign country. This saves on the costs of establishing new design and manufacturing facilities that focus on the new country. Investing in exportation can be viewed as buying a call option that gives the firm the right to invest in the second stage—offering modified end products.[8] During that first stage the firm can find out more about the stability of the government of the country, how well the product is received, and what it is, if anything, that customers in this country would like to see changed in the next version of the product. After seeing how well the product has done, the firm can decide whether to take the next step or pull out—it can exercise its call option or let it expire.

If it decides to exercise the option to invest in stage 2, it can make the additional investment to modify end products for the market. In making country-

FIGURE 14.4. Options approach to entering emerging economies.

specific modifications to satisfy customers in a specific country, the firm is making irreversible investments and demonstrating its commitment to serve that country. These investments are now a call option that gives the firm the right to invest in stage 3. Depending on the stability of the government and other factors, the plants to modify these products can be at home or in the foreign country. As the market develops, the firm can see whether it is worth its while investing in the next step—stage 3.

In stage 3 the firm uses the core components to build new products. By this time the firm has learned more about the market, about building products in the foreign country, and it can establish plants there. It can import the core components from home and, using other local components, build end products to suit local tastes. If the products are well received and the future looks good, the firm can move on to stage 4—investment in the facilities and people to develop and manufacture products from scratch in the foreign country.

It is important to note that a firm does not have to start with end products. It may decide that enough of its uncertainties have been resolved for it to go straight on to using capabilities to enter without going through end products, modified end products, and core products.

Role of ITC

Information and communications technologies (ITC) can have an impact on product specificity and therefore an influence on what types of strategies firms use to exploit foreign markets. That is, how deep a firm goes into its value stock or how fast up Vernon's life cycle it wants to go in exploiting an innovation can be a function of the type of information technology it uses. ITC impacts product specificity in two ways. First, these technologies can help influence worldwide consumer tastes. This was Levitt's argument.[9] Worldwide television networks such as CNN, the World Wide Web, and networks of travelers and multinationals can be used to influence consumer tastes, preferences, and needs worldwide. By homogenizing customer wants, a firm is effectively reducing product specificity. This is equivalent to shifting *aa* and *bb* upward in Figure 14.5. Effectively, the area where end products were used is increased whereas that where capabilities and underpinning technological and market knowledge were used is decreased. Thus where the economic differences are low but product specificity is medium, customers whose tastes have been influenced can buy unmodified end products.

Second, it can be argued that with the proliferation of ITC and product technologies, firms can collect information on foreign consumer tastes more easily and develop products that reflect more than one region's tastes.

IMPLEMENTATION

Having chosen the strategies to use in entering the market, a firm must now carry out the decision to enter. This implementation can be seen as having two parts: (1)

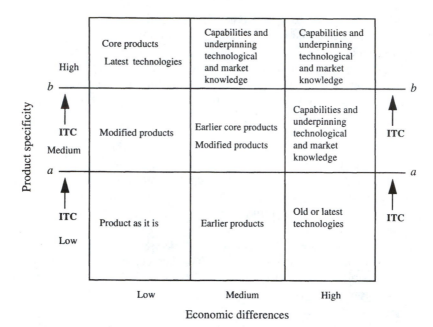

FIGURE 14.5. The impact of information and communications technologies (ITC) is to increase the area over which products can be sold as they are.

transferring the technology and (2) commercializing it. That is, given the technology, how does the firm get customers to buy the product at prices that render a profit?

Technology Transfer

The type of technology transfer that takes place depends on which level of its value stock the firm is using to enter the new market. If the firm is exporting "products as they are," then the knowledge that underpins these products is encoded in them. For example, if a German firm is exporting cars to China, knowledge of the car's engine, transmission, electronic fuel injection, and cooling system, and the linkages between them, is already embedded in the car. So is knowledge of the manufacturing processes that were used to build the car. In either case, the technology transfer is said to be product embodied since the physical product itself is being transferred.[10]

If a firm uses core products to enter the market, the results of the technology transfer are the same as those for exporting fully assembled products if all the firm does is sell the core components to the emerging economy. If it uses the core components to build products for the foreign market, the firm must also transfer the knowledge of how to link the components and manufacture the end product. In the automobile example, the German firm not only exports the drive trains for cars, it also transfers the manufacturing knowledge that is needed to produce the cars locally. The manufacturing knowledge is said to be process and people embodied. The process being transferred is in the form of equipment, flowcharts, blueprints, microcodes, software, routines, and the knowledge embedded in employees. It is more tacit than product-embodied knowledge. The transfer of such knowledge requires personal interaction between the transmitter and the receiver and relatively more absorptive and delivery capacities than the transfer of the more explicit product-embodied knowledge.

If the firm decides to transfer capabilities and the knowledge that underlies them, then the knowledge is a lot more people and process embodied than product embodied. It also has a much larger tacit component to it than the other forms of transfer. This suggests that most of the measures proposed in Chapter 4 for improving the effectiveness of technology transfer apply. For example, prior to the transfer, employees of the receiver nation can be sent to the transmitter country to study at universities, or to work at research centers or related industries to better prepare for receiving the technology. Training sessions in which members from both nations explore their cultures can help diffuse some of the tensions that occur. The transfer can take the form of joint ventures or acquisitions. During the transfer, continued workshops in the challenges of cultural differences can help keep reducing the impedance mismatch between the two entities.

Commercialization

Innovating in the Back End: Marketing and Distribution

In our discussion so far we have concentrated on the technological aspects of offering a product to a country with a certain economic level. Transferring the product technology is only part of the story. The other is commercialization—all the other activities, such as marketing, distribution, and financing of purchases, that will get the invention to the customers.

In marketing to a foreign country, a firm may be tempted to do one of two things: (1) follow the same pricing, promotion, positioning, and distribution methods that local competitors have pursued; or (2) use the same pricing, promotion, positioning, and distribution methods that worked so well before in its home country. Should one do as the Romans do while in Rome? Terpstra offers two reasons why it may not be wise to do as the Romans do if you are out there to compete with them for market share.[11] First, trying to imitate them means they will always trounce you in the competition to be Roman since they are already very good at being Romans—they are much further up the learning curve. Second, Rome may already have a lot of Romans and probably does not need any more. Any Egyptian who tries to be a pseudo-Roman may not contribute that much to Rome. Being different in some way may be better. The Egyptian may have to be innovative. As we will see shortly, however, the Egyptian also has to be very careful not to assume that Romans are going to be very receptive to Egyptian ways of doing things.

Economic, cultural, competitive, and legal factors all make pricing, promotion, and distribution in a foreign country necessarily different from those at home (Table 14.1). The same differences in income levels between the two countries that

TABLE 14.1. Some barriers to standardized international marketing.

Obstacles to uniformity	Marketing ingredients		
	Price	Distribution	Promotion
Economic factors	Varied income levels	Different retail structures	Media availability
Cultural factors	Price negotiating habit	Shopping habits	Language, attitude differences
Competitive factors	Competitors' costs and prices	Competitors' monopoly of channels	Competitors' budgets, appeals
Legal factors	Price controls	Restrictions on distribution	Advertising and media restrictions

Source: Adapted from *International Dimensions of Marketing* by V. Terpstra. Copyright © 1988 PWS-Kent. By permission of South-Western College Publishing, a division of International Thompson Publishing Inc., Cincinnati, Ohio 45227.

necessitated different entry strategies also suggest different pricing strategies.[12] For example, in a relatively poor country, bundling of products may not be as easy since personal incomes may only permit buying stand-alone products. While providing a one-stop shop approach may have been a viable approach at home, in an emerging economy it may not be. In some cultures all prices are negotiable. While price controls are legal in some countries, they may not be in others. For example, while the prices of medicines in the United States are determined by their manufacturers, in many countries prices are set or controlled by the government.

Cultural and language differences can turn innocent translations from one language or culture to another into not so flattering advertisements. David Ricks offers some interesting examples of how big businesses blundered in marketing their products in other countries.[13] In marketing its new automobile to Germany, Britain's Rolls Royce decided to use the name "Silver Mist." As appealing as the name was in English, when translated to German "mist" becomes "dung" or "garbage." America's Sun Beam also translated its mist-producing hair curling iron "Mist-Stick" into German. Not that many German's were interested in the "dung" or "manure" wand. Then there is American Motors Corporation's car called the "Matador." While in the United States it evokes images of virility and strength, in Puerto Rico it means "killer." Media availability also differs greatly from one nation to the other. While almost everyone in the United States has access to television, some people in emerging economies have never seen a television set, let alone own one. And even when media are available, there may be restrictions on what can be advertised and what cannot.

Distribution channels can also vary greatly from one country to another. While in the United States soap from Procter & Gamble can go from the manufacturer's plant straight to a retailer like Wal-Mart, in Japan the system is different. The manufacturer must sell to a general wholesaler, who sells to a product wholesaler, who sells to a product-specialty wholesaler, who sells to a regional wholesaler, who sells to a local wholesaler, who sells to retailers.[14] In some countries distribution channels are monopolized by powerful firms or families. In the United States, some stores are open 24 hours a day, seven days a week. In many countries all stores are closed at 8:00 P.M. on weekdays, half the day on Saturdays and all day Sunday.

All these differences suggest that a firm's competitive advantage in entering a foreign market can come from innovations in pricing, promotion, and building distribution networks.

Establishing Co-opetitors

Transfer of the technology, pricing, promotion, and distribution in and of themselves may not be enough to profit from the innovation. The system of suppliers, complementary innovators, customers, financial institutions, and related industries that supported the innovation at home, or something similar to it, must be in place in the developing country if the innovation is going to succeed in the foreign country (Figure 14.6). Hurdles similar to those that have to be overcome to transfer the technology may also have to be overcome to build this system of co-opetitors. At the supplier level, a firm must ask itself if there is a network of suppliers with the right capabilities. For example, a German car maker that opens an automobile plant in China must also worry about having suppliers nearby with whom it can maintain the close relations that are important to on-time delivery and supplier-sourced innovations. In some countries, the firm may have to integrate vertically to produce the components it needs.

The firm must also worry about whether there are complementary products or services to match its innovation. While in the more advanced countries a consumer credit system can be taken for granted, in some emerging economies such a system might not exist. Local customs may frown on debt. This can hurt sales of high-priced innovations. In fact, *the* innovation that makes the difference may come from something as unrelated to the product as establishing a consumer credit system to help customers finance their purchase of the product.

A firm may also need the cooperation of competitors to establish the credibility of its innovation or lobby the government to build such complementary assets as good roads or stave off price controls.

OTHER FACTORS

There are other factors that can greatly influence a firm's ability to innovate in an emerging economy. Kotler suggests looking out for several others factors when entering foreign markets.[15]

Firms operating in countries with unstable governments face additional risks of expropriation, nationalization, and limitations to how much of their profits they can repatriate back home. Some country's currencies fluctuate or depreciate in

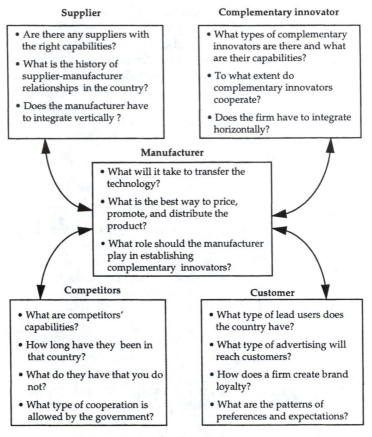

Supplier
- Are there any suppliers with the right capabilities?
- What is the history of supplier-manufacturer relationships in the country?
- Does the manufacturer have to integrate vertically?

Complementary innovator
- What types of complementary innovators are there and what are their capabilities?
- To what extent do complementary innovators cooperate?
- Does the firm have to integrate horizontally?

Manufacturer
- What will it take to transfer the technology?
- What is the best way to price, promote, and distribute the product?
- What role should the manufacturer play in establishing complementary innovators?

Competitors
- What are competitors' capabilities?
- How long have they been in that country?
- What do they have that you do not?
- What type of cooperation is allowed by the government?

Customer
- What type of lead users does the country have?
- What type of advertising will reach customers?
- How does a firm create brand loyalty?
- What are the patterns of preferences and expectations?

FIGURE 14.6. Success also means having the right systems of co-opetitors.

value too often, making it difficult for firms operating in them to repatriate their profits in hard currency.

Some governments place many regulations on foreign firms that can severely constrain the strategic decisions that a firm needs to make in order to profit from an innovation in those countries. They can, for example, interfere in technology transfer issues, dictate what share of joint ventures local partners must have and how many nationals must be hired, and put limits on profit repatriation.

As we will see in Chapter 15, governments often use tariffs, quotas, and subsidies to protect domestic industries. They can also introduce bureaucratic bottlenecks to slow down import approval and inspection or clearance of arriving goods, as France did with Japanese video cassettes in the 1980s.[16] In some countries bribery is part of doing business. This puts firms from a country such as the United States at a disadvantage since the U.S. Foreign Corrupt Practices Act of 1977 prohibits U.S. firms from practicing bribery while their competitors' governments have no such law.

In locating its innovation activities in a foreign country a firm is further exposing its intellectual property to pillage. Some employees from foreign countries may join a firm just to learn enough to leave and start competing firms. If copyright and patent protection is not tight in these countries, they may be profit sinks rather than sources of profits.

PRACTICE CASE: CHINA FAMILY CAR

In 1994 the Chinese government invited 20 American, European, South Korean, and Japanese automobile makers to submit proposals to develop and build in China a low-cost ($5000–6000) fuel-efficient family car.[17] The car would be designed specifically for the Chinese market and use 1990s technology, emphasizing modern safety and pollution control standards. The decision as to who would build the family car would be made by 1996 and production would start by 1999.

The Chinese Market for Family Cars

The potential of the Chinese car market was seen as being huge (Table 14.2). First, the country's economic growth rate was very high. Second, the car market was far from being saturated; there was about one car for every 640 people, compared to Germany's one car for every two people. More than 70 percent of the vehicles sold were trucks or vans. More than 90 percent of the cars sold were for government or business use.

In China there were 914 kilometers of roads per million people, compared to 25,326 kilometers per million in the United States and 9,096 in Japan. It was estimated that by the year 2010, 80 million Chinese families would buy their first car.

Potential Competitors

Twenty firms presented their entries to the China Family Car competition in the China Family Car Forum held in Beijing in November 1994. *Daihatsu* offered its three-cylinder, 0.993-liter Charade, which was already in production in China and very well received as a passenger car. The car had 70 percent local content. Daihatsu would have the capacity in China to produce 300,000 of the Charade by the year 2000. It had been in China since 1984, when it signed an agreement to start

TABLE 14.2. 1994 automobile forecast in China.

	1990	1991	1992	1994*	1996*	1998*	2000*
Growth in registrations (%)	21.2	98.7	2.8	8.6	19.8	15.9	11.1
Cars in use ('000)	1150	1225	1500	1850	2500	3400	4450
Growth of cars in use (%)	8.5	6.5	22.4	10.4	17.6	15.3	12.7
Cars in use per 100 of population	0.10	0.11	0.13	0.15	0.20	0.27	0.34
Production ('000)	38	67	47	315	575	825	1100

*Forecasts.

Source: Data from *Financial Times*, November 23, 1994.

producing its Charades and minivans in Tianjin. It was expected to produce 60,000 Charades and 100,000 minivans in 1994.

Ford was offering its Fiesta line, which had been developed in Europe for European markets. *General Motors* offered its 1.1–1.4-liter Opel Corsa line of cars, which had been developed and built by Adam Opel AG, its German subsidiary. Because of the car's fuel efficiency and low price, it was doing very well in Brazil and Mexico and other Latin American countries. *Mercedes-Benz,* not known for inexpensive cars, offered the FCC (Family Car China). The four-door FCC was designed specifically for China and looked like a "squished" minivan. The car was based on its A-Class line. A three-cylinder, 1.3-liter version with antilock brakes built from local parts could cost as little as $10,000. *Mitsubishi Motors* offered a small hatchback minivan that doubles as a cargo vehicle. The firm called the car the X-concept car derived from its Chariot/Space Wagon small multipurpose vehicle. *Nissan* offered the Micra.

Peugeot-Citroen SA offered the Fukang, derived from the firm's Citroen ZX. The car, already being assembled from kits in China, would go into full-scale production in China in 1995. A rather unlikely candidate for making an inexpensive family car was *Porsche AG,* the carmaker known for its speedy expensive sporty cars. Working with Chinese engineers, it developed a prototype from scratch. Dubbed the CC88, the 50-horsepower 1.1-liter five-seater reached 60 miles per hour in 22 seconds. *Suzuki* had the Alto, already being produced in China. *Toyota Motor Corp.* offered its large Crown Corona model for business executives, promising to offer the very popular Corolla later. *Volkswagen* already had the Chinese market leader in its full-size sedan, called the Santana. It was however used largely for company cars and taxis. Volkswagen had been in China since 1984, when it entered a joint venture, Shanghai Volks Wagon, with China to produce passenger sedans. In 1994 the venture was expected to produce more than 100,000 cars. It also had another venture established in 1991 with First Auto Works of China, with Volkswagen owning 40 percent of the venture. Volkswagen estimated that by the year 2000 it would have the capacity, from these two ventures, to produce 660,000 cars and 830,000 engines. Local content at the Shanghai factory exceeded 80 percent.

What Next?

At the end of the conference, each car company was wondering who the lucky winners to build the China Family Car would be. Many could not avoid asking themselves if they should have entered China as early as Volkswagen did or if they should have designed a car from scratch as Porsche and Mercedes did.

SUMMARY

Each firm has a value stock—the stock of end products, modified end products, core products, and capabilities—that it can use to enter an emerging market. There are three different strategies that a firm can pursue in using this value stock to exploit an emerging market. In the first, the firm introduces its products at home first, and as the product matures and the price falls, it can introduce it to other nations that now have the absorptive capacity to learn to build the product. In the second strategy, a firm uses one of the stages of its value stock to enter the market. Which of these stages it uses depends on the specificity of the product that it wants to offer, and on the economic differences between the country in which the firm's value stock presently resides (home) and the foreign country it wants to enter. (Product specificity is the extent to which the use of a product depends on local sociotechnical conditions.) The higher the product specificity and the larger the economic differences, the later in its product life cycle a firm may want to reach and the deeper into its value stock it may want to dig.

In the third strategy, the firm enters in a sequence of stages. Investing in the first stage, is like buying a call option. At the end of that stage when some of the uncertainties associated with innovating in the foreign country have been resolved, the firm can decide to invest in the next stage (exercise its option), or not (let the option expire). The use of information and communications technologies can alter effective strategies.

Implementation of these strategies is in two stages: technology transfer and commercialization. Effectiveness of the transfer depends on which stage of the value stock is being transferred and the measures taken to overcome the factors (see Chapter 4) that handicap effective technology transfer. Commercialization also has economic, cultural, competitive, and legal factors to contend with.

KEY TERMS

Core product
Emerging economy
End product
Options approach to international
  technology transfer

Pricing, promotion, and positioning
Product specificity
Value stock

QUESTIONS AND EXERCISES

1. Pick an industry other than automobiles. Develop a value stock for it for a firm in a country of your choice.

2. How important are co-opetitors in exploiting innovation in a developing country? How does this vary from industry to industry?

NOTES

1. *China Statistical Year Book.* 1995.
2. "The long drive into the middle kingdom." *The Economist,* June 8, 1996.

3. Kotler, P. *Marketing Management.* Englewood Cliffs, NJ: Prentice Hall, 1994, p. 412.

4. Kotler, P. *Marketing Management* (1994, p. 412).

5. Kotler, P. *Marketing Management* (1994, p. 412).

6. Vernon, R. "International investment and international trade in the product life cycle." *Quarterly Journal of Economics,* 190–207, May 1966.

7. Keagan, W. J. *Multinational Marketing Management,* 4th ed. Englewood Cliffs, NJ: Prentice Hall, 1989, pp. 378–81.

8. Chapter 11 provides more details on using options theory to explore investments.

9. Levitt, T. "The globalization of markets." *Harvard Business Review,* May–June 1983.

10. Keda, B. L., and R. S. Bhagat. "Cultural constraints on transfer of technology across nations: Implications for research in international and comparative management." *Academy of Management Review,* **13**(4):559–71, 1988. Hall, G., and R. Johnson. "Transfer of the United States aerospace technology to Japan." In *The Technology Factor in International Trade,* R. Vernon (Ed.). New York: Columbia University Press, 1970, pp. 305–58.

11. Terpstra, V. *International Dimensions of Marketing.* Boston: PWS-Kent Publishing, 1988.

12. For detailed treatment of pricing strategies, see Kotler, P. *Marketing Management* (1994). Terpstra, V. *International Dimensions of Marketing* (1988).

13. Ricks, D. A. *Big Business Blunders.* Homewood, IL: Dow Jones–Irwin, 1983.

14. Hartley, W. D. "How not to do it: The cumbersome Japanese distribution system stumps US concerns." *Wall Street Journal,* March 2, 1972. See also Kotler, P. *Marketing Management* (1944, p. 425).

15. Kotler, P. *Marketing Management* (1944, p. 410).

16. "Import or die." *The Economist,* February 19, 1983.

17. This case is based on the following: Mitchener, B. "German automakers learn to adopt; they are starting to tailor new models to Asian tastes." *International Herald Tribune,* February 20, 1995. Cheng, A. T. "Cruise control." *Asia, Inc.* November, 1995. Walker, A., and K. Done. "Chinese roads paved with gold: A look at a market that western carmakers are eager to enter, in spite of the risks." *Financial Times,* November 23, 1994. "The long drive into the Middle Kingdom." *The Economist* 63–64, June 8, 1996. "Coming together." *The Economist* 64–65, June 8, 1996. Kahn, J. "Creating a wonder for China; family car." *Wall Street Journal,* November 21, 1994.

15

ROLE OF NATIONAL
GOVERNMENTS IN INNOVATION

Throughout this book we have hinted on the role that national governments play in providing an environment that is conducive to innovation. In this chapter we outline that role in more detail. We start by exploring some of the reasons why governments have a role to play in innovation. We then outline some government policies that impact innovation. Next, we explore how firms can benefit from these policies. Finally, we present the case of the global pharmaceutical industry highlighting both the intended and the unintended outcomes of public policy on innovation in that industry. Throughout the chapter, the point is not to judge whether government policies are good or bad for innovation and how government ought to go about its job as regulator. Rather, the goal of this chapter is to suggest how a firm can best take advantage of the opportunities and threats in innovation that government policies present.

WHY A GOVERNMENT ROLE

There are several reasons why a national government may want to play a role in the process of innovation: (1) the "public" nature of the knowledge that underpins innovation, (2) the uncertainty that often plagues the process of innovation, (3) the need for certain kinds of complementary assets, (4) the nature of certain technologies, and (5) plain politics.

"Public" Nature of Knowledge

Scientific knowledge has certain "public" properties that make it difficult to appropriate the rent from it.[1] First, suppose a firm wants to buy a new idea. That buyer cannot determine the value of the idea until it knows what the idea is. But once it knows the idea, the potential buyer may no longer have an incentive to pay for it, especially if he is opportunistic. He already has the idea. Such a situation may discourage potential suppliers of knowledge from investing in its generation. Second, knowledge has a nonrivalrous aspect to it. If A gives B some knowledge, it does not reduce the amount of knowledge that A has. What is more, B, the buyer, will always have the knowledge. That is, unlike products or services that get used up and the producer can sell more of them, knowledge remains in circulation no matter how many people consume it. This may also discourage potential suppliers from investing in knowledge generation. Third, if a seller of knowledge found a buyer, it may leak during the process of transfer. Or once the buyer starts making money from it, the idea can be quickly copied. In either case, appropriability of the knowledge is reduced. This leakage is a function of how explicit or tacit the knowledge is. If it is tacit and therefore requires learning by interacting over time with the generator of the knowledge, the risk of leakage is reduced. Leakage of knowledge, also called spillovers, may not always be bad. It allows firms not to have to invest to duplicate each others' past efforts.

There are several things that could be done to alleviate these problems.[2] The first is for the government to grant and protect intellectual property rights to producers of knowledge. Second, the government can engage directly in idea generation itself and give the output freely to its firms and entrepreneurs. Third, it can provide subsidies for firms and individuals alike to encourage private production of knowledge. We will discuss all three later in this chapter.

Uncertainty

As we saw in Chapter 6, the process of innovation is often fraught with both technological and market uncertainty. Will the R&D result in any discoveries or inventions? If it does, can the discoveries be commercialized? What is the potential of the innovations? When will the profits start flowing in to satisfy investors and the chief financial officer? Unfortunately, breakthroughs like the DNA or the Web are difficult to anticipate, and it would be difficult to convince many firms to invest—without some help from the government—in the hope of maybe making such a discovery some day. Moreover, when such discoveries are made, it sometimes takes too long for the benefits to materialize. For example, the structure of the DNA was discovered in 1953, and almost half a century later the full benefits of biotechnology are not quite here yet. Research on the Internet, which would later give us the Web, started in the 1960s, and no one anticipated the type of Web we have today.

If the uncertainties inherent in an innovation are very large, firms may not be willing to invest in it. One solution is to shift the risk of failure to insurers. But this also has some problems. The potential innovator has more information about the innovation than the insurer. Opportunistic innovators may decide not to give the insurer all the information that it needs to write a good policy. And even if the potential innovator had good intentions of doing so, he may not be able to articulate all of the information, given that he is only boundedly rational. The insurer may not be able to absorb and process all of the information from the innovator either. This information asymmetry leads to two potential problems: *adverse selection* and *moral hazard.* Only firms that are not good at innovation may decide to obtain insurance while good firms stay away. Since the insurer does not have all the information about the firms and the innovation, it cannot tell bums from the innovators. This is the adverse selection problem that we saw in Chapter 11. It is also possible that the insurer succeeds in selecting the right innovators. But once the contract has been signed, the innovators may become complacent and not work as hard as they would if they were not insured. Given the uncertainty associated with the innovation, it is difficult to tell if the innovator is shirking. This problem of firms behaving opportunistically once they have signed a contract is the moral hazard problem.

If firms are afraid of investing in highly uncertain innovations and insurance companies do not want to take some of the risk, these innovations may not be undertaken. There are several things the government can do to help. First, it can undertake some of the risky R&D itself. Second, the government can help firms cooperate in R&D ventures. Third, it can subsidize R&D for such high-risk ventures to attract more innovators. Fourth, it can extend the patent life of innovations from such ventures to increase the length of time over which firms can recoup their R&D investments.

"Public" Complementary Assets

As we saw in Chapter 2, it takes more than R&D to innovate. It takes complementary assets, some of which are more likely to be undertaken only by government, given their public nature. These include roads, electricity, gas, water, and communication systems. In some cases these require so-called natural monopolies because the minimum efficient scale for producing them is equal to or larger than the whole market. Minimum efficient scale is the smallest output that minimizes unit costs.[3] Having many firms compete in such a market may not be prudent. The government can have one firm offer such services under its regulation or it can offer the services itself.

Network Externalities

A technology exhibits network externalities if the more people that use it, the more valuable it is to them.[4] One disadvantage of such technologies is that if a new superior one comes along but has a smaller network, users may prefer to stay with the old one for fear of being the only ones to switch to the new technology and losing their network benefits. They may be effectively stuck with an older technology. If this continues so long that a nation starts to lose its competitive edge because of the inferior technology, a government might want to intervene.

There is also the more traditional type of network externality. This is the cost or benefit imposed by the actions of one firm on others.[5] It is called a negative externality if a cost, and a positive externality if a benefit. A classic example is that of a power plant that, in burning coal to produce electricity, also produces sulfur dioxide, which in turn rises into the air and eventually falls as acid rain. The acid rain is a negative externality since, in calculating the cost of the electricity that it sells, the electric company does not factor in the cost of the acid rain to the people on whose properties or bodies the acid rain falls. By regulating the amount of sulfur that coal can have, a government can reduce the amount of this negative externality. Pollution from cars is also a negative externality.

Politics

Of course, many of the innovation-related regulations can be sociopolitically motivated. Safety regulation is an example.

GOVERNMENT ACTIONS

As we have just seen, government intervention may be needed at certain stages of the innovation process. In general, this intervention can be in the form of financing R&D, acting as a lead user, providing complementary assets, regulating the firm's activities, educating the workforce, maintaining macroeconomic fundamentals, and maintaining political stability to attract investment in innovation (Figure 15.1).

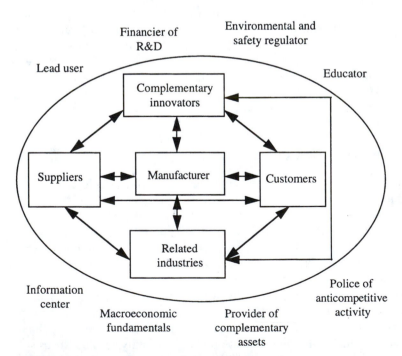

FIGURE 15.1. Government as environment for innovation.

Financing R&D

One solution to the public good aspect of invention, as we saw earlier, is to have the government perform the research. That is, since the difficulty to appropriate invention can prevent firms from investing in R&D, the government can perform the R&D and make it available to all the firms. Government sponsors two kinds of R&D: basic research and applied research. The research is conducted largely in government laboratories, universities, within firms, or at consortia made up of some combination of the three. In 1995, for example, the U.S. budget for R&D was $71.4 billion dollars, to be spent on defense, health, space, general science, energy, transportation, energy, environment, and agriculture.[6] While some of these funds are spent on production, advanced testing, and incremental innovations on weapons and space systems at the Department of Defense, the Department of Energy, and NASA, many of them go to industry research laboratories, federal intramural laboratories, universities, nonprofit laboratories, and federally funded research and development centers (FFRDCs) for the generation of new scientific and technological knowledge. Government financing of R&D is not always direct. Some firms receive indirect financing through tax breaks, government subsidies, loan guarantees, export credits, or artificial price ceilings that ensure profits. For example, Boeing not only paid no taxes between 1970 and 1984, but also received a $285 million tax refund during that period.[7] Quotas, tariffs, and subsidies, as we will see shortly, are also sources of indirect financing.

Government-sponsored R&D has been instrumental to the creation of whole new industries and many innovations within existing industries. The Internet and the Web, both tenets of the information superhighway that promises to give birth to thousands of different firms all over the world, both grew out of government-sponsored research. The Internet originated in the U.S. Defense Department's Advance Research Projects Agency (DARPA), which sponsored research on computer networks. Berners-Lee invented the Web while working at CERN, a government-sponsored European particle-physics laboratory in Geneva. The discovery of the double-helix structure of genes, or DNA, that underpins today's biotechnology industry also grew out of government-sponsored research conducted at universities. UNIX, computers, semiconductors, RISC technology, jet engines, and jet planes have all benefited from government financing. DARPA alone is credited with funding more than half of the computer field's key innovations.[8]

Financing R&D has other benefits besides solving the problems of the "public" properties of knowledge. First, in financing R&D, the government is also educating its workforce with the knowledge and skills that firms need to innovate. Once the Web took off, for example, it was easier to find employees with computer science and networking skills, partly because of the many students trained at many universities with DARPA funds. Second, spending by the governments on R&D also spurs private firms to invest in related invention or commercialization activities. Third, by focusing attention on specific areas, government R&D projects can enjoy the economies of scale that come with large R&D projects. Finally, the government can considerably reduce the cost for firms to enter certain markets. By 1996, when Airbus Industrie, the German, French, British, and Spanish consortium, won a third of the market share for airplanes, it had been subsidized with $20 billion.[9] The Boeing 747, the world's commercially most successful plane, was initially designed as a military cargo aircraft and most of that tab picked up by the U.S. Department of Defense.

Although government intentions may be good, the results of their actions are not always positive. Stories of failed projects also abound, and questions about just how much R&D the government should undertake haunt policy makers.

Lead User

As we pointed out in Chapter 2, early in the life of an innovation, there is a lot of technological and market uncertainty. An innovator may not be quite sure about what goes into the product and what customers want. Many customers may not even know what they want in the product either. Thus interaction between innovator and customers is critical to allow the customer to know what the possibilities are and help the innovator flesh out what the customer needs. Von Hippel suggested that lead users can be critical to the process of innovation.[10] These are users whose needs are similar to those of other customers, except that they have these needs months or years before the bulk of the marketplace does, and they stand to benefit significantly by fulfilling these needs earlier than the rest of the customers.

In some critical areas, governments have needed certain innovations earlier than the public and have been willing to pay the high prices that innovations in the early stages command. What is more is that governments, as lead users, have been willing to work closely with firms to shepherd inventions into innovations. The U.S. Department of Defense saw many benefits in the transistor replacing the bulky vacuum tube. Because transistors were much smaller and consumed less power than vacuum tubes, electronic systems built from them would not only be lighter and provide more functionality, they would also require smaller power supplies, further reducing the weight of the whole system. This made the transistor and, subsequently, integrated circuits particularly attractive to the Defense Department and NASA. The U.S. government's willingness to award contracts to both incumbents and new entrants, and to work with them, helped the U.S. semiconductor industry into its early industry lead.[11] The U.S. role as lead user has not been isolated to semiconductors. Jet engines, airplanes, and computers have all benefited from this shepherding. This role is not limited to the United States. Rothwell and Zegveld found that purchases by European governments play a significant role in innovation.[12]

Provider of Public Complementary Assets

An excellent highway system, for example, can encourage innovation in the automobile industry. An information superhighway facilitates communications not only between different functional units of a firm, but also between different units throughout the world and between firms and customers. Chip design can now take place twenty-four hours a day, with people in Israel, Japan, and the Silicon Valley taking turns in designing the same product. Sometimes the complementary asset is a by-product of some other government project. For example, one of Caterpillar's strengths in the 1970s was its strong worldwide service and dealership network. One reason for this network was the fact that Caterpillar's bulldozers had been the Army's standard equipment during World War II. When the Army withdrew, it left behind many of Caterpillar's machines for local use, and local mechanics learned how to service these machines—a valuable asset in the earth-moving equipment industry.[13]

Regulator

The other solution to the problem that firms have in appropriating rents from their inventions is to accord the inventor some monopoly privileges over its invention. In the United States the need for such a privilege is written in the constitution: Congress grants "for limited times to authors and inventors the exclusive rights to their respective writings and discoveries" so as "to promote the progress of science and useful arts" (Article 1, Section 8). This privilege is accorded via intellectual property protection such as patents and copyrights. Thus, as argued by Schumpeter, anticipation of the market power that can be acquired via patents is a strong incentive for firms to invest in invention. The effectiveness of the protection granted by patents varies from industry to industry. It is considered weak in semiconductors, as imitators can invent "around" patents. Another reason for the low appropriability is that patents from many different owners are so interrelated that it is difficult for a firm to enforce its patents without effectively violating another firm's own patents. In pharmaceuticals, patents have better protection, although by studying a patent, a firm can narrow the range of chemical compounds that it has to search in order to come up with a similar drug.

Giving a firm monopoly privileges via patenting raises the prospect that a firm can engage in so-called preemptive patenting, whereby it patents its inventions but does not commercialize them. It thus effectively prevents other firms from offering products that utilize those patents. If such patents are potentially radical in the economic sense, in that they can render the firm's existing products noncompetitive, preemptive patenting allows a firm to keep collecting monopoly rents while retarding the rate of innovation. Thus although ex post monopoly privileges are supposed to promote innovation, they can also retard it if not well managed.

Ironically, another regulatory job of government is to prevent monopolies that can result in underinnovation. In mergers, for example, antitrust legislation in the United States seeks to prevent any mergers that can unduly increase the market power of one organization. Such market power can result in a firm keeping prices artificially high and a lack of incentive for the firm to innovate. Other activities that can result in keeping prices artificially high, such as collusion and predatory pricing, are also illegal in some countries. In the United States, for example, the Sherman Act makes illegal any agreements among competitors that allow them to keep their prices artificially at some level by fixing the prices or coordinating their outputs. Tacit collusion is also illegal. In it, rather than having explicit formal agreements, firms can, for example, send signals as to what their actions are going to be, inviting competitors to follow suit. In predatory pricing a firm deliberately takes actions that are not profitable, such as lowering its prices, just so that it can drive out competitors. Then, after competitors have been driven out of the market, it raises its prices to start making profits. This is difficult to prove, especially early in the life of an innovation, because innovators can claim that they are lowering their prices to attain the kinds of volumes that can take them down the learning curve (up the S curve) rapidly, resulting in such lower cost that they can afford to offer the lower prices. This was Japan's plight when accused of dumping—selling products overseas at below domestic prices—chips in the United States.

Another regulatory area that can affect innovation is pricing by governments. This can come in the form of price floors, price ceilings, tariffs, quotas, and subsidies. A price floor is the price below which a firm may not set its price. A government may resort to price floors, for example, when it wants to prevent dumping by foreign firms. The United States and Japan agreed on DRAM floor prices in 1986 as part of the settlement for antidumping charges against Japanese semiconductor makers. By keeping prices artificially high, governments can assure local firms of higher profits while the floors last. A price ceiling stipulates the price over which a firm may not set its price. Such price ceilings may be prompted by the need for governments to keep certain costs low. For example, the prices of pharmaceutical medicines are set by the government in certain countries. The effect can be to lower profits for sellers and therefore innovation, as we see later in the practice case at the end of the chapter. In tariffs a government imposes a fee on imports, thereby increasing the prices of imports. This allows local firms to raise their prices and earn higher profits. Instead of tariffs, a government may decide to set the quantity of the good that can be imported from some country at some level or quota. The level is chosen to be small enough so that the total quantity sold locally is low enough for prices to rise. The effect on local prices and on the profits of local firms is similar to that of tariffs. The difference is that in quotas, the foreign firm also makes more profits, while the big loser is the government since it collects nothing. Finally, to keep profits for local firms high, government can also use subsidies. For each quantity of the product sold, the government pays the firm a certain amount of money, a subsidy.

The way financial markets are regulated can also have an impact on the level of innovation. For example, an initial public offering (IPO) can be a very good way for a firm to raise money. More importantly, as we saw in Chapters 5 and 11, anticipation of cashing in at an IPO is an incentive for venture capitalists to invest in new ventures and for entrepreneurs to pursue their ideas more faithfully. When and how firms can go public varies from country to country. In Japan, for example, firms must show several years of decent profits in order to be listed on the over-the-counter (OTC) market.[14] That can take as many as ten years, compared to five in the United States. Most investors would rather cash in in five years than in ten.

Then there is environmental and safety regulation to ensure the safety of citizens at work, at home, and in the products they use. In the pharmaceutical industry—which we will discuss at length later—before firms can market any new ethical drugs, they must prove to the government that the drugs are safe and cure the ailment that they are supposed to. Regulation can also introduce technological discontinuities. Los Angeles's decision to require that a certain percentage of cars sold there by the year 2000 must have zero emission can mean, for some manufacturers, a technological discontinuity from internal combustion engine automobiles to electric cars.

As quickly as governments can regulate, they can also deregulate. Such deregulations can change radically the nature of competition in an industry. Deregulation of the telecommunications industry in the United States, for example, is changing the way voice, data, and images are delivered.

Macroeconomic Fundamentals

Sound macroeconomic fundamentals can be just as critical for innovation. Economic policies that spawn expectations of low inflation, low interest rates, increased growth, and higher profits encourage firms to invest more in R&D and complementary assets such as plant and equipment that are critical to innovation. Expectations of such profits encourage venture capitalists to invest in entrepreneurial activity. Low expected interest rates make it easier for projects to make firm hurdle rates. Low rates and higher economic growth mean that there will be more customers to buy the products or more lead users willing to work with innovators. Innovative activity may be the engine of economic progress.[15] But it is also true that economic process can feed that engine.

Baby-Sitter and Godfather

As we saw earlier, quotas, subsidies, tariffs, and price floors can be used by governments to protect fledgling industries until they can compete well locally against foreign imports. They can also breed complacency. Governments can also help obtain access to foreign markets for local firms. The United States, France, and Great Britain all help local defense firms win foreign arms sales. Government can also play a critical role in opening up opportunities in foreign countries. Allowing U.S. carriers that fly from the United States to pick up passengers in Europe and fly to other countries, for example, may require special agreements between governments. Governments may need to intervene when the intellectual property protection of their firms is violated by firms from other countries. A government can also intervene when its firms' investments are expropriated in foreign countries.

Educator, Information Center, and Provider of Political Stability

As we suggested earlier, university laboratories, in performing R&D, are also training future innovators. In addition to running R&D laboratories, universities also teach. By providing guidelines, funding, and rewards for education, governments can help not only in formal education, but also in on-the-job training and retraining of displaced workers. Governments can also be the source of tremendous amounts of information. Firms going to some developing country may find out that their best source of information is their embassy in that country. Another role of government is to provide a stable political environment that assures investors that their investments will not be expropriated, that citizens will not riot and destroy the investments, and that it is safe to do business in that environment.

TAKING ADVANTAGE OF THE OPPORTUNITIES AND THREATS OFFERED BY GOVERNMENT

The fact that government can be idea generator, financier of R&D activity, shepherd, provider of complementary assets, lead user and customer, source of opportunities and threats, and partner in seeking global opportunities or protecting intellectual property can have profound implications for the formulation and implementation of innovation strategies. We examine some of these implications.

Idea Generation and Recognition of the Potential of Innovation

The question is, how can a firm exploit the knowledge generated with public funds? Specifically, how can a firm transfer this knowledge from the generator to its organization? First, the firm must perform its own R&D since it needs some absorptive capacity if it is going to be able to correctly search and capture ideas.[16] Second, physical interaction with the generators may be necessary. Although the results of scientific and technological discoveries can be published in journals, there are still many reasons why a firm would want to stay in close contact with researchers at universities and at government and other public laboratories. For one thing, as Allen showed, many engineers get their information from colleagues through informal interaction and not from journals.[17] On the other hand, by the time the results of the research are published in journals and presented at conferences it might be too late for industries, where first-mover advantages are important. Moreover, not all of the knowledge from the research—especially the tacit portions of the methodology—is presentable in papers.

Close contact with public research institutions has been achieved via several mechanisms. Some firms have located their facilities or research departments close to universities, whereas others have performed joint research. Others have sponsored applied research at universities to take advantage of the basic research being performed there.

Although the research conducted by a government is usually intended for the benefit of the firms in that country, it can also be the source of ideas and knowledge for other countries. In the 1970s and 1980s Japanese firms used several mechanisms to access U.S. scientific and technological knowledge.[18] They sent their employees as visiting scientists to U.S. university research laboratories, supported university research in return for access to new research results, hired U.S. personnel from U.S. firms, licensed technologies from U.S. start-ups, and sent their employees to study at top U.S. universities.[19] Firms can also locate branches in foreign countries to maintain a window on advances in knowledge in those countries.

Gatekeepers are particularly important in acting as transducers between the scientific laboratories and the firms transferring the technology, especially between different countries since the impedance mismatch can be a lot larger.

Protecting Profits

In carrying out all the generic strategies for protecting entrepreneural rent, a firm may need its government's help. In *blocking,* for example, a firm needs strong intellectual protection enforcement when such protections are violated. Texas Instruments sued Japanese companies for violating its semiconductor patents and won. This enabled it to collect royalties, which between 1987 and 1994 amounted to $1.9 billion compared to $1.4 billion in operating profits during that period. As detailed in Chapter 10, the microprocessor industry would be very different had U.S. courts, in the case of Intel versus NEC, not ruled that microcode is copyrightable in the United States. In *running,* a firm surrounded by government-sponsored laboratories is more likely to have ideas to run with than one that is not. Finally, in *teaming up,* a firm sometimes needs government approval or even support. In 1987, when U.S. semiconductor firms decided to team up to remedy their shortcomings in manufacturing, they turned to the U.S. government for both approval and financial support. Earlier, in 1984, U.S. antitrust law had been rewritten to allow firms to share know-how.[20] With $100 million from industry and another $100 million from the U.S. government, Sematech was started to help U.S. firms boost their semiconductor manufacturing capabilities.

PRACTICE CASE: THE CASE OF THE GLOBAL PHARMACEUTICAL INDUSTRY

Governments of different countries have, for sociopolitical and socioeconomic reasons, instituted policies that have had major impacts on the development of the global pharmaceutical industry (Figure 15.2).[21] These regulations have had both intended and unintended effects. For example, strict U.S. FDA regulations on safety and efficacy were intended to keep unsafe and ineffective drugs out of the U.S. market, and in this they have largely succeeded. However, they may also have had the unanticipated effect of making U.S. firms more competitive globally while keeping small firms out of the market.

This case explores the effects of public policy on the global pharmaceutical industry. In order to focus the discussion, we first discuss policies that affect the supply of new drugs and then turn to a discussion of policies that affect the demand for pharmaceuticals. Policies that affect supply include public investment in R&D, patent protection, and regulatory approval of the introduction of new drugs. Policies that affect demand include pricing regulation, payment methods, and government reimbursement. Of course since supply and demand are directly related, poli-

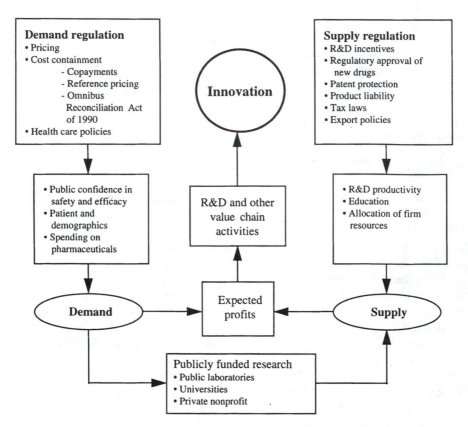

FIGURE 15.2. Public policy and innovation.

cies that affect demand will also have an indirect effect on supply, and vice versa. For example, efforts to control demand may reduce industry profits, which may in turn limit the supply of innovative drugs.

Policies Affecting Supply

Three policy instruments have had critical effects on the "supply side" of the pharmaceutical industry: public investment in R&D, patent policy, and the nature of the regulatory regime surrounding the introduction of new drugs.

R&D Incentives

Many governments fund basic research in the life sciences. A number of studies suggest that public funding of basic research has very significant implications for the productivity of the local industry. In a ten-nation study of government industrial policies and corporate pharmaceutical competitive advantage, for example, Thomas found that the ratio of a nation's R&D spending to corporate R&D spending was correlated significantly with the nation's innovativeness.[22]

His results are confirmed by the work of Ward and Dranove.[23] Using data on funding of the National Institutes of Health (NIH) from 1962 to 1988, medical journal articles, and Pharmaceutical Manufacturing Association (PMA) member spending from 1968 to 1988, Ward and Dranove showed that spending by U.S. pharmaceutical companies on applied R&D was directly correlated with medical journal articles, which in turn were correlated with NIH spending on basic research. For every 10 percent increase in basic research spending, the number of medical journal publications increased by 2.5 percent, and several years later, the amount spent by PMA members on applied research increased by 7.5 percent. They interpreted these results as evidence that basic research stimulates substantial increases in privately funded research.

Patents

Several studies have examined the effect of patent policy on the innovativeness of the local pharmaceutical industry. In a study of Japanese health policy as industrial policy, Reich suggests that the lack of adequate patent protection for chemical compounds may have retarded Japanese innovativeness in pharmaceuticals and delayed the development of globally competitive firms.[24] Before 1976 Japanese law did not allow for the patenting of chemical compounds; firms could only patent unique processes. Thus a Japanese company could develop a new process for a competitor's compound and obtain a patent to manufacture and sell it in Japan. Reich suggests that this substantially decreased the incentive to invest in research. Japanese patent law was changed in 1976 to provide for the protection of unique compounds. In 1988 Japan followed the example of the U.S. 1984 Patent Restoration Act and passed legislation allowing for the extension of the life of a patent depending on how long it took to process the firm's application for approval of the drug in question. To date there have been no studies of the impact of either piece of legislation.

Regulatory Approval of the Introduction of New Drugs

Several researchers have suggested that stringent regulatory requirements for the approval of the introduction of new drugs have positive effects on the innovativeness of the local pharmaceutical industry. In one study, for example, Thomas compared the industrial policies of ten nations and suggested that the stringent local pharmaceutical regulation in the United States made U.S. pharmaceutical firms better global competitors.[25] In a later study of the effects of pricing and safety regulations in the United Kingdom and France, Thomas found that pro-innovation pricing and stringent regulation in the United Kingdom made U.K. firms more globally competitive, whereas lenient safety regulations and low prices in France made French pharmaceutical firms less competitive globally.[26]

Before a drug can be marketed in the United Kingdom, he noted, it has to be formally tested for safety and efficacy through well-controlled clinical trials, which are difficult, costly, and time-consuming. In contrast, the French system was initially designed to restrict access of foreign firms to the French market, rather than to restrict ineffective and dangerous drugs. Decisions on access to the French market are made by employees of drug firms already selling products in the French market, rather than by the committee of independent experts who make the same decisions in the United Kingdom. Moreover, the French evaluate safety and quality using traditional methods of assessment by individual doctors in place of the British insistence on scientific demonstration of efficacy and safety. As a result, a firm that can launch a drug in Britain can easily launch it in France, but drugs that can be introduced to the French market cannot be easily introduced to the British. Thomas suggests that the United Kingdom's stringent local drug approval requirements may have forced out weaker firms, leaving stronger firms that are more innovative and globally competitive, whereas the more lenient French regulations have encouraged the existence of many small firms that are neither very innovative nor very competitive.

Reich's findings support Thomas's conclusions. He points out that prior to 1967, Japan did not require domestic trials for safety and efficacy for any foreign drugs listed in an accepted official pharmacopoeia. This meant that Japanese companies could easily license a foreign drug and get it quickly approved for sale in Japan. Reich suggests that this may have encouraged Japanese firms to license foreign drugs at the expense of the development of any significant innovative capability.

Both Reich and Thomas suggest that stringent local regulations shelter local firms. Thomas argues, for example, that the huge battery of tests and the specialized knowledge required to satisfy the requirements of the FDA constitute an entry barrier into the U.S. market, especially to foreign firms. He suggests that both foreign firms and several smaller U.S. firms have been forced to license their drugs to U.S. firms or to establish some form of partnership with a larger U.S. firm in order to gain access to the infrastructure that they have in place for clinical testing. Similarly, Reich points out that in Japan, after the 1967 change in the law to require efficacy and safety tests for foreign drugs, foreign companies were not allowed to apply on their own for the first step of drug approval *(shonin),* the demonstration of efficacy and the safety review. Clinical trials had to be conducted in Japan on native citizens. This law was changed in the mid-1980s under pressure from the United States in the process of trade negotiations.

Policies Affecting Demand

Many countries have instituted policies whose results have a direct effect on the demand for pharmaceutical products. Most of these have resulted from government efforts to provide health benefits for a larger proportion of the population, particularly the poor, and in general these policies have increased demand substantially.

However, some policies have been instituted to hold down escalating health care costs, and have thereby reduced demand.

Price Regulation

Pricing policies vary greatly from country to country, ranging from complete freedom in the United States and Denmark to freedom with some restrictions in the United Kingdom, Germany, The Netherlands, and Sweden to product-by-product control in Australia, Belgium/Luxemburg, France, Greece, Italy, Japan, Portugal, Spain, and Switzerland. In general the existing literature suggests that there is a strong link between pricing regulation and the innovativeness of the local industry. Countries that do not regulate pharmaceutical prices or that tie prices to research investment or global competitiveness appear to have much more innovative local industries than their counterparts.

For example, Thomas found that differences in pricing regulation between the United Kingdom and France were a key factor in shaping the innovativeness of the local pharmaceutical industry. In the United Kingdom pricing regulation has been through voluntary cooperation between the pharmaceutical industry and the Ministry of Health. Prices have been calculated as a rate of return on an agreed-upon level of investment, with the rate of return being set higher for export-oriented firms. Foreign firms that try to sell drugs in the United Kingdom without investing locally are penalized. Thomas suggests that this encourages competitive foreign firms to invest in the United Kingdom, which in turn makes the U.K. environment more competitive, and leads to the development of globally competitive local firms. In France, in contrast, prices are constrained to a markup over manufacturing costs. Thomas suggests that this policy encourages high manufacturing costs, while at the same time discouraging investment in leading-edge research. He concludes that the effects of those policies have been to concentrate innovative effort in the United Kingdom into a few firms that are globally competitive, whereas the French industry is highly fragmented and has introduced many minor, derivative products.

In related work, Redwood draws on two data sets to explore the relationship between the innovativeness of new drugs and the containment of health care costs.[27] The first data set is Barral's 1992 study of 775 new drugs that were first introduced between 1975 and 1989. Barral identified those new drugs that were "innovative and globalized" (available in seven of the markets covered by his study).[28] Redwood noted that the United States and the United Kingdom dominated the innovative and globalized category during the 15 years covered by the study, having introduced 45 and 17 percent of the innovative and globalized drugs, respectively, compared to their shares of total drug introductions of 27 and 5 percent. He further noted that Japan's share of innovative and globalized drugs was 5 percent, compared to a share of total introductions of 20 percent; and that France's and Italy's shares were 5 and 1 percent, respectively, compared to shares of total introductions of 12 and 9 percent.

The second data set Redwood draws on is his own study of 453 internationally accepted drugs introduced between 1970 and May 1992, where he defined "international acceptance" as introduction in at least four of the world's seven leading markets, or progression to the postclinical stage in at least six of the same seven markets. He divided these drugs into two groups: 265 "major global drugs" that were marketed or reached at least the postclinical stage (preregistration) in at least six of the seven markets; and 188 "other international drugs" with a presence in only four or five of these markets. He found that U.S. firms introduced 43 percent of the drugs sold globally, or a total of 114 drugs, and that they led the market in nearly every therapeutic category, while Japan was a distant second with 29 drugs, and the United Kingdom was third with 25.

Redwood attributes the U.S. lead in both studies to the "pricing freedom" that U.S. pharmaceutical companies enjoy and that acts as an incentive for innovation in therapeutic areas where the risks of pioneering failure are at their highest. He also argues that pricing regulation stifles pricing competition. He suggests that in countries such as France, Japan, and Italy, which practice stringent pricing regulation, "developing non-innovative new drugs for the local market with a 'contemporary' price tag becomes an attractive low-risk option." While these countries are three of the seven largest spenders on pharmaceutical R&D, they have a significantly below average record of finding drugs with global marketing and therapeutic potential. He concludes that "there is an indisputable link between pricing freedom and successful innovative research and development in the pharmaceutical industry."

Redwood then turns to the question of whether health care can afford pharmaceutical pricing freedom. He notes that the United States spends a lower proportion of health costs on drugs than any other industrialized country (8.2 percent in the United States versus 16.3 percent in the European community, for example), and that in countries where total or partial pricing freedom was permitted in 1989, pharmaceutical expenditures per person were 22 percent lower than in countries with strict regulations. He suggests that these figures reflect structural changes in the consumption pattern of price-controlled drugs. Price controls contribute to an increase in drug expenditure, he argues, because R&D is reoriented toward developing noninnovative new products with contemporary price tags to replace older drugs with low controlled prices. In contrast, he suggests, pricing freedom is nearly always combined with pressures designed to moderate consumption expenditure: generic competition is encouraged, and serious efforts are made to persuade physicians to prescribe rationally and economically. As a result, pricing freedom is associated with much higher levels of innovativeness.

Cost Controls

Existing studies of the impact of cost controls on pharmaceutical consumption suggest that direct controls may have paradoxical effects in that while drug costs may fall, hospital or other care costs may rise, and that the institution of copayments or reference pricing may also have disappointingly small effects.

In a dramatic example of the unintended effects of public policy, Soumerai et al. studied the effects of Medicaid drug-payment limits on admissions to hospitals and nursing homes.[29] They analyzed 36 months of Medicaid claims data on 411 patients from New Hampshire, who had a three-drug limit per patient for eleven of those months, and 1375 patients from New Jersey who had no such limit. In New Hampshire there was a decrease of 35 percent in the use of the drugs under study, but this was followed by a substantial increase in the rate of admission to nursing homes. The New Jersey cohort had no such changes. In both cases there was no significant increase in the rate of hospitalization. When New Hampshire ceased requiring the three-drug limit, levels of medication use and rates of admission to nursing homes reverted to their precap levels. The authors conclude that limiting reimbursement for effective drugs puts frail, low-income, elderly patients at increased risk of institutionalization in nursing homes and may increase Medicaid costs.

In a study of cost containment measures in the European pharmaceutical market, REMIT Consultants Ltd. examined three methods used to control public spending on pharmaceuticals: patient copayments, reference pricing, and the stimulation of competition from generic products.[30] They found that implementation of copayment policies varies from country to country, but that in all cases the elasticity of demand for drugs is rather small—on the order of 0.2 to 0.3.[31] They speculate that the long-term price elasticity may be even lower as the effects of increased copayments may have less impact over time, and conclude that copayment policies may have disappointingly small effects on the total demand for drugs.

Reference pricing, a form of indirect price controls in which the patient's choice of drug is unlimited but reimbursement rates are driven by a "reference price," was introduced in Germany in 1989 and in the Netherlands in 1991. In Germany it was applied initially to multisource products, and firms that had introduced drugs at greater than the reference price were forced to reduce prices to the reference level or lose market share. However, the German government only realized a small saving from the introduction of the scheme, partly because the existing flat-rate copayment was simultaneously abolished and partly because firms raised the prices of other drugs not covered by the reference pricing legislation. Overall, spending was reduced by 2.5 percent. The authors speculate that an extension of reference pricing to other products could have serious consequences for the research-based industry.

REMIT also briefly examined direct price controls, noting that an alternative to direct price controls is to stimulate competition from generic products. The United States has followed this path with some success, with generics now having some 30 percent of the value of nonhospital prescriptions. In contrast generics constitute only 5 percent of the European Community's market. They suggest that generics are more successful where prices are high to begin with.

In a meta-analysis of the impact of consumer fees on drug consumption, Smith and Kirking found that the demand for drugs tends to be insensitive to consumer fees; but cautioned that care must be taken in generalizing the results to the uninsured population, since most of the data in the studies they examined were for insured subjects.[32] From the literature they estimated that the demand elasticities are around 0.1 to 0.3 for prescription drugs. The overall cost savings to health care are minimal, as cost savings tend to be passed on to third parties in the health care system. They cite Roemer et al., who found that copayments on drugs and physician services in 1972–1973 decreased drug and physician costs, but increased total costs because of higher hospital costs.[33]

Conclusions

Nearly every available measure, including scientific papers, patents, number of new chemical entities, and market share, suggests that U.S.-based pharmaceutical companies are more innovative than their global rivals. The literature reviewed for this case points to four policies as critical determinants of this innovativeness: government funding of basic research, strong patent protection, stringent drug approval regulation, and unregulated pricing. All four policies appear to be associated with the maintenance of a globally competitive, innovative local industry.

Government funding of basic research provides a rich scientific base for the industry. Strong patent protection provides an incentive for innovation, and may also be a source of economic rents that can be reinvested in research. Stringent drug approval regulations appear to foster a demanding local environment that favors the development of globally competitive firms, and unregulated pricing appears also to foster a strongly innovative local industry (Table 15.1).

These studies also point to some of the unanticipated effects of public policy. The imposition of price controls may actually increase the share of the health care budget devoted to pharmaceuticals, and health care cost-containment measures that seek to regulate expenditures on pharmaceuticals directly may increase health care costs by increasing the demand for other health care services.

More research into the effects of different forms of price control would certainly be of interest. The existing work suggests, for example, that price review boards are probably different in their effects than more direct forms of price control. These results are thought provoking, but further research is clearly needed in this area. One important question that this research leaves unanswered, for example, is the degree to which publicly funded basic research benefits local firms disproportionately. It may be the case, for example, that as the scientific community becomes increasingly "global," publicly funded basic research will benefit all of the major pharmaceutical firms. In such a case the benefits a firm derives from publicly funded basic research may be more a function of its own R&D spending than of its geographical location.[34]

Another shortcoming of the available literature is its failure to address a number of additional public policies that may also have important effects on the innovativeness of the local pharmaceutical industry. For example, export restrictions may have a negative impact on domestic firms, particularly when they are coupled with other regulations. Up until 1986, U.S. firms could not export drugs unless they had been approved for use in the United States, even if the drugs had been approved by the importing country. This regulation forced US pharmaceutical companies to build plants abroad for the manufacture of drugs that had received foreign approval but had not been approved by the FDA. Pisano suggests that tacit knowledge developed through the manufacture of some pharmaceutical products may be difficult to transfer, suggesting that countries that force domestic firms to build plants overseas may be penalizing themselves by reducing the amount of knowledge that is generated locally.[35]

Product liability laws are another set of government policies whose implications for the strength of the pharmaceutical industry have not been studied system-

TABLE 15.1. Policies with their intended and unintended effects.

Policy	Intended effect	Unintended effect
Supply		
Regulatory approval	Protect consumers from unsafe, ineffective, and fraudulent drugs	Approval takes too long, thus reducing patent lengths and incentive to innovate Makes U.S. firms more competitive globally Entry barrier to small new entrants and foreign firms Increases market concentration Larger firms mean economies of scale and scope and more innovation
Patents	Encourage innovation	May encourage patent races and overspending on R&D
Product liability	Protect consumers	Higher health care costs
Export policies	Protect other countries from unapproved and unsafe drugs	Export technology and jobs May decrease innovation in the United States
Demand		
Pricing	Make drugs more available Lower health care costs	Price controls discourage innovation and may actually increase health care costs Pricing freedom encourages innovation
Cost containment Copayment Reference pricing Omnibus Reconciliation Act of 1990	Keep health care costs low	Actually discourages demand for certain drugs (reference pricing in Germany; not sure whether it actually reduces health care costs) May discourage innovation and global competitiveness as in the case of France
Health care policies	Lower health care costs Provide better health care	May actually increase health care costs and provide less care May indirectly decrease innovation

atically. Product liability laws regulate a patient's right to take legal action against pharmaceutical companies for injuries received as the result of defects in a drug. It is estimated that for products such as childhood vaccines in the United States, liability insurance and litigation defense costs are an extremely high fraction of the costs of these drugs, accounting for over 95 percent of the price of vaccine.[36] Since pharmaceutical companies bear the brunt of product liability suits, this threat probably limits the supply of such drugs. U.S. firms may be disadvantaged by the fact that foreign liability laws tend to be less stringent.

Most importantly, the existing literature throws little light on the interrelationships between the various policy mechanisms described. What is the relative role of NIH spending, FDA regulation, and pricing freedom in supporting a globally competitive U.S. industry, for example? Japanese prices are almost double those in the United States, yet the U.S. industry is clearly more innovative. Can this be ascribed to lax local regulation, to unsatisfactory patent protection, or to inadequate support of basic research? Public policy in this area clearly has both intended and unintended effects. We need to know much more about both before we will be in a position to make predictions with any confidence.

SUMMARY

It is important to reiterate the fact that the goal of this chapter was not to judge how much of a role, if any, a government should play in the innovativeness of its country's firms and how best to go about it. Rather, the goal was to explore what the role of government can be when it decides to get involved in the innovation process and how best a firm can exploit the opportunities and threats that government actions offer. Why would a government want to play a role in innovation? We offered several answers to this question. First, the public nature of knowledge makes it difficult for firms to appropriate certain kinds of innovations. Without intervention by the government, such innovations might not take place. The government can intervene either by performing the research itself or by granting innovators temporary monopoly rights (patents) for certain innovations. Second, because of the uncertainty that often plagues innovations, the amount of money needed to perform the research, and the sheer amount of time that it takes to see any results, most firms may be reluctant to invest in such research. The government can also perform such research or pay private industry to carry it out. Third, complementary assets such as highways, electronic highways, and schools are best undertaken by the government. Finally, politics can be a good reason why governments play a role in innovation.

KEY TERMS

Adverse selection
Moral hazard
Network externality
Public "nature" of knowledge
Quotas

R&D scale economies
Spillovers
Subsidies
Tariffs

QUESTIONS AND EXERCISES

1. Do you think that the role of government as lead user may have hampered technological progress in some cases? Name one.
2. Which of the roles of government do you think is the most critical?
3. What would your advice be to a firm that wants to maximize its exploitation of the benefits that the government bestows on its firms?

4. How does one of the following help finance innovation for local firms: (a) capital gains tax cuts, (b) quotas, (c) tariffs, (d) subsidies, and (e) performance of R&D by the government?

NOTES

1. Arrow, K. J. "Economic welfare and the allocation of resources for invention." In *The Rate and Direction of Inventive Activity;* R. Nelson (Ed.). Princeton, NJ: Princeton University Press, 1962, pp. 609–26.

2. See, for example, Dasgupta, P., and P. Stoneman, "Introduction." In *Economic Policy and Technological Performance;* P. Dasgupta and P. Stoneman (Eds.). Cambridge, UK: Cambridge University Press, 1987.

3. For an excellent discussion of minimum efficient scale (MES), see Oster, S. *Modern Competitive Analysis.* Oxford: Oxford University Press, 1994.

4. Katz, M. L., and C. Shapiro. "Network externalities, competition and compatibility." *American Economic Review* **75**(3):424–40, 1985.

5. Oster, S. *Modern Competitive Analysis* (1994, p. 316).

6. Meeks, R. L. "Federal R&D funding by budget function fiscal years 1993–1995." NSF 94–319, 1995.

7. Dussauge, P., S. Hart, and B. Ramanantsoa. *Strategic Technology Management.* New York: John Wiley, 1992, p. 123.

8. See, for example, Katz, B. G., and A. Phillips. "The computer industry." In *Government and Technical Progress;* R. N. Nelson (Ed.). New York: Pergamon, 1982.

9. "Airbus. Growing up." *The Economist,* p. 58, July 13, 1996.

10. von Hippel, E. *The Sources of Innovation.* New York: Oxford University Press, 1988.

11. Borrus, M. G. *Competing for Control: America's Stake in Microelectronics.* Cambridge, MA: Ballinger, 1988.

12. Rothwell, R. and W. Zegveld. *Industrial Innovation and Public Policy.* London: Frances Pinter, 1981.

13. Rangan, U. S., and C. A. Bartlett. "Caterpillar Tractor Co." Harvard Business School Case #9-385-276, 1985.

14. "Japanese venture capital. In need of funds." *The Economist,* October 16, 1993.

15. Schumpeter, J. A. *Capitalism, Socialism and Democracy,* 3d ed. New York: Harper, 1950.

16. Cohen, W. M., and D. A. Levinthal. "Innovation and learning: The two faces of R&D." *The Economic Journal* **99**:569–96, 1989.

17. Allen, T. *Managing the Flow of Technology.* Cambridge, MA: MIT Press, 1984.

18. Ferguson, C. H. "Technological development, strategic behavior and government policy in information technology industries." Unpublished Ph.D. Dissertation, MIT, 1989.

19. Ferguson, C. H. "Technological development, strategic behavior and government policy in information technology industries." (1989).

20. The change in this law has been prompted by several factors including the fact that the United States had been overtaken by Japan in several technologies, including semiconductors. Japan's spending of $1.3 billion on their "fifth generation" computer project was cited as the reason for why the United States could no longer hang unto its old antitrust laws that punished sharing of know-how.

21. This case draws heavily on Afuah, A. N. "Public policy and pharmaceutical innovation: A literature review and critique." Working Paper, Program on the Pharmaceutical Industry, MIT, November 1993.

22. Thomas, L. G. "Spare the rod and spoil the industry: Vigorous competition and vigorous regulation promote global competitive advantage: A ten nation study of government industrial policies and corporate pharmaceutical advantage." Working Paper, Columbia Business School, 1989.

23. Ward, M. and D. Dranove. "The vertical chain of research and development in the pharmaceutical industry." Mimeo, Northwestern University, 1991.

24. Reich, M. R. "Why the Japanese don't export more pharmaceuticals: Health policy as industrial policy." *California Management Review,* Winter 1990.

25. Thomas, L. G. "Spare the rod and spoil the industry . . ." (1989).

26. Thomas, G. L. "Implicit industrial policy: The triumph of Britain and the failure of France in global pharmaceuticals." Working Paper, School of Business, Emory University, February 1993.

27. Redwood, H. *Price Regulation and Pharmaceutical Research—The Limits of Co-existence.* London: Oldeicks Press, 1993.

28. Barral, P. E. (Collège des Economistes de La Santé, Rhône-Poulenc Rorer). "18 ans de résultats de la recherche pharmaceutique dans le monde (1975–1992)." Presentation at CREDES & CES European Conference "From Economic Analysis to Health Policies." Paris, December 18, 1992.

29. Soumerai, S., et al. "Effects of Medicaid drug-payment limits on admission to hospitals and nursing homes." *The New England Journal of Medicine,* October 10, 1991.

30. REMIT Consultants. *Cost Containment in the European Pharmaceutical Market: New Approaches.* 1993.

31. The elasticity of a product is the percentage change in its demand given a percentage change in price. An elasticity of 0.2, for example, implies that a 10 percent increase in price will only reduce demand by 2 percent.

32. Smith D. G., and D. M. Kirking. "Impact of consumer fees on drug utilization. *Pharmacoeconomics* 2(4), 1992.

33. Roemer M. I., C. E. Hopkins, and F. Gartside. "Copayments for ambulatory care: Pennywise and pound foolish." *Medical Care* 13:457–66, 1975.

34. Cohen, W. M., and D. A. Levinthal. "Innovation and learning: The two faces of R&D" (1989).

35. Pisano, G. "The R&D boundaries of the firm: An empirical analysis." *Administrative Science Quarterly,* 35:153–76, 1990.

36. "Global competitiveness of U.S. advanced-technology manufacturing industries: Pharmaceuticals." USITC Publication 2437, September 1991. Huber, P. *Liability: The Legal Revolution and Its Consequences.* New York: Basic Books, 1988.

16

THE INTERNET: A CASE IN
TECHNOLOGICAL CHANGE

In 1997, 1998, and 1999, many dot.coms—Internet start-ups—could not do wrong. So-called experts predicted the imminent arrival of a new economy in which dot.coms were going to displace old economy brick-and-mortar firms. In 2000, however, the bottom fell out of many of the start-ups and, in many cases, it appeared that brick-and-mortar incumbents might retain their competitive advantage after all. This prompted many questions: Should the rise and fall of these dot.coms have been expected? Is there anything that dot.coms could have done to improve their chances of survival? When can one expect brick-and-mortar firms to win over dot.coms? Does the Internet have any impact on globalization? In this chapter, we use the concepts of this book to explore these questions and more.[1] We start the chapter by defining the Internet and exploring some of those properties that can help us understand its impact on organizations.

WHAT IS THE INTERNET?

The Internet is a network of interconnected computer networks that allows users who are connected to it to exchange information (Figure 16.1). It was developed by the Advanced Research Project Agency (ARPA), a U.S. Department of Defense research program, to allow different computers and their users to communicate with each other even in times of war. Before the invention of the World Wide Web, the Internet had four primary applications: electronic mail (e-mail), file transfer protocol (ftp), discussion lists or newsgroups, and telnet or remote login. *Electronic mail* (e-mail) allowed a user at a computer that was connected to the network to send a text message at any time to a recipient's computer where it was stored for retrieval by the recipient at any time. *File transfer protocol (FPT)* allowed users to transfer files (usually large blocks of data) from one computer on the network to another at fast rates. The *discussion lists* or *newsgroups* service allowed users to post messages on electronic bulletin boards or have the messages sent to lists of subscribers. *Telnet* or *remote login* allowed users to log in to a remote computer and use it as if he or she were sitting at that computer. If a user wanted information from another

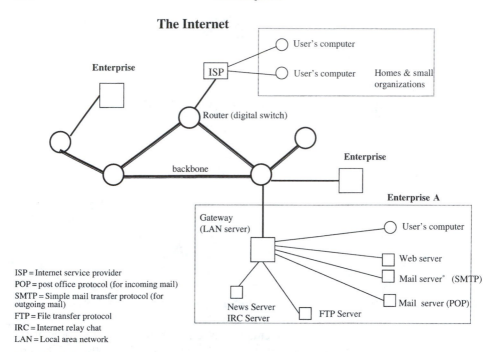

FIGURE 16.1. The Internet.

computer on the network, he or she had to specify the computer node in question, the directory, and the file in which the information was stored.[2] This was not an easy exercise for most potential users and so the Internet remained largely a tool for engineers, scientists, and some academics. With the invention of the *World Wide Web* and the introduction of the Web browser, however, users could access information on any computer anywhere in the world by clicking a mouse on highlighted words or pictures without having to specify the name of a file, a directory, and which of the millions of computers in the network had the information.[3] Employees located anywhere in an organization could now have access to information located in computers anywhere else by clicking on highlighted words and images.

No one firm or individual owns or controls Internet protocols, the rules for connecting to the Internet, and using it. This makes it a low-cost common standard. Therefore anyone anywhere can connect to it as long as he or she complies to the protocols. Previous networks such as electronic data interchange (EDI) were proprietary and therefore costly to join or access, limiting the number of people that could join them. As a low-cost open standard network, the Internet exhibits the property of network externalities. The more people that connect to it, the more valuable it is to each user, offering users network benefits that previous information technologies could not. Each user not only has access to text, voice, and video information at relatively low cost, but each of them could also broadcast to others on the network— something that no previous information or communication technology could allow so many users to do. The combination of the Internet's e-mail, World Wide Web, electronic file transfer, and online chat, coupled with the fact that it is a low cost standard, have the potential to influence the way organizations communicate, collaborate, and coordinate activities in ways that previous information technologies did not. They give the Internet the potential to change interfirm, intrafirm, and seller-buyer interactions in ways that previous information technologies could not.

PROFIT SITES OR VALUE NETWORK

In the face of a new technology such as the Internet, an important question for many entrepreneurs is, how does one make money from it? To make money from the Internet, a firm must add value somewhere in the technology's value network. Such a firm must add value at one of the value-adding stages that collectively create value for the Internet end-user. There are three major parts to the value network: communications network or infrastructure firms, users of the Internet, and suppliers to infrastructure and users (Figure 16.2).

Communications Network Providers

Communications network providers are the hardware and software firms that develop and maintain the infrastructure over which Internet messages can be sent and received. This consists of several segments: backbone, routers, points of presence (POPs), computer servers, last mile providers, users' computers, Internet service providers (ISPs), and portals (Figure 16.2). The backbone is a collection of high-speed telecommunications lines, usually made up of fiber optic cables or large-bandwidth wireless channels, that are connected by high speed computers. Routers are the high-speed digital switches or dedicated computers that route or direct signals from one backbone line to another. Typically, a user at home or at a small busi-

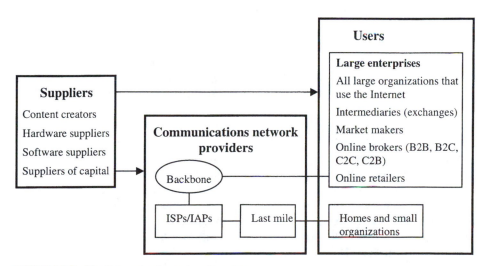

FIGURE 16.2. The Internet value network system.

ness who wants to access the Internet passes through an Internet service provider (ISP). The ISP connects the user to a router through a point of presents (POP)—a dedicated computer that acts as an interface between the high-speed routers and the user at home or small organization. The hardware connection between a home user and an ISP server is usually known as the last mile. Depending on where the home user is located, he or she has several choices in the last mile: the old twisted copper wire that phone companies used to use to transmit voice signals, an asynchronous digital subscriber line (ADSL), cable television's coaxial cable, wireless, and fiber optics.

Large users such as Enterprise A in Figure 16.1 have their own local area networks. Such a network is usually made up of users' computers and several servers. Web servers store the enterprise's Web pages and transmit them in response to requests from Web browsers, also called Web clients. Two e-mail servers manage outgoing and incoming electronic mail. Post office protocol (POP) servers, also known as POP3 servers, store incoming mail. Simple mail transfer protocol (SMTP) servers store outgoing mail. Mail clients or the e-mail programs that reside on the user's computer enable the user to read, write, store, print, send, and receive messages. ftp servers store files that a user can transfer to or from a computer using an ftp client. News servers store newsgroup articles that users can read or send using news clients. IRC servers control access to online chats in which participants must have IRC clients. The local network servers are connected to a router via a local area network (LAN) server.

Suppliers

Suppliers can be divided into three groups: hardware suppliers, software suppliers, content creators, and suppliers of capital.

Hardware suppliers consist of communications equipment manufacturers, computer equipment manufacturers, and component equipment manufacturers. Communications equipment providers are the firms that supply infrastructure firms with the routers, other digital switches, wireless systems, and fiber optic cables that are used to build and maintain the infrastructure. Computer hardware suppliers supply the servers, workstations, and other computers that users and infrastructure firms need. Hardware component providers supply components such as microchips to infrastructure and computer hardware companies. These include Intel, AMD, and Motorola.

Software suppliers supply software of all types for infrastructure and users. Different categories of software suppliers are still emerging and include providers of infrastructure operating systems/browsers, applications software, and applications services. Infrastructure operating systems/browser providers are firms such as Microsoft or AOL/Netscape that develop and market software to help people manage or use the Internet. Software in this category includes browsers such as Microsoft's Internet Explorer and Netscape Communicator that facilitate surfing the Web. Applications software providers develop software targeted at specific applications on the Internet. These include developers of different e-mail packages and e-commerce applications packages such as shopping carts and micropayments. Applications service providers (ASPs) offer software on their own servers that individuals can rent instead of buying the software outright. The application is usually delivered to the customer on demand.

Content suppliers develop music, games, movies, videos, news, sports, other entertainment, written works, art, books, and results of research that can be delivered over the Internet. That is, any works or intellectual property that can be reduced into bits and transmitted over the Internet is considered content.

Capital suppliers. are the investors who provide the money that is needed to finance Internet-exploiting activities. Firms are in business to make money. But until they start making money, they need money to finance their activities. For this, they turn to, as we saw in Chapter 11, angels, venture capitalists, banks, individual and institutional investors, and other financial institutions. These investors expect some return on their investment in the infrastructure firms, suppliers, or users in which they invest.

Users

Of the three profit sites—infrastructure, suppliers and users—users is the largest category. It includes not only the millions of individual users but also the thousands of enterprises that use the Internet.

THE INTERNET BUBBLE OF 1998, 1999, AND EARLY 2000

Table 16.1 gives a glimpse of some of the excitement that dot.com companies created in 1998, 1999, and early 2000. The reception of start-ups that went to the public to raise money through initial public offerings (IPOs) was phenomenal. For example, on November 13, 1998, theGlobe.com went public with its shares priced at $9 each. The public wanted to pay much more than the $9. Investors wanted to pay ten times as much. The stock price shot up to $90 before eventually settling at $63.50 at the end of the day. Such a high stock price should not have made sense because the firm was not making money and did not have the potential to make that much money. Recall that a firm's valuation is the present value of future cash flows, and high valuations mean that investors expect the firm to earn a lot of money. The Globe's business model was easy to duplicate. There was nothing distinctive or inimitable about how the firm planned to make money. Slightly more than a year later, on December 9, 1999, VA Linux Systems, a company that built computer servers, also went public with an IPO offer price of $30. Again, investors wanted to pay about ten times as much and the price shot up to a high of $299 before settling down to $239.25 at the end of the day. There was nothing distinctive about VA Linux's business model either. It planned to build systems using commodity components and a free operating systems in Linux. In general, most Internet-related

TABLE 16.1. Spectacular first days.

Company (ticker)	IPO date	Offer price	1st day open	1st day close	Close over offer
VA Linux Systems, Inc. (LNUX)	12/9/99	$30	$299	$239.25	697.50%
theGlobe.com, inc. (TGLO)	11/13/98	$ 9	$ 90	$ 63.50	605.56%
Foundry Networks, Inc. (FDRY)	9/28/99	$25	$109	$156.25	525.00%
webMethods, Inc. (WEBM)	2/11/00	$35	$195	$212.63	507.51%
Free Markets, Inc. (FMKT)	12/10/99	$48	$248	$280	483.33%
Akamai Technologies, Inc. (AKAM)	10/29/99	$26	$110	$145.19	458.42%
Avanex Corporation (AVNX)	12/3/99	$36	$175	$172	377.78%
Ask Jeeves, Inc (ASKJ)	7/1/99	$14	$ 72	$ 64.94	363.86%
Priceline.com Inc. (PCLN)	3/30/99	$16	$ 81	$ 69	331.25%
Healtheon/WebMD Corp. (HLTH)	2/11/99	$ 8	$ 21.88	$ 31.38	292.25%
Etoys (ETYS)	3/20/99	$20	$ 78	$ 76.56	282.80%
Red Hat, Inc. (RHAT)	8/11/99	$14	$ 46	$ 52.06	271.86%
Redback Networks Inc. (RBAK)	5/18/99	$23	$ 67.25	$ 84.13	265.78%
Turnstone Systems, Inc. (TSTN)	2/1/00	$29	$ 94	$ 97	234.48%
iVillage Inc. (IVIL)	3/19/99	$24	$ 95.88	$ 80.13	233.88%
OpenTV Corp. (OPTV)	11/23/99	$20	$ 56	$ 62.75	213.75%
Aether Systems, Inc. (AETH)	8/20/99	$16	$ 50	$ 48.44	202.75%
Commerce One, Inc. (CMRC)	7/1/99	$21	$ 66	$ 61	190.48%
Autoweb (AWEB)	3/23/99	$14	$ 21.63	$ 40	185.71%

IPOs that were issued in 1998, 1999, or early 2000 were enthusiastically received. It seemed no dot.com company could go wrong even though most of them did not make any money and had no potential to do so. Sometimes, all it took was the suffix ".com" to get some investors to invest.

By April 2000, however, things had changed (see Table 16.2). The Internet bubble, as the inflated stock prices had come to be known, had burst. On March 20, for example, theGlobe.com's share price had dropped to $3.56, a drop of 94% from its first day closing price, while that of VA Linux Systems had dropped to $38.02, a drop of 84% from its first day closing price. By 2001, the valuations of many dot.coms had dropped considerably and many had filed for bankruptcy. In fact, VA Linux Systems' value had dropped to less than $5.00. Many more firms had died without reaching the IPO stage and with them the dreams of many entrepreneurs. Many individuals who invested in these dot.coms lost a lot·of money.

Should the Bubble Have Been Expected?

This rise and crash of dot.com valuations begs the question: Should one have expected these events? The answer is yes. New technologies such as the Internet, as we saw in Chapter 2, often allow firms to offer their customers better value than ex-

TABLE 16.2 First signs of the crash.

Company (ticker)	IPO date	Offer price	1st day open	1st day close	52 week high	4/20/00 close	3/5/01 close
theGlobe.com, inc. (TGLO)	11/13/98	$ 9	$ 90	$ 63.50	20.38	$ 3.56	$ 0.38
Etoys (ETYS)	3/20/99	$20	$ 78	$ 76.56	86	6	$ 0.09
Autoweb (AWEB)	3/23/99	$14	$ 21.63	40	$ 18.50	3.97	$ 0.40
iVillage Inc. (IVIL)	3/19/99	$24	$ 95.88	$ 80.13	$ 67.88	$12.16	$ 1.03
VA Linux Systems, Inc. (LNUX)	12/9/99	$30	$299	$239.25	$320	$38.02	$ 3.90
drugstore.com, inc. (DSCM)	7/28/99	$18	$ 65	$ 50.25	$ 69	$ 8.06	$ 1.50
MP3.COM, Inc. (MPPP)	7/21/99	$28	$ 92	$ 63.31	$105	$10.56	$ 3.00
cdnow (CDNW)	2/10/98	$16	$ 22	$ 22	$ 23.27	$ 3.81	$ 0.00
Free Markets, Inc. (FMKT)	12/10/99	$48	$248	$280	$370	$59.81	$17.00
Webvan Group Inc. (WBVN)	11/5/99	$15	$ 26	$ 24.88	$ 34	$ 5.75	$ 0.25
1-800-FLOWERS.COM, Inc. (FLWS)	8/3/99	$21	$ 21.75	$ 18.19	$ 23.19	$ 4.50	$ 6.00
BUY.COM INC (BUYX)	2/8/00	$13	$ 30.13	$ 25.13	$ 35.44	$ 6.25	$ 0.38
Varsity Books	2/15/009	$10	$ 12	$ 9.88	$ 13.12	$ 2.81	$ 9.25
pets.com (IPET)	2/11/00	$11	$ 13.50	$ 11	$ 14	$ 3.38	$ 0.00
Palm Inc. (:ALM)	3/2/00	$38	$165	$ 95.06	$165	$30.06	$18.00
Avanex Corporation (AVNX)	12/3/99	$36	$175	$172	$273	$55.06	$20.00
webMethods, Inc. (WEBM)	2/11/00	$35	$195	$212.63	$336.25	$90	$33.00
Ask Jeeves, Inc (ASKJ)	7/1/99	$14	$ 72	$ 64.94	$190.50	$29.38	$ 1.67
Red Hat, Inc. (RHAT)	8/11/99	$14	$ 46	$ 52.06	$151	$26.25	$ 7.00

isting technologies. Entrepreneurs who recognize this value or its potential locate at various stages of the innovations value configuration (value network in the case of the Internet). In the fluid phase of the technology, there is a lot of entry. In 2000, for example, there were over 9,000 ISPs; and ISPs are just one of many profit sites. The larger the potential of the technology and the lower the barriers to entry, the more the entry. As the number of entries increases, competition for resources such as capital, talented employees, and standards increases. So does competition for market share, customers, and suppliers. Each firm usually wants to win. If one firm plans to win, say, a 20% market share, the chances are that each of the hundreds of other new entrants in the market also want 20% of the market. If all of them work toward investing for a 20% share, artificial demand is created for all resources. As competition heats up, some firms are forced to exit or to be bought by rivals with better potential. In those segments where a dominant design emerges, those firms that did not win the dominant design may have to exit. The automobile industry offers a good example. From the late 1800s to the early 1900s, more than 1,000 automobile companies were started in the United States. Often, all that one needed to attract investors were the words "Motor Company," just as the magic words in 1997, 1998, and 1999 were dot.com. As of 2001 there two U.S. automobile companies. Along the way, hundreds of them were forced to exit. Others had to merge to form larger companies.

So far, our analysis of the bubble has been limited to dot.coms. An interesting question is, why did incumbent non-dot.com firms also suffer huge losses in their valuations in 2000 and 2001? For example, in June 2001, Cisco's share price dropped by more than 80% from its 52-week high. The drop in valuations of these incumbent firms can be explained by focusing the analysis on the whole value network—by considering how the different profit sites of the Internet interact with each other. Take Cisco, for example. Since it supplies routers and other digital switches to infrastructure and users of the Internet, any inflated market share expectations by dot.coms that result in over investment (e.g., all 30 firms in an industry believing that they will each capture 20% of the market results in six times more capacity than is needed) will be translated into over-inflated demand for Cisco's products. When reality eventually sets in, Cisco also suffers.

What Should Firms Have Done to Increase Their Chances of Survival?

A natural question is, what should firms do to increase their chances of maintaining high market valuations and surviving during a shakeout as a technology evolves? In other words, what increases a firm's chances? A firm's chances of surviving and thriving are determined by its ability to make money or its *potential* to do so and chance events. Since a firm's ability to make money is determined by its macro or regional environment, competitive environment, and business model, we can say that its chances of surviving and thriving in the face of a technological shake-up is a function of four factors: macro or regional environment, competitive environment, business model, and chance events.

Macro or Regional Environment

As detailed in Chapter 5, some environments, by their nature, are more conducive to innovation than others. Thus, firms in such environments have a better chance of surviving than firms in less endowed environments. As we saw in that chapter, four factors determine whether an environment is conducive to innovation or not: a system that provides financial support and rewards for innovation; a culture that tolerates failure; the presence of related industries, universities, and other research institutions; and government policies.

The Competitive Environment

Some industries are more profitable than others. For an industry to be profitable, firms in it must offer products or services whose value to customers considerably exceeds the cost of providing them. But as Michael Porter pointed out, there are five forces that can prevent firms in the industry from being profitable.[4] The impact of these forces on firm profitability, as we saw in Chapter 7, can be understood by considering the simple relationship of Equation 1. The equation states that the profits that firms in an industry make are equal to the revenues that they receive from customers in exchange for the products or services that they offer, less the costs of offering them.

$$\text{Profits} = \text{revenues} - \text{costs} = P(Q)*Q(P) - C(Q) \tag{1}$$

If customers are powerful enough to impose lower prices on industry firms, these firms' revenues are lower, reducing their profits. If powerful customers instead extract higher quality products for the low prices, industry firms must incur the cost of higher quality products, thereby reducing their profits. Powerful suppliers have an analogous effect on firm profitability. They can extract higher prices for their products or force lower quality products on industry firms. Higher costs of supplies mean less profitability. Lower quality components mean that industry firms may have to ship lower quality products to their customers, which will fetch lower prices and fewer sales. Both also result in lower profitability. The threat of new entrants forces firms to lower their prices. They may also be forced to take costly measures such as advertising to create barriers to entry or differentiate their products. Either way, firm profitability is reduced. Similarly, increased rivalry leads to price wars or costly attempts to differentiate products, both of which reduce profitability. Substitute products provide an alternative for customers, thereby putting pressure on industry prices. A profit site in which suppliers and buyers have bargaining power, rivalry is high, the threat of new entry is high, and the power of substitutes is high is said to be unattractive. A firm that locates in such a profit site, on the average, increases its chances of not surviving a technological shakeout. This is because if a site is viewed as not having the potential to be profitable, venture capitalists may, for example, decide not to invest in firms at the profit site. Start-ups that are starved of financing have a much smaller chance of surviving. Such a site may not attract savvy employees who understand industry analysis.

Business Model and Competitive Advantage

A firm's business model details how it makes money now and how it plans to do so in the long term. To gain and maintain a competitive advantage, a business model is critical. There are ten components to a business model (Figure 16.3).

Profit Site. The choice of a profit site, as we have just seen, is critical. Locating in an attractive profit site where, on the average, firms are more profitable than firms in less profitable sites increases the chances of the firm making money. Recall from Chapter 7 that an industry or market is attractive if the market forces exerted on market firms by suppliers, customers, substitutes, rivals, and potential new entrants are weak. Being in an environment that is conducive to innovation or locating in an attractive profit site, however, is no guarantee to survive and thrive. A critical factor for doing well, whether in an attractive or unattractive environment, is for a firm to have a competitive advantage. A firm has a competitive advantage if it is more profitable than its rivals or has the potential to do so. To gain and maintain a competitive advantage, a firm also needs the other nine components of a business model.

Customer value. Customers would prefer a firm's product over rivals' products only if the product offers them something distinctive—something that competitors'

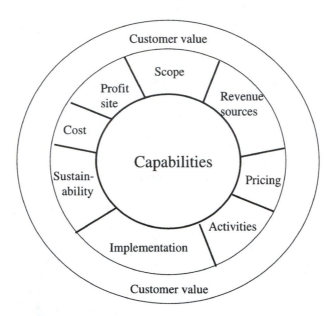

FIGURE 16.3. Components of a business model.

products do not[5]. This something, or distinctive *customer value*, can be in the form of differentiated or low cost products/services. If the value is not distinctive, it would be difficult to convince customers to keep coming.

Scope. A firm must also decide which market segments to offer the value to as well as how many types of products that embody versions of this value should be sold. A firm can, for example, market to either businesses or households. Often, a firm must also decide where in the world it wants to market its products: in North America, Europe, or Africa. Within each continent, a firm must decide which country to serve. The choice of market segment is just one decision that a firm must make. The firm must also decide how much of the needs of each segment it can profitably serve.[6]

Price. A bad pricing strategy not only can leave money on the table, it can also kill a product. A critical part of pricing is understanding the nature and dynamics of the underpinning technology. With so-called knowledge-based products—products that are heavy on know-how and whose up-front costs are very high relative to the variable cost of producing and offering each unit to customers[7]—a firm may decide to give away the product earlier on in order to build a large market share and high customer switching costs. It may decide to give away one product and charge for a related less imitable one.

Sources of Revenues and Profits. Isolating a firm's sources of revenues *and* profits is critical. For example, a computer maker's profits may come not so much from the hardware boxes that it ships but from the after-sales services. Understanding these sources makes for a better strategy.

Activities. Offering customer value to different segments of the market requires performing the activities of the firm's value configuration—value chain, value shop, or value network. To offer better value to the right customers, a firm must carefully choose *which* activities it performs, which ones it *does not* perform, and *when* it performs or does not perform them. One criteria for performing an activity is if a firm's capability in the activity is distinctive or if the firm can build a distinctive capability in the activity. If a firm has neither the distinctive capability nor the potential to build such a capability, it may want to outsource the activity provided there is more than one firm that can perform the activity better than the firm. eBay offers a very good example. Its distinctive capabilities rest in its core base of registered users and brand name. Although the back-end technology on which access to its Web site rests is critical to the firm, other firms can provide the technology better than eBay. Thus eBay decided to outsource provision of the back-end technology to Abovenet Communications and Exodus Communications.

Implementation. Offering the right value to the right customers, pricing that value effectively, identifying the right sources of revenue, and choosing which activities to perform and which ones not to perform are extremely important but not sufficient. A firm must execute if it is going to exploit a technological change. Implementation entails the right fit between strategy, structure, systems, people, and environment (S^3PE), which we discussed in Chapter 5. A firm's strategy is defined by how it uses its capabilities to perform the connected activities of its value configuration and offer customers lower cost or differentiated products so as to keep earning a higher rate of return than its rivals.

Capabilities. For a firm to offer its customers distinctive value, reach the customer segments that it wants to, price its products appropriately, exploit its sources of revenues, implement its strategies effectively, and do so in a way that gives it a competitive advantage, the firm needs distinctive capabilities. That is, for a firm to have a competitive advantage, there must be something distinctive about the firm that allows it to perform value-creating activities better than its rivals.

Sustainability. If, as we discussed in Chapter 10, a firm is to sustain its competitive advantage, it must pursue some combination of block, team-up, or run strategies.

Cost. A firm must always strive to be efficient, no matter whether it is offering low cost or differentiated products. Costs must be carefully managed. A start-up that has a very high burn rate, for example, may not survive long enough to fulfill its potential of making money long term. That is, all the components of a firm's business model may be on the mark, but if execution is unnecessarily costly, the firm may still fail.

Chance Events. Firms that offer their customers the best value do not always win. The stories of VHS versus Beta and of Apple versus the IBM-compatible PC, as recounted in Chapter 12, illustrate the fact that although strategy is important, luck may play a role in whether a firm survives and thrives in the face of a technological change. In any case, the firms that were "lucky" either put themselves in a position to be that lucky or were very good at exploiting their luck. For example, Microsoft was lucky to have been in the process of buying QDOS from Seattle Computer when IBM came to it for software. It was, however, Microsoft's strategy from then on that allowed it to profit as much as it did from operating systems software.

WHO SHOULD WIN THE DOT.COM VERSUS BRICK-AND-MORTAR WAR?

As dot.coms invaded some brick-and-mortar industries, the question that many researchers pondered was, would incumbents lose their competitive advantages to upstart dot.coms? To answer this question, we need to recall two things from the previous chapters. First, it takes more than technology to profit from technology. It also takes complementary assets. Recall that if a firm is to make money long term, it has to offer customers some value. Technology is just one of the many things that are needed in a value configuration—be it a value chain, value shop, or value network—to offer a customer value. It also takes complementary assets such as distribution channels, marketing, manufacturing, logistics, brands, installed base, relations with clients, content, and so on to offer customer value. Second, recall from the Teece model that when imitability of a technology is high and complementary assets are important and difficult to come by, the owner of complementary assets makes money. Since the use of the Internet is easy to imitate in many cases, the owner of complementary assets in these cases should win. Since complementary assets in many markets are owned by brick-and-mortar incumbents, we can expect them to win. Thus the answer to the question, who should win the dot.com versus brick-and-mortar war? is those incumbents who have distinctive complementary capabilities in markets where complementary assets are important and difficult to come by and where the Internet is easy to imitate.

What Should the Impact on Sustainability Be?

As we argued in Chapter 10, it takes a combination of block, team up, and run to sustain a competitive advantage. Figure 16.4 presents one model of the impact of the Internet on sustainability. With information that is more easily available to more people at lower cost, the likelihood of imitation is higher. For example, reverse engineering a product is easier with the Internet for several reasons. First, information on the core concepts that underpin the product is now more easily available to potential imitators through the Internet. A firm that needs to learn more about the chemical structure and mechanism of action of a new drug is more likely to find the information with the Internet than before it. Second, imitators can more

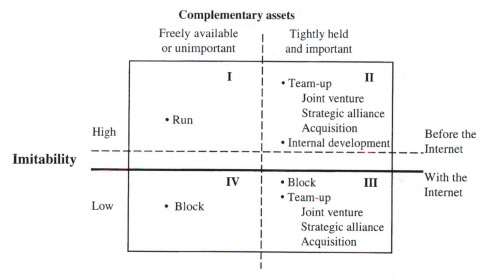

FIGURE 16.4. The impact of the Internet on sustainability.

easily find the tools for reverse engineering and people who are willing to help reverse engineer the product for a fee. Since, on the average, imitability increases, the area over which a block strategy would work decreases while the one over which a run strategy should work increases. This suggests that to sustain a competitive advantage in the face of the Internet, firms may have to pursue a run strategy in cases where a block strategy was appropriate prior to the Internet.

What Should the Impact on Globalization Be?

In Chapter 13, we explored the impact of information and communications technologies (ICTs)—which include the Internet, wireless devices, and hand-held devices—on globalization. In this section, we focus on the impact of the Internet. Recall from Chapter 13 that four different strategies can be used to better innovate on a global basis: multidomestic, global, transnational, and international. The *multidomestic* strategy is appropriate for innovations that depend more on understanding local customer preferences, tastes, expectations, distribution channels, and local government regulations than they do on the technological knowledge on which they rest.[8] If the technological information requirements for an innovation are high relative to market information requirements, a firm may want to pursue a *global* strategy.[9] Firms can locate their facilities where the environment is most suitable for technological innovations or at home where they have home assets that give them some advantage. If both market and technological information demands are low, a firm can pursue the *international* strategy. If both market and technological information needs are high, the *transnational* strategy is best.

The Internet can be used to locate, collect, and share certain kinds of market

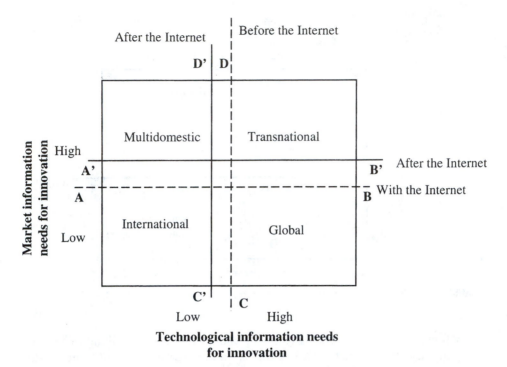

FIGURE 16.5. Impact of the Internet on globalization.

information in foreign countries inexpensively rather than move to these countries. Thus, in area ABB'A' in Figure 16.5, where a firm would have used the *multidomestic* or *transnational* strategies to pursue innovations in foreign countries, firms can now pursue *international* or *global* strategies. By integrating Internet technologies into their organizational technologies, however, firms are increasing their technological information needs. Effectively, they are moving the line CD to C'D' in Figure 16.5. Overall, the Internet increases the range over which the *global* strategy can be pursued while reducing the area over which the *multidomestic* strategy can be pursued. Whether it increases or decreases the area over which the *international* and *transnational* strategies can be pursued or not is a function of the extent to which the information needs of the firm are more marketing than technological. The more marketing the information needs, the larger the area over which the *international* strategy can be pursued rather than the *transnational*.

THE INTERNET'S LIMITATIONS

It is important to understand that because the Internet is an information technology, there is a limit to the type of information that can be transmitted and received over it. What is sent over the Internet must at one point be encoded into bits (ones and zeros) in order to be transmitted and received. That means that information sent over the Internet, sooner or later, must be handled by people. Thus, the types of transactions that can be performed over the Internet are a function of the nature of the knowledge on which the transactions rest and of the type of people undertaking the transactions. Thus, the nature of knowledge and people limit the extent to which people can exploit the Internet.

Tacit Knowledge

Whatever is transmitted over the Internet has been, at one time or the other, knowledge that had resided in individuals or in organizational routines. E-mail messages sent by individuals come from their stock of knowledge. The design of a car that is sent over the Internet is knowledge that had resided in individuals at the automaker or in its organizational routines and archival knowledge banks. Effectively, for knowledge to be transmitted over the Internet, it must be encoded in a form that can be transmitted. That is, knowledge transmitted over the Internet is explicit, not tacit. As we saw in Chapter 3, knowledge is explicit if it is codified, spelled out in writing, verbalized, or coded in drawings, computer programs, or other products. It is tacit if uncoded and nonverbalized. In trying to carry out transactions over the Internet, then, a problem arises when the tacit knowledge on which the transactions rest cannot be encoded into a form that can be put unto the Internet and transmitted. Thus, a *multidomestic* strategy will be replaced by an *international* one only to the extent that the knowledge of market and local conditions is explicit or encodable into a form that can be transmitted over the Internet.

People

The other problem with transacting over the Internet, as we also saw in Chapter 3 is that as smart as human beings and their organizations can be, they are still cognitively limited. They are boundedly rational, and not as rational as most people might think.[10] Because individuals and organizations are cognitively limited, they may not be able to encode their knowledge contribution in a transaction in a form that can be transmitted over the Internet. And even if they could articulate their knowledge very well, boundedly rational individuals at the receiving end may not understand. How does one describe the smell of a car to another person and give him or her the feel that he or she would get by himself or herself? Even if one could describe it, would the receiver understand? Tacit knowledge and cognitive limitations of people make it difficult to perform some transactions over the Internet. Technological advances such as virtual reality may remove some of these limitations.

Summary

Like most major new technologies, the Internet offers the potential to create and deliver superior customer value. Creating and delivering this value entails adding value at various profit sites. Entrepreneurs locate their start-ups at these profit sites to make money. But as these start-ups compete for customers, market share, talent, financing, and other resources, some of them are forced to exit. To increase its chances of surviving and thriving as a technology evolves, a firm needs a business model with the right components: profit site, customer value, scope, pricing, sources of revenue, activities, capabilities, implementation, sustainability, and cost structure. Brick-and-mortar incumbents also must fend off competition from start-ups or use the Internet to reinforce their competitive advantages. In any case, they too need the right business models. Where complementary assets are important and difficult to come by, these incumbents have an edge since they can use their existing complementary assets.

KEY TERMS

Backbone
Business model
Competitive environment
Content providers
Customer value
Internet service providers
Last mile
Network externalities
Online brokers

Point of presence (POP)
Post office protocol
Profit site
Routers
Sources of revenues
Sustainability
Tacit knowledge
World Wide Web

QUESTIONS AND EXERCISES

1. Does the disruptive technology model that we saw in Chapter 2 explain why so many bricks-and-mortar firms performed so much better than their dot.com counterparts in head-to-head competition?
2. To which of the following industries is the Internet likely to be (a) a radical innovation and (b) a disruptive innovation?
   1. Investment banking
   2. Travel agencies
   3. Automobiles
   4. Publishing
   5. Software distribution
   6. Semiconductors
   7. Business school education

NOTES

1. This chapter draws heavily on Chapter 2 of *Internet Business Models and Strategies: Text and Cases*, by Allan Afuah and Christopher Tucci. Chicago: McGraw-Hill/Irvin, 2003.

2. A user of the Internet who wanted to access information on a computer connected to the network had to specify a "path" of the format *node.ext/directory/subdirectory/file*. Typing *node.ext* took the user to the computer. Once logged into the computer, the user had to specify the directory path (*directory/subdirectory/file*). This required the user to know what he or she was looking for and where it was located. Contrast that with today's Internet, where, with the help of the World Wide World, users only have to point and click highlighted words to access information.

3. Each highlighted word or picture on the Web represented a file, directory, and computer address that one would have had to specify in the pre-Web days. A user still had to specify the name of a Web site by typing its domain name, but for the most part, users just had to point and click.

4. Porter, M. E. *Competitive Strategy: Techniques for Analyzing Industries and Competitors*. New York: The Free Press, 1980. McGahan, A. M., and M. E. Porter. "How much does industry matter? Really?" Strategic Management Journal **18** (Summer special issue): pp. 15–30, 1997.

5. Porter, M. E. *Competitive Strategy: Techniques for Analyzing Industries and Competitors*. New York: The Free Press, 1980.

6. Porter, M. E. "What is Strategy?" *Harvard Business Review*, November–December 1996.

7. Arthur, W. B. "Increasing returns and the new world of business." *Harvard Business Review*, July–August 1996.

8. The terminology of multidomestic, global, international, and transnational are from Bartlett, C. and S. Ghoshal (1989). *Managing across Borders*. Cambridge, MA: Harvard Business School Press 1989.

9. The words *global* and *international* as used in this categorization of different strategies can be confusing given the normal everyday uses. Hence, these two words will be italicized whenever referring to a strategy.

10. Williamson, O. *Markets and Hierarchies*. New York: Free Press, 1975, p. 21. Conner, K., and C. K. Prahalad. "A resource-based theory of the firm: Knowledge versus opportunism." *Organization Science* **7** (5): 477–501, 1995.

17

STRATEGIC INNOVATION PROCESS

In this chapter we offer a systematic process for strategy formulation and implementation that will allow us to profit from innovation. We will call it the *strategic innovation process* in honor of its predecessor, the *strategic management process* (Figure 17.1).[1] In this process a firm has a mission and some goals. To achieve these goals, it scans its environment and other sources of innovation for any opportunities and threats that it can exploit. After analyzing its ability to exploit some of these opportunities and threats, the firm chooses a profit site—that is, whether to be a supplier, manufacturer, complementary innovator, distributor, or customer. Next the firm formulates several strategies. In its business strategy, it decides whether the product—the outcome of the innovation process—will be low cost, differentiated, or both. In its innovation strategy, it decides whether to be the first to introduce the innovation or to be a follower of some kind. Business and innovation strategies help drive functional strategies—resource allocation and the actions taken by each function along the value chain (R&D, manufacturing, and so on). A firm's globalization strategy provides a road map of how the firm will take advantage of worldwide sources of innovation and markets.

All these strategies constitute a strategic direction, which drives the implementation process that follows. Implementation entails having the right organizational structure, systems or processes, and people. A strategy, no matter how fundamentally sound, must be implemented well if its full benefits are to be realized.

A STRATEGIC INNOVATION PROCESS MODEL

I. Mission and Goals

Most firms have goals, and the role of innovation within the goals is sometimes also spelled out. This role varies from firm to firm. At some, innovation is at the core of the firm's products and services, and therefore an integral part of its mission and goals or their pursuit. 3M, Intel, Merck, and General Mills are examples. In any case, innovation can play one of two roles. The first can be characterized as *goal pull*. A firm sets some goals—for example, to be number one or two in any market it enters—and then uses innovation to achieve these goals. The second can

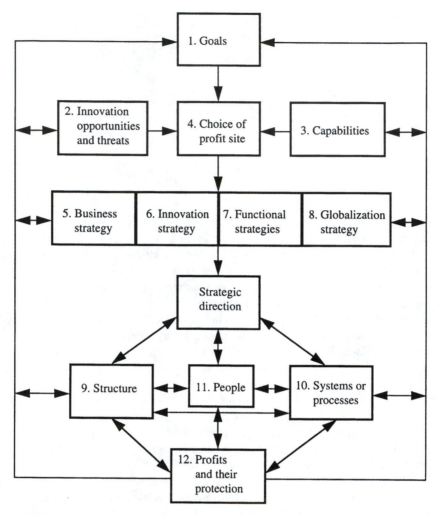

FIGURE 17.1. Strategic innovation process.

be termed *innovation push.* Here, for example, a firm that is endowed with some unique capabilities, which enable it to recognize and exploit innovation, may make it its goal to be the most profitable firm in the world, or to have the highest market share in any market that it uses its capabilities to enter.

2. Innovation Opportunities and Threats

The first step in attaining its goals is for a firm to scan its suppliers, customers, competitors, complementary innovators, related industries, research laboratories, universities worldwide, and its own value chain for any ideas or inventions that can be turned into profitable innovations. Technological discontinuities, deregulation, regulation, globalization, demographic changes, macroeconomic movements, competitors' strategies, and changing customer tastes, preferences, and expectations, all present opportunities and threats.

3. Identifying Capabilities

Once an idea or invention has been spotted and the rationale behind it as well as its applications are understood, the firm then determines three things: (1) what types of capabilities are required to exploit the innovation as a supplier, manufacturer, complementary innovator, distributor, or customer; (2) its capabilities and the extent to which they meet those required to exploit the innovation in each of these industries; and (3) potential co-opetitors' capabilities. The firm's capabilities and those of its co-opetitors are determined using the VIDE (customer *v*alue, *i*mitability, competitor *d*ifferentiation, and *e*xtendability) analysis of Chapter 9.

4. Choosing a Profit Site

Next the firm chooses a profit site—whether to be a supplier, manufacturer, customer, complementary innovator, or distributor. For each of these possible profit sites, the firm must answer several questions: How attractive is the industry over the life cycle of the innovation? What capabilities are needed to be profitable over the life cycle of the product? Does the firm have these capabilities, and if not, can it build them quickly? How about its co-opetitors? With whom can it collaborate and at what level? Finally, the choice of a profit site should be in line with the firm's *corporate strategy*. A firm's corporate strategy answers the question: what businesses should the firm be in? Knowing its goals, its capabilities, the extent to which its capabilities meet those required to exploit the innovation compared to those of its potential competitors, and its corporate strategy, the firm can choose a profit site.

5. Business Strategy

Having chosen a profit site, a firm must now decide what its business strategy will be. What industry should the firm be in and where in the industry should it position itself? Should the products from the innovation be low cost, differentiated, or both? This decision, for example, enables the firm to better allocate resources for the different functions along its value chain.

6. Innovation Strategy

The firm also determines whether it will follow an offensive innovation strategy in which it is the first to introduce the innovation or follow a strategy in which it waits for others to go first. Which of these strategies it follows is a function of its capabilities and strategic intent.

7. Functional Strategies

Having decided whether to offer low-cost or differentiated products, and whether to introduce the products first or be a follower, the firm must allocate resources and direct the different functions along its value chain in accordance with these business and innovation strategies. Differentiated products and offensive strategies, for example, may require investing heavily in R&D to pioneer new products. It may also demand speeding up the product development process. A low-cost, follower strategy may require focusing on manufacturing processes.

8. Globalization

An important part of the decision to adopt the innovation concerns the questions of when and how to go global, in particular, where and when to locate what functions of the value chain, that is, where to locate what functional activities so as to best use both technological and market knowledge in order to offer low-cost or differentiated products worldwide. The firm can use one of four globalization strategies: international, global, multidomestic, or transnational.

9. Organizational Structure

With the business, innovation, functional, and globalization strategies in place, the firm can now turn to their implementation. It must find an organizational structure, build systems and processes, and put in place the right people to match the strategies. In finding the right structure, the firm faces several questions. How do worldwide functions keep increasing their specialization in their functional areas while at the same time coordinating their activities so as to speed product development and keep cost low? How should the tasks be organized? Who goes where?

10. Systems or Processes

Management must be able to monitor performance and to reward and punish individuals, functions, divisions, and organizations in some agreed upon and understood way. It must establish systems whereby information will flow in the shortest possible time to the right targets for decision making.

11. People

Ultimately it is people who will carry out the strategies. A firm must ask several questions about these people. What type of gatekeepers, boundary spanners, champions, sponsors, and project managers does the firm have or need? To what extent do employees share the same goals as their firm? Does the manufacturing group see R&D as a "bunch of ivory tower, money-spending snobs" or colleagues with whom they can work to build the best cars in the shortest possible time at the lowest cost? To what extent do the employees have the knowledge that underpins the various activities of the firm's value chain? How much is such knowledge valued? What does it take to motivate employees? Paychecks, job security, stock options, seeing their ideas implemented, being respected, or being "seen" as a person? Are managers leaders or systematic planners?

12. Profits and Their Protection

These steps are designed to allow a firm to offer low-cost or differentiated products better than its competitors and therefore earn profits. Once a firm starts earning the profits, however, its competitors are likely to want some of them. Moreover, technological and other discontinuities can render the firm's profitable capabilities useless. To protect its profits, a firm uses a combination of three generic strategies: (1) *team up*, in which a firm allies with others to, for example, improve its chances of gaining a standard or dominant design; (2) *block*, in which the firm prevents others from imitating its innovation; and (3) *run*, in which the firm frequently introduces new products, cannibalizing its own products before anyone else does.

NOT SO SYSTEMATIC

Our discussion so far suggests a top-down flow of activities from a firm's innovation goals to protecting profits, and a feedback loop, as illustrated in Figure 16.1 (vertical arrows), to reinforce or change goals and strategies. Such a process would be best during relatively stable conditions, with little uncertainty, as is the case with many incremental innovations, and if organizations and their managers are rational and therefore can foresee all future contingencies. Given that firms are boundedly rational and that radical innovation is often fraud with uncertainty, such a top-down process may not be very practical for such innovations. Rather, any one of the boxes shown in Figure 16.1 can be the starting point of a firm's strategic innovation process. For example, when Intel started out with its microprocessor, it did not explicitly have as its goal to be one of the most profitable and most admired firms in the world. Its first microprocessor, the 4004, was designed for Busicom, a Japanese calculator manufacturer. Intel did not recognize the potential of the innovation as the brain of a personal computer until years later. Since that realization it has adjusted its strategic innovation process accordingly, including the way it protects its profits, which we detailed in Chapter 10.

KEY TERMS

Business strategy	*Strategic fit*
Corporate strategy	*Strategic innovation process*
Functional strategy	*Strategic management process*
Globalization strategy	*Structure, systems, process,*
Innovation strategy	*and environment (S^2PE)*

QUESTIONS AND EXERCISES

1. Pick a firm of your choice and develop a strategic innovation process for the firm.

2. What is the difference between a firm's strategic innovation process and its strategic management process? When should there be a difference?

NOTE

1. In particular, this *strategic innovation process* parallels the strategic management process presented by Hill, C. W. L., and G. R. Jones. *Strategic Management: An Integrated Approach.* Boston: Houghton Mifflin, 1995.

1

DOMINANT DESIGNS
AND STANDARDS

In Chapters 2 and 7 we suggested that in some industries, one important goal of a firm may be to win the dominant design or standard for the product it offers. The goal of this appendix is to define dominant designs and standards, distinguish between them, discuss what it takes to profit from them, and review what we know about attaining them.[1]

DOMINANT DESIGN

The concept of a dominant design was developed by Utterback and Abernathy.[2] According to Utterback,[3] a dominant design "in a product class is the one that wins the allegiance of the marketplace, the one that competitors and innovators must adhere to if they hope to command significant market following." Such a design marks the end of the period of experimentation when, because of both technological and market uncertainty early in the life of the product, manufacturers had to interact with co-opetitors to resolve the uncertainties. For example, personal computer (PC) makers such as MITS did not quite know what should go into a PC. Many business customers did not know whether they needed one at all and, if so, what they wanted in it. Following IBM's entry and the subsequent emergence of its architecture as the dominant design, however, it became clearer what should be in a personal computer, and many business customers had a better idea of what they wanted. A dominant design also incorporates certain choices about the design that are not revisited in every subsequent design.[4] Makers of the IBM-compatible PC do not have to rethink the microprocessor, operating system, or type of memory system each time they design a new PC.

Since a design is usually a system that incorporates many components, some of these components are also dominant designs in their own right. For example, in the PC, the Intel microprocessor, Microsoft's DOS and Windows 95 operating systems, and the DRAM (dynamic random-access memory) are all dominant designs. Sometimes these dominant component designs emerge at the time the system's dominant design emerges, as was the case with the microprocessor and the operating system. The DRAM had emerged earlier.

STANDARDS

There are two kinds of standards: interchangeable standards and product standards. *Interchangeable* standards are dimensional, timing, electrical, or other specifications that allow two or more components to work together. For example, the socket into which most American households screw their lightbulbs is a standard since anyone can go to a store and buy a bulb, and it will fit into the socket. It would not be a standard if lightbulbs from GE could only fit in certain sockets (probably manufactured by GE) and those from any other manufacturer could only fit in their own sockets. The standard socket allows any lamp from any manufacturer who complies with the standard to work with any lightbulb from any manufacturer who complies with the standard. As far as the standard socket is concerned, the lamp and the bulb are black boxes. Thus firms can differentiate their bulbs or lamps, although the socket is standard. For example, the 110-volt 60-Hz power socket in the United States is a standard since an appliance, for example, a hair dryer, will work when plugged into any house anywhere in the United States. Yet the appliances can be very different in function. Europe and Africa have the 230-volt 50-Hz standard, and therefore appliances designed for U.S. households will not work in Europe or Africa without an adapter.

Like a dominant design, a *product* standard emerges when one of a variety of products beats out competing designs to become the most common in the industry. In that sense, product standards and dominant designs are used synonymously. Like dominant designs, a standard can consist of more than one standard. The PC and its components—microprocessor, DRAMs, and operating system—are an example. Interface standards imply compatibility whereas a dominant design does not necessarily imply compatibility. For example, IBM's and DEC's minicomputers all utilize the single-processor (so-called von Neuman architecture) dominant design. But the minicomputers from the two computer makers are incompatible.

BENEFITS OF STANDARDS
AND DOMINANT DESIGNS

In Chapters 2 and 3 we emphasized the desirability of winning the standard. The question is, why is winning a dominant design so important? What really are the benefits of standards?

Winners of Standards

The winner of a standard stands to gain in several ways, depending on its capabilities. If a standard is difficult to imitate or if the intellectual property that underlies its offering is protected, its owner can collect monopoly rents. Even if the standard is open in that anyone can copy it without repercussions, its innovator can still make money by building complementary products better than its competitors. The innovator can also use the technological knowledge that underlies the standard to establish another standard. For example, theoretically, any other firm could have designed a graphical user interface (GUI)–based operating system for the PC to beat out Microsoft's Windows. The fact that Microsoft owned DOS made it easier for them to develop a GUI-based operating system that was compatible with DOS. If a firm controls a standard, it can, all else being equal, introduce complementary products faster. Microsoft gained ground on Lotus in spreadsheets after it introduced a Windows version of the program well before Lotus. As the innovator of Windows, the program on which the spreadsheets sit, Microsoft had better access to the critical information that is needed to develop the spreadsheets.

There are also some drawbacks to owning a standard. First, if newer generations of the standard must be compatible with older ones, performance may have to be sacrificed. In Windows 95, for example, a large part of the code (and therefore memory space and speed) is there just to assure compatibility with DOS and its applications. Second, as detailed in Chapters 5 and 12, paying so much attention to its standard can blind a firm from recognizing the potential of radical innovations or from successfully adopting them. Mainframes are often blamed for IBM's difficulties in exploiting personal computers, workstations, and now the Web. Third, antitrust regulation may hinder the owner of a standard from innovating in some areas since such moves may be considered anticompetitive.

Benefits to Others

Winners of standards are not the only ones who benefit from them. Customers also benefit in several ways. First, for some products the benefits are network externalities. It can be recalled from Chapter 2 that a product exhibits network externalities if the more customers that own it, the more valuable it is. Take the PC example again. The PC has a larger network than the Macintosh since more people own it. If you bought a PC, your chances of finding software are better since more people are developing software for it. If you learned how to use it and bought software that only runs on it, your chances of finding one when you need it are higher given their sheer availability. Second, the more people that make the product, the cheaper it becomes for the customer. The disadvantage for customers is that they may actually be missing out on the latest and best technology by being locked in the standard. There is also less variety to choose from.

WINNING THE STANDARD OR DOMINANT DESIGN

If standards can play such a critical role in the profitability of firms, the question is, how do they come about, and can a firm do anything to improve the chances of its design emerging as a dominant design or standard? Government can mandate standards or help tip the balance in favor of a group. For example, in 1949 the U.S. Federal Communications Commission (FCC) chose the CBS color television configuration as the standard. It played a role in the 1993 alliance of AT&T, General Instrument, Philips, Thomson, Zenith, the David Sarnoff Research Center, and MIT that has a good chance of winning the HDTV standard. Industry has two ways of doing this. The first is through standards bodies, which negotiate with industry and governments to arrive at a standard. Standards set by governments and standards bodies are sometimes referred to as *de jour* standards. The other way industry can set standards is to let the market decide, that is, let a standard emerge through the interaction of customers, manufacturers, suppliers, and complementary innovators. These are called *de facto* standards. An example is the emergence of the IBM PC as the standard. The government or standards bodies had little to do with it. The question is, what can a firm do to improve the chances of its design emerging as the standard?

Improving a Firm's Chances

There is no sure bet on what a firm can do to assure itself of winning a standard. However, there are certain things that it can do or count on to improve its chances. We group them under capabilities (competences and endowments), strategy, chance events, and environment, as illustrated in Figure A1.1.

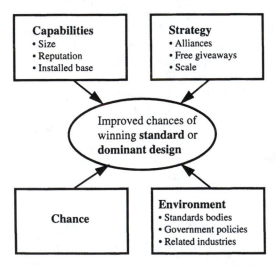

FIGURE A1.1. Determinants of emergent standards.

Capabilities

A firm's assets, such as its size, its installed base of compatible products, and its reputation, can play a significant role in helping its design emerge as a standard. Before IBM entered the personal computer market in 1981, many companies were already in the market. But when it introduced its PC, the design quickly emerged as the industry standard. One reason for the quick emergence was IBM's sheer size and reputation at that time, having established a standard in mainframes earlier. Until IBM's arrival on the PC market, there had been some doubt, especially among customers, as to how real personal computers were. In entering the PC market, IBM was said to have "legitimized the PC." To many customers, if a reputable IBM, the company that had established a standard for the mainframe computer, believed enough in PCs to offer one, there had to be something good about them. In addition software developers were quick to make commitments to develop software for the PC. Since the more software a computer has, the more valuable it is to customers, many potential computer users would opt for the IBM PC. It rapidly became the standard, winning a very large fraction of the market.

Although the product that emerges as the standard is not always technologically superior, developing such a product still requires a certain level of competence. Thus although the quality of JVC's VHS format was inferior to Sony's Beta, it was a good machine compared to what incumbents like Ampex had to offer. As another example, take the Intel microprocessor standard. One reason IBM chose it was because Intel had been smart enough to build a version of its 16-bit machine that could use existing low-cost complementary 8-bit chips, instead of the expensive, sometimes unavailable 16-bit complementary chips. Competing 16-bit microprocessors did not have the 8-bit interfacing capability with complementary chips.

Strategy

A firm's strategy can play an important role in helping its product emerge as a standard. One of the best documented cases demonstrating the role of strategy in winning a standard is that of the triumph of JVC's VHS over Sony's Betamax.[5] Sony kept its technology proprietary, whereas JVC sought strategic alliances with other manufacturers worldwide, licensed out its technology, and took advantage of rental stores to offer more customers the opportunity to try its products. Another example is Sun's RISC (reduced instruction set computer) strategy. When the company decided to adopt RISC technology, it developed its own version of the technology internally, but licensed it to anyone who wanted it. This helped make its RISC technology a standard of sorts in the workstation world.[6] Despite the assault from HP, IBM, and DEC, Sun has held its own in the workstation market. More recently, Sun decided to give away, for "free," its Java software. This is software that people on the Web can use to create their own applications software.

Environment

A firm's local environment of suppliers, customers, competitors, complementary innovators, and government can also play an important role in a firm's product emerging as a standard. It is no accident that winners of the key standards for the PC, for example, were all American companies. One reason is the tacit nature of technological and market knowledge. The microprocessor was invented by Intel, and although the instruction set was spelled out in manuals, developing software for it (operating systems, programming languages, and applications) required lots of tacit knowledge that could be more easily exchanged or passed around by local firms and hobbyists. Thus some of the first software developed for the PC was in the United States. And when IBM wanted an operating system and a microprocessor for its PC, it went to local U.S. firms, Microsoft and Intel. It was therefore no accident that the microprocessor and operating system standards were won by local firms.

Government policies can have a direct or indirect impact on the emergence of standards. Directly, as we saw earlier, a government can mandate standards. Indirectly, antitrust legislation can prevent a firm from using endowments such as size or installed base to win a standard. Recent suits against Microsoft may hurt is ability to use its reputation and other endowments to gain a standard in new markets such as the Web.

Chance Events and Positive-Feedback Effects

In some cases chance has played a key role in the emergence of a standard. But chance alone is not enough. In 1980 when IBM went to Microsoft to look for software for its upcoming PC, Microsoft just happened to be negotiating the buying of Q-DOS (quick and dirty operating system) from Seattle Computer. Microsoft would buy the operating system, turn around, and sell it to IBM (as DOS). But it should be remembered that IBM went to Microsoft because of Microsoft's "reputation" as a PC software company since the BASIC sold on MITS's Altair, the first PC, was Microsoft's. (Gates, Microsoft's CEO, had also grown popular in the PC world partly because of the letters he had written to magazine editors condemning software piracy.) Moreover, buying Q-DOS and selling it to IBM was not enough to guarantee a standard. As detailed in Chapters 7 and 12, Microsoft drew on its experience to take some strategic steps that were instrumental to DOS emerging as the standard.

Combined Effect

It is important to note that although we have listed these factors separately, more often than not it is a combination of them that helps a firm's chances of winning a standard. For example, as stated earlier. Sun's strategy of pursuing open standards led it to make its RISC technology available to anyone who wanted it. But one reason the technology quickly gained acceptance was because Sun already had a huge compatible installed base of workstations. Thus for potential cloners, adopting the technology meant instant access to a huge customer base that had its own libraries of software and that had learned to use Sun's operating system.

NOTES

1. This appendix draws on several works on standards and dominant designs. See, for example, Tripsas, M. "The effect of standardization on competition and strategy: A review of the literature." Term Paper for 15.365, MIT, 1991. Link, A. N., and G. Tassey. "The impact of standards on technology-based industries: The case of numerically-controlled machine tools in automated batch manufacturing." In *Product Standardization as a Tool of Competitive Strategy*; H. L. Gabel (Ed.). Amsterdam: North Holland, 1987. Farrell, J., and G. Saloner. "Standardization, compatibility and innovation." *Rand Journal of Economics* **16**(1):70–83, 1985. Katz, M. L., and C. Shapiro. "Network externalities, competition and compatibility." *American Economic Review* **75**(3):424–40, 1985.

2. Utterback, J. M., and W. Abernathy. "A dynamic model of process and product innovation." *Omega* **33**:639–56, 1975.

3. Utterback, J. M. *Mastering the Dynamics of Innovation*. Cambridge, MA: Harvard Business School Press, 1994.

4. Clark, K. B. "The interaction of design hierarchies and market concepts in technological evolution." *Research Policy* **14**:235–51, 1985.

5. Cusumano, M. A., Y. Mylonadis, and R. Rosenbloom. "Strategic maneuvering and mass-market dynamics: The triumph of VHS over Beta." *Business History Review* **66**:51–94, 1992.

6. Khazam, J., and D. Mowery. "Commercialization of RISC: Strategies for the creating of dominant designs." *Research Policy* **23**:89–102, 1994.

2

SOME ORGANIZATIONAL
STRUCTURES

In innovation research three types of organizational structures are frequently referenced: functional, project, and matrix.[1] We discuss each.

FUNCTIONAL STRUCTURE

In the functional organization people are grouped and perform their tasks according to traditional functions such as R&D, manufacturing, marketing, and so on. As shown in Figure A2.1, a chief executive officer (CEO) has a vice president that heads each of the functional areas, from R&D to finance, reporting to her or him. Each of these vice presidents has many managers reporting to her or him. These managers, in turn, have other people reporting to them. The number of people that report directly to a manager is called the manager's span of control. The number of levels of management in the firm is called the depth of the hierarchy. By grouping people with similar competences and knowledge, they can learn from each other and increase the stock of knowledge of the firm in the particular function. They can also monitor each other since they possess similar technological or market knowledge. If there is a task that requires only the specialized knowledge of the area, the task can be performed very effectively. For example, if a chip maker wants to reverse engineer a chip, the engineering group can handle that without much help from marketing and sales.

The functional structure has several disadvantages when a firm must perform an activity such as product development that requires the capabilities of all the different functional areas. First, since the allegiance of an employee is to its functional group where his or her performance evaluations and compensation come from, employees are not likely to devote the type of energy that is needed to offer a competitive product or service. Second, functional groups can be physically and virtually isolated from each other, making communications between them difficult. Each of these functions may be housed in a different building with very little personal interaction between employees from other functions. Since, given its tacit-

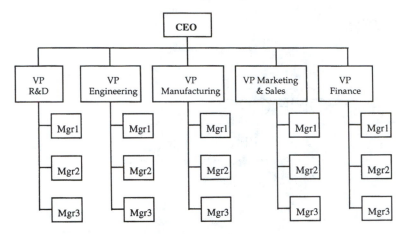

FIGURE A2.1. Functional structure.

ness and stickiness, technological knowledge and market knowledge are best transferred by some form of physical interaction, the design group, for example, may be starved of vital marketing information, which could turn a product into a blockbuster. Arranging to meet from different physical locations can be very costly, especially if the frequency of interaction is high. Functions can also be virtually separated in the way they perceive each other. For example, manufacturing may view R&D as "those ivory tower academics,"[2] whereas R&D perceives marketing as "those free-spending salespeople with flashy suits." Such prejudices can also make information exchange very difficult. Third, given their differences in experiences and capabilities, functional groups may have goals that are not consistent with developing the product or service or cooperating with other functions. For example, if the head of one of the functional areas got to that position by virtue of existing products or services, he or she is less likely to be cooperative in the development of a product that might cannibalize existing products and his or her power. For all these reasons, the functional structure is conducive for product or service developments that require very little or no interaction between the different functions. For those that do, the project structure, which we explore next, is better.

PROJECT STRUCTURE

The project structure, shown in Figure A2.2, is more practical for tasks that require frequent and a high degree of interaction between functions. Each group of projects is under a vice president for program management. Each of these vice presidents has project managers working for him or her. In each of these projects there are employees with the different functional competences deemed important for the project. These employees are assigned to the project for the duration of the project and report to the project manager. Their performance evaluations and compensation are the responsibility of the project manager, not the functional group from

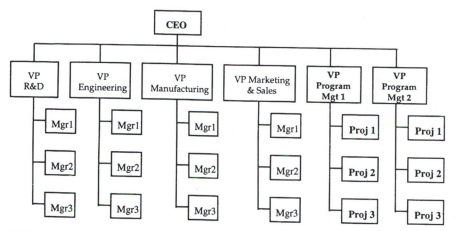

FIGURE A2.2. Project structure.

which they came. Thus for the duration of the project, their allegiance is to the project and the project manager and not to the function. Since members of the same project team are usually located in the same physical location, they can interact and exchange information more easily. Improved information flow is not the only advantage of the project structure. It can also be used to keep away the effects of political power, the fear of cannibalization, and the emotional attachment to existing products that can sap the blood out of implementation. Once the decision to adopt has been made, the project team that supports that project can be selected from the different functions and, when possible, located in a different geographic location. IBM's development of its PC is a good example. The program was located in Boca Raton, Florida, away from IBM's mainframe power bases in New York and elsewhere. Key members of the team were "renegades" who believed that there was life after mainframes.

The project structure has one major drawback: while working on the project, employees from functional areas whose underlying technological or market knowledge changes rapidly, may fall behind, especially if the project duration is long. That is, if the rate of change of the knowledge that underpins a functional area is high and the project's duration long, project members may find their functional skills outdated. The tail, and maybe wings, of their T-skills may be clipped. Given how important these skills can be in product or service development, the question is how such loss of skills can be prevented. One answer lies in the matrix structure.

MATRIX STRUCTURE

In the matrix structure, shown in Figure A2.3, there is a vice president for program management who reports to the CEO. Reporting to her or him are project managers, just as in the project structure. The difference, though, is that these project managers and their subordinates have two bosses, one from their functional areas

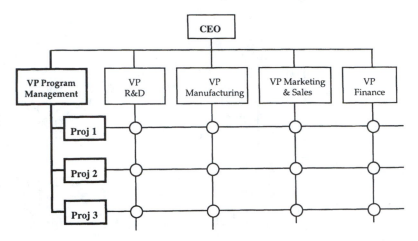

FIGURE A2.3. Matrix structure.

and the other from the project management group. Members of the same project team may or may not reside in the same physical area. This structure has three advantages. First, since the rate of change of knowledge is likely to vary from one function to the other, employees can spend time on project management commensurate with the rate of change of the knowledge in their functional areas. For example, if the rate of change of the underlying design technology is high while that for manufacturing is not, employees from design can spend less time on the project and be physically located in the design engineering area, whereas employees from manufacturing can move to the project's location and spend most of their time on the project. Second, employees can keep their T-skills sharpened since they have a chance to interact with both their project teams and their functional groups. Third, talented employees can be assigned to more than one project. The disadvantage lies in the difficulty in managing two bosses and allocating allegiance.

NOTES

1. See, for example, Allen, T. *Managing the Flow of Technology.* Cambridge, MA: MIT Press, 1984. Hill, C. W. L., and G. R. Jones. *Strategic Management: An Integrated Approach.* Boston: Houghton Mifflin, 1995.
2. Allen, T. J. "People and technology transfer." Working Paper #10–90, International Center for Research on Management of Technology (ICMOT), MIT, 1990.

GLOSSARY

Italicized words can also be found as main entries in the glossary.

Absorptive capacity. A firm's ability to assimilate new knowledge. The more related knowledge a firm has, the easier it is for it to assimilate the new knowledge.

Adverse selection. Problem caused by information asymmetry in which only the less desirable (who happen to have an information advantage) are attracted to a contract placing the other party (without the information) at a disadvantage. For example, there is an adverse selection problem when only firms with very risky innovation projects go for outside financing and the financier knows very little about those projects.

Ambiguity. Problem-solving situation in which the variables have not be identified.

Angels. Wealthy individuals who invest in private companies.

Appropriability regime. Extent to which a technology can be protected from imitation and therefore allow an innovator to collect rents from it.

Architectural innovation. Innovation in which knowledge of components and the core concepts underlying them remains fundamentally the same but knowledge of the linkages between the components has changed.

Architectural knowledge. Knowledge of the linkages between the components of a system.

Asymmetric information. Important information to a bargain or contest that is held by one party but not by the other.

Backward integration. Start producing some own inputs.

Bargaining power of buyers. Extent to which buyers can effectively determine the price–cost relationship between manufacturers and customers, giving the buyer lower prices and higher quality.

Bargaining power of suppliers. Extent to which suppliers can effectively determine the price–cost relationship between suppliers and manufacturers, giving suppliers higher prices and the right to ship lower quality supplies.

Beta. Measure of market risk from the capital asset pricing model (CAPM).

Block. Strategy in which a firm seeks to protect its technology from imitation or to prevent entry into its product-market space.

Boundary spanner. Individuals within a team who acts as the transducer between the team and the rest of the firm (organization) during the exchange of information that takes place during the process of innovation.

Bounded rationality. Conjecture that individuals are cognitively limited and therefore do not always know all that they need to know in order to make decisions. Thus two parties to an agreement or contract end up holding different information, creating room for *opportunism*. The underlying assumption in transaction cost economics.

Breakthrough knowledge. Knowledge that never existed before, e.g., the transistor and DNA when they were discovered.

Business strategy. Answers the question: what industry should the firm be in and where in the industry should it position itself? Should it offer low cost or differentiated products, or both?

Call option. Right to buy an asset at a specified price (the *exercise price*) on or before a specified date (the *exercise date*).

Cannibalization. Loss of revenues from an existing product or service as a result of introducing another product or service that renders a firm's own existing products noncompetitive.

Capabilities. *Competences* and *assets*.

Champions. Individuals who take an idea for a new product or service and do all they can within their power to ensure the success of the innovation and, in the process, risk their positions, reputation, and prestige.

Circumstantial sources of innovation. Answer to the question: when or under what circumstances can one expect the innovation?

Competence. Skill or aptitude. Ability to perform an activity. This skill or aptitude is core (i.e., a *core competence*) only if it provides customer value, differentiates a firm from its competitors, and is extendable to other products.

Competence destroying. Renders existing ability to perform an activity obsolete.

Competence enhancing. Builds on existing ability to perform an activity.

Competitive advantage. What it is about a firm that makes it outperform its competitors.

Competitor differentiation. One of three criteria for a competence or asset to be classified as core (the others being *customer value* and *extendability*). Requires that the competence or asset be uniquely held or, if widely held, the firm's level of the competence (or asset) be higher than that of its competitors.

Complementary assets. *Capabilities*—apart from those that underpin a technology—that a firm needs to exploit the *technology*.

Complementary innovations. Other innovations that play an important role during an innovation process.

Complexity. See *product complexity.*

Co-opetitors. Suppliers, customers, competitors, complementary innovators, and related industries with whom a firm must collaborate or compete in order to succeed.

Core competences. Skill, ability to perform an activity that meets three criteria: customer value, competitor differentiation, and *extendability.* The customer value criterion requires that the competence make an unusually high contribution to the value that customers perceive. Competitor differentiation requires that the competence be uniquely held or, if widely held, the firm's level of the competence be higher than that of its competitors. Extendability requires that the competence be applicable to more than one product area.

Coreness. Extent to which a competence or an *asset* meets the three criteria of *customer value, competitor differentiation,* and *extendability.*

Corporate culture. System of shared values (what is important) and beliefs (how things work) that interact with the organization's people, organizational structures, and systems to produce behavioral norms (the way we do things around here).

Corporate strategy. Answers the question: what businesses should the firm be in?

Core product. Intermediate product between a *core competence* and the *end product,* e.g., laser printer engines and microprocessors.

Creative destruction. Phenomenon in which a technological change offers an order of magnitude performance advantage over previous technologies but, in the process, results in capabilities obsolescence.

Cross-functional teams. Teams made up of people from different functions such as R&D, manufacturing, marketing, and sales.

Defensive strategy. Pattern of activities that leads to and includes offering a product or service only after another firm was the first to introduce it.

Differentiated product. Product that a customer perceives as having something that other products do not have.

Discontinuity. See *technological discontinuity.*

Discounted cash flow (DCF). Present value of future cash flows.

Dominant design. Design whose major components and underlying core concepts do not vary substantially from one product model to the other, and which commands a high percentage of the market share for the product.

Dominant logic. See *managerial dominant logic.*

Drastic innovation. Innovation that renders existing products noncompetitive. Same as a *radical innovation* in the economic sense.

Dynamic analysis. Analysis that takes a longitudinal view, looking at events over time.

Educational acquisition. Buying of a firm not so much for the profits that it can make but for what can be learned from it. Reverse engineering of a firm.

Elasticity. Measure of the percentage change in one variable in response to a 1 percent change in another variable.

Entrepreneurial rents. Profits from *innovation*.

Environmental determination. Extent to which a firm's environment determines its success in innovation.

Era of ferment. Phase of a technology life cycle that follows a *discontinuity*. In it, there is a significant amount of technological and market uncertainty, with competition between the different designs that use the new technology. Same as the *fluid phase*.

Era of incremental innovation. Phase of a technology life cycle, following the emergence of a *dominant design*, when technological uncertainty is considerably reduced and attention is focused largely on incremental product innovations. Same as the *specific state*.

Exercise price. Price at which a *call option* can be exercised.

Exit costs. Costs of quitting from a market.

Extendability. One of three criteria for a *competence* or *asset* to be classified as core (the others being *customer value* and *competitor differentiation*). Requires that the competence or endowment be applicable to more than one product area.

First-mover advantage. Advantage held by a firm by virtue of being the first to introduce a product or service.

Fluid phase. Phase of a technology life cycle that follows a *discontinuity*. In it there is a significant amount of technological and market uncertainty, with competition between the different designs that use the new technology. Same as the *era of ferment*.

Forward integration. Performing the innovation value-added chain functions that were previously performed by customers or distributors.

Functional sources of innovation. Where, within a firm's value chain or environment, *innovation* originates.

Functional strategy. Answers the question: what kinds of activities should each of the functional units (R&D, manufacturing, marketing, and so on) be engaged in and what kinds of resources should be allocated to them?

Functional structure. Organizational structure in which people are grouped and perform their tasks according to the traditional functions such as R&D, manufacturing, and marketing.

Gatekeeper. Individual within a firm who understands the idiosyncrasies of the firm and those of the outside, and therefore acts as the transducer between a firm and the outside world during the exchange of information that takes place during the process of innovation.

Global. Strategy in which firms locate their development facilities where the environment is most suitable for technological innovations and from there, they develop products for world markets.

Globalization strategy. Answers the question: when and where (in what country) should a firm locate what functions in order to better innovate for worldwide customers?

Hurdle rate. Minimum acceptable rate of return on a project set by a firm.

I already know it (IAKI). Situation where an individual puts up mental defenses and refuses to give new ideas a chance. Attitude that does not give new ideas an objective look.

Idea generation. Process of finding and articulating new ideas that may lead to new products or services.

Idea generators. Individuals who have the ability to sift through jungles of market and technological information to find ideas that lead to new products or services.

Idiosyncratic assets. Assets whose value is limited to very narrow use.

Imitability. Extent to which a firm's *competences* or *assets* can be imitated or substituted for.

Incremental innovation. Innovation is incremental in the organizational sense if the knowledge required to exploit it builds on existing knowledge. It is incremental in the economic sense if it allows existing products to remain competitive.

Information channels. Sources to which a firm turns for data.

Information filters. Screen that lets in data that a firm believes it needs and keeps out what it believes it does not need.

Initial public offering (IPO). A firm's first offering of common stock to the public.

Innovation. Use of new knowledge (technological or market) to offer new products or services that customers want.

Innovation strategy. Pattern of activities about when and how to use new knowledge to offer new products or services.

Innovation value-added chain. Suppliers, manufacturers, complementary innovators, distributors, and customers that each add value to an innovation as it makes its way to the final end user.

Intellectual property. Patents, copyrights, trade secrets, and other know-how that underpin innovation.

Internal venture. Unit within a firm that is given the same kind of entrepreneurial "environment" that start-up firms thrive in.

International. Strategy in which a firm develops products at home first, and enters foreign markets only when it has learned enough about the product.

International product life cycle. As espoused by Vernon, a product is usually developed in a developed country and, as costs drop and competition grows, the product can be moved to less developed economies and finally to developing countries.

Invention. New idea, concept, technique, device, or process that has not been commercialized.

Joint venture. Separate legal entity set up by two or more firms with ownership rights to its outputs.

Knowledge-based products. Products such as pharmaceuticals, computers, software, telecommunications equipment, missiles, factory automation, and biotechnologicals that are low on natural resources and heavy on know-how, and whose up-front development costs are very high, but per-unit production costs low.

Lead users. Users whose needs are similar to those of other users except that they have these needs months or years before the bulk of the marketplace does, and stand to benefit significantly by fulfilling these needs earlier than the rest of the customers.

Licensing. Renting of a technology to or from another firm.

Limit pricing. When incumbents lower current prices to discourage new entrants from entering a market.

Local environment. Suppliers, customers, competitors, complementary innovators, government, and related industries with which an innovator interacts as an innovation evolves.

Managerial dominant logic. Common belief among a firm's managers about what industry their firm is in, how money is made in that industry, what types of people to hire, what technologies are best for the firm, and how to approach the business in general.

Market information bound. Products with high *market uncertainty*.

Market uncertainty. Additional information on who the customers are, what their needs and expectations are, how to get them to buy the product, and how to get the product to them.

Matrix structure. Organizational structure in which individuals from different functional areas are assigned to a project, but rather than reporting only to the project manager, they report to both their functional managers and the project manager.

Mechanistic structures. Inflexible organization that emphasizes vertical communications, rigidly defined responsibilities, and hierarchy-based influence.

Minimum efficient scale (MES). Smallest output at which a firm is producing at minimum cost.

Monopoly rents. Profits that come from deliberate limitation of output (contrast with *Ricardian rents*).

Moral hazard. Situation in which the behavior of one or more parties to a contract changes to exploit an information advantage, e.g., a driver with theft insurance on a car decides not to be careful about where he parks the car.

Multidomestic. Strategy in which each country has its own organization (with complete value chains) that is almost independent of the parent company.

Network externality. Property of a product or technology that makes it more valuable to users, the more people that use it.

New knowledge. Knowledge that the firm in question has not used before to offer a product for the market in question. Includes, but is not limited to, *breakthrough knowledge*.

Not-invented-here (NIH) syndrome. Situation in which a group or firm rejects an idea, technology, or innovation, regardless of its merits, just because it is from outside the organization.

Offensive strategy. Pattern of activities that leads to and includes being the first to introduce a product or service.

Opportunism. Situation where there is information asymmetry and an individual with the information advantage exploits it.

Option. See *call option*.

Option purchase date. Date on which a *call option* was bought.

Organic structure. Flexible and adaptive organization that emphasizes loosely defined responsibilities, lateral communications, and expertise-based influence.

Political power. Ability of an individual or group to have its interests reflected in the decisions of a firm.

Positive-feedback products. Products that are heavy on know-how, exhibit network externalities, can lock-in customers, and for which an early lead or chance events can propel an otherwise inferior technology to emerge as the dominant technology (or standard), beating out superior technologies.

Principal-agent problem. Problem faced by a principal and controlling authority (e.g., shareholder) in ensuring that an agent (e.g., manager) acts on her behalf. The manager has more information on how the firm is being run than the shareholder does.

Problem-solving strategies. Proven methods of solving problems that a firm has used frequently before.

Process innovation. Use of new methods, techniques, materials, task specifications, or equipment in an organization's manufacturing or service operations to offer a lower cost or better quality product.

Product champion. See *champion*.

Product complexity. Combination of a product's dimensions of merit as perceived by its local environment, the number of interfaces between the product and complementary products, its components and linkages between them, and the number of organizations in the product's local environment that are impacted by it.

Product-market position. View that a firm's profitability rests primarily on choosing the right industry and positioning its products in the right markets within the industry (contrast with *resource-based view*).

Product specificity. Extent to which the use of a product depends on local sociotechnical conditions.

Profit chain. Framework that links new knowledge (from within and outside a firm) to profits. Effectively, profits come from low-cost or differentiated products which, in turn, rest on competences and asset, which also rest on technological and market knowledge. The knowledge comes from a firm's value chain and its environment.

Profit site. Position in an *innovation value-added chain* (whether as a supplier, customer, complementary innovator, manufacturer, or distributor) that a firm chooses to exploit an innovation from.

Project manager. Individual responsible for the overall coordination of the activities that underpin the development of a product or service.

Project structure. Structure in which employees from different functional areas are assigned to a project and work for the project manager, not their functional managers.

Prove it to me (PITM). Situation in which an individual, group, or firm has already made up its mind about something and does not want to give other ideas a chance.

Public "nature" of knowledge. Property of knowledge that makes it difficult for individual firms to appropriate new ideas that they generate.

Quality of knowledge. Measure of how explicit knowledge is.

Quantity of knowledge. Measure of how much knowledge must be collected and processed in the process of innovation. A function of the complexity of the innovation.

Quota. Upper limit of a quantity of a good that a country is allowed to import from another country.

Radical innovation. An innovation is radical in the organizational sense if the knowledge that underpins the innovation is very different from existing knowledge. It is radical in the economic sense if it renders existing products noncompetitive.

Rate of technological progress. Rate at which some generally accepted dimension of merit for a technology increases as the effort put into improving the technology increases.

Resource. A firm's assets.

Resource-based view (of the firm). View that sustained profits come from having distinctive *competences* and *assets*.

Ricardian rents. Profits that come from reduced output that is a result of scarce inputs.

Risk. Problem-solving situation in which the variables are known but the relationships among them can only be estimated.

Rivalry among existing competitors. Degree of competition among rivals.

Run. Strategy in which a firm introduces new products frequently, sometimes cannibalizing its own products.

S curve. Description of the shape that technological progress takes, given the effort put into it: starts off slowly, then increases very rapidly, and then diminishes as the physical limits of the technology are approached.

Second source. Second supplier for a product or technology.

Sibling S curves. *S curves* of related industries.

Skunkworks. Small operation, usually "hidden" away, used to develop a new product without the burden of ongoing firm activities.

Specific phases. Phase of a technology life cycle, following the emergence of a *dominant design,* when technological uncertainty is considerably reduced and attention is focused largely on incremental product innovations and major process innovations. Same as the *era of incremental innovation.*

Spillovers. Leakage of knowledge from one firm to another.

Sponsor. Senior-level manager who provides behind-the-scenes support, access to resources, and protection from political foes during an innovation.

Static analysis. Analysis that only takes a cross-sectional view, looking only at a point in time.

Sticky information. Information that, because of its sheer volume or tacitness, is very costly to transfer.

Strategy implementation. Carrying out the actions stipulated by a strategy.

Strike price. *Exercise price* of an *option.*

Tacit knowledge. Uncoded and nonverbalized knowledge that is often imbedded in actions and routines.

Team up. Strategy in which a firm allies with others in introducing an innovation instead of keeping its technology proprietary and going it alone.

Technological discontinuity. Unpredictable fundamental changes in the knowledge that underpins the offering of products or services and that result in new products with a decisive cost, performance, or quality advantage over existing products.

Technological knowledge. Knowledge of components, linkages between these components, methods, processes, and techniques that go into a product or service.

Technological uncertainty. Additional information on the components, relationships among them, methods, and techniques that go into making a new product or service work according to some specification that must be determined.

Technology driver. Product that helps a firm learn more about a technology that underpins its other products.

Technology information bound. Products with high *technological uncertainty.*

Threat of new entrants. Extent to which new firms can enter an industry and reduce incumbent profits.

Threat of substitute products. Extent to which one product or service can be a substitute for another.

Top management team (TMT). Those upper level managers with overall responsibility for the firm.

T-skills. Deep expertise in one functional area combined with broad enough knowledge in others to see and exploit the linkages between the functional areas.

Transaction costs. Costs associated with contractual relationships within and among firms in a world where information asymmetries exist, individuals and firms are boundedly rational and can be opportunistic, and contracts for uncertainty-ridden activities (e.g., R&D) are costly to write, monitor, and enforce.

Transitional phase. Stage of a *technology life cycle* in which a *dominant design* emerges.

Transmission capacity. Ability of a firm to transfer knowledge from its organization to another firm's organization.

Transnational. Strategy where each stage of a firm's value chain is located wherever (in the world) the environment is most conducive to the firm's innovation activities.

Uncertainty problem. Problem in which even the innovator, given how rife with uncertainty an innovation can be, does not know if it is worthwhile investing in the innovation at all.

Value chain. Series of activities within a firm, each of which adds value to what will eventually be a product or service.

Value stock. Repertoire of *end products, core products, capabilities,* and *knowledge* that a firm has accumulated and that it can use to exploit new markets.

Venture capital. Capital to finance a start-up firm.

Venture nurturing. Situation in which a venture capital firm provides not just financing, but also managerial expertise to a start up.

Venture partnership. Partnership between a party (e.g., *venture capital* firm) that has the expertise to minimize the *adverse selection* and *moral hazard* problems associated with financing ventures, and a financier (e.g., *angel* or pension fund) with the money.

VIDE analysis. (customer *v*alue, *i*mitability, competitor *d*ifferentiation, and *e*xtendability). Analysis that determines the extent to which a firm's capabilities can allow it to exploit an innovation long term.

INDEX

Abernathy, W. J., 33–34, 43n6, 44n16, 46n44, 353, 359n2
Abernathy–Clark model, 17–18, 27, 30, 31t, 32
Abovenet Communications, 339
absorptive capacity, 7, 107, 365
  innovation transfer and, 75–76, 79–80, 82
  spillovers and, 71
acquisitions, 24, 196, 197, 202, 204, 205
  educational, 24, 205, 278, 367
  in emerging economies, 299
  international, 276, 277
Acura, 140
Adam Opel AG, 304
administrative innovations, 14
Advanced Research Project Agency. *See* ARPA
adverse selection, 9, 236–237, 238, 240, 241, 308–309, 365
Afuah, A. N., 44n22, 44n25, 46n51, 46n58, 113n15, 114n39, 131n16, 150, 151n6, 189n1, 189n4, 189n5, 221n28, 264n31, 328n21, 344n1
Airbus Industrie, 29, 311–312
Alcoa, 72
Alexander, P. L., 112n3
Allen, P., 61, 145–146, 151n20, 151n21, 152n22, 206–207, 220n18, 220n19, 220n21, 220n22
Allen, T., x, 46n54, 82, 87n11, 87n20, 88n23, 88n26, 101, 104, 113n24, 113n29, 254, 263n23, 263n24, 316, 327n17, 364n1, 364n2
Allergen, 63
ALPHA, 169, 170–171
Altair, 30, 358
Alto, 304
ambiguity, 365
AMD, 3, 52, 144, 208, 209, 332
American Motors Corporation, 300
America Online (AOL), 125, 332
Ampex, 124, 127, 357
Ancona, D. G., 263n25
Anderson, P., 15, 43n10, 43n11, 44n14, 151n17, 263n27, 263n29
Andrews, P., 152n22, 152n23, 152n24, 152n25, 220n20

angels, 365
Ansoff, H. I., 45n42
antitrust legislation, 313, 317, 327n20, 355, 358
AOL. *See* America Online
Apollo workstations, 163, 164, 167
Apple Computer, 30, 55, 63, 67n22, 92, 144, 147, 157, 192–193, 196, 226, 238, 340
Apple II computer, 196
applications service providers (ASPs), 333
applied research, 73, 84, 107, 311, 319
appropriability regime, 71, 365
architectural innovations, 7, 18, 19, 30–32, 40, 41, 365
architectural knowledge, 18–19, 30, 365
Argentina, 215
ARPA, 329. *See also* DARPA
Arrow, K. J., 44n13, 46n43, 112n8, 131n9, 327n1
Arthur, B., 45n29
Arthur, W. B., 345n7
ASIC, 283
aspartame, 99
asset specificity, 207–208
assets, xi, 2, 3, 47–48, 52, 53–54, 64–65
  competences and, 56–58
  complementary. *See* complementary assets
  coreness of, 53
  financial, 53
  human, 53
  idiosyncratic, 194, 207–208, 369
  intangible, 53
  limited, 60–61
  physical, 53
  sources of, 61–62
  tangible, 53
asymmetric information, 9, 207, 225, 308, 365
  ex ante and ex post, 229, 236–240
asynchronous digital subscriber line (ADSL), 332
AT&T, 163, 185, 356
Australia, 321
automobile industry, 77, 80, 257, 291–293, 298, 303–304, 335

backbone, 331
backward integration, 365

DATE DUE

Trexler Library
Muhlenberg College
Allentown, PA 18104

DEMCO